DEVON LIBRARIES

Please return/renew this item by the due date.
Renew on tel. 0345 155 1001 or at
www.devonlibraries.org.uk

LONDON'S
HOLLYWOOD

The Gainsborough Studio in its heyday during the 1920s
Courtesy Ronald Grant Archive

London's Hollywood

The Gainsborough Studio in the Silent Years

Gary Chapman

Edditt Publishing

www.eddittpublishing.com

First published in 2014 by Edditt Publishing

Paperback
ISBN: 978-1-909230-10-1

Other formats available:
ebook (epub) 978-1-909230-11-8
ebook (mobi) 978-1-909230-12-5
Hardback 978-1-909230-13-2

Visit the websites
www.eddittpublishing.com
www.jazzageclub.com

Printed in the UK by Print on Demand Worldwide
9 Culley Court, Orton Southgate, Peterborough, PE2 6XD, UK

CONTENTS

Author's Note

Commonly called 'Hollywood by the Canal' and even 'Los Islington', it cannot be forgotten that although the studio was originally owned by Famous Players-Lasky and simply referred to as 'the Islington studio', it was bought by Gainsborough Pictures Limited in 1926 and thereafter also called 'the Gainsborough studio'. Nowadays it is more commonly known as 'the Gainsborough studio' hence the sub-title of the book. However, for ease, I have tended to refer to the Islington studio rather than the Gainsborough studio throughout.

My aim has been to provide a complete history of the Islington studio and the films that were made there. However, there are a few anomalies in the book that need to be aired. I have taken the liberty of discussing certain films that were not made at Islington but nevertheless are important to the overall narrative, for example, *The Wonderful Story* and *Cocaine* (both 1922), directed by Graham Cutts before he began work at Islington, and some Gainsborough films that were filmed in Germany and America. There are also a few films that were made by Gainsborough and should have been filmed at Islington but filming was forced to take place elsewhere, such as *The Sea Urchin* (1926) and *The First Born* (1928). Since Gainsborough bought the studio in 1926, the inclusion of all these films is vital as Gainsborough and the Islington studio were interlinked and it is necessary to place everything in clear perspective. For the purpose of continuity I have also mentioned the films that Graham Cutts made after he left Gainsborough in 1927 as he did resurface to direct *The Return of the Rat* (1929) at Islington for Gainsborough..

I have tried to follow a broadly chronological pattern, dividing up the book largely by film, and have grouped everything together, including the development, filming, trade shows and reviews despite the fact that often this spanned up to a six-month period. Formatting the text to fit this chronological perspective was a challenge but I felt this would be neater and easier to follow. However, for clarity I have grouped some films together out of chronological context, for example, the George Pearson's films with Betty Balfour, Gainsborough's adaptations of Noël Coward's plays and Cutts' later movies.

All reasonable effort has been made to ensure accuracy of detail. If there are any errors please advise by email via info@eddittpublishing.com.

A timeline or chronology for the main events described in this book will be available as a pdf on the Edditt Publishing website within the page for *London's Hollywood*.

As this book was nearing its final edit, news emerged of the discovery in Holland of a print of George Pearson's previously lost film *Love, Life and Laughter* (1923), starring Betty Balfour. Part of this movie was filmed at the Islington studio. For silent film buffs and Betty Balfour fans this is a remarkable find indeed and viewing will be eagerly awaited.

INTRODUCTION

I first became aware of the Islington studio twenty years ago while researching the Graham Cutts' film *Woman to Woman* (1923) for a biography about the British designer Dolly Tree, who had created the costumes. Following this, I became a little sidetracked and pieced together a brief outline of the formation and development of the studio and then moved on. At the same time, finding it difficult to unearth much information about specific stars of British silent films, I made a note to evolve a concept for a book.

Later, I watched as the old Islington studio was bought and converted into luxury apartments, and finally I began doing some rather leisurely research for a book to be titled *Stars of the British Silent Screen.* The one studio that kept popping up with increasing regularity was Islington and it became obvious that the story of the studio was significant because, from its creation in 1919 to suspension of activity due to a fire just as sound became established, it presented a microcosm of the evolution of the British film industry during the silent era. Of all the studios in the UK, Islington became the most iconic of its day. As a result I felt it necessary to document its fascinating, formative history.

Many of the most important films of the silent era were filmed at the Islington studio, and many of the leading luminaries of the film industry swept through its doors, including Graham Cutts, Michael Balcon, George Pearson, Victor Saville, Adrian Brunel, Walter West, Herbert Wilcox and Alfred Hitchcock. Of the stars that graced the floors there were many, both American and British, including Betty Balfour, Mae Marsh, Betty Compson, Dorothy Gish, Ivor Novello, Isabel Jeans, Marjorie Daw, Alice Joyce, Miles Mander, Carlyle Blackwell, Mabel Poulton, Benita Hume and Clive Brook.

Of course it cannot be overlooked that the early history of the Islington studio encompasses the emergence of Alfred Hitchcock as he made his first steps toward becoming an internationally renowned director. I also chart the early career of Graham Cutts, a somewhat shadowy figure, and later somewhat maligned by Hitchcock and others, but in my opinion deserving of more recognition for his talent and achievements.

There are four important themes running through this book. The first is the battle against American influence, the second the advent of the 'Quota act', the third the creation of large-scale film combines and finally, the arrival of talking films. The most poignant theme is the struggle faced by the British immediately after World War I to revive the film industry against overwhelming American competition. This dilemma continued throughout the 1920s despite some clever and effective strategies to circumvent the stranglehold of Hollywood's movie moguls.

The war had severely curtailed British production and the five-year hiatus meant that America gained advantage in all aspects of production and distribution, not least in terms of dominating the domestic market with its product. It was the policy of block booking that prevented effective distribution of British films and became a huge issue. Making a film was easy in comparison to getting it screened and for British film producers this had serious implications.

In 1919 the number of British films released was 103, by 1923 this had dropped to 75. A serious slump took place, with production plummeting to 56 films in 1924 and only 45 in 1925. In late 1924 the situation was so dire that all the studios were idle and in desperation, good performers were enticed to American or Continental studios to gain work.

The British National Film League organised British Film weeks throughout 1923–24 to stir up enthusiasm among exhibitors and enable British films to be seen but even this could not stop the Depression. A national debate ensued between organisations, leading producers, the Board of Trade and the British government and it became a public issue. Even David, Prince of Wales, championed the cause. A variety of options to remedy the situation and effectively encourage indigenous film production were aired and discussed. It was not a smooth or easy ride to formulate a resolution but finally the Board of Trade's Cinematograph Films Act of 1927 became law on 1st January 1928. Popularly known as the 'Quota Act', it introduced a requirement for renters to show a minimum of 7.5% British films. Before and after its introduction the act had a significant impact. However, this was not the only issue affecting the British film industry. Despite early optimism immediately after the war, production was also hampered by a lack of finance, facilities, equipment, good stories and most importantly, vision and commercial savvy. The adverse trading conditions and eventual slump weeded out many of the old-style producers and methods of working and a new breed of rose to prominence in the early 1920s.

None were more significant than Michael Balcon and Herbert Wilcox. Both men looked beyond the confines of the UK and struck deals with American and German companies for distribution and finance. Right from the outset they used key American stars to attract attention and interest globally. They did not opt for the sausage factory approach in churning out multiple films in quick succession, but instead carefully chose subjects and spent considerable time, care and effort in making them well-made, productions all geared to generating maximum income. They also employed the top technicians and performers of the day and appear to have had their fingers on the nation's pulse. And yet, like many others they were slow to adapt to changing conditions and the challenge of the talkies. As always, it became a battle between creativity and artistic expression versus big business and profit making.

Balcon was shrewd in basing himself at the Islington studio, the most technically advanced studio in the UK, built and fitted out with all the latest advanced equipment by the American company, Famous Players-Lasky in 1919. After forming Gainsborough Pictures he eventually purchased the studio and became one of the most imaginative and energetic of British producers. Without doubt it was Balcon and Wilcox who rose to the challenge and confronted the problem of how to make British pictures successfully with vigour, verve and creativity, demonstrating it could be done and thus inspiring a whole new generation.

Graham Cutts (with microphone) and team filming *The Rat* (1925)
Courtesy J.W. Mitchell Collection / Brian Twist

1 FAMOUS PLAYERS-LASKY'S LONDON EXPERIMENT

With the end of the Great War in November 1918, the country naturally fell into jubilant mood as a feeling of renewed optimism reigned in all walks of life, not least in the British Film Industry.

Before the war, production in all areas including photography, acting and design had improved, along with some technical and artistic progress in an attempt to match the growing excellence of America. But when war was announced, actors, carpenters, scenic artists and directors all flocked to the front. Production carried on, albeit on a diminished scale, but was further hampered by an amusement tax and since there was no plant making actual film in Britain at the time, stock became scarce. Far more damaging was the growing American influence on the distribution and renting networks.

During the war imports of American films had doubled and the leading firms tried to monopolise film distribution in Britain by using attractive prices as successful bait combined with an aggressive policy of blind and block booking. Such contracts sealed exhibitors into showing their films without prior viewing and for periods in excess of six months. This created a big gap between the time a picture was shown to the trade (the trade show was the first stage in the release process when a film was screened to relevant parties in the industry including renters, exhibitors and media) and the time when it was seen in the cinema. By the end of the war, 90% of films exhibited came from America. By 1919 there were 100 British pictures made against sixty in 1918. When over 1,000 new films were shown the percentage of British films was substantially low and even then, because of the distribution set-up, many had a restricted theatrical release. The general effect pushed British films out of their own market.

With the end of the war some companies carried on as before in the confined space of their insubstantial studios, with meagre facilities and an old-fashioned vision. For others with a more progressive view, a new way of making films with better resources, finance, facilities, script properties, performers and technical know-how evolved.

With the arrival of 1919 there was huge commercial activity and a frenzied rebuilding of older, existing firms and the financing of new ones. Companies like Broadwest, Hepworth, Gaumont, Ideal, British and Colonial (B&C) and Samuelson increased production but newer concerns, such as Welsh-Pearson, Astra and George Clark Productions, arrived. Two further significant developments marked this expansion with the advent of Stoll and Alliance.

After dipping his toe in film production in 1919, Oswald Stoll formed Stoll Picture Productions in mid-1920 and bought an old airplane factory in Cricklewood, converting it into three floors comprising various studio spaces, the largest of which was 400 x 700 feet. With full modern facilities, there were departments for printing, developing, cutting, stills, wardrobe, lighting, property and art, plus a screening theatre, changing rooms, a canteen and executive offices.

The Alliance Film Company, a million-pound venture, was an ambitious project spearheaded by the business tycoon Charles F. Higham, MP and a board of directors comprising theatrical magnates and bankers, which also emerged in late 1919. Alliance took over the British Actors Film Company and secured a deal with First National Exhibitors Circuit to distribute their films in America. They announced plans to build a new studio in Harrow Weald Park Estate at a cost of over £100,000 and engaged several American directors with the idea that they would become a British Hollywood. They were very quickly forced to abandon their grandiose plans and instead bought the old London Film Studio at Twickenham in early 1920, spending over £22,000 on renovations. Under the direction of Sydney Reynolds, formerly a leading Fox producer in the US, the studio was completely re-equipped with every modern appliance with the intention of making pictures to compete with America.

But by far the most momentous event was the announcement in April 1919 of the formation of the Famous Players-Lasky British Producers Limited (FPLBPL) with a capital of £600,000. The purpose was to increase the prestige and visibility of Famous Players-Lasky (FPL) and its output of Paramount-Artcraft pictures abroad, and in Europe in particular. They knew that they could bring American expertise and guarantee American distribution for the British films they would make, thus consolidating their market share in Great Britain and the Commonwealth territories. To justify this strategy, they propagated the idea that the British film industry needed an infusion of superior American technique, experience and knowledge, which they would share.

John Cecil Graham was made managing director and Chester A. Clegg the business manager and on the board were a mix of personalities largely identified with banking, manufacturing and theatrical institutions in England and these included: Major David Davies, MP, Major Norman Holden, Albert Hirst, A.W. Kerley, Alexander Nesbit and W.J. Burdon Evans, Thomas Wrigley, J.H. Kippax, J.G. Thompson, George Isaac and Abraham Collins.

FPL had evolved through the tireless efforts of two men: Adolph Zukor and Jesse L. Lasky. Hungarian-born Zukor had been an early investor in nickelodeons and formed Famous Players in 1912, while Lasky formed Lasky Feature Show Company in 1913. From 1914, both released their films through Paramount Pictures Corporation (it is by this name that we know FPL today) and in 1916 Zukor merged the three companies into one to form the Famous Players-Lasky Corporation, which became the most significant film concern in the world. Through sheer dominance of the market, Paramount introduced the concept of block and blind booking, which meant that an exhibitor had to buy up to a year's worth of other Paramount productions. The decision to open a studio and produce in London had been a scheme that Zukor had in mind for many years but the war had prevented him from implementing this.

Beside his new duties, J.C. Graham remained as general foreign representative for Famous Players-Lasky in Europe, responsible to the American partners Lasky and Zukor, with Lasky due to direct the production activities from the US. Graham was held in high regard as one of the pioneers of film business. He had formed a film distribution company in St Louis in 1910 and had later been associated with the Reliance Motion Picture Company in New York and several other companies; at one time he was also a representative for Fox in Australia. In 1917 he became head of FPL European activities, based in London.

According to business manager Chester Clegg, the new organisation's immediate plans were to open a new studio and start producing pictures in England with British settings and a British atmosphere but with a universal appeal; they would work closely with the parent company in America. Clegg said: 'The company is setting out with the idea of becoming the pioneer of British thought, ideals and talent throughout the world and will adopt as its motto "Nothing but the best".' He added that American and European actors would take part in photoplays staged in picturesque parts of the old world, including the Alps, France, Belgium, Spain, Wales and Scotland.[1]

The ethos of their strategy was made clear in another statement 'the intention is to do all that lies in its power to raise the standards of production in this country at least to the level of that of leading studios of the US. The productions will be of the highest possible standard of technical and artistic excellence'.[2]

It was felt that because Famous Players-Lasky had produced some of the best films on the market, the aim of the British concern was to live up to their reputation by producing British films of equal stature. Concerning these plans, one of FPL's directors, Emil E. Shauer (assistant treasurer and manager of the foreign department), who concluded arrangements in London, said: 'the worldwide affiliations of the Famous Players-Lasky British Producers Limited will enable it to keep in touch with the desires of audiences in every part of the globe. Special bureaus for this purpose will be established. Special importance is attached to the possibilities of cementing international friendship through this medium. The future of the motion picture is dependent upon its opportunities to grow. This affiliation for the first time will place leading directors, authors and artists in the position of co-operating in work with the leaders of European thought along the same channels.'[3]

The new company began discussions with key technicians to come to England and take charge of production work, including directors. It was recognised that because of the war those selected had the advantage of many years' pioneering work denied their counterparts in England. The intention was to use some FPL American players but also to engage existing and new British talent and encourage British writers. The idea of using American talent in England was not a new one since the London Film Company, established in 1913 in Twickenham, had been set up with largely American staff, including directors George Loane Tucker and Harold Shaw.

By July 1919 a building in Islington had been found that was suitable for conversion into an extensive studio complex and a twenty-eight year lease was taken on an old power station in Poole Street. Renovation work began immediately with the intention of creating production facilities comparable to those in the FPL Hollywood studio.

It was planned that the new studio was to become the production headquarters of FPL Europe, with pictures to be made wherever possible in the actual locations called for by the stories but this was just the start because they envisaged opening studios in other European capitals producing films on a scale never previously attempted. At the same time it was announced that FPL intended to construct a new studio on Long Island, New York to become the largest studio in the East. It was to handle eight companies at once, and to be equal to the Hollywood production plant allowing artists who could not go to Hollywood due to New York theatre contracts to make pictures where an appropriate metropolitan setting was required.

Albert A. Kaufman was made European production supervisor and duly dispatched to London to look after preparations for the development of the new studio and begin work on initial productions. These were to be adaptations of stories and plays by Henry Arthur Jones, Arthur Wing Pinero and other English dramatists. Somewhat ambitiously, it was reported that arrangements had been completed for the filming of the first story and that work would commence following his arrival in London from New York on 7th July 1919.

Kaufman was in a secure position as brother-in-law to Zukor and had been a producer for FPL from 1914 in the Hollywood studio. He was described as being 'one of the best known and most capable production experts in the film industry'. During the war he had spent two years as captain, supervising the work of all the cameramen in the Signal Corps in France and had directed the US government's official motion picture work.

In a rather grandiose gesture to justify their expansion policy, FPL made it clear in *The Film Daily* that they believed pictures could bring closer and friendlier relations between the nations of the earth: 'The success of the League of Nations, they feel, will depend in a large measure upon the abolishment of narrow creeds and prejudices, and the motion picture camera is expected to be the gun which will hold sway over the hundreds of millions who will be guided by the League of Nations'.[4] Interestingly, it was reported that the first production to be made by FPL in London was to deal with the question of a League of Nations.

Shortly after Kaufman's arrival, other key production personnel joined him. Richard Murphy, scenic artist, who had been in charge of the art department in the Hollywood studio, arrived on 20th July 1919, along with his assistant William Cameron Menzies (later to become an influential production designer and art director) and Clinton Murphy, described as a 'carpenter'. This advance party of technical staff was due to help design the new studio and work on the League of Nations film; it was also reported that some American stars were expected to sail for England. Perhaps they made arrangements to rent a studio to begin work but the film did not materialise nor did any of the stars arrive and everyone, including Kaufman, returned to New York at the beginning of December 1919.

Before leaving, Kaufman visited the Riviera to look at locations where the exteriors of one of the first productions would almost certainly be made. He also made arrangements with a well-known Italian firm, for the future visit of one of the FPL companies in Italy. Passing through Paris, Kaufman met the actress Ethel Levey and her daughter, Georgette Cohan. There were rumours that the latter would become the first FPLBPL British star.

A portrait of Eve Unsell c.1921
at the time of her arrival in London

The other important arrival was that of Eve Unsell, aged twenty-nine, the well-known scenario writer who arrived from New York on 2nd August 1919 as head of the new FPL scenario department in association with Robert E. MacAlarney, chief scenario editor of the parent company in America. Unsell's arrival initiated an FPL policy of sending over key scenario personnel from Hollywood to London for almost a year and many others followed her. Significantly, this was one department ruled virtually by women.—Her work was 'characterised by conscientious effort, deep study and a keen appreciation of dramatic values'.[5] She had written over 100 screenplays in America over a seven-year period and her brilliance was acknowledged throughout the film world. 'Human feeling is the note of her personality and of her work, together with a wonderful range of sympathy and imaginative power – gifts so much needed in getting to the core of another author's work and translating it without depreciation of artistic values'.[6]

Before her film career Unsell had been a short story writer, dramatist and also edited her college magazine. Through her friendship with David Belasco and Mrs DeMille she acquired extensive and practical knowledge of stagecraft. Her first success in screen work came with scenarios for Alice Joyce. She was then asked to join FPLBPL as scenario writer. One of her aims in London was to produce the works of the greatest continental writers on the actual locations specified by them.

In an interview Unsell outlined her views on writing for the screen. She believed that women had a greater facility to bring out the human interest in a picture story because they could 'successfully create domestic scenes and situations which parallel real life and give to a picture the simple little touches which, combined with a strong theme bring tears and laughter into the hearts of the audience'. Any film writer must also study film technique and cultivate a critical attitude to achieve anything marketable 'for the art of the silent drama is subject to more rapid evolution than anything else in the world and only by striking a new note and giving something better than it already has, can a new writer win success in its spheres'.

To achieve this she advocated every writer should be true to herself, putting her own personality into her plot and creating good themes and characters drawn with a conscientious study of human nature: 'Love interest must always be the main theme of a picture story. A simple story with a new turn of plot or an unexpected finale is always the most popular. The most wanted film at present is the modern society drama with a story that grips and entertains, has a clean outlook on life and a dependence on heroism and courage of the moral kind rather than the physical'.[7]

After she had found her feet Unsell sent word to *The New York Times* via her husband, Lester Blankfield, that she found English scenarios better written than American but not strikingly original in plot. She added, 'They all seem to centre around illegitimate children, betrayed ladies, insane wives that prevent the union of true soul mates, peers who threaten to lower the family crest by marrying daughters of tradesmen and hopelessly antiquated costume stories.'[8]

As the visitors started to settle in the FPL offices on Wardour Street in London, trouble was brewing as some in the media began to use alarmist language in describing the new developments as an invasion. FPL did not help matters in becoming embroiled in a very sensitive issue by launching Picture Playhouses Limited in mid-1919 with the objective of building up their own picture circuit in the UK. In an interview Major Davies stated that the new company 'was promoted with the sincere desire to develop the cinema-exhibiting business in this country on higher and better lines.'[9] He added that any insinuations of sinister intent to control the exhibiting company through the producing company were unfounded but his reassurances did little. Although the shareholders and directorate (including Graham and Clegg) were British, the interconnection with the rest of FPL was viewed with general disdain and outrage by British exhibitors, who feared exclusion by FPL product. Eventually the new studio and British production were viewed as more of a priority and the plans for a picture circuit were dropped although the damage to the integrity of FPL was already done.

Into the fray stepped the new general manager of the London business, Milton E. Hoffman. Previously general manager of the Hollywood studio, Hoffman arrived on 13th November 1919, shortly after it was announced that the first FPLBPL production would be a screen version of Marie Corelli's *Sorrows of Satan*, along with plans to adapt *The Great Day*, a drama running at the Drury Lane Theatre.

Hoffman had joined Jesse L.Lasky at his original Feature Play Company in April 1916 and was thus engaged in the same capacity under the merger for FPL.

He had demonstrated his production skills with initiative, the ability to make quick decisions and a thorough knowledge of the industry, while his engaging personality acquired the friendship and confidence of many.

Hoffman explained the contrast between American and British production in light of the war, during which time production in England had naturally been at a standstill. During this time America had been able to acquire wide experience and to carry out much experimental work that had resulted in bringing production to its present high form. If it hadn't been for the war he had little doubt that British production would have been on a par with America.

Pictures made before the war had shown a real quality and with this foundation he believed that there would be no difficulty in reaching the highest standards. His purpose was to make the company one of the country's biggest producing concerns and optimistically, he thought this could be done in a little over twelve months. Hoffman was keen to give the full benefit of his experience gained in the five-year gap: 'I do not wish it to be imagined that I have come over with the intention of teaching the British producer his business – he already knows it. What I desire to do is to assist him to avoid the mistakes and difficulties which we have experienced in our own progress.'[10]

After he had succeeded in giving the British producer the full benefit of his experience, Hoffman said he would return to Hollywood. How long this would take would depend on how soon native producers reached the stage of being able to make pictures that would be marketable in America. In line with his views, he appointed Major Charles Hugh Bell as assistant general manager. Trained as an engineer, Bell had been with the Royal Flying Corps during the war and at the relatively young age of twenty-nine took up his new post with relish with the view that he would ultimately take over from Hoffman.

As renovation work progressed on the creation of the studio, by early 1920 it was being suggested that production would begin immediately and by March of that year it was probable that at least three companies would work simultaneously, with additional accommodation for even more producing units still in reserve. However, the mood was somewhat ebullient and it was not until early May 1920 that the studio was complete and ready for use.

2 THE ISLINGTON STUDIO

A twenty-eight year lease was concluded in October 1919 on a massive glass-roofed structure in Poole Street, Islington comprising two buildings, each containing three floors. Originally a power station of the Metropolitan Electric Supply Company, since the end of 1914 it had been a factory devoted to the manufacture of tent and tarpaulin material for the war effort. It was now abandoned, dirty and dilapidated; also surrounded by slums in an area that would not have pleased the FPL management, no doubt preferring a somewhat less working-class address. However, it was stressed that it was located within a fifteen-minute journey by Tube from the West End on the Metropolitan line to Essex Road or Old Street.

It was impossible to find a contractor prepared to carry out the reconstruction work within the specified time and so it was decided to carry out the work with direct labour, which proved entirely successful. The reconstruction was completed in six to eight months according to the latest plans, with the most up-to-date devices from the United States. The interior of the building was practically gutted, with little except the outside walls remaining.

One of the initial difficulties was that the London County Council classified the building as a theatre, not as a factory and therefore it was necessary to keep an eye on safety with appropriate means of escape in an emergency.

The first major alteration was the removal of the three floors in each building to make space to construct two immense stages. Incredible difficulties were encountered from the outset as huge girders and brick pillars ran from floor to ceiling. Naturally it was impossible to film in a building with pillars and girders in obvious positions that reduced the open space available for staging a set. These obstacles – the stanchions – had to be carefully removed and two lattice girders built to support the roof.

On entering the main brick building, the casting director's office was right in front and here, artistes were detailed to their dressing rooms and to the wardrobe department and fitting rooms. The principle carried throughout the building was to enable people to pass through any department with which they had business and out at the other, thus reducing crowding to a minimum.

There were two studios of sufficient size, each over 100 feet for the largest interior sets. No. 1 studio on the ground floor was 102 x 68 x 40 feet. In the floor was a sunken concrete tank, 50 x 17 x 12 feet. To provide the opportunity of filming water effects, the tank was fitting with sliding covers so the whole of the floor space was available when not in use. An ingenious arrangement of windows in the side of the tank allowed underwater scenes to be taken. Glass walls were installed on one side of this studio space, with adjustable awnings to utilise natural light. Alongside was a lofty scene dock from which painted scenes could be dispatched either direct to the No. 1 studio or by elevator to No. 2 studio.

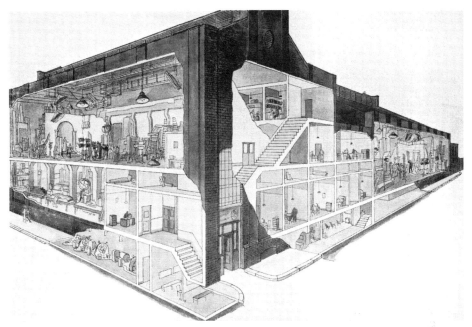

A section of the Islington studio showing some of the internal layout
Courtesy of the Ronald Grant Archive

No. 2 studio on the first floor was 115 x 48 x 35 feet and reserved for comparatively small sets but was large enough to allow six sets to be used at any one time. At one end was a balcony containing at least forty dressing rooms with full facilities, rooms for technical purposes and the offices of the art director.

Every detail of comfort and convenience had been considered and each dressing room was encircled with hot water pipes, supplementary electric radiators and hot and cold running water. The rooms for star players were even more luxurious, being equipped with considerable comfort and furnishings that included a bath; there was even a room for a maid. Each dressing room had a small window just above floor level so that long shots could be made from any angle down into studio No. 2.

Underneath No. 2 studio was the carpenters' shop, which provided accurate woodworking. It was fitted with all the latest mechanical and labour-saving devices, such as band saws, mechanical mortising, moulding and planning machines. In the basement were the paint shops, darkrooms, electrical supplies, printing and chemical labs, dressing rooms for those involved in crowd scenes and a projection theatre.

At the end of studio No. 1 was a huge area for incoming goods, with space to receive and unload properties and furniture that could then be transferred to the property store forming an entirely separate building. Here, all items were checked and registered.

Above: No. 1 studio showing the water tank

Below: No. 2 studio

Since all the work of the studio would be done by artificial light, and in order to obtain sufficient power, the Shoreditch generating system laid down a special plant and cable a mile and a half long to give the studio the power it required. The current was received at 8,000 volts and transformed down by means of two 250 k.v.a, static transformers to 220 volts, which fed four motor generators and was thus capable of giving 800 amps at 125 volts.

There was an enormous heating plant fuelled by coal brought into the works by a private underground subway from the nearby railway station and the general temperature of the studio was kept at at a steady 60 degrees Fahrenheit, even in winter.

All administrative offices, including writing and conference rooms, were to be found on the ground floor, effectively between studios 1 and 2. These included offices for all managers, secretaries, company secretary, assistant managers, casting director, purchasing manager, audit department, directors, assistant directors, as well as stock rooms. All were connected by an extensive intercommunicating telephone system.

One of the major features of the new studio was its equipment and the lighting inventory was exceptional for the time, with 24 stands of Cooper-Hewitt tubes of a special design, the only ones of their kind in the country (some cost as much as a Rolls-Royce!). There were also 24 Klieg light lamps and Wohl broadsides and a sunlight arc of 2.5 million candlepower, the only one in the UK.

Behind No. 1 studio was a two-storey annexe and on the ground floor was a garage with space for up to six motorcars. As the studio was not situated in a district where food could be easily obtained, above the parking bay was the staff restaurant with space to seat sixty, organised on the most up-to-date lines, with a chef from Simpson's providing meals at cost price.

Air pollution would have made photography very second rate and the onslaught of London fog was the cameraman's greatest enemy so an elaborate system of prevention was devised with a unique air washing and filter plant that was constructed in consultation with heating and ventilation experts. Pressurised hot water pipes were introduced around the outside walls and on the roof and placed at narrow intervals from each other. Water at high temperature and high pressure was forced through these pipes. It was hoped that the mist would be almost entirely overcome.

When the studio opened local people were glad to see a bit of glamour, with stars arriving in chauffeur-driven cars. Children would congregate outside to get autographs that they could sell on. In their breaks the actors often visited the Earl of Aberdeen on the corner of Penn Street. With their thick pancake make-up, they looked somewhat bizarre in the local pub.

The excellence of the studio and its facilities was also matched by the organisation within. Assistant studio general manager Major Charles Hugh Bell described the complexities of their centralised organisation: 'The whole of our system in the direction of its various energies into the proper channels is nothing but a practical realisation of the value of time. Studio organisation is nothing more than a specialised system applied to the production of motion pictures, a system by which

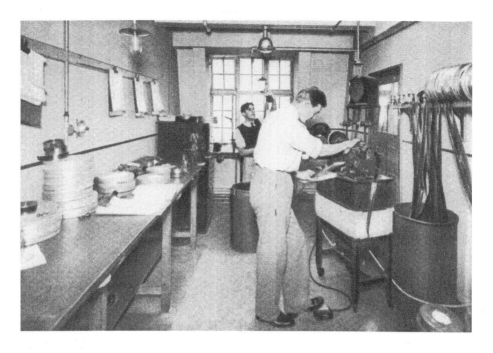

Above: The cutting-room at the Islington Studio

Below: The art department at the Islington Studio

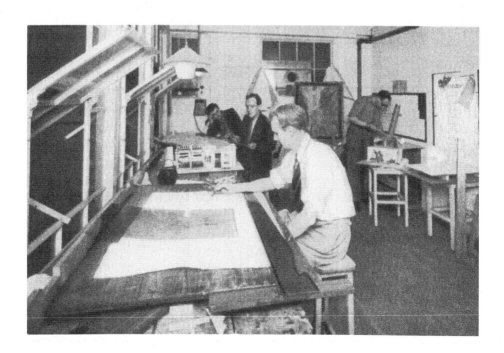

energy, time and money are husbanded by steady concentration in one direction and not dissipated in a number of extraneous issues. The director of today should be able to give his entire attention to his story and its production without having to worry about such matters as getting a cast together, running up a set or superintending the exigencies of the leading ladies screen magazine.'[1]

Staff received their orders from each departmental head and were directly responsible to them in all matters pertaining to their respective duties. The department heads were in direct touch and responsible to Milton Hoffman, the studio manager. For example, L.R. Lestocq was in charge of the casting department and made a point of stressing that he only employed those with at least twelve months' practical film experience, including crowd work. Chief art director Leslie Dawson was the head of draughtsmen, carpenters, painters, property men and engineers. A Londoner, Dawson had begun film work in 1906 and had been employed by numerous British firms before joining FPLBPL. His assistant, Norman G. Arnold, had trained in architecture before joining the Royal Flying Corps during the war. Chief cameramen Hal Young (from FPL in America) and Mr B. Kingston were attached to their own particular directorial group during the making of a picture, taking orders from the director who became their head of department. When the picture was finished they came under the studio manager, who, after consultation with producing staff, decided under which director they would work next.

When a scenario of a new production was passed into the hands of the studio management, a conference to discuss it was held by all heads of department. After half an hour each person would know what was expected of him and the assistant director had only to notify the various departments when the different sets and costumes or other effects would be required.

Major Bell affirmed 'the value of time is possibly the most important consideration'[2] and went on to explain that with the system of centralised organisation any director gaining inspiration at 5pm which necessitated a slight alteration in the story could call for a new set to built by 9am the following morning and his rush call would be dealt with and everything would be ready.

Art director Leslie Dawson also outlined his views about the art department. He started by explaining that one of the reasons for the failure of the British film industry to keep pace with the progress of American competition had been the lack of sufficient capital 'to carry on its enterprise on a commensurate scale of lavishness in the matter of production'.[3] This important aspect of film production had been grasped at an early stage by American art directors who had realised a sense of responsibility with regard to accurate settings. Dawson saw his role as ensuring that every production was as artistically correct as possible. He explained that when a director planned his scenes he would outline the type of thing he needed from the art department based on the story. Sketches were then prepared for approval. If an elaborate set was called for, a model would be made in cardboard or plaster by the model department. Once approval was granted, working plans and scale drawings were made and then given to carpenters and the set constructed with the best procurable materials. When painting the set, careful study was given to the selection of colours and toning. It had been observed that sometimes better photography was secured if the upper panelling and columns of a room were darker than the lower portions 'by this graduating and the judicious blending of the shades employed we achieve better lighting effects and that subtle quality known as atmosphere'.[4]

The dressing of the more luxurious sets was based on a careful study of style and period – columns, windows, mouldings and panelling all designed to be strictly in character. Dawson noted that the camera relentlessly picked up cheapness in textures so it was necessary never to economise over curtains and hangings, which were usually made of the finest damasks, silks and brocades. Most of the furniture was hired from stores specialising in period artifacts.

Once renovation work was finished, and the internal management structure and staffing complete, the studio was officially opened on 6th May 1920. Expected to surpass anything in England or America, it was viewed as the most completely and perfectly equipped producing studio in the country. It became the envy of other British studios due to its array of excellent facilities, adequate backing and good distribution.

Islington à la Mode

One of the major features of the new FPLBPL studio was the emphasis placed on costume and a fully functioning wardrobe department was regarded as essential: 'It seems now that producers are at last recognising the importance of this adjunct to the studio'.[5]

Milton Hoffman had appointed Madame Langfier to run wardrobe but in February 1920 he visited Paris to arrange the setting up of an atelier for the making of costumes in the latest Parisian styles for use in the new studio at Islington. Hoffman was rather pleased that they were the only ones in the country to accomplish such a venture.

Since it had to be remembered that fashions must be anticipated, otherwise the films would look out of date when released, special care was taken to introduce fashions into the films in advance of the times so that when the pictures were released, the styles would be the popular thing of the moment. All the new dresses were delivered by airplane to the studio. As a result the studio had 'successfully overcome the notorious difficulty of dress fashions in films by making its own costumes' and in so doing they had become 'blissfully independent of Dame Fashion's whimsical decrees'.[6]

At the first dress parade along with many others a representative of the trade press viewed professional mannequins exhibiting the dresses to be worn in *The Great Day* (1920), among them garden party frocks, evening gowns, négligées and walking dresses: 'These creations unquestionably outshine the best thing that Bond Street can offer and are highly fashionable without being tied down to any particular period. That is to say they are not committal enough to be unfashionable a year hence when the film is released. Milton Hoffman rightly plumes himself on the fact that the Islington studio are the only ones in this country to attempt such a venture and he is confident also that the establishment of the atelier in Paris will astound America'.[7]

Marcelle de Saint Martin

The one detail we are not told is who actually designed these costumes. However, exactly a year later, the French dress designer Marcelle de Saint Martin (who had already made a name for herself designing costumes for London stage shows) made it quite clear in various interviews that she was the costume designer for the Famous Players-Lasky studio and as such, must be regarded as the first true British studio designer.

Born in Paris in 1898, de Saint Martin was a creative, talented and striking beauty. Her education encompassed a thorough study of drawing, painting, modelling, anatomy and the history of art, which laid the foundations for her later career as a dress designer. During the war, de Saint Martin and her mother moved to England and she began designing for some actresses and stage shows, at the same time becoming aligned to the couture outlet of Hockley of Bond Street. Her undeniable flair for costume design and considerable stage experience was soon recognised and FPLBPL appointed her as the studio designer. It is not clear where she was based since in one of the features she referred to her workshop at the Islington studio, so perhaps the atelier in Paris was abandoned. It was more than likely that Saint Martin was secured as designer from the outset of production in early 1920 and began working at the Paris atelier before relocating to London.

Some examples of Marcelle de Saint Martin's costume designs
for Famous Players-Lasky British Producers Limited

Marcelle de Saint Martin made numerous fascinating points about her working methods. She made it clear that the studio spared no expense in ensuring she had everything at her disposal, including reserving her a seat in the Grand
Stand at Ascot and encouraging her to attend the Bal de l'Opéra in Paris, organised by the legendary couturier Poiret on the eve of the Grand Prix. She returned 'with my notebook filled with sketches which will prove an inspiration to me for some months to come'.[8]

She started the design process by viewing the entire script 'so that I have ample time to study the characters, their portrayers and those points of the story which call for particular care in the choice of textures, styles and colours'. De Saint Martin also placed great emphasis on conferring with the other production staff – 'team work is essential if the studio dress designer is to be in any way successful'.[9]

Discussions with the art director were vital to ensure she had an accurate idea of the kind of background against which her creations would be grouped. She was also assisted by the camera and lighting men to make the most of filming certain fabrics to advantage. Most costumes would be constructed by de Saint Martin's own team of workers but a Bond Street firm (most likely, Hockley) would occasionally assist, where necessary.

Outlining her work ethic, Marcelle de Saint Martin stressed the need to circumvent the vagaries of fashion trends and made the point that many women found a film interesting if the characters were well dressed since many visited the cinema for their fashion tips. This was a useful lesson for other British producers to observe: 'One of my desires is to do away with the fashion problem which so unfortunately dates a film. I am now designing costumes which more than keep pace with the vagaries of Madame La Mode. In this way the "movies" will become to the picturegoer the mirror of fashion wherein will be reflected the graceful gowns of world famous stars clothed in styles which will be authoritative as those issuing from the famous ateliers of Paris. And instead of buying fashion magazines, the up-to-date woman of the future will pay a visit to her favourite picture house, there to watch society heroines garbed in frocks and frills which she herself will later reproduce for her own personal adornment.'[10]

Not to be outdone, the fledgling Alliance Film Company, presumably encouraged by FPLBPL policy, engaged their own in-house costume designer, the previously unknown Gladys Jackson, while other producers also began to acknowledge the importance of good costume and to appoint specific designers for specific projects.

3 FAMOUS PLAYERS-LASKY: THE BRITISH FILMS

As the studio raced towards completion Adolph Zukor arrived in March 1920 for a few weeks to assess progress on the studio renovation and approve pre-production plans for future films among a myriad of other activities.

To take care of the initial productions Milton Hoffman brought over director Hugh Ford, who arrived from New York on 16th April 1920, along with his assistant director, J.C. Boyle. Ford had initially worked as a stage director in London and New York before joining Famous Players in 1913, joining Edwin S. Porter as assistant director and screenwriter. He had worked with many major stars, including Pauline Frederick and Marguerite Clark. In the summer of 1914 he had sailed for Europe to make a series of spectacular films, including *Her Triumph* (1915) with the famous French star Gaby Deslys, filmed in a Paris studio.

It was reported in America that when Ford was asked to go to England to produce pictures 'the other directors held up their hands in horror, for they knew that he would be up against untold difficulties. In the first place because of the war, the British had been prohibited from making any strides in their methods of picture making and America had sailed along ahead of them by several years'.[1] Thankfully, the construction of the studio, the installation of the latest equipment and the employment of skilled technicians made this task less of a problem and certainly not the horror that was predicted.

Initially it was still being announced that the first film to be made was *The Sorrows of Satan* and that Ford would be using prominent British artists with exteriors in France. However, he made it clear that he would produce two pictures and by that time they would 'have discovered native producing talent capable of following in his footsteps'.[2]

Outlining a few of his thoughts, Ford said that it was 'hopeless for artistes to play in pictures when they are working in a stage production because they are not able to give the necessary time and attention to their screen work with their minds principally on their stage engagements'. He also believed all stage players could 'benefit by acting for the films because the photoplay teaches the art of pantomime'.[3]

Following the visit of Adolph Zukor, Jesse L. Lasky arrived from New York on 8th June 1920 for a visit to London and Europe lasting about a month. In an interview he admitted that the new studio was not the largest in the world but it did possess the finest equipment and was comparable to other studios in America.

One objective of FPLBPL was to ensure that the appeal of the screen was international. It was noted that current American films representing foreign elements portrayed local colour purely from an American angle and lacked authenticity – 'They know the world is surfeited with the American view'[4] – and although America had bought the rights to numerous English novels and plays, the resulting screen efforts were not true to the originals. It was therefore important to produce films in Europe and Lasky wanted to engage British authors and dramatists to specifically write for the screen, noting that he saw three stars in picture making: authors, artistes and directors. He was to meet many well-known authors and dramatists and secured Sir James Barrie (author of *Peter Pan*) and Henry Arthur Jones with plans for them to be actively involved in turning their stories into films at the Islington studio.

Shifting slightly from his original intention, which was to bring American artistes to the UK, Lasky suggested only British artistes would be used and that it was hoped to develop stars. However, although keen to engage largely British players, a little later they did import American stars: Anna Q. Nilsson, Ann Forrest and the British-born David Powell. Although seemingly averse to building up a typical stock company, they did engage two British actresses and appeared to be grooming them for greater things. Of the eleven films that FPLBPL released in the early 1920s, six starred Mary Glynne and three starred Marjorie Hume.

Mary Glynne   Marjorie Hume

Mary Glynne was in private life Mrs Dennis Neilson-Terry, part of the famous theatrical family and had started her stage career in 1908. She was strident in her view that stage training had been essential to prepare her for film work as 'there is a high degree of technique and a depth of experience that one gets on the stage which becomes at once an inestimable asset. I strongly advise all screen aspirants to go into pictures via the footlights – it will save years of worry and disappointment.'[5] Glynne was highly regarded and excelled in both romantic and adventurous parts.

Marjorie Hume was a young, cultivated and beautiful girl blessed with brains and 'much charm of personality doubtless due to having inherited the best qualities of a varied ancestry – English, Irish and Welsh'.[6] Like Mary Glynne, she had been a stage actress and the celebrated Shakespearean actress Ellen Terry had taken an interest in her and had been instrumental in helping her gain entry into British films.

Besides the high-profile visit of Zukor and Lasky, that summer also attracted other important figures in the form of the actor Bryant Washburn, the renowned actress Mae Murray and her husband Robert Leonard, Emile Shauer, FPL assistant treasurer and the actresses Marguerite Clark and Ethel Clayton.

At this time an ambitious and enthusiastic young man by the name of Alfred Hitchcock visited the studio in search of a job in motion pictures. Alfred Joseph Hitchcock was born on 13th August 1899 in Leytonstone and his father, a typical cockney, had a retail fruiterers business but followed his brothers (who were fishmongers) in opening up a fish and chip shop. His mother was second-generation Irish and brought up her children with a strict Catholic sensibility yet she gave him, as the youngest child, doting affection.

Alfred Hitchcock in the mid-1920s

Although life was hard, he was pampered and excused from shop work, which may have caused his older brother and sister to feel some resentment and Alfred in turn may well have felt left out. He grew into a solitary and quiet child, developing huge needs and insecurities. But the extended family was full of fun and from them he developed a love of music halls, plays and moving pictures. Although staunchly Catholic, they displayed irreverence for everything, including Catholicism.

From the age of seven Hitchcock went to two convent schools before entering St Ignatius College at the age of eleven, run by Jesuits known for order, discipline and a rigorous curriculum. During this time he visited cinemas more and was reading the London screen trade papers. He also developed a taste for American magazines and began to think of himself as an 'Americophile'. A quiet, chubby boy who excelled academically, he kept himself to himself and was secretive, sensitive and watchful. He calmly observed and absorbed everything and enjoyed pursuing his own slightly eccentric private interests but he wasn't what he appeared for inside he was tough, sensitive and wise, that self-knowledge crucial to his make up.

On leaving St Ignatius in 1913 he expressed an interest in engineering and was sent to study at the London County Council School of Engineering and Navigation for a year. In late 1914, he found a job as a technical clerk at the Henley Telegraph and Cable Company, which manufactured electric cable. The death of his father shortly afterwards changed everything and with his older siblings living away, Hitchcock, who was still at home, had to provide for his mother. The war had little effect on him and he was excused from service for various reasons, including his weight, a glandular problem, and the fact he lacked physical fitness.

At Henley's he excelled and graduated to the sales section, where he proved diligent at planning and organisation and learned about publicity and promotion. The job educated him technically, artistically and commercially, and later he was promoted to the advertising department in charge of writing or editing the copy for newspaper and magazine advertisements and brochures. Hitchcock became known as a 'natural humourist and clown'[7] with a sparkling wit and he developed a new persona in public, being smartly dressed and taking long lunches at West end restaurants. He read widely, began to study photography and became a devoted film buff, admiring the technical superiority of American films; he also began to develop his own ideas about how to tell a story visually. But he was bored with his job and on reading about Famous Players-Lasky building their new studio in Islington, he saw this as the perfect opportunity to get into films and to learn the art of film-making for himself.

On learning that the first film would be *The Sorrows of Satan*, he read the novel by Marie Corelli and produced a series of title cards for the film as part of his portfolio aided by Henley's advertising manager, agreeing to split any fee received. He visited the studio to show them his work and after finding out that their plans had changed and they were to film *The Great Day* instead, he made new drawings and went back to the studio with them. It was his own 'grit and endeavour' that had 'opened the magic doors of movie-land'[8] and although he continued at Henley's full time, Hitchcock was hired on a freelance basis by Norman G. Arnold, assistant art director, and designed the title cards for the films that included printed dialogue, explanatory captions, decorative borders and backgrounds.

The Great Day

For whatever reason, filming of *The Sorrows of Satan* was abandoned. As early as November 1919, it was clear that FPLBPL would film *The Great Day*, a war melodrama being staged with great success at the Drury Lane Theatre and starring Sybil Thorndike. Each autumn, Drury Lane usually staged a conventional melodramatic story of simple virtues presenting a realistic picture of human life and *The Great Day* was no exception.

FPLBPL made a bold statement in acquiring the screen rights for £4,000, a staggering amount in those days when £500 was usually deemed adequate for London producers. But film rights were going for over £10,000 in America. For example, D.W. Griffith had paid £35,000 for *Way Down East*, while Samuel Goldwyn had paid £21,000 for *A Tailor Made Man* and £20,000 for *The Wanderer*.

As part of the contract with Arthur Collins, who staged the play, it was agreed that all the original scenery, properties and costumes could be used if necessary when filming was due to commence in May 1920 after the show had finished its West End run. The chief plot of the stage play concerned the making of special steel for war purposes, the secret of which is greedily noted by a German spy. The Drury Lane show featured several spectacular scenes, including a steel foundry with the rush of the glowing molten metal, the Clemenceau Paris Peace Conference, an Apache cellar in Paris and the rising of the Seine, from whence the heroine is rescued.

Eve Unsell adapted the story and filming began at the end of June 1920 with exterior filming of a garden party scene. Location manager Alec Stewart secured permission to use the grounds of a private school in Bushey, which proved an ideal setting with its spacious, well-kept lawns, masses of flowers, abundant trees and an imposing mansion. The players were assembled by Major Bell, the assistant manager at the studio, and given ample time to change to dress and make up.

Most of the gowns worn by the ladies were exquisite creations from the costume workshops in Paris. When everyone was ready – in total about 100 people – they were driven out to Bushey in almost a dozen conveyances, including three private buses and several roomy motorcars. There, under the direction of Hugh Ford, the company could work eight hours under the happiest of conditions. There were some occasions when the sky clouded over but it was mostly sunny. Lunch and afternoon tea was provided under the supervision of FPLBPL's own caterer. At the end of the day the whole party returned to the studio, where they were able to change in the dressing rooms.

The story revolved around Frank Beresford (Bertram Burleigh), a young chemist in an engineering firm who invents a new method of treating steel that will establish British supremacy. Beresford falls in love with his employer's daughter Clara (Marjorie Hume) and tells her about his past. He has escaped from a German war prison with his friend Dave Leeson (Geoffrey Kerr), who perishes on a glacier. Beresford goes on to marry his friend's widow (Meggie Albanesi) but she deserts him for a dancer and together they too perish on a lost liner. Despite his past, Clara and her father (Arthur Bourchier) agree to the marriage and there is a quiet ceremony. But then the 'missing' wife re-appears. Beresford receives a mysterious letter about a man who has lost his memory yet somehow remembers his name. He goes to Paris to discover his 'lost' friend. After thrilling sewer escapes from apaches acting on behalf of a German agent wanting to steal the steel formula, Beresford brings his friend home, confesses all to Clara and life carries on.

Filming was swift and a trade show given in November 1920 (released 9th January 1922) but despite admiration for the lighting, photography and good technical production values, sadly the overwhelming reaction was not positive. It was felt that it hardly came up to expectations and was full of missed opportunities: 'If this is the best FPL can do, British film-makers can heave a sigh of relief... A very disappointing piece of work'.[9]

For most Eve Unsell's scenario was undistinguished, the story thin and not progressive in its action, the quality of photography uneven and the studio sets inferior. By far the biggest criticism was that many of the strongest and most impressive scenes in the original play had been omitted. For example, the scene with the Seine flooding and the strike at the works and a raid on the banqueting hall of the proprietor of the steel works by starving workers was entirely eliminated. Although there was praise for some effective scenes, taken in a real Sheffield steel works, it was felt that the stage make-believe was more dramatic.

Furthermore, in the play, the climax came in London on Peace Day, with cheering crowds in St James's Park and realistic rockets hurtling in the air. In the film the Peace Day idea was never suggested, the drama concluded without any spectacular effect and the audience were perhaps left wondering as to the special significance of the title, *The Great Day*, although obvious in the play.

The acting was regarded as being reasonably good but sometimes the characters' motives appeared somewhat confused, especially in the case of Bertram Burleigh. However, Geoffrey Kerr as the soldier who loses his memory was greatly admired, while Meggie Albanesi, though regarded as hopelessly miscast as the villainess, gave an entirely charming performance.

As filming began on the first FPLBPL production, Major Bell (newly promoted to studio manager) was sent to America for nearly three months on 15th July 1920 as part of the overall scheme of FPL to train English managers and technicians in American methods. His trip was designed so that he could learn as much as possible about film production on the East and West Coast studios. On arrival in New York he was met by Howard Turrell, manager of the Eastern Studio, introduced to Adolph Zukor, renewed his acquaintance with Jesse L. Lasky and met all the heads of department of the FPLBPL organisation. He then set out for the West Coast, stopping off at some cities en route to visit principal cinemas and learn about the American trade from the viewpoint of exhibitors, renters and the general public.

In Hollywood he was put up at the Hollywood Hotel, where he stayed for one month studying motion picture production from a strictly studio standpoint and gave special attention to the technical side. He met Jesse L. Lasky again and other luminaries such as Cecil B. DeMille, Charles Eyton, Fred Kley and Frank Woods. Returning to New York he spent more time in the Eastern studio under the guidance of Walter Wanger, the production director. Bell finally returned to the UK on 7th October 1920 and brought back with him two of the latest pattern sunlight arcs and three of the newest overhead wohls (8-arc type), allegedly the only lights of their kind in the country at the time. He had also persuaded Mr Hamrer, president of the Sunlight Arc Corp, to visit the UK to give his expert advice on lighting.

The Call of Youth

Following *The Great Day*, Hugh Ford began work on his second picture, *The Call of Youth*, in August and September 1920. Eve Unsell adapted an original story by the well-known author and dramatist Henry Arthur Jones about a wealthy man who tries to force a poor young woman into marrying him by sending her ailing boyfriend away to Africa. Unsell said that when working with Ford she always found fresh inspiration in his 'sympathetic handling of film dramas'.[10]

FPLBPL were no doubt hoping to adapt other novels by Henry Arthur Jones such as *The Liars, The Case of Rebellious Susan* and *Mrs Dane's Defence*. It was observed that at last dramatists were beginning to realise that the screen could have much in store for them if they made full use of the new method of interpretation of their ideas.

The simple story was about a family in financial distress that see salvation when James Agar (Malcolm Cherry), a Park Lane millionaire, shows signs of interest in one of their girls. However, Betty Overton (Mary Glynne) is in love with a penniless young man called Hubert Richmond (Jack Hobbs), who is trying to pay off his father's debts. Betty reluctantly agrees to marry the millionaire but when she shows signs of wavering, he despatches the boy to an unhealthy part of Africa. On the morning of the wedding Betty realises that the call of youth is too strong and so she visits her prospective husband and begs to be released. With extraordinary magnanimity he agrees, takes the blame on himself and promptly sets out to bring the sick Hubert back from Africa, reuniting the young lovers.

As part of FPL policy to appoint and train up English technicians Robert James Cullen was appointed assistant director since Ford's previous assistant, J.C. Boyle, was busy on the editing and cutting of *The Great Day*. Before the Great War Cullen had theatrical experience and toured the world prior to entering the film business but naturally the war had interfered with his career. He served with the Black

Watch on the Western Front and later with the Royal Air Force. However, he had been discharged from the army in the early part of 1918 and subsequently assisted in the production of several films at Stoll and Ideal for Maurice Elvey and A.V. Bramble. At FPLBPL he was keen, energetic and resourceful and 'his appreciation of American methods of film-making is a good omen for the future work of the studio'.[11]

After taking some interiors at the studio, Ford's unit left for North Devon and Lynmouth and Lynton in mid-September for a week to take exteriors. The picturesque location of Waters-Meet provided scenes for the opening of the film in which the hero and heroine meet by chance just below a waterfall, where the heroine accidentally loses a shoe while crossing some stepping-stones.

One of the last shots was done in early October. The story required that the heroine should have a brief imaginary picture of a wedding at St Margaret's Westminster in her mind's eye but Ford was due to leave for America in forty-eight hours. Art director Leslie Dawson and his team started work at 9am and by 5pm the wedding scene was being shot. By the next afternoon the set was dismantled and the floor cleared so that Hugh Ford could leave for New York on 5th October 1920.

The trade show was given quite soon after the film was complete in November 1920, along with *The Great Day*, but the reception was mixed for the story was regarded as conventional and tiresome. It was thought the principle of simplicity was carried too far and in the end the plot became unconvincing, with the handling of incidents and character showing little imagination. Described as 'an American sentimental melodrama but technically only an average one', its one redeeming feature was that it was pictorially appealing. The photography was beautiful, with effective settings in the Devon countryside. In terms of the acting, Malcolm Cherry's charming performance was highly praised as being full of sympathetic touches, with excellent support from Mary Glynne and Jack Hobbs but the rest of the cast (including Marjorie Hume as Joan Lawton) were not given much opportunity.

Interestingly, on his return to New York, Hugh Ford abandoned his film career and was placed under contract by Charles Dillingham to stage his shows. By 1923 he had produced the Kaufman-Connelly success *Merton of the Movies* in New York and London.

As the filming of *The Call of Youth* drew to a close there were many changes in studio personnel besides the departure of Hugh Ford. Eve Unsell, who had set up and run the scenario department for a little under a year, departed for New York on 8th September. To replace her came Margaret Turnbull, Scottish by birth and a novelist and playwright who had abandoned the New York stage for the movies to join Cecil B. DeMille in January 1915.

With over sixty scenarios to her credit, Turnbull possessed a wide knowledge of English life and literature and had earned distinction with her stage plays. In addition, Roswell Dague, another scenarist, arrived at the end of September from New York with Robert E. MacAlarney, head of the scenario department of FPL Corporation and formerly city editor of the *New York Tribune*, the *Evening Post* and the *Evening Mail*. MacAlarney was to become general production manager responsible for all new productions and would work closely with Major Bell.

Another arrival at this time was director Donald Crisp and when Major Bell returned from America in early October he was accompanied by another director: Paul Powell. On taking up the role of studio manager, Bell relieved Milton Hoffman, who left for New York on 23rd October. In his place Bell hired James Sloan as assistant manager and Fred Errol as location manager. The studio was ostensibly being run by a British man but clearly under the watchful eye of MacAlarney.

Before production resumed a new lighting gallery was added to studio No. 1 running right round the walls, some twenty-two feet from the ground. With a floor space of ten feet from the wall, it was designed to provide ample accommodation for Kliega and spotlights, sometimes the great sun arc and scene flats and other accessories. This was designed to bring No. 1 studio more into line with No. 2 since the latter already had an art director's room and dressing rooms built some way up the wall at one end, providing a number of specially constructed portholes, through which lights could be thrust to concentrate on the floor below.

Margaret Turnbull   Donald Crisp

Appearances

Margaret Turnbull's first assignment was to adapt Edward Knoblock's novel *Appearances* for the screen; a story dealing with the struggles of a young architect and his wife to appear better off than they really are. Directed by Donald Crisp, the third FPLBPL project starring Mary Glynne and David Powell began filming in late October and ran for a few weeks through December 1920. Claude H. Mitchell was to be assistant director. Australian-born Mitchell had attended Aberdeen University and joined FPL in 1915, becoming head of the assistant director's department.

Donald Crisp was highly regarded as one of the veterans of the film world. On arrival he said, 'I'm over here to give to my own country the benefit of the knowledge and experience that I have gained in America. England is capable of making quite as good pictures as America.'[12] Born George William Crisp in Bow, East London, he claimed to be of Scottish descent. After completing his education at Eton, he became an officer in the British army and fought in the Boer War as a captain with the 10th Hussars. He was wounded: at the Battle of Tugela Heights at Kimberley and during the siege of Ladysmith. In 1906 he travelled to America, performed in Grand Opera and became a stage director before befriending D.W. Griffith and moving to Hollywood to become an actor and director.

Crisp firmly believed film-making must be recognised as a business proposition. He also observed one of the difficulties was 'the fact that actors and actresses on the stage have not yet taken the films seriously and consequently stand aloof from them'.[13] After making some films in London it was planned that in the summer of 1921, he would travel to Bombay, where FLP would establish another studio. One of his duties in London was to form a unit to take to India for that purpose.

The story followed Kitty Marshall (Mary Glynne), who, having been secretary to Lord Thornleigh (Langhorne Burton), marries Herbert Seaton (David Powell), an aspiring young architect. Seaton believes it is necessary to spend in order to earn and so the young couple begin a social existence that entails 'keeping up appearances' and soon their domestic finances become unstable. Although heavily in debt, they give a dinner party and all the guests display similar attempts at keeping up appearances. Lady Thornleigh (Mary Dibley) is jealous of her husband's secretary and relieved when Kitty marries. But even when Lady Thornleigh dies, Lord Thornleigh still cannot declare his secret love for Kitty because of family honour. The finale entails a dubious financial investment that goes wrong. Lord Thornleigh sends Kitty a blank cheque for her last salary but her husband intercepts it and fills it in for £500. Kitty appeals to Lord Thornleigh on his behalf. However, the real villain of the story is Percy Dawkins (Percy Standing), who promotes fraudulent companies and causes the ruin of Kitty and Herbert. Lord Thornleigh finally forgives Herbert for his deception.

The male lead, David Powell, was an American import although Glasgow-born of Welsh parentage. He deserted a business career in London for the stage and studied dramatic technique at Sir Herbert Beerbohm Tree's school and then played for Tree for nearly two years in Shakespearean roles. With Forbes Robertson he toured America for the first time and there he became interested in motion pictures and decided to devote himself exclusively to film. He had risen from the ranks of a leading man to a long-term contract and featured roles.

At the trade show in June 1921 (released 26th June 1922) the overall reception was moderate with the observation that there was nothing essentially English about the production and it could have been filmed just as well in America. The story was regarded as effective with a plot that was developed skilfully and sequentially; the sets were classed as magnificent with the illusion of a motor accident well crafted. The film displayed the admirable capabilities of Crisp and he was praised for 'deft touches' masking some defects and scrappiness. The actors were all admired for being polished if somewhat stereotypical. Marjorie Hume shone in a small part and deserved more, while David Powell came off better in showing 'decided personal individuality'[14]

During the filming of *Appearances*, Major Bell gave the novelist Arnold Bennett a tour of the studio and observed Crisp at work. Jesse L. Lasky's mission to lure British authors to the screen was clearly in operation and Bennett, the author of *Sacred and Profane Love* and other novels and plays, took a keen interest in movie-making. It was becoming increasingly evident that an author's work would be made known to far more people through the medium of the screen than either via the spoken play or the greatest bestseller.

Another visitor was the FPL director George Fitzmaurice, who was combining business and pleasure. For months he had been studying George du Maurier's *Peter Ibbetson* and planned to produce the film of the novel in London. He was also working with another prominent author on another story that he was also planning to film in the spring of 1921. His wife, Paramount scenarist Ouida Bergère, was currently in Rome and he was going to meet her and then spend some time with her in the South of France before returning home to America. The following year he and Ouida returned to commence production on two films.

As Donald Crisp neared completion of *Appearances* in mid-December 1920, he announced that he was to take a trip to Nice and Cairo afterwards to look at possible locations for his next production, due to start in January.

During filming one event that caught the studio unawares was the 'troublesome weather conditions'.[15] Despite creating a unique air washing and filter plant when the studio was constructed to combat the London fog, it wreaked havoc on Crisp's production schedule with the loss of time conservatively estimated at more than £11,000.

Studio manager Major Bell had never been happy with the system of air purification that had been installed when the studio was first built. Although supposed to eradicate the effects of London fog, it didn't work. In fact, it was acknowledged that when FPL decided to build the studio the difficulties of the British climate were only partially realised. From the outset they were handicapped by creating the studio well within the London fog-belt but also on the banks of a canal that naturally experienced the drastic effects of the water-mists.

To improve matters Major Bell re-examined the situation and consulted Mr W.E. Riley, who for twenty years had been the chief architect to the London County Council and was responsible for large ventilating installations such as that of the London Underground. Mr S.L. Groom of the Carrier Engineering Company also submitted a practical tender for a carrier humidifier.

For six months Bell, Riley and Groom worked together to try and resolve the problem. After three attempts and six months later, they finally had a system and plant that appeared to work by keeping the building free of fog during winter and circulating pure air all the year round. It maintained a given temperature and a certain percentage of humidity – namely eight degrees of outside wet bulb temperature – and could automatically answer a variation in temperature of one degree, including when lighting raised the temperature. The plant circulated 3.5 million cubic feet of washed pure atmosphere per hour, the air being drawn from outside or re-circulated from inside as required; a complex control board regulated the proportion of outside and inside air to be circulated.

The Mystery Road

A story of love, attraction and intrigue, the fourth FPLBPL production was Paul Powell's *The Mystery Road* and was based on an adaptation by Margaret Turnbull from an original story by E. Phillips Oppenheim. Powell had arrived in mid-October and as he settled down and waited for Donald Crisp to move forward with his first production of *Appearances* it was announced that he was to make a short feature showing the growth and progress of the FPL organisation, in both the UK and France. After some preliminary work in studio No. 2 he headed off with Turnbull and his assistant director, Robert James Cullen, in search of locations in Paris and elsewhere.

Paul Powell was a reporter for sixteen years and had worked for the *Chicago Tribune*. After he wrote a story about the local mafia, his life was threatened and so he fled to California, where he worked for the *Los Angeles Express*. He then wrote screenplays based on his life in Chicago and joined Siegmund Lubin's West Coast plant in 1911. After a while he transferred to D.W. Griffith and made Fine Arts films for Triangle, directing Dorothy and Lillian Gish, Mae Marsh, Bessie Love, Marie Doro and Douglas Fairbanks. He then directed Mary Pickford in *Pollyanna* (1920) before joining FPL.

Powell expressed the view that the real purpose of the motion picture was 'eavesdropping on life'[16] and added that films should be entertainment but there was no reason why they should not have a purpose and express an idea too. He was not particularly in favour of adaptations of novels and stage plays, but thought they could be used as a basis for a film as long as time was given to the writing of the scenario using the theme or central idea instead of following the usual practice of hurriedly and slavishly adapting the play or novel incident by incident. One wonders what he thought of the first FPLBPL British film, *The Great Day*, and his own efforts.

There was at the time conflicting opinion about the virtues of adapting novels and plays and in contrast to Powell's view, *Motion Picture Studio* argued that many were spoilt by introducing unnecessary variations and omitting essentials. They believed that often the producer took it for granted that the public who see a film have seen the play or read the book, when in fact it is best to assume they are totally unfamiliar with it and what should be done is to present a clear and easily followed story and alter types and characters – 'The essence of adaptation is not mutilation but simply the art of knowing what to leave out'.[17]

The rather convoluted story followed Gerald Dombey (David Powell), son of Lord Farringdon, who proposes to Lady Susan (Mary Glynne), his father's ward. He confesses that on holiday he had an affair with a local girl, Vera (Ruby Miller). Lady Susan says she will give him an answer, warning him that she will not forgive further digressions and leaves for the Riviera. On his way to Nice with his friend Christopher Went (Pardoe Woodman), Gerald comes across a peasant girl called Margot (Nadja Ostrovska), who has escaped from ill treatment by her father. He takes pity on her and installs her in an expensive hotel in Nice, convincing Susan to welcome her as a friend but she is not receptive to the suggestion and discovers that she is becoming attracted to Went.

Gerald visits Margot's father and persuades him to release her. Vera turns up at his father's villa with an alleged brother, Luigi (Percy Darrell Standing), with whom she runs a gambling saloon. Gerald becomes hopelessly entangled with both Vera and Margot and then loses all his money. Vera kills herself and Gerald, also driven to suicidal thoughts, is saved by Margot. Realising real happiness lies with her, he confesses everything to Susan, who releases him and so he starts a new life with Margot, while Susan ends up with Went.

With his well-groomed appearance, strikingly handsome face and talent for portraying romantic and tragic figures it was no surprise that David Powell had been singled out as a leading man. He hoped that the film would be attractive to British picturegoers and that it would show America what could be done with picturesque England as a setting.

The Mystery Road took some time to film, from December 1920 through to May 1921. Perhaps this was because Donald Crisp was filming *The Princess of New York* at the same time with the same leading players. Casting finished in early December and Powell's unit left for exterior filming on the Riviera. His stars were Mary Glynne and David Powell and there was much amusement about the similarity of names between director and leading man that became a trifle confusing at times. Back at Islington some costly, elaborate and beautiful sets were being prepared for the interior shots, including a full-sized corner of an opera house with boxes and a stage set for a performance and a cabaret. When FPL Film Service held their first conference in London in mid-January 1921, Major Bell escorted delegates on a tour of the studio and showed them the sets.

The unit arrived back in London in February and started to shoot interiors. One impressive set was the hall of a famous cabaret with wonderful dances symbolic of the tempting of Eve by the serpent, played by Phyllis Bedells along with the dancer Espinosa and a chorus of the sixteen Palace Girls. Eventually, in mid-May Powell announced he had finished filming. But was it all worth it?

At the trade show in October 1921 (released on 23rd October 1922) the reaction was polarised. For some it was thought to be a grotesque caricature of E. Phillips Oppenheim's original novel with a story that was sordid, mediocre and tawdry and merely a picturisation of weak-minded moral laxity. Crisp was questioned as to why he had completely lost the author's idea. Once again, despite 'the high state of efficiency and the importation from America of persons who are regarded as being experts in their various departments'[18] there were doubts about the output of FPLBPL and this was seen as another disappointing production.

However, completely out of line, *The Bioscope* thought the story was of considerable interest and was made plausible and interesting by the 'admirable manner in which it was presented and played'.[19] It was thought that the production compared very favourably with other films from the FPLBPL studio. They praised the acting and loved David Powell's performance, which made Dombey a thoroughly interesting character and despite the fact he makes a dreadful mess of things, he was really a good chap who would find himself eventually.

In early 1921 a significant addition was made to the FPLBPL staff in the form of a petite, four foot eleven, vibrant young woman with long Titian curls called Alma Reville, who joined to look after editing and continuity, becoming floor secretary to Donald Crisp.

Born 14th August 1899 in Nottingham, Reville's parents both worked in the famous Nottingham lace industry but when she was young, her father became the London representative of a local lace firm and the family moved south, first to Lewisham and then to Twickenham. At an early age she was diagnosed with a manifestation of acute rheumatic fever and she had to stay out of school for two years. As a reaction to her illness she developed into a bit of a tomboy and was drawn to exercise and physical activity. Despite becoming extremely self-conscious and sensitive about her lack of formal education, she had the inner resolve to get what she wanted out of life.

Her mother and grandmother took her to the movies at early age and she acquired a passion for film. Since her family lived near the Twickenham studio owned by the London Film Company, Alma made regular visits and watching the actors fascinated her. Eventually, Harold Shaw, a friend of her father, secured a job for her in the cutting room and here, she multi-tasked, doing typing, filing, shorthand, cutting, prompting, recording and script changes and minor writing tasks. The job was precise and tedious but even so she thoroughly enjoyed it. She tried to make herself useful to everyone and also worked as a floor secretary on the sets and evolved into editor and continuity girl. Alma was a pioneer in this field, having a sharp and creative eye with an innate grasp of the art of continuity. This involved maintaining the logical progression of scenes, consistency from shot to shot, of clothing and background and gesture and the general adherence to the film treatment.

One important film during this early period that she worked on was *Hearts of the World* (1918) with the legendary American director D.W. Griffith. She also worked for Maurice Elvey as his assistant or floor secretary for two years before joining FPLBPL. Her first assignment in the studio was working in the cutting room on Donald Crisp's *Appearances*. One day she noticed a young man with a confident air, who walked into the studio with an enormous flat package under his arm. Immediately she knew he had the inter-titles for *Appearances* and was delivering the artwork.

Alfred Hitchcock strolled across the set without a word and without paying attention to anyone, went into the design department.

The Princess of New York

Shortly after Paul Powell commenced work on *The Mystery Road*, Donald Crisp also began work on his second film, the fifth FPLBPL production. Called *The Princess of New York*, it was a light comedy drama. An adaptation of a story by Cosmo Hamilton by Margaret Turnbull, it described the adventures and dangers that beset an American heiress on a visit to Europe. Filming took place between January and March 1921. Since his leads were also Mary Glynne and David Powell, the production overlapped with *The Mystery Road*, which meant considerable attention to detail and continuity.

The story opened on board a ship as Helen Stanton (Mary Glynne), an American steel millionaire's daughter, known as 'The Princess of New York', together with her chaperone (Saba Raleigh) travel to London. She swiftly finds two suitors: a virtuous Oxford undergraduate Geoffrey Kingswood (David Powell) and the dubious Allan Merstham (Ivo Dawson). Helen is entertained by the Merstham family, who are 'society' crooks and soon Allan is out to win Helen's love but his father, Sir George Merstham (George Bellamy) extorts money from her. To his credit, Allan shows remorse and genuine attachment. Sir George backs horses with Helen's money, loses and then persuades her to pawn her jewellery, which has not yet been paid for, before running off with the proceeds. When a detective attempts to arrest Helen for fraud on the jeweller, the gallant young Geoffrey saves her. Somewhat foolishly, he drives her into the country, where they spend the night in a wood. In the morning they are arrested but the court case is dismissed with a caution when Helen's chaperone pays the jeweller. Geoffrey's reluctance to propose to an heiress is then overcome by Helen herself, who makes it clear that she loves him.

In early January Donald Crisp joined Paul Powell in the Riviera, sharing Margaret Turnbull's guidance and the help of assistant director Robert James Cullen. The combined units of thirty people stayed at the famous Riviera Palace Hotel in Beausoleil, Monte Carlo. Crisp was shooting for most of January in excellent weather conditions and one big scene was filmed on the Promenade des Anglais in Nice with the crowd conforming to his wishes in a manner that reflected hugely on his tact and good management. Back in the UK in February more exteriors were taken around Oxford and then he took only fifteen days to film fifteen interior sets in the studio.

After the trade show of *The Princess of New York* in June 1921 (released 10th February 1920), it received the typical mixed reception of previous FPLBPL offerings and in general was thought to show little outstanding quality. The conventionally themed story and treatment – the usual triumph of virtue over vice – was thought to be somewhat convoluted and slight. As for the acting, David Powell was regarded as satisfactory and Mary Glynne as colourless, with insufficient character to grip attention. However, Dorothy Fane as Allan's sister was seen as exceptionally good with a real sense of character.

Donald Crisp indulges in some humorous by-play between sets
most probably during filming of *The Princess of New York* (1921)
(Mary Glynne facing)

On a more positive note the English scenery and Oxford exteriors were viewed as admirable and the photography by J. Rosenthal was excellent. Although for some the film gave an essentially American version of British social folk and ways, the technical work illustrated striking evidence of the efficiency of the Islington studio and its organisation.

While the two units were filming on the Riviera in early 1921 another scenarist, Mary O'Connor, arrived from New York on 16th January to join the studio and assist Margaret Turnbull and Roswell Dague. She was designated to work with the productions of Paul Powell, with whom she had been closely associated at the old Triangle film company with D.W. Griffith. O'Connor had been in the industry for ten years, of which four had been spent with Griffith, working in every department. She was a keen student of the stage, which she watched with an eye to the application of motion picture technique. O'Connor was expected to stay for a year and would visit Spain, France and Italy, where she and Paul Powell were due to make most of their pictures. Their first collaboration was to be shot in the south of Spain.

Another visitor was Jeanie MacPherson, another scenarist, who visited Europe from March to April 1921. An actress who retired in 1917 to concentrate on screenwriting, she had worked with prominent directors Cecil B. DeMille and D.W. Griffith and was seemingly on vacation rather than assigned to the FPLBPL studio.

At the same time the young man who had been producing title cards on a freelance basis was given a full-time job. Clearly the art department were impressed by his work and on 27th April 1921, Alfred Hitchcock left his secure job at Henley's and stepped into the dream factory at Islington to take charge of all art titles. It was a job that combined the skills of writer and sketch artist and was perfect training since he was to work closely with the art and scenario departments. Gradually he began to help out in other areas to broaden his knowledge base.

A little later, in July 1921, Hitchcock wrote a feature about the importance of title design for *Motion Picture Studio*. Firstly, he said that although incredibly obvious, the most important aim was to make a title readable and that the choice of style or typeface should also make easy reading with 'bold' being best. Hand-lettered titles had an advantage over printed ones as letters could be spaced and balanced better and look more effective without the hard appearance of a typeface. But once again they must be readable and not too ornamental. With regard to illustration, art titles were helpful because you read the title and then looked at the picture, giving continuity to the story. Subtitles benefit from some kind of picture to give colour to the action of the story and help space the episodes, but adding an image to a spoken title can confuse as it needs to be read quickly, not holding up the action.

A large ornamental index letter for each subtitle was also found useful as it draws the eye to the text first. He thought that choosing the right illustration was best done with the director and that the best forms of illustration were still life, which was easily interpreted by the audience and symbols as long as they were not be too subtle. A landscape background could also suggest the locale of the current action but required careful treatment, avoiding white behind the actual title. For example, using a silhouette of a large tree in the foreground and a black background for the title itself was a good model. Hitchcock concluded by saying that the most effective surface for artwork was black canvas as it gives a richness, depth and softness – 'Bad titles can harm a picture; they create an indifferent atmosphere and look shoddy. Good titles will create a harmonious setting and help the picture run smoothly.'[20]

He later observed of these early days, 'I'm American trained…All of the personnel at the studio was American. As soon as you entered the studio doors you were in an American atmosphere.'[21]

Dangerous Lies

After finishing *The Mystery Road*, Paul Powell assembled his cast for the sixth FPLBPL production, entitled *Dangerous Lies*, with the starring team of Mary Glynne and David Powell. Mary O'Connor adapted E. Phillips Oppenheim's *Twice Wed*, a story with a strong lesson about the folly of concealing the truth. On the advice of Leonard Pearce (Warburton Gamble), the Reverend Farrant (Ernest A. Douglas), a country clergyman, invests all his money in a bogus company and loses everything. He does not have the courage to tell his daughters, Olive (Minna Grey) and Joan (Mary Glynne), and has a heart attack and dies. The dubious Pearce marries Joan but when Olive discovers her father has been swindled by Pearce, she tells Joan. Blaming Pearce for their father's death the girls decide to leave home and flee to London. After failing to discover them, Pearce goes to Australia.

Joan gets a job as a secretary to Sir Henry Bond (David Powell) and he falls in love with her. The sisters learn that Pearce has been killed and when Sir Henry proposes to her, Joan accepts without disclosing the fact that she has been married. Olive goes back home to obtain evidence to get her sister's previous marriage annulled. After the wedding she learns that Pearce is still alive and in London, looking for his wife (he pretended to be dead to evade lawyers). Joan goes to his hotel to implore him to leave the country. He drinks heavily and during a struggle with his wife, falls dead. Under the impression that she has killed him, Joan takes refuge in a room occupied by Sir Henry's cousin. The cousin summons Sir Henry and Joan makes a full confession but the doctor certifies that Pearce died of heart failure. Following an estrangement Sir Henry and Joan find happiness after a second marriage.

Filming took place between May and June 1921 and was largely shot in the studio with a few exterior locations in London. Robert James Cullen was assistant director and a new cameraman, Claude L. McDonnell, made his debut for FPLBPL.

Quickly given a September trade show (released 11th September 1922), *Dangerous Lies* gained favourable reviews. It was thought to be 'an excellent, well told, clean, well acted story'[22] and was a 'well produced film of dramatic interest and strong appeal'.[23] At last there was a FPLBPL British film that would compare favourably with the work of the American company from a technical point of view – 'It has the advantage of dealing with types familiar to the British public and will appeal to their sympathies'.[24] Perhaps viewing the film more as a feminine attraction it was suggested that women might well ask, 'what would I have done in her case?'[25]

The staging, interior sets and photography were all admired and the acting highly regarded. David Powell's portrayal of Sir Henry was convincing and it was thought that Mary Glynne showed a very fascinating creation.

On 13th May 1921, the director John Stuart Robertson arrived from New York. Robertson was a Canadian-born actor who took up film directing in 1915 with Vitagraph and then FPL, working with such stars as Mary Pickford and John Barrymore.

John Stuart Robertson

His arrival was of major interest since it was announced that FPL had bought the film rights to Sir James Barrie's *Peter Pan* and Robertson was to shortly begin filming. Undoubtedly regarded as the most important film to made by FPLBPL in the UK to date, it must have been given a lot of attention in pre-production. However, by July it was clear that production was being held up because Sir James was so upset over the death of his son that he had been unable to give the matter as much attention as he would have liked. The project took a few more years to materialise and was finally filmed in America.

Beside the Bonnie Brier Bush

As Paul Powell drew to a close with *Dangerous Lies*, Donald Crisp began filming the seventh FPLBPL production, entitled *Beside the Bonnie Brier Bush*, in which he also took the male lead. Adapted by Margaret Turnbull from a classic Scottish novel by Ian Maclaren and two separate plays by James MacArthur and Augustus E. Thomas, the film evolved into a story about a shepherd's daughter who is beloved by a laird.

Lachlan Campbell, a rugged shepherd (Donald Crisp), is a widower and his beautiful daughter, Flora (Mary Glynne), was the very embodiment of feminine charm and grace. She loves and is beloved by Lord Malcolm Hay (Alec Frazer), whose ambitious and aristocratic father hopes to marry him to the wealthy Kate Carnegie (Dorothy Fane). But Kate is in love with the romantic-looking pastor (Langhorne Burton) and she is accustomed to having her own way. Equally, Lachlan distrusts Lord Hay and forbids Flora to continue the relationship. Flora and Lord Hay meet secretly but her father discovers them and duly banishes Flora, striking her name from the family bible. At the same time Lord Hay's father sends him to London, out of harm's way. Flora follows, but fails to find him and when her father repents, she is brought home. Lord Hay finds out and follows her back. True love eventually triumphs and Flora and Lord Hay, Kate and the Parson are united in a double wedding with the aid of a pageant of pipers.

Filming took place from June to September 1921. At first, in June, Crisp's unit, with assistant director Claude H. Mitchell and photographer Claude L. McDonnell, were filming exteriors, though not in Scotland, as one might expect but Devon instead – not a particularly good move on the part of FPLBPL, who had stressed the importance of authenticity and accuracy. By mid-July the unit were filming interiors in the studio for several weeks running into September. These scenes included a massive highland ball in the banqueting hall of a mock Drumtochty Castle with 300 extras and music from twenty regimental pipers of the London Scottish and Scots Guards.

A scene from *Beside the Bonnie Brier Bush* (1921)

Reaction after the trade show in November 1921 (released 13th November 1922) was good overall. The film, praised for its good direction, excellent staging and photography, powerful acting and picturesque settings, was described as Crisp's 'best British picture'.[26] However, the story, although well adapted and told in a straightforward, unaffected manner, was regarded as somewhat weak and ordinary, lacking in dramatic suspense. The acting was what powered the film and Crisp gave a performance of great dramatic simplicity and force. While Mary Glynne was simply viewed as appealing, Dorothy Fane was regarded as more convincing and natural.

It was no surprise that the countryside of Devon was perceived as not really portraying a realistic vision of Scotland. Rather amusingly, when screened in Canada, the various scenes and settings scored a big hit with the Scottish contingent for it was 'the Scotland they remembered and loved',[27] despite being Devon!

Once again there was movement of FPLBPL staff and during filming Paul Powell and Mary O'Connor were recalled to America and once completed, Donald Crisp, Robert MacAlarney, Roswell Dague and Margaret Turnbull were also recalled, with MacAlarney leaving on 10th September and Crisp leaving on 24th September for New York. However, George Fitzmaurice arrived on 2nd August from New York with his wife Eula (Ouida Bergère). Along with John S. Robertson, these formed the new directors who planned to begin work in the studio on the next batch of films. Ouida also settled down in the scenario department alongside Roswell Dague.

Later, Thomas Jefferson Geraghty, described as 'editor', arrived on 21st August 1921 from New York. Tom Geraghty had been a reporter for the *New York Herald* and the *New York Tribune* before becoming a film publicist and later started writing for Douglas Fairbanks. He was sent to New York to work as a supervising director of the scenario department at the FPL studio there before travelling to London to take up the role of supervising editor. Another interesting employee was allegedly Mordaunt Hall. Frederick William Mordaunt Hall was English but emigrated to America in 1902 and became a newspaper man working for the *New York Press* and *New York Herald*. During the war he did intelligence work, arriving back in the UK with his wife Helen in October 1916. They returned to New York in September 1917 and then came back to the UK again in November 1919.

Alfred Hitchcock said that when he became head of the title department, presumably after he joined FPLBPL in a full-time capacity, he went to work for the editorial department and the head of department had two American writers under him. Although he was taken on by the design department, it must have been felt that it was better for him to report to Tom Geraghty, acting supervising editor, who wrote the titles. Hitchcock thrived in the scenario department and learned how to write scripts; he may well have helped out too.

Flirtations with Sound

As Donald Crisp filmed *Beside the Bonnie Brier Bush* there was renewed interest in talking pictures. We often assume that sound emerged out of nowhere when Al Jolson sang on the screen in *The Jazz Singer* in October 1927. In fact there had been tremendous efforts to produce sound on film or to synchronise the film with a phonograph since the beginning of picture making. Films had always been seen in conjunction with sound from an orchestra accompaniment and in some instances actors were utilised to sing or speak parts behind the screen with amplification.

The various attempts towards introducing sound were fraught with difficulties and the whole process proved a minefield of patents, litigation and continued refinement. One of the biggest stumbling blocks was the overall resistance by exhibitors and producers to adopt a given system and spend money in implementation when there was still no real 'perfection'.

As Lee De Forest perfected his Phonofilm system in the US and Germany, two interesting developments occurred in England. On 30th April 1921, after five years of experimentation, the inventor Claude Hamilton Verity gave demonstration of two short films titled *A Cup of Beef Tea* and *The Playthings of Fate* using his sound-on-disc system called Veritphone in Harrogate and then in June at the London Philharmonic Hall. The *Daily Mail* remarked, 'there was no mistaking the accuracy of voice and lip movement.'[28] A little later, on 16th September 1921 another inventor, Harry Grindell Matthews, interviewed and recorded Sir Ernest Shackleton in his laboratory in Harewood Place, London. Matthews' system recorded an optical soundtrack alongside the photographed image and he claimed to have invented the first true talking picture.

The Stage was engrossed by these developments and announced 'to introduce voice would be to revolutionise all present ideas, both in production and presentation of the kinema.'[29] However, it was believed emphatically that any vocal effect would spoil the movies because many enjoyed the silence; voice and orchestral accompaniment could never be combined and film scenes were so short that any conversation would be ludicrously brief as a result.

Three Live Ghosts

George Fitzmaurice began shooting exterior scenes for *Three Live Ghosts*, the eighth FPLBPL production almost immediately after his arrival from New York on 2nd August 1921. Filming was virtually concurrent with John Robertson's *Perpetua* and so studios No. 1 and 2 were in use at the same time through to mid-October.

Fitzmaurice was born in Paris, studied fine arts and saw art and sculpture as intimately related to film. He began designing stage sets and after relocating to America dabbled in screenwriting and then directed many leading stage actresses, who moved to film. Specialising in romantic drama, after a period with Pathé, he joined FPL in 1919.

Adapted by Ouida Bergère and Margaret Turnbull from a play by Frederick S. Isham, staged on Broadway in 1920, *Three Live Ghosts* was a sort of comic melodrama based upon War Office muddling in respect of men who were wrongly reported dead during the Great War. The leading lady, Anna Q. Nilsson, was Swedish-born and one of the very first Hollywood imports. She had been a much sought after model before entering the movies in 1911.

Reported 'missing', three soldiers – Jimmy (Edmund Goulding, who became a celebrated Metro-Goldwyn-Mayer director), Billy (Norman Kerry) and Spoofy (Cyril Chadwick) – escape from a German prison camp and reach London on Armistice night. They begin to pick up the threads of their old lives. Billy is American, Jimmy a cockney and Spoofy's mind is still a blank from shell shock, though he is in fact the Earl of Mannering. For various reasons they all have to hide from the police, entailing a variety of complications. Jimmy claims his back pay at the War Office but is told he is officially dead. He is in trouble, for his mother has spent the insurance money. By joining up, Billy prevented his prosecution for the 'murder' of a man shot in a quarrel, but the 'deceased' is really alive and means to marry Jimmy's American sweetheart, Ivis (Anna Q. Nilsson). Billy discovers Ivis living in Park Lane. She is with Peter Larne (John Miltern), for whose misdeeds Billy is in hiding and in a struggle between the two men, Larne is shot. Spoofy develops kleptomania, robs a house of clothes, money and jewels, and on seeing a baby, takes the child as well. He becomes a great asset to Jimmy's family, who want him to remain 'dead'. During a police raid it is found that 'Spoofy' has burgled his own house and he falls on his head, promoting sanity. Ivis is able to clear Billy's character satisfactorily and Jimmy is made happy by a romance of his own.

Fitzmaurice began shooting scenes in London with his cameraman, Arthur C. Miller, with an amusing sequence outside the Royal Exchange with the immaculately dressed Spoofy, an aristocratic-looking gentleman, wheeling a baby carriage across the busy thoroughfare and at the same time dragging a reluctant lamb by a piece of rope. Afterwards it was found that the scene had been spoilt by a baker's van that had crossed the line of vision and so they had to do a complete retake. So, Spoofy, his pram and the lamb had to be whisked back by motorcar from the Islington studio to cross the busy thoroughfare another time, with a burly policeman holding up the traffic and hundreds of people watching.

By the mid-September Fitzmaurice was shooting interiors for four weeks. One day Fitzmaurice announced that he would be taking a big crowd scene the next morning. Because there was a little mist about, Major Bell turned up at 8am to ensure that the new air washing device was in good working order before Fitzmaurice was due to start. All was fine but 'Fitz' began registering agitation, which bemused Bell, and so Fitz sent an SOS to stop the machine. He explained that he was shooting a scene showing Armistice celebrations in a big Whitechapel public house. Forty extras were smoking their short clay pipes and it was hard to get the proper bar atmosphere because the air washing machine was dissipating the smoke as fast as they were producing it!

Arthur Miller, the cameraman on Fitzmaurice's unit, told Patrick McGillan, one of Hitchcock's biographers,[30] that he recalled meeting Alfred Hitchcock when he bought the furniture from an old lady, replacing it with new for a set at the studio, thus implying he may have done some of the art direction on *Three Live Ghosts*.

According to Donald Spoto, another Hitchcock biographer,[31] the young Alfred Hitchcock, increasingly being called 'Hitch' for short, learned a lot from Fitzmaurice and he observed his quietly professional approach to the chaotic and undisciplined atmosphere of a film set in being calm, slightly detached, quietly insistent and well prepared. He also learned what to look for in sets, lighting, the development of a coherent script and the emphasis on character analysis and detailed storyboards for each shot.

Claire Greet and Edmund Goulding in *Three Live Ghosts* (1922)
Courtesy Townly Cooke Collection

During this time Hitchcock wrote his first script, adapting a novella owned by the story department, directing some 'crowd' scenes and did little shoots such as entrances and exits in interiors. He often stayed at the studio after his own work was finished to widen his scope through watching and learning and making himself familiar with the essentials of scenario writing and art direction in particular.

Three Live Ghosts was greeted warmly after the trade show in March 1922 (released 12th February 1923) as excellent entertainment and a delightful comedy with well thought-out detail, clever acting and thrilling tension. The main appeal was in all the amusing situations and incidents arising from the official 'death' of the three men. It was also praised for portraying a really convincing British atmosphere previously caricatured by American producers, the fine characterisation of London East End types and the admirable vision of Limehouse atmosphere, including the riotous Armistice night scene.

Anna Q. Nilsson and Norman Kerry were viewed as excellent leads and Cyril Chadwick supplied a rich vein of humour. Claire Greet as Mrs Gobbins (Jimmy's mother) was one of the biggest attractions and small parts were given to other rising British stars, Malcolm Tod and Annette Benson.

It was thought to be the best production from FPLBPL: 'It is the sort of subject we have been expecting from the unique financial and technical resources of the Islington studio which has not been previously forthcoming.'[32]

Perpetua

After languishing since May in pre-production on the delayed film of *Peter Pan*, John S. Robertson finally took on another project and by 13th August 1921 was making preparations to leave for Le Havre, France to film exteriors of *Perpetua*, the ninth FPLBPL production. His wife, Josephine Lovett, adapted Dion Clayton Calthrop's novel, a crime drama of love and intrigue starring the Danish-born, actress Ann Forrest and once again, the suave David Powell.

A scene from *Perpetua* (1922)

Twelve-year old Perpetua Mary (Ann Forrest) is left alone in the world and is adopted by the artist Brian McCree (David Powell). She travels with him to France and they lead a carefree life as members of a circus before she is sent away to a convent to gain an education. Meanwhile, swindler Russell Felton (John Miltern) is trying to obtain the fortune of his latest dupe, Saville Mender (Geoffrey Kerr), a young millionaire and drunkard. Felton recognises Perpetua as the daughter of his abandoned wife and introduces his friend Mender and induces McCree to paint Mender's portrait. Mender is strongly attracted to Perpetua. Although Perpetua loves McCree, Felton reveals her parentage and brings about her marriage to Mender, something she agrees to out of pity. Felton knows that Mender is bound to die through the effects of drink and causes him to make out a will in Perpetua's favour. To add to the drama, Felton is under the influence of a man worse than himself called Christian (Lionel d'Aragon), an ex-convict who compels him to poison Mender and implicate Perpetua. She is found guilty but is then exonerated by Felton's confession before Christian kills him. Once Perpetua is acquitted, she falls into the arms of McCree, who has always loved her.

After taking exteriors in France, Robertson was back in the studio by mid-September 1921 to film interiors, which continued for several weeks. Later, in light of his experiences in London, Robertson observed, 'England will soon take a leading place among the foremost countries of the world in the picture making industry. There are numerous clever actors with splendid training and expert helpers in every other branch of the profession.' Robertson had an easy confidence in himself, thought to be typically American but combined with real modesty, which was not quite so typical. 'There is no cut and dried method of making a film,' he said, 'I may make one picture one way and another film another way. I think the artistes ought to have a good general idea of the story before starting to work.' One of his directorial interests was lighting. The actual management of lighting was usually the domain of the cameraman and carried out by electricians, 'but the American director seems to take a general supervision of the lighting effect to an extent which is not common among British directors.'[33]

Following the trade show in May 1922 (released 7th May 1923) *Perpetua* (renamed *Love's Boomerang* for the American market) was described as 'a masterpiece'[34] with a strong and dramatic story that would 'make a good bid for popularity'.[35] The opening when the young Perpetua visits McCree in his studio was regarded as charming and the plot developed in an interesting and original way. Although there was some criticism about continuity the handling of the incidents was effective. The settings and exteriors were all thoroughly British in character and beautifully photographed by Roy Overbaugh, including some enchanting circus scenes. The acting was admired, with David Powell making a pleasant figure as the artist who gained sympathy on account of a natural and restrained performance. Ann Forrest was perfectly delightful and effective, John Miltern a suave rogue, Geoffrey Kerr was realistic and Bunty Fosse as the young Perpetua who presented herself as an artist's model to McCree was singled out as being excellent, presenting a very 'finished little study'.[36]

The Man From Home

The shooting schedule for the last two FPLBPL pictures followed a similar pattern to the previous two films and both were shot virtually concurrently with Alfred Hitchcock allegedly working on the art direction for both. George Fitzmaurice was first with *The Man From Home*, the tenth FPLBPL production, once again starring Anna Q. Nilsson and Norman Kerry and with cameraman Arthur C. Miller. Shooting began in mid-October 1921 and lasted ten weeks, with exteriors being taken in Rome, Naples and other picturesque parts of Italy in December.

Fitzmaurice's wife Ouida Bergère adapted a play of the same name, by Booth Tarkington and Harry Leon Wilson. It was a romantic drama about an American who sets off on an adventure to rescue the heart and fortune of a countrywoman from a scheming foreign prince and convinces her in the end that the man from home is the better choice.

Opening in Kokomo, Indiana, Genevieve Simpson (Anna Q. Nilsson) and her younger brother Horace (Geoffrey Kerr) decide to spend their father's millions and visit Europe to acquire that old-world culture so dear to provincial rich Americans. They visit Italy and Genevieve becomes entangled with an impecunious aristocratic family. Although engaged to Daniel Pike (James Kirkwood), she cannot resist the son, Prince Leone Kinsillo (Norman Kerry), whose impoverished family view the prospective match with some relish. Soon Genevieve writes to Pike, her guardian and lover, announcing her engagement and requesting him to arrange a wedding settlement. To complicate matters, the Prince is finding it hard to shake off Faustina (Annette Benson), a fisherman's wife. Pike rushes to Italy to take charge, meets a king travelling incognito and quickly sees through the schemes of the Italian family and the Prince. Discarded, Faustina stabs the Prince, who in turn strangles her and escapes. The fisherman husband (Jose Rubens) is arrested for her murder, but escapes assisted by Pike. Eventually the Prince's schemes are exposed and he is found guilty of the murder. Genevieve finds that 'A Man From Home' is really her man.

The trade show of *The Man From Home* was 27th June 1922 (released 11th June 1923) at the New Gallery Kinema, London and the reviews were positive. The story, although novelettish and intricate, was seen as well worked out and maintained attention, offering considerable dramatic scope to all the artists and provided excellent pictorial effects crowded with stirring incidents. All the players were hugely admired: James Kirwood was breezy and gave an effectively conceived character; the beautiful Anna Q. Nilsson played in a straight, unaffected manner and Annette Benson's Faustina was a lively rendering. One of the best features of the film was the local scenery, with beautiful Italian coastal and garden scenes adding to the overall atmosphere.

The Spanish Jade

Shortly after George Fitzmaurice started on *The Man From Home*, John S. Robertson began work on the eleventh, and final FPLBPL production, originally called *Love's Boomerang* but later changed to *The Spanish Jade*, with cameraman Roy Overbaugh and David Powell and Evelyn Brent in the lead roles.

Evelyn Brent was an American film actress who had arrived in Europe on vacation in late 1919. Once in London she gained employment in a show at the Comedy Theatre. When C. Aubery Smith, the male lead, suggested she should play opposite him in the British Actors production of *The Shuttle of Life* (1920) she accepted, thus securing her fate in about eleven further British films.

Like his previous film, Robertson's wife Josephine Lovett created the scenario and adapted the book by Maurice Hewlett and the play by Louis Joseph Vance which was an adventurous love story of a Spanish peasant girl. Sold by her disreputable stepfather to Esteban (Charles de Rochefort), the dissolute son of an impoverished grandee, Manuela (Evelyn Brent), runs away and takes refuge in the country. She is befriended by a wandering vagabond called Pérez (David Powell) and an American tourist by the name of Oswald Manvers (Harry Ham). Esteban finds her and tells her he is going to kill Manvers. As she struggles and tries to shield Manvers, Esteban is stabbed and killed.

Esteban's father Don Luis (Marc McDermott) swears a vendetta against Manvers. Fearing for her life, Manuela gives herself up and is tried and sentenced to life imprisonment for the murder of Esteban. Don Luis still demands a life in exchange for that of his son and Manuela secretly arranges to submit herself to his vengeance on condition that he allows Manvers to go free. He procures her release and she comes to him, followed by Pérez. Don Luis is about to kill her when Pérez offers his life instead. Touched by his devotion, Don Luis allows Manuela and Pérez to go free and declare their love.

Shooting began towards the end of October and continued into January 1922, with exteriors being taken in Spain towards the end of the year. In fact Mrs Robertson, along with the assistant director Shaw Lovett and Harry Ham as interpreter, went on a scouting mission beforehand and at first contemplated filming in the Segovia district but this was swiftly discounted as being unsuitable in terms of climate and lighting and after exhaustive investigations Carmona was found as the ideal location. As a result, Robertson and his unit spent part of Christmas at Carmona, thirty-five miles from Seville, which was regarded as a primitive place boasting only one picture theatre.

Unlike all the other productions where the costumes were designed by Marcelle de Saint Martin and made in the Islington studio, Mrs Robertson took on the task and had them all made in Seville – 'She made a careful study of any peculiar national touches in the dresses of the women and in the attire of the men whom she saw in the street. If the costume of a peasant girl struck her as particularly effective for screen purposes, that girl was tactfully approached and her entire wardrobe was purchased outright'.[37]

Evelyn Brent and David Powell had to learn the steps of a dance called the 'Sevilliano' to their own accompaniment with castanets. The dancing was to be seen in the big 'fiesta' scene staged in the market place of Carmona and they received special training from Señor Otero, an expert on Spain's national dances.

The trade show of *The Spanish Jade* took place on 1st August 1922 (released 27th August 1923) and it was slammed by the critics as being slow-moving, rambling, undramatic and somewhat pointless. Although the acting was admired, it was thought worthy of better material. Evelyn Brent was well suited as the heroine, David Powell had little to do as the lover, missing most of his opportunities for real heroism, Marc McDermott and Charles de Rochefort conveyed the Spanish spirit as the vengeful Spanish grandee and his dissolute son and Harry Ham (Manvers) was ineffective due to a purposeless role. However, there was praise for elements of genuine novelty and the fact that it was one of the few pictures made in Spain by a foreign company. The beautiful Spanish settings of many town and country exteriors and glimpses of Spanish life proved the outstanding feature.

4 CHANGE IS IN THE AIR

During filming of *The Man From Home* and *The Spanish Jade*, and while both pictures were being edited and cut, clearly something happened at the FPLBPL studio as no provision was made for new productions to be filmed in 1922. Thomas Geraghty, along with George Fitzmaurice and Ouida Bergère, left for New York on 18th February 1922, followed by John S. Robertson and his wife Josephine on 1st March. The studio remained dormant in the spring and initially nothing was said about its future.

Perhaps part of the hesitancy was a slump in confidence in the summer of 1921. From just over 100 films being made in 1919, the number rose to 145 in 1920 and then dropped to 136 in 1921, with a further drop to 95 in 1922. There had been some strides from British directors releasing films of unusual character that captured artistic initiative and originality, yet overall production qualities were not good and there had also been a drop in the quality of American films. It was thought that the American big studio system was churning out films of a repetitive nature and the public wanted something different. A mixture of this and the unfavourable economic and weather conditions caused the general public to protest at bad films. It was stressed that the mass production route was not a good model for British producers and thankfully many were 'showing the superiority of the single feature method of production over the American wholesale method'.[1]

There was still some debate about the efficacy of British film-making and in the summer of 1921, for example, *The Stage* argued that to compete with American, French, Italian and German manufacturers, British companies needed to employ first-rate producers, imaginative scenario writers and witty subtitlers. At the same time the idea of 'knocking out a picture' without expert control in each particular branch was viewed with disdain. Overall the average home production was regarded as 'weak, struggling, half competent, half inefficient, often pretentious and generally low grade. With a few exceptions the British output is rightly despised'.[2] And yet an editorial in *Movie-Land* was more positive. Here, the generally-held belief that British films were hopeless and they could not compete or aspire to equal American and continental film was deemed incorrect. The belief was that the British film industry had outstanding qualities and there were many companies producing excellent films and there was a 'credible and encouraging record of past achievements'.[3]

At the same time there was also a challenge issued to producers championing British players. *Motion Picture Studio* argued that 'British players in British films have not, nor never have had, a fair chance. The British film star is every bit as handsome and talented as any foreigner but suffers from lack of opportunity, lack of publicity (of the right kind) and lack of understanding in producers.'[4]

Change was clearly in the air and one major casualty was Walter West's Broadwest. The company had specialised in racing dramas with Violet Hopson but its debenture holders called in the official receiver in October 1921. The reason for its failure was attributed to West's 'sausage' output of adaptations from unwanted and unsuitable novels.[5] Another failure was the Alliance Film Company, which folded in late 1922 after producing just three superb features. Alliance had attempted to introduce a large scale and modern style of production but the figures for its prospectus were based on pre-war estimates and no 'super production' could be made at the time with a budget of merely £7,425. The management were clearly not experienced enough and inline with modern thinking and their calculations were invalid. They ran out of money and folded. *The Stage* observed that Alliance 'did nothing but pay salaries to Americans who had never held positions in their own country. Its solid incompetence was revealed and the ambitious enterprise did a lot to damage the prestige of British films.'[6]

One positive development was the establishment of The Kinema Club in late 1921, a members-only organisation for those involved in the British Film industry and designed to be more social than professional. In January 1922 they opened premises at 9 Great Newport Street in the West End, with four floors of dining rooms and lounges, serving lunches, teas, dinner and suppers. It was a place where everyone involved in the film business could meet in a convivial atmosphere providing a greater opportunity of getting together and exchanging ideas. The opening night was packed with 500 people having a great time, with music and dancing until midnight. Much was made of the first Kinema Club ball from 9pm to 3am at the glamorous Hotel Cecil, which had a superb ballroom with the 800 attendees reading like a 'who's who' of British studios.

With no immediate plans for further productions, at FPLBPL Major Bell was forced to close various departments and many people lost their jobs. Since the directors George Fitzmaurice and John S. Robertson had brought their own cameraman it was likely the studio cameramen – Hal Young – had already been released. The wardrobe department under Marcelle de Saint Martin was wound up, already the scenario department had been disbanded and Alma Reville left. However, a skeleton staff remained, although exactly who was part of this team was not revealed. One survivor was Alfred Hitchcock, who 'through thick and thin slyly positioned himself at the very heart of the studio'.[7]

When Jesse L. Lasky of FPL arrived on 20th May 1922 for a European tour of five weeks the situation became a little clearer. He denied that the idea of producing in England had been abandoned and said it was improbable that the studio would re-open that summer and confirmed they would not open any more European studios or the projected Bombay project – 'It is not our intention to embark upon a complete British programme but whenever we have a story that required a British background we shall make it at Islington. Far from being dissatisfied, the results so far achieved have encouraged us to continue. We are particularly pleased with our last three British pictures – *The Man From Home, Three Live Ghosts* and *The Spanish Jade*.'[8]

The modern consensus has been that the eleven FPLBPL films did not do well at the box office and were incomparable with FPL American output or good

British films of the time, and that this was the reason why British production stopped. Although there had been criticism of some of the early films, the comment was mixed and certain pictures were regarded as acceptable. Perhaps if the studio had continued, the quality of product would have advanced. The real reason for the abandonment of local production cannot have been poor product, but rather a mix of other factors. What Lasky did not mention was the fact that FPL had, in effect, overreached itself in terms of its very ambitious expansion plans. The construction of the new studio on Long Island (Astoria) almost simultaneously with London had been too much from a financial viewpoint. FPL was pausing and taking stock of its situation before deciding what to do next.

Tell Your Children/Lark's Gate

After a few months the Islington studio began renting out its studio space and facilities to other production companies. The first of these productions was *Larks Gate* based on a novel by Rachel S. Macnamara, which was a painful but moving story of how two young people ruin their chances of happiness. It was to be directed by actor and writer John Gliddon (previously running Gliddon-d'Eyncourt Productions) for International Artists Films and had a rather intriguing development finally being re-titled and released as *Tell Your Children*.

The star was to be the American actress Doris Eaton, a young beauty who had risen to fame in the *Ziegfeld Follies* and had appeared in two previous films, *At the Stage Door* (1921) with Billie Dove and *The Broadway Peacock* (1922) with Pearl White, before being signed by Gliddon. Eaton and her mother set sail from New York on 1st February 1922 and on arrival in London had a big press reception at the Piccadilly Hotel. She met her male co-star Walter Tennyson d'Eyncourt, a true descendant of Lord Tennyson, and he invited them both to a weekend away at the d'Eyncourt Castle in the English countryside. Following ten days of costume fittings and briefings with the director, Gliddon's unit with cast and crew left London for two months in mid-February 1922 to film exteriors in Egypt and the Riviera.

When exteriors were complete at Luxor, Cairo and Alexandra, the unit returned to London in early April to begin shooting interiors at the Islington studio. But then something happened. By May 1922 there was the surprising announcement that Donald Crisp would be joining International Artists to remake *Lark's Gate*. Was Gliddon's vision and footage not liked or not up to scratch and was Crisp brought in to salvage the production? According to Martin Sabine who was the general manager of International Artists, the start of the company had not been good but a recent reconstruction had salvaged affairs, the implication being that Glydden's activities were not acceptable. Sabine stressed that Crisp had 'neither made nor remade the picture and in fact in the new feature… not a single inch of the old stuff had been used'. *Tell Your Children* had been adapted from the same novel as *Lark's Gate* 'but it was in every way entirely new and the story had been launched upon from an entirely different angle'. [9]

Crisp set to work and with the help of Alma Reville as editor and cutter and perhaps Alfred Hitchcock as art director, swiftly made the picture but was forced to make an inexplicable trip to New York and back with Tennyson in mid-July 1922 to complete some of the scenes.

The story of *Tell Your Children* was viewed as a great moral drama with the idea of explaining the dangers of allowing children to remain ignorant of sex. Rosny (Doris Eaton) is the young daughter of Lady Sybil Edwards (Margaret Halstan), a woman of high social ambitions. She goes to stay on a farm for her health and there she falls in love with John Haslar (Walter Tennyson), the equally young and innocent farmer's son. They run away to be married but are stopped by John's father (Cecil Morton York), who sends John to America and Rosny to her mother's country house, where a child is born. The child is taken away and Lady Sybil tells Rosny it is dead and later forces her to marry Lord Belhurst (Warwick Ward), with whom she leads an unhappy life. During a holiday in Egypt, Lord Belhurst is killed in a brawl. John, since adopted by a wealthy American, learns that his aunt has the child that he believed had died. On his return he visits Rosny and they are happily reunited with their offspring.

Following the trade show in September 1922 (released 19th March 1923), the sum total of any praise was that it was 'technically a beautiful production'.[10] The story was regarded as improbable, mechanical and wearisome and in trying to avoid all offence nothing was interesting or convincing. The novel itself was viewed as a crude and sentimental novelette and the film in following the book, particularly John Haslar's seduction of the child, the episode of the birth and callous cruelty of her mother and the death of Rosny's husband, rendered some of the scenes exceedingly distasteful.

The acting was not admired either. Although Doris Eaton's performance was 'charming and attractive',[11] she was regarded as much too youthful to be convincing, particularly in the latter part of the film as the wife of Lord Belhurst. She failed to bring out the real drama of her role, being too placid and not arousing any sympathy or interest. Walter Tennyson was amateurish and lacked screen experience and Margaret Halstan's incessant superciliousness proved irritating.

Somewhat surprisingly, Doris Eaton said that this was not the only movie made by the same cast and crew and that another film was made without her knowledge: 'I suppose the days of silent film-making allowed moviemakers to patch together the second film without the actors' knowledge and without any contractual discussions.'[12] Clearly her observations allude to something rather strange. Directed by Bert Wynne for International Artists, the second film was *Desert Sands* re-titled *Call of the East* and was given a trade show in October 1922. Described as a story of love and tragedy by the waters of the Nile, the film featured exterior settings in Cairo, Thebes and by the banks of the Nile and perhaps this is where the exterior footage from *Lark's Gate* ended up.

5   GRAHAM-WILCOX'S WONDERFUL STORY

As Donald Crisp filmed *Tell the Children* in June 1922, two very different men came to visit the studio to look around. Graham Cutts and Herbert Wilcox were the driving force behind the newly formed Graham-Wilcox Productions Limited (registered in July 1922, in association with Rudolph Solomon) and they were planning to make two big budget films. Cutts, highly educated, cool, debonair and already in his late thirties, was in stark contrast to the short, fast-paced and frenetic Wilcox, aged thirty. Both would have a profound affect on the British film industry and Cutts in particular on the Islington film studio.

Between them they were a good combination: Cutts with over twelve years' experience as an exhibitor and showman with a unique instinct for what the public was eager to see and Wilcox with solid experience in distribution and production, who believed in giving the audience what they wanted and not challenging them. The pair had also achieved some staggering success with two films – *The Wonderful Story* and *Cocaine* – that had just been given rapturous trade shows.

John Henry Grahame Cutts (sometimes called 'Jack') was born in Brighton on 19th February 1884 to Henry Whitmore Cutts (who appears to have had a varied career as an artist, wood engraver, author, journalist and even dental surgeon) and Mary Maud Colclough Cutts (formerly Jackson), living at 47 Park Crescent. His grandfather was the Yorkshire-born clergyman Edward Lewes Cutts, who was a curate in Coggeshall, Essex, from 1850–57, and an author of many works on Church history. He later lived and worked in Hammersmith, London.

After living in Brighton, the family moved back to Essex and a daughter called Maud Primrose was born in 1886. By 1911, they had moved again, this time to Croydon. Cutts was educated from an early age at a private school in Eastbourne and then at St John's College, Hurstpierpoint from 1898–1901. Being privately educated at one of the most famous schools in the UK indicates his well-off, middle-class family background.

Cutts originally trained as a marine and electrical engineer and pursued this career for a while in Croydon until he visited an acquaintance's cinema out of curiosity. The business of showing pictures interested him and he therefore abandoned engineering and started managing a cinema. By 1909 he was living in Hartlepool and married to Charlotte Maud Palliser. By 1911 they had moved to Sevenoaks, Kent. He was listed as a 'Picture Theatre Manager' and she as a 'Picture Theatre Pianist' and now called 'Lizzie'. From Kent, Cutts moved to Devon and in late 1911 through to early 1913, he was the manager of the Empire Electric Theatre in Exeter.

Later, Cutts was an exhibitor around Newcastle and Birmingham in association with Solomon Levy, an important cinema impresario. Levy had a small chain of cinemas, including the Scala and Futurist in Birmingham, where he lived; he also controlled the Palace Theatre in London.

Graham Cutts
Courtesy Ronald Grant Archive

Cutts managed Levy's picture palaces and so became actively interested in six of the leading cinemas in the UK. He turned the Pavilion Theatre in Newcastle upon Tyne into one of the finest houses of cinematic entertainment in the country and spread his magic touch to the Futurist in Birmingham, where the decor (in futuristic style by Val Prince) was the outcome of recommendations that he himself had made. Levy also controlled a film distribution business called Sol Exclusives and was shrewd in gambling a large sum of money to secure the UK rights to D.W. Griffith pictures *Birth of a Nation* (1915) and *Intolerance* (1916). Cutts was prominently in the public eye during this process and personally toured the whole of the UK and presented the films at all the big centres. At some point he also worked for George Black, who controlled a chain of twelve cinemas, in and around Newcastle.

After more than ten years in rental and distribution, Cutts had earned a reputation as 'the master showman of the North'[1] and in the early 1920s became interested in diversifying into film production itself. A colourful character, pushing forty but with energy and stamina, he had quite the reputation for his love of life and also for being a womaniser.

Herbert Wilcox

Herbert Wilcox was born on 19th April 1892 and brought up in London and Brighton, although his mother was from County Cork. Both his parents had died in quick succession from TB and he was looked after by his step-mother. He soon found his vocation excelling at billiards and played exhibition games all over London but gained another reputation as 'the Camberwell Casanova'.[2] His hectic lifestyle and drinking took its toll and in the summer of 1914, he took a break to Gibraltar and Cairo to rest and recuperate.

When war broke out he enlisted and joined the 17th battalion of the Royal Fusiliers. He saw action in France before being posted, ironically enough, to Dublin to help quell the Irish Rebellion of Easter 1916, where he was shot. When he recovered he was commissioned as a pilot in the Royal Flying Corps and served again in France. Towards the end of the war he was back in England as a flying instructor and when peace was declared, he went to London to see the Armistice night celebrations and never flew again for a long time.

Wilcox was at a loose end when his brother Charles, who had been declared unfit for military service, telephoned him from Leeds and said he was a salesman for moving pictures. Herbert went to join him and his business associate Victor

Saville. Both were ace salesmen and Charles was hailed as the super salesman of Yorkshire. Herbert's first job was selling American films to Yorkshire exhibitors, including the first serial of *Tarzan the Ape Man*. Saville was later to be pivotal in the formation of the production unit Balcon-Salville-Freedman.

Herbert and his brother raised £500 and started Astra Films Limited. Although specialising in distributing American films one of the very first British films they took on was *A Peep Behind the Scenes* (1918), a Masters production starring Ivy Close and Gerald Ames. They became so engrossed in the film industry that eventually in July 1920 the brothers decided to embark on production and in conjunction with a Northern exhibitor called H.W. Thompson proposed to make twelve films in the first year with a good list of novels to adapt. Upon engaging a fine array of names, they hired a studio and their first film was *The Breed of the Treshams* (1920) with Kenelm Foss as director (they went on to make other films with him). Later, the two Wilcox brothers formed an auxiliary company called Astra National Productions Limited designed to secure and exploit films and secured the UK rights to *Bohemian Girl* (1922), made by Alliance. Their intention was to acquire big films of any nationality for exploitation. Soon they were renting offices in London and had even grander plans. Independently of Astra Films, Wilcox had decided to enter film production himself. On a more personal note he had married in late 1916 but divorced in 1917, before marrying Maud Bower in 1920, with whom he had four children.

The British Film industry was a small community and so Wilcox already knew of Cutts. Before long the pair began discussing the idea of producing a British film together. Wilcox wanted to expand into production, while Cutts was keen to switch to directing. Cutts had a book called *The Wonderful Story* written by I.A.R. Wylie that he was eager to adapt and so Wilcox stepped in to help, laying the foundations for the formation of Graham-Wilcox Productions a year later.

The Wonderful Story

Herbert Wilcox raised a budget of £1,400 and casting for *The Wonderful Story* began in mid October 1921. Three leads were finally signed – newcomer Herbert Langley, Lilian Hall-Davis and Olaf Hytten at a cost of only £78 – and filming started in early November at the old B&C studio in Hoe Street, Walthamstow, lasting only eight days. The production unit consisted of six people: Graham Cutts as director, cameraman L.G. Egrot, a continuity girl, a property man, a boy to carry the camera and Wilcox as producer.

Adapted by Wilcox, it was a simple story about the humble, everyday life of narrow-minded country folk, with two actors and one actress (and some other minor parts). Brothers Robert (Herbert Langley) and Jimmy (Olaf Hytten) live together in a small cottage. The grim and morose Robert is surly and self-centred in his determination to make a village girl, Kate (Lilian Hall-Davis), his wife and appears to have no romantic foundation for this. She accepts his attentions, realising his determined strength of character rather than any real affection.

Jimmy is a foolish rustic, with an optimistic smile and entirely under the domination of his brother, who treats him with brutal contempt.

On the eve of his wedding Robert has an accident that results in paralysis and over time Kate loses her admiration for him and instead transfers her affections to his brother. Robert is helpless and doomed to lie and watch the gradual courtship and ultimate marriage of his brother and the girl he loves. However, the couple's limited means compels them to share the small cottage with Robert and they refuse to put him in an institution. Robert nurses his hatred and they are forced to live under his malevolent eye. It never occurs to them to pluck up and the courage to defy Robert. His hatred dominates them and although helpless, he is their master. But when the couple's first child is born, Kate places it in Robert's arms and as he holds the infant, his hatred is dispelled and he becomes forgiving.

Herbert Langley in *The Wonderful Story* (1922)

Distributed by Astra-National, it was given a trade show in May 1922 and was described as 'irresistible, interesting and absorbing',[3] 'a masterpiece'[4] and 'an exceptionally good British eternal triangle story'.[5]

It was acknowledged that Cutts and Wilcox had taken a good deal of risk in producing a picture based on a simple story that for some might have lacked 'punch' without lavish expenditure on sets, crowds, stars and other accessories. The film itself however was gripping 'even though there is no wonderful sensation of stunt',[6] and the powerful little story was thought to belong 'to *The Miracle Man* class'.[7] It was readily seen that Cutts was in a position to know what the cinema-going public required and Wilcox was 'congratulated upon his foresight and the courage of his convictions in discovering the latent production ideas manifest in *The Wonderful Story*'.[8]

The scenario, continuity, sets and photography were regarded as being perfect and the acting exemplary. Herbert Langley gave fine work, mostly done lying on his back in bed as an invalid and 'his sincere though at times sinister personality makes him an outstanding figure at once'.[9] Olaf Hytten, who usually played villainous characters, showed himself in a new light as a farm labourer, while Lilian Hall-Davis was simply excellent. As a result of the highly positive reaction Wilcox was offered £4,000 to sell the film, which he accepted. But according to him, despite the huge fanfare and glowing reviews from the trade, the film did not appeal and proved a box-office flop when released.

Cocaine (When London Sleeps)

After filming *The Wonderful Story* in late 1921 there was a gap before Graham Cutts directed his second picture. The death of the actress and socialite Billie Carleton from a drug overdose in November 1918 after the Armistice Victory Ball at the Albert Hall provoked enduring press headlines. The resulting fascination with vice, London night life and Chinese gangs continued unabated. It was this sensational background that interested Cutts and Herbert Wilcox as a suitable frame for a film. No doubt both would have frequented the major cabarets such as Murray's on Beak Street, Ciro's of Orange Street and other seedier joints in the West End such as Mrs Meyrick's 43 Club in Gerrard Street. They would have had first-hand experience of the events and environment they were to recreate.

Cutts gained backing from H.B. Parkinson for Masters Films for his film called *Cocaine*, written by the prolific Frank Miller. It was distributed by Wilcox's Astra National, who may have had a hand in financing the project too. Described as 'a stirring story of London Night Life',[10] the film starred Hilda Bayley and Flora Le Breton. Filming began in mid-March 1922 at Weir House, Teddington, with cameraman Theodore Thumwood.

The film opened with an effective colour sequence of Piccadilly Circus with a blaze of flashing and revolving lights to kaleidoscopic effect. Montagu Webster (Teddy Arundell), known as 'Number One', is a man who owns a string of nightclubs and a drug organisation but lives a life of ease and respectability in the country. His pretty daughter Madge (Flora Le Breton) is carefully guarded from his business life but when he tries to marry her off to his business partner she rebels and runs away to her old school friend Jenny (Hilda Bayley), a pleasure-seeking actress and a slave to drugs. Both girls visit a nightclub owned by Madge's father. While there, a man with a grudge against her father persuades Madge to take cocaine and then informs her father and the police. The police thus discover the identity of Number One but on arrival at his club he shoots his enemy before killing himself. The girls escape to a chapel next door, where Jenny dies a horrible death from an overdose of 'snow' while Madge accepts protection from a faithful young man who loves her.

Cutts had an impressive nightclub set constructed and did some exterior scenes in the local countryside. By mid-April filming was complete. A month later it was rushed out for a trade show in May 1922 (at the same time as *The Wonderful Story*) and the reaction was unanimously good. Although the story was thought to be somewhat sordid and a little too conventional, it was not depressing nor too lurid and the production and acting was regarded as outstanding. Hilda Bayley gave a convincing and natural performance that was perhaps a little too temperamental, Flora Le Breton was good in her lighter moments but rather stiff in her more dramatic scenes but much praise was heaped on Tony Frazer and Ward McAllister, the Chinese assistants (the former, deformed and menacing; the latter, smart and debonair). The only criticism was that Cutts had prolonged the nightclub scene.

Astra gained extensive bookings for *Cocaine* all over the UK and though displayed in some London halls, the British Board of Film Censors refused to grant it a certificate. The London County Council confirmed the ban but other leading cities permitted its exhibition. Wilcox showed the banned film to the L.C.C committee and said in its defence that the film had 'a good moral story'.[11] Although he noted that the members expressed surprise at the censor's action, they then upheld the decision. With distribution in London suspended, Cutts and Wilcox were forced to revise the film to meet the requirements of the censor.

Retitled *When London Sleeps*, it was given a new trade show in July 1922. The image of the effects of a glass of champagne was substituted for cocaine and although the story remained the same, it was tame in comparison, painting a picture of the dangers of dancing and drink.

Even though the company was formed after the release of the film, *The Wonderful Story* was described as the first Graham-Wilcox production. *Cocaine* did not go out under the same banner, despite the fact that Cutts was the director and Wilcox pulled a lot of strings behind the scenes. For both men, having two films – each very different, but receiving glowing reviews from the trade – reaped huge rewards. Wilcox was offered substantial financial backing for future productions and as a result, in the summer of 1922, Cutts and Wilcox decided to make another film. A story had been developed and preliminary casting took place in mid-June 1922, with the old Alliance studio at St Margaret's cited as being secured for filming. A few weeks later Wilcox and Cutts entered the Islington studio and clearly thought this would be a better base. It was announced that arrangements had been made to take a lease of the whole studio with the organisation remaining in the hands of the old FPLBPL staff. Preparations were then made to start work on the next production that was to be called *Flowers of Passion*, later changed to *Flames of Passion*.

Flames of Passion

In accordance with Herbert Wilcox's determination to get into the American market, he and Graham Cutts thought big. Cutts declared he would make *Flames of Passion* as lavish as *The Wonderful Story* was simple with a budget of £45,000. By far the biggest decision was to secure a high-profile American star and in mid-June 1922, the well-known agent Sidney Jay was sent to America for the specific purpose of booking Mae Marsh, an actress both Cutts and Wilcox hugely admired and star of such D.W. Griffith classics as *Intolerance* (1915) and *The Birth of A Nation* (1915).

This decision precipitated some heated debate with the thought that there appeared to be an unnecessary vogue for bringing American artistes to the UK and citing the earlier import of Ann Forrest and Anna Q. Nilsson by FPLBPL. Interesting in a way because American stars had visited the UK before including Edward Godal's casting of Marie Doro in *Twelve Ten* (1919) and both Josephine Earle and Malvina Longfellow made London their professional home during the Great War and had become successful film stars.

To avoid any controversy, Cutts made it clear that the all-star cast had been chosen after a lot of consideration and only when they felt sure that the artistes were entirely suited to the parts selected for them – 'Cutts is a firm believer in the policy that it pays to engage artistes first and foremost for their suitability to portray a given role. Should they possess names which are of value to the box office in addition, so much the better. A name alone would not induce Cutts to engage an artist'.[12] The idea of blending British and American artistes was seen to be 'in pursuance of the new idea of blending the talent of both countries in order to arouse international interest in the picture'.[13] Yet Mae Marsh's name was a huge asset that was seen as a means of getting into the American market.

In real life Mrs Mary Arms, Mae Marsh arrived in Southampton with her husband Louis and child Mary from New York on 3rd July 1922. At Waterloo she was greeted by huge crowds, estimated to be in the region of 100,000. Filming began in earnest at the height of the summer.

The Flowers of Passion was based on an original story especially written for the screen by Herbert Wilcox and his wife Maud and was described as powerful, dramatic and with a universal appeal. However, it was in essence a lurid tale about baby murder, reflecting high and low life. Dorothy Forbes (Mae Marsh), daughter of the wealthy John Forbes (Allan Aynesworth), is neglected. Arriving home from school, she finds herself left to her own devices. She is friendly with her father's chauffeur, Henry Watson (Herbert Langley), but they became far too intimately involved and eventually she finds herself pregnant. She confides in her practical and worldly-wise aunt (Eva Moore), who manages to make arrangements to keep the birth of the child secret. Dorothy retires to the country for the birth and the child is then sent out to nurse; she returns home. She pines for the baby and it is brought from its original foster parents.

The chauffeur is still besotted with Dorothy. He sinks considerably lower and spends his spare time bullying his wife Kate (Hilda Bayley) and getting drunk whereupon he is dismissed from his job. His wife begs for his reinstatement but her request is refused. However, Dorothy's aunt gives her the child to look after, saying it belongs to some friends of hers who have gone to India. Meanwhile, Richard Hawke (C. Aubrey Smith), a famous barrister, falls in love with Dorothy and marries her but she keeps her secret to herself. In a drunken fit the chauffeur kills the child, not knowing that it is his. Hawke is Counsel for the Prosecution and amid fears that he will find out about the child or that the murderer will escape, Dorothy confesses all. He then calls on her as a witness to prove the motive for the murder. Hawke forgives his wife but gives up his career. The last scene shows the couple in a rural retreat, happy in their love and family.

Robert James Cullen assisted Cutts and Norman G. Arnold conducted the art direction (both had been part of the old FPLBPL team). This leads to the question, where was Alfred Hitchcock? Since he was allegedly still part of the studio team at the Islington studio, it is likely he worked on this film and *Paddy the Next Best Thing*, perhaps once again designing the titles and helping out in other capacities, maybe assisting Arnold with properties. And so this must have been his first association working with Cutts.

Photographed by the Frenchman René Guissart, exterior shots took place at Goodwood, Henley, Maidenhead, Cowes and other society rendezvous, with the two major interior scenes in a ballroom and the Old Bailey. At the finale and the ballroom scene, the film burst into colour – described as 'Prizma colour' – similar to the other films made in the same year by John Stuart Blackton.

It was noted that 'frocks are a feature of the production'[14] and all the gowns for Mae Marsh, and presumably the other leading ladies, were created especially by Lucile (Lady Duff Gordon), the world-famous couturier. Mae Marsh explained: 'I always have my clothes made at Lucile's in New York, they understand my personality and now they are just as charming here.' She had up to twenty-five costume changes and had to endure countless hours in dress fitting operations at Lucile's establishment.[15]

Another vital member of Cutts' crew was Renie Morrison, who was his continuity expert and remained with him for many years to come. On *Flames of Passion* she noted the scenario had to be re-written every day and she never had more than one day's script in her hand from which to prompt the director. Morrison observed that few people knew what continuity was and many thought it merely semi-creative work done at a desk revising a scenario. She summed up the job neatly and poetically as being 'the hired memory of the film director'[16] and said that armed with a pencil and notebook, she was there to watch, record and remind. Her role was to observe everything and note the thousand and one details of the production that the director, concentrating as he does on the acting, cannot remember.

Two scenes from *Flames of Passion* (1922)
Left: Eva Moore and Mae Marsh
Right: Herbert Langley and Hilda Bayley

Morrison said that the professional implements of the continuity writer were a notebook, a pencil and observant eye.

An interesting part of her work was on location going over the ground with the cameraman and the director the day before, noting decisions of the best shots and background and camera angles and when the players arrived, recording all relevant details. When filming finished, the continuity writer retired to the cutting rooms with her logbook and from this and memory, cuts and matches up all the scenes so there is no jerkiness in the action and it can be assembled to make the finished film.

In order to do the job it was essential to know the technique of cutting and assembling the negative because all the continuity writer's work was in preparation for this. It demanded hard work, long hours and dedication being responsible for the detection of any inaccuracy in detail and the entire decor of a setting and the progress of action.

Flames of Passion was given a trade show on 10th November 1922 and was a big success. It was highly regarded for staging, direction and acting and was thought to be the most ambitious and successful British picture attempted to date. Comparable with any foreign standard it was seen as 'a venture that looks like making film history in England'.[17] Although a masterly and capital entertainment, *Variety* thought that it did not approach 'the art or value of the same producers' *The Wonderful Story*.'[18]

Displaying the shadier side of life, the subject matter was carefully handled but there was criticism of the story that was seen as slight, sordid, full of improbabilities and implausible plotlines: 'it loses interest as a story and only holds the attention by the excellence of the acting… it is a pity that the skill and care bestowed on the picture could not have been given a worthier object than the story chosen.'[19] Thankfully, there were lighter moments in the film 'which help one forget the somewhat gloomy nature of the story'.[20]

The exteriors and interiors were highly praised, especially the replica of the Old Bailey, which reflected 'a wealth of grim realism'.[21] But the fancy-dress ball was criticised for being colourised, distorting the beauty of the scene. The slightly incongruent ballet sequence was staged by Miss Purcell, a celebrated terpsichorean instructress, and was 'something of a milestone' for it represented one of the first occasions on which dancing had been taken seriously on the screen by introducing movement that could be synchronised effectively with picture-theatre orchestras. The dancers swayed rhythmically to the music and 'do not flicker across the screen with an irritating indifference to the time of the kinema hall orchestra accompanying their appearance'.[22]

There were glowing comments about the acting, with one or two slight reservations. Mae Marsh was admired for showing feeling and a real sense of what was required. In her ingénue scenes as a light, frivolous girl, she was unapproachable but there were doubts about her keeping up to the standard in the heavier scenes.

Hilda Bayley had an exceedingly difficult part but acquitted herself admirably. She evidenced sympathetic insight into the character and her performance had a finesse that made it a pleasure to behold. Herbert Langley was a little too heavy in his bad man role but his performance was polished, while Eva Moore played the aunt with her usual grace and charm.

Towards the end of August 1922, a farewell dinner was given with Mae Marsh as the guest of honour at the Criterion Restaurant, off Piccadilly Circus, before she left for New York. During the course of the evening Herbert Wilcox announced that he had purchased the film rights of *Paddy the Next Best Thing* and everyone agreed that Marsh would be ideal as Paddy.[23]

According to Wilcox *Flames of Passion* went on to make a substantial profit, especially after it was sold to America. He believed that it was the first British film to be sold to the US after World War I. Referring to *The Wonderful Story*, Wilcox remarked that he had 'made a great little picture then; now he has made a great big picture.'[24] Without doubt, it was one of the earliest groundbreaking British silent films.

Paddy the Next Best Thing

Graham-Wilcox's second film with Mae Marsh was *Paddy the Next Best Thing*, a romantic drama about a young tomboy and her growing love for a rich landowner. It was set in Ireland and London. Although Mae Marsh had returned to New York towards the end of August 1922, her stay was extremely brief because she was back in London on 9th September. Like its predecessor, this was a lavish production and once again the same crew were used – including Lucile, who created all the costumes.

The film was adapted from Gertrude Page's novel and play that had been staged at the Savoy Theatre in 1920. Amid picturesque countryside the Adair family live in Mourne Hall and the story centres around the romance of Paddy Adair (Mae Marsh), a kind, yet impulsive and wild Irish girl. She is a 'son' to her father (Sir Simeon Stuart), who would dearly have liked a boy and hence Paddy as 'the next best thing'.

The opening of the film shows a yacht race between Paddy and her father, in which she nearly gets drowned. After being rescued by her father they arrive back on dry land, where she meets Lawrence Blake (Darby Foster), polished man of the world and the owner of a neighbouring estate. In her eyes he has disgracefully neglected the land of his birth in shooting big game in India in preference to leading the life of an Irish gentleman. She takes an immediate dislike to him. For Paddy, Lawrence exudes a self-satisfied superiority and she delights in trying to bring him back down to earth. In the meantime, Paddy encourages Jack O'Hara (George K. Arthur) in his quest for her sister Eileen (Lillian Douglas), but she has fallen for Lawrence. There are various social gatherings at Mourne Hall, including a lavish birthday party, a fox hunt, a ball featuring an elaborate ballet and an Irish country dance. Throughout, verbal skirmishes between Paddy and Lawrence take place.

Eventually, Lawrence tells Paddy that he does not care for her sister and she is the woman he loves. 'One day I will break down your defences,' he says. Paddy calls him a cad for leading her sister on and adds defiantly, 'I despise you.'[25] This forces Lawrence to leave for Europe and India, while Jack also goes abroad to seek his fortune.

When Paddy's father dies it transpires he has saved little of his fortune and she is forced to leave the desolate shuttered mansion and live with her doctor uncle in Shepherd's Bush, working as a dispenser.

When Blake returns, he finds Paddy and again declares his love for her without success as she judges him to be a mere philanderer. In a realistic street fight, Lawrence proves his mettle and Paddy, binding up his wounds, impulsively kisses him. She realises that perhaps she does love him after all but still resists.

Paddy receives a telegram announcing that Jack has returned home with a fortune and is now engaged to her sister Eileen. She rushes back to Ireland. One evening, leaving Eileen and Jack, Paddy wanders off alone into the hills, feeling lonely and unloved. She is soon lost in a dense fog on the edge of a treacherous bog. Lawrence, who has immediately followed her to Ireland, arrives to learn the tragic news that Paddy is lost and heads the search party with the villagers. Their torchlight procession shows hundreds of points of light moving across a mist-shrouded moor. Lawrence arrives just in time to snatch Paddy from the claws of death and Paddy at last confesses her long repressed love.

Once filming was complete Mae Marsh returned to New York, arriving on 17th November 1922; a trade show was given in January 1923. Regarded as being as good technically in terms of staging and photography as *Flames of Passion*, *Paddy the Next Best Thing* became another big success: 'This is one of the best British films yet made... Graham Cutts has done his work admirably'.[26] It was thought to be outstanding, delightful, splendidly presented, 'a genuine triumph'[27] and another film that marks 'a milestone in the improvement of British screen art'.[28]

The story itself, although it had a deep human appeal, was thought to be slight and disjointed in places. And yet it was believed the screen version gained additional power to convey the sentiment more convincingly than the written word or the stage: 'Cutts has succeeded in evolving a charming entertainment from slender material and is the best evidence of his skill'.[29]

Mae Marsh as Paddy in
Paddy the Next Best Thing (1922)

A social gathering at Mourne Hall in
Paddy the Next Best Thing (1922)

Two scenes from *Paddy the Next Best Thing* (1922)

Visually, there was huge praise: 'the pictorial qualities throughout are as pleasing as they are artistic'[30] and the photography of René Guissart was thought to be 'some of the best seen'.[31] Cutts captured Paddy's beautiful home 'vividly with its spacious surroundings of moorland, lakes and rocky coast and the incidents of country life like the fox hunt and the ball' were a delight.[32]

Mae Marsh as Paddy was regarded as being at her best and a delight, illustrating the heroine's many moods with art and realism, from tomboy high spirits to hot-tempered anger and gentle sympathy. Her methods were infinitely varied, her work was never monotonous and she created a consistent and carefully worked-out characterisation of a likeable, yet feisty young woman.

Once again Graham-Wilcox Productions scored a big hit on both sides of the Atlantic and immediately the next project was announced: an all-colour film version of the huge stage success, *Chu Chin Chow*. As John Russell Taylor, one of Hitchcock's biographers, wrote, 'Wilcox and Cutts had developed, almost alone of contemporary British film-makers, some real know-how in the film business'.[33]

Mrs Peabody and Always Tell Your Wife

Following the two Graham-Wilcox productions, a new unit was established in late 1922 to film *Mrs Peabody* at the Islington studio. A modest low-budget project directed by Alfred Hitchcock and funded initially by Hitchcock's uncle Joseph, little is known about the film or who was in fact producing and releasing it. Apparently the enigmatic Anita Ross came up with the idea and script that Hitchcock referred to as '*Number Thirteen*'. Perhaps this referred to the fact it was the thirteenth film Hitchcock had worked on, although that does not account for the two Graham-Wilcox films. Ross was allegedly an American publicity lady from FPL and it was claimed she had worked with Charlie Chaplin.

Conceived as a two-reel comedy, it featuring Clare Greet and Ernest Thesiger. The story concerned low-income residents of a building financed by the Peabody Trust, which offered affordable housing to needy Londoners. Greet was the daughter of actor-manager John Greet and was a popular older character actress who featured in George Fitzmaurice's *Three Live Ghosts*. When the budget started to run out, she financed the film with her own money but even this was not enough to maintain production and only a handful of scenes were shot. The film was believed to be unfinished and shelved. However, Adrian Brunel remembered that Hitchcock did show it to him in an incomplete form, so perhaps more was accomplished than is generally known.[34] Hitchcock never forgot Greet's generous spirit and featured her in many of his later films.

In early 1923, the Edwardian musical comedy star Seymour Hicks decided to produce his own films starring himself and his wife, Ellaline Terriss. He rented the Islington studio intending to make ten short two-reelers based on his past stage successes. Hicks, the famous performer, playwright, screenwriter, theatre manager and producer, was not new to film-making for in 1913 he had worked with Zenith, a company specialising in producing film versions of stage successes out of their studio in the grounds of Woodlands, an old country house in Whetstone. Only two of these films are known: *David Garrick* (1913) and *Scrooge* (1913). Later, Zenith was taken over by British Empire Films and Hicks appeared in their first production – a film version of *Always Tell Your Wife* (1914), a marital farce written by E. Temple Thurston, preformed at the Coliseum in 1913. Hicks and Terriss appeared in another short film called *Prehistoric Love Story*, also produced by the same company in 1915.

Ten years later Hicks attempted to recreate the idea of Zenith/British Empire Films and set to work filming another version of *Always Tell Your Wife* in February 1923 with Hugh Croise as director. It was a comedy sketch about a devoted married man who is confused by the unwelcome return of an old flame. Hicks would appear as the husband, American actress Gertrude McCoy was to play the wife and Ellaline Terris would be the old flame.

During filming, either Croise fell ill or had a disagreement with Hicks over the handling of the picture. Hitchcock stepped in. As John Russell Taylor, commented, Hitchcock was well aware of Hicks as he was an enthusiastic theatre-goer and knew enough of his background and experience to make himself helpful and sympathetic.[35] Hicks described him as a 'fat youth in charge of the property room', who was 'tremendously enthusiastic and anxious to try his hand at producing'.[36] The film was completed but it is not clear how much of it Hitchcock directed and it does not appear to have been released. Nor did Hicks realise his ambitions and sadly, the nine remaining films in the series were never made.

6 WELSH-PEARSON TIP-TOE IN WITH BETTY BALFOUR

In March 1923, the enterprising British film-maker George Pearson leased the Islington studio, still under the control of Major Bell, to create the first of his higher budget pictures titled *Tip-Toes*, starring the incomparable British actress Betty Balfour.

George Pearson's vision of film-making was similar to that of Graham Cutts and Herbert Wilcox. He had enthusiasm and creative ability, thought big and believed in producing well-made, interesting, individual projects and not mass-produced product. Born in 1875 in London, his first profession was teaching. He became a headmaster in 1902 at the age of twenty-six. On seeing a travelling film show, he became aware of the new medium as a means of education and was entranced. He began writing scenarios for the Pathé film company and in 1913 at the age of thirty-seven accepted a job with them as a producer. After a year he moved to work for G.B. Samuelson and then Gaumont, where he met Thomas Welsh, general manager. In early 1918, Pearson went into business with Welsh and they formed Welsh-Pearson with the slight capital of £6,000, optioning a music hall sketch from Charles B. Cochran called *The Better Ole* (1918) as their first film venture. Next, they bought an old school in Craven Park, Harlesden, and converted it into a modest-sized studio opening in the autumn of 1919. Various productions followed, usually numbering three to four a year.

Pearson was regarded 'as a leader in thoughtful and artistic film-making'[1] and the popularity of his films rested on down-to-earth humour and working-class characters with an acknowledgement of the highs and lows of life. He was inventive in using visual and symbolic effects with limited resources and possessed the ability to gain charismatic performances from his actors. Of all of these, Pearson found his muse in Betty Balfour, who became one of the most popular screen stars in Britain in the 1920s.

Balfour was born in London in 1903 and began singing and making a nuisance of herself from the age of three. Gifted with a talent for mimicry and comedy, she imitated street characters such as the milkman and dustman. She began performing at charity events and then in a children's pantomime, where she proved such a success that she was snapped up by an agent and placed in a sketch with Syd Chaplin at the Wood Green Empire at the age of twelve. The theatre producer Charles B. Cochran noticed her and placed her in his revue, *Odds and Ends*, at the Ambassadeurs Theatre in 1914. More stage appearances followed through the war.

During this period Thomas Welsh at Gaumont saw Balfour and thought she was ideal screen material but nothing happened until 1920, after Welsh-Pearson was formed, when Welsh signed her to play a small character part in *Nothing Else Matters* (1920). As the cockney skivvy she was a huge hit and was

Betty Balfour in *Squibs* (1921)

signed to a long contract, appearing in a more serious role in *Mary-Find-the-Gold* (1921). Pearson believed that comedy was essential to Balfour's development and wanted to find something more suitable. Through the scriptwriter Eliot Stannard, he found a music-hall sketch with a jolly and brazen daredevil and bought the right to use the character name – Squibs. With Stannard, he wrote the first Squibs' escapade, a simple tale of a Piccadilly flower girl who is madly in love with a policeman and also the daughter of a very shady father who earns a precarious living as a street corner bookie. While her character Squibs was a rough cast, ragged little East Ender, in real life Balfour was a smartly-attired, highly polished little West Ender.

Squibs (1921) was a huge success and Pearson was persuaded by William Jury of Jury's Film Service, who handled the distribution of Welsh-Pearson films, to turn the character of Squibs into a series. So the exuberant cockney urchin, roguish and with a heart of gold, appeared once again in *Squibs Wins the Calcutta Sweep* (1922). Besides the Squibs' films Pearson also cast Balfour in the comedies *Wee MacGregor's Sweetheart* (1922) and *Mord Em'ly* (1923). Before long, Betty's charming and effervescent screen personality made her 'Britain's Queen of Happiness'.[2] She was hailed as the British Mary Pickford and 'the finest comedy artiste on the British screen'.[3]

Love, Life and Laughter

For Balfour's next project, Pearson sought inspiration from the famous music-hall star Marie Lloyd. He was convinced that Betty would be perfect as a child of poverty who rises through sheer ability to become the Queen of Musical Comedy. He began writing an unconventional story that was christened *Tip-Toes*, and renamed *Love, Life and Laughter*. It had a typical boy-meets-girl theme set in the slums but then moving to spectacular heights with a daring fantasy climax. Although a risk placing Balfour in a different environment to her former escapades as Squibs and mixing imagination and realism, it paid off handsomely.

The story followed the fortunes of two people divided for two years. The hero (Harry Jones) is a novelist struggling for fame. Tip-Toes (Betty Balfour) is a chorus girl who wants be a star. Both live, one above the other, in the attic of a tenement. They meet and Tip-Toes shows the boy that there is laughter in life. He writes a story about them both and reads it to her. As he reads, it becomes real and he makes her journey a fairytale of success, while he himself is a failure. His book is a success but he never knows it. They make a contract to meet on a certain day two years from the day they part. On that day Tip-Toes waits for the boy in her old rooms, only to receive word from an old musician friend that he is dead. Having finished the story, we are brought back to reality; Tip-Toes embraces the boy and tells him there must be a happy ending in real life.

Pearson set a budget of £18,000 and decided to film the less ambitious scenes at the small Craven Park studio and other, grander ones at the Islington studio. His strategy paid off and the film was produced on a far more lavish scale than any of Betty Balfour's preceding pictures. Filming began in Harlesden in late February, with Claude McDonnell as cameraman. For four weeks the emphasis was capturing 'Tip-Toes' in her cheap attic lodgings as she danced behind footlights of her own making as a struggling, but optimistic member of a vaudeville troupe.

Two scenes from *Love, Life and Laughter* (1923) featuring Betty Balfour

At the Islington studio filming took place in March 1923 and a complete up-to-date music hall, the ballroom of a West End restaurant of the Carlton scale, an open-air East End jazz palace and a crowd of down and outs in an underground embankment doss-house were recreated. The open-air East End jazz palace scene featuring a big area at night at the rear of an inn with a crowd of happy dancers and musicians was achieved by illusion. The studio was dark and a high camera held the whole floor in view, with one strong searchlight only for illumination capturing the festivities.

Night-time revelry was depicted in the cabaret scene: a gorgeous ballroom. Crowded with pretty woman and distinguished-looking men at daintily laid tables, an exhilarating atmosphere of smart, polite Bohemianism and carefree enjoyment was created. Tip-Toes arrives, wearing a wonderful gown and astonishing head-dress, and accompanied by friends. She enters the set at the top of a broad and beautiful staircase to be greeted by admiration and a crescendo of popular applause. Charmingly, she acknowledges the tributes and moves with her entourage to a reserved alcove table to watch the show. In the centre of the great hall emerges a troupe of scantily-clad dancers in alluring, shimmering costumes and led by the graceful Dacia to the exotic strains of a coloured orchestra. At the end of the show many silvery streamers descend on Dacia and her companions like a huge fairy shower bath.

With a distinctly Hogarthian atmosphere, Pearson charmingly evoked the lives of humble stage folk and the romantic glamour of small triumphs and failures in almost epic dimensions. The action was really a series of intriguing and vivid interludes all peppered with delightful cockney humour. These scenes included episodes of the lodging house keeper (Annie Esmond) and her hen-pecked, balloon making husband (Frank Stanmore); the tragic comedy of the fallen star (Sydney Fairbrother) and the quiet beauty of the scenes in the house with the old musician (Harding Steerman) and his daughter (Audrey Ridgwell).

After the trade show in May 1923 (released 22nd October 1923), the reaction was complimentary and *Love, Life and Laughter* was deemed a challenge to the world: 'British supremacy would be assured if all native productions approximate to this standard'.[4] It was viewed as charming, distinguished, packed with excellent entertainment qualities, splendidly produced, full of masterly touches and clever characterisations. Pearson's lighting created an illusive fairyland in utilising the effects of candlelight and firelight perhaps to enhance the crude raw edges of life. The main criticisms concentrated on some 'jumpy' continuity and a plot that needed to be stronger and more carefully thought out.

Betty Balfour brought all the grace, lightness and vivacity distinguishing her work to portray the charming, blithe and sprightly little dancer effectively, naturally and quaintly. Her performance was so good that it was made clear that it would 'silence all those who would suggest that we have no actresses to compare with American screen idols'.[5]

The film was a huge success and Erich Pommer, head of UFA (Universum Film Aktiengesellschaft) in Berlin (who had been present at the trade show), booked it for Germany. He didn't like the happy ending and so he scrapped the last section of the return to reality, saying without this it would appeal more to the German audience. At the same time Gaumont made a generous offer to distribute the film, taking over from Jury's Film Service. And the stage was set for even bigger things for Pearson and Balfour as more films of a similar nature were to be filmed as previously at Craven Park and Islington.

Squibs M.P.

Squibs M.P. was the third Squibs' film and was, as the title suggests, a hilarious account of how Squibs, the former cockney flower girl, became a Member of Parliament. At the time there was much discussion about female suffrage since women had just gained the right to vote in 1918, but only qualified if they were over thirty and met a minimum property qualification. It was the perfect frame for Squibs and a story was written by Will Dyson, Leslie Hiscott and George Pearson.

They circumvented the problem of Squibs' age (she was twenty) by introducing the theme of her crafty old father (Hugh E. Wright) having a financial incentive for Squibs winning a seat. He had to tell her that she was actually thirty and had suffered from long trances, one of which lasted ten years, although they had not informed her of this before then. The issue of her birth certificate and how she got it, and how Squibs became an M.P. provided much amusement.

The film featured a series of disconnected incidents, some trivial and others far-fetched, which served as a vehicle for Squibs' characteristic exploits. Squibs starts a rival milk company to Miss Fitzbulge (Irene Tripod) and gets her fiancé to stand for Parliament. Through her father's efforts he is accused of bribery and Squibs, by lying about her age, stands instead. She is elected, makes a speech and goes to stay with some wealthy Parliamentary people. Here, Miss Fitzbulge chases Squibs' father and discovers the truth about her age; Squibs subsequently resigns.

George Pearson started work on *Squibs M.P.* at the Craven Park studio in late May 1924 and transferred to the Islington studio in early July. There was a kaleidoscopic variety of scenes including an East End election scene with 300 'rough types', a visit to a cabaret, shopping inside a couture establishment of tasteful magnificence, a range of Paris exteriors and at the end of the film, a midnight pyjama romp through a country house.

One of the most impressive scenes featured the House of Commons in session, where Squibs makes her maiden speech advocating government expenditure on the health of the nation's babies rather than battleships. There was also a night-party in Willesden, with a quaint and eerie forest comprising large and tall mossy tree trunks with lanterns and moving lights.

A crowd of people incongruously attired dance and are dwarfed by the trees 'as if fairies had decided to hold a fancy-dress ball'.[6] Betty Balfour, surrounded by the rest of the cast, was dressed as a French soldier in slate blue and scarlet, complete with moustache.

Charles Penley, George Pearson's new assistant, explained the real economies of a big studio and the new system where big scenes were hardly ever extended into the second day due to the organisation of Major Bell and his efficient technical studio staff. During filming, Pearson would often disappear at lunchtime to Alfred Hitchcock's little office (calling him the art director) and 'a very friendly young man', where they would gamble with pennies on a little toy race game that Hitchcock had created.[7]

Two scenes from *Squibs M.P.* (1923) featuring Betty Balfour

Pearson believed that the trade show in September 1923 (release date unknown) was a huge success, but although seen as 'good light entertainment – a riot of light humour'.[8] The reaction was in fact lukewarm and thought not to be up to the general standard of previous productions. Despite skilful direction, good lighting and photography, elaborate and artistic staging and clever acting, it was viewed as a disappointing instance of clever people and elaborate material wasted upon an unworthy scenario. The story was of no consequence and so there was a lack of continuous dramatic interest. Instead the numerous farcical episodes were haphazard and contained little humour or intrinsic human appeal. It was a slapstick comedy, where the talent of the fine players was wasted.

In terms of the acting, Betty Balfour was joyous, bright and clever and avoided the temptation of too much clowning around. Overshadowed by Balfour's prominence, the other players had little to do. Hugh E. Wright was quaint as the erratic but loveable cockney father; Irene Tripod played the badly used, yet rather likeable Fitzbulge with great energy and enthusiasm but Fred Groves as the jolly policeman sweetheart received only background treatment. Despite the criticism Squibs was in great demand and there was a clamour for more.

Squibs Honeymoon

George Pearson thought there was a danger of overdoing a good thing and decided the only way to end the Squibs' series was marry Squibs off to her policeman lover and so *Squibs Honeymoon* was devised. In the late summer of 1923, Pearson and Thomas Welsh went away to the seaside for a rest and to formulate the plot that evolved into a frustrated honeymoon idea. It opened with the frantic and complicated preparations for the ceremony, then the wedding itself, followed by a mix-up at the railway station with Squibs and her husband (Fred Groves) at Calais, en route for Paris. While Squibs found her seat on the train, her husband was making purchases from the station stall and missed the train. Squibs returns to Calais from Paris in search of her husband while he chases her to Paris with the two trains passing each other. They take one sensible action in wiring Squib's father in London (Hugh E. Wright), affording the excuse of bringing him and his delightful friend Honeybun (Frank Stanmore) to join the search for the disconnected honeymooners. The confusion is compounded and leads to a whole chain of outrageously comic situations including a gang of Apaches in a barge who kidnap them, followed by Squibs' escape, Monte Cristo fashion, in male attire. On the French country road she has a car smash and discovers her husband is in the colliding vehicle. Unharmed and overjoyed, they begin their honeymoon in a local cottage.

Filmed mostly on location in Calais, Boulogne and Paris and at Craven Hall, the wedding scene with the exterior of the church was shot at the Islington studio in early October 1923, but because finances were limited, they could only commit to this one scene. The whole of the big floor at the Islington studio was taken up with a lovely old village church set with real shady trees and bushes and laid lawn, cobbled path leading up to the church through a lychgate with perched doves. The church in the crest of the slope seemed centuries old but had in fact been erected in just a few hours. Among the spectators were a number of uniformed policemen all 'attending' the wedding, including husband-to-be Fred Groves and Hugh E. Wright as Squibs' father in his comic Sunday best. There were cheers from the crowd when Squibs arrived and Betty Balfour looked radiant in a cream wedding dress. Accompanying her were a few young girls in plain black straw hats and shawls, attire that was practically the insignia of the Piccadilly Circus flower seller.

It was a slow motion wedding for Balfour as Squibs for she must have gone into the church at least twenty times and came out six. Each time the bodyguard of flower girls and 'bobbies' threw confetti and cheered; each time Balfour had to be dusted over with a big feather duster to remove all the confetti for retake after retake.

Rather than follow the usual idea of an altar and stained-glass windows and pews, Pearson focused on illusion and the imagination of the audience in using a length of white stone wall and one stone column for the church interior and a near shot of an organist at his keyboard. With suitable lighting, the diffused shadow of Squibs in her wedding gown moved across the old church wall while outside peeping through the church doors were her cockney admirers.

The unit filmed exteriors for *Squibs Honeymoon* in Paris for three weeks. They worked several days at the Pre-Catalan and made it their base. A real old French farm inn and a showplace beloved of Parisians and tourists alike, the Pre-Catalan was one of the most chic summer society rendezvous in the Bois de Boulogne. Balfour discovered all the locals knew who she was and affectionately dubbed her 'La Petite Marchande de Fleurs de Piccadilly'. It was not summer but late autumn and there was scarcely one fine day; sadly, Betty caught a cold and when she returned to London, she was in bed for ten days.

At the trade show of *Squibs Honeymoon* in December 1923 (released 24th March 1924), it fared better than Pearson's previous offering and was thought to fully maintain the high reputation of Welsh-Pearson company as wholesome British farce of the best kind: 'one of the cheeriest British films made for some time'.[9] The film had all the distinctive George Pearson touches of spontaneous humour, well-drafted character and swift action. Balfour was adored as being 'impish, charming, masterful and excitable'[10] and it was observed that she 'had never had a part which has given more scope to her talents as an actress or her personal charm'.[11] Fred Groves was at his best and Hugh E. Wright and Frank Stanmore were splendid in the ridiculous and half-pathetic comedy parts.

The final screen farewell to one of Britain's most loveable characters drew to a close: Squibs was no more - until the talkie remake of *Squibs* in 1935.

Reveille

During the latter part of 1923, George Pearson had been preoccupied with a lawsuit concerning plagiarism over the story of *Love, Life and Laughter* but the case was without foundation and he won. It did hold up making a new picture, though. Finally, he started thinking about what to do next and sought inspiration. The film critic George Atkinson talked about the war tragedies among the poor and Pearson caught the phrase 'the poor old widow lost her three sons'.[12] This provided the idea for his next film, titled *Reveille*, and he wrote the script in Saint-Raphael, on the Riviera, in early 1924.

Reveille was a drama of war and its after-effects on a closely-knit group of family and friends in London during a month in 1918 and a month in 1923, with episodes at the front. There was no definite story and the plot was neither strikingly original nor complex but instead leant on the development of a series of truthful pictures of everyday life with humour and tragedy. Regarded as the biggest picture attempted by the Welsh-Pearson, the characters were humble folk and the main setting was a greengrocer's shop in the East End. Before the war, an aged widow (Henrietta Wilson), mother of three fine sons – Sam (Charles Ashton), Ted (Donald Searle) and the Kid (Ralph Forbes), kept the business going. Mickey (Betty Balfour) is a loveable young girl lodged over the shop with her brother Fred (Guy Phillips). On the top floor of the dilapidated house are two elderly spinster sisters Sophia (Sydney Fairbrother) and Amelia (Buena Bent), who live on a small inheritance from their father.

The three sons and Fred are called away to serve in the war. Mickey and the mother are left to continue daily life with the two maiden aunts. The boys come home on seven days' leave with two friends, Nutty (Stewart Rome) and Whelks (Frank Stanmore), in September 1918. This admirably captured London's hectic days when the war was drawing to a close and the optimistic 'home on leave' spirit. Mickey spends much of her time with the Kid and becomes romantically involved. But the men must return to the front. Within two months the Armistice is signed but the three sons and Mickey's brother never return. The tragedy of a telegram and finally, the long, drawn-out struggle for things to come right are all depicted with a realistic fidelity. Five years later Mickey is working as a seamstress to keep herself and her little son, while her mother works as a charwoman. It was a bold move to portray an unmarried mother in such circumstances and Balfour no doubt helped somewhat in removing the stigma. Whelks and Nutty find themselves among the great number of unemployed. Nutty gives way to despair and becomes a revolutionary but Mickey intervenes and through her courage brings him to a more positive frame of mind. Finally, on Armistice Day, the Reveille sounds a note of hope.

The film was a risk because it was a departure from previous Welsh-Pearson offerings, but Gaumont nevertheless chose to back it. Most of the filming took place at the Islington studio from mid-February through March 1924. Further minor interiors were then filmed at the Craven Park studio thereafter. Described as 'a smart piece of floor work',[13] one scene involved the whole studio floor being covered in realistic trenches and sandbags. Pearson worked until after 10pm one evening to get it right but by 10.30 the next morning, the whole studio had been cleared and in its place was a big joy wheel (specially imported from a fun-fair) with circus seating for an audience of 400, especially recruited from the surrounding area and many of them proud of the fact that they had played in previous Betty Balfour pictures. Another big scene was the frivolities of Armistice night in a mock Trafalgar Square with the studio floor covered in sheets of grey three-ply to represent the pavement and a replica of the Landseer lion.

At the trade show in late July 1924 (release date unknown), attended by David, Prince of Wales, the reaction was universally good: 'The appeal to crude emotions, very good comedy incidents and star's star's name (Betty Balfour) will make this picture a big attraction'.[14] It was thought to capture something of the spirit of the trenches and of wartime London, with its anti-aircraft searchlights and hectic gaiety, and then dealing with problems such as the unemployment of former service men: 'Pearson has the gift of knowing what the public wants and the ability of presenting it in an effective and convincing manner'. [15]

The performance of all the players was admired, but Stewart Rome had little to do and his characterisation was thought to be vague with little chance to display his usual qualities. Betty Balfour as the jolly flapper of the war period and a plucky woman in the lean times of peace 'never acted better' and played her part 'with the freshness and vivacity that is the secret of her popularity'.[16] But there was criticism suggesting that the vivacity she continually exhibited was a little too artificial.

Betty Balfour in her wedding dress from *Squibs Honeymoon* (1923)

7   BALCON-SAVILLE-FREEDMAN

Following the success of *Paddy the Next Best Thing* at the trade show in January 1923, Graham Cutts and Herbert Wilcox were planning to film a version of the stage show *Chu Chin Chow*. But something happened and Cutts decided to leave Graham-Wilcox Productions. Perhaps they had a disagreement over future strategy although it is more likely it had become evident that Wilcox wanted to direct and so Cutts felt there was no room for two directors. Indeed, Wilcox went on to direct *Chu Chin Chow* (1923).

At the same time, a new company called Balcon-Saville-Freedman based on the surnames of its three founders – Michael Balcon, Victor Saville and John Freedman – rose to prominence. In their twenties, enthusiastic and optimistic, both Balcon and Saville came from struggling Jewish families in the industrial Midlands and were the driving forces behind this new venture. They were destined to become major players in the British film industry.

Free from pretension, benevolent, a nurturer of talent, generous with opportunities, sensible but also imaginative, Balcon was always smartly dressed with a neat moustache and receding hairline. Although very cosmopolitan in outlook due to his roots, he looked more like a sober bank manager and was careful and shrewd with money. Saville was dashing, tall, blue-eyed, well-built and had a showman's instinct for promotion and advertising; also a keen appreciation of the American market.

Victor Saville

Born Victor Salberg (he changed his name to Saville when he married) to a respectable middle-class Jewish family in Birmingham on 5th September 1897, Saville's father was an art dealer who travelled all over Europe and had shops in Harrogate and later in Bond Street, London. He was educated at King Edward VI Grammar School in Birmingham and in his younger days enjoyed visiting the Alexandra Theatre (owned by his Uncle Leon) and local cinemas. At the age of seventeen he went to work in a shipping office in London through a business connection of his grandfather in South Africa, but only stayed a few weeks as war broke out and he enlisted.

Assigned to the 18th Regiment the London Irish Rifles, his military life was cut short when he was badly injured at the Battle of Loos. He was invalided out of the army in mid-1916 and was lucky to get a job with Soloman Levy, a friend of his father, who worked in the film business. Levy, as we have seen, employed Graham Cutts to manage his cinemas and also ran a film distribution company called Sol Exclusives. When Levy financed two films for G.B. Samuelson, he went there to observe and saw the inside of a studio for the first time. Over the next two years Saville worked in London for Pathé, Gaumont and Oswald Stoll, but then returned north to work with Charles and Herbert Wilcox in Leeds.

Michael Balcon was born in Birmingham on 19th May 1896 to a respectable but impoverished family. In 1907 he gained a scholarship to Birmingham's George Dixon Grammar School. When family finances became even tighter, he was forced to leave in 1913 and gained work as a jeweller's apprentice. By then he already had a lively interest in the cinema. When war broke out he was turned down for service because of defective eyesight and joined the Dunlop Rubber Company, becoming assistant to the managing director.

Balcon and Saville had been friends in their earlier years and at this point in time they renewed their friendship. When the Wilcox brothers formed the distribution company Astra Films Limited, they secured the UK rights to a block of twenty-four films from the Mutual Company of America. Saville was offered the franchise to sell these films in the Midlands. He raised some capital and in 1920 formed Victory Motion Pictures with Balcon. The chairman was another mutual friend, Oscar Deutsch, from a family of prosperous metal merchants, and another director was Sam Bodlender, a shrewd Yorkshireman, who was on the board of Standard Life Assurance Company. As the company expanded, they took on the distribution rights to some of the films that Soloman Levy controlled and also represented the interests of W&F Distribution Company in Birmingham.

W&F was founded by Charles Moss Woolf, S. Freedman, D. Tebbitt and J.ulius Hagen in February 1919 with a capital of £10,000, using the surnames of Woolf and Freedman to form the company name, Woolf and Freedman Film Service (abbreviated to W&F). Charles Woolf was the more visible and controlling partner and still had one foot in the family fur business in the City of London. One of his first steps was to take the UK franchise for the first *Tarzan of the Apes* film and the Harold Lloyd Comedies. Balcon described Woolf as 'a high tension man', adding that he was capable of great charm and generosity but could

Michael Balcon
Courtesy Ronald Grant Archive

reduce a strong man to tears: 'He was regarded with a mix of awe and affection. He hated holidays abroad. Rarely visited the studio. But he knew about the end product and had an unparalleled talent for film business. He was the shrewdest film salesman of his time.'[1]

The director Adrian Brunel described Woolf as 'a courageous backer with faith in British films' and added that he was by no means an infallible judge of pictures and like many other Wardour street businessmen made great mistakes, but his faith and support set the pace to encourage the British Film Industry and film production.[2] Woolf spent his career imposing his taste on a succession of film companies in which he invested heavily and was hugely significant in the development of the Islington studio and its unfolding story.

Significantly, Saville had met and married a cockney called Phoebe Vera Tiller in mid-1920, who was niece to Charles Woolf, thus cementing further connections. Not long afterwards Saville and Balcon left Victory in the hands of Balcon's elder brother 'Shan' Chandos (Samuel) and relocated to London with the intention of breaking into film production. Although their contacts in the film industry were slight and they only had a small capital of £200, they set themselves up in business with John (or Jack) Freedman, son of S. Freedman at W&F, who allegedly was also a nephew to Woolf. They rented a small office in Cranbourn Street, off Leicester Square with a staff of three – a secretary, a salesman called Turner and a young man called Cedric Belfrage as an assistant, who later made a name for himself as a film critic and author.

Balcon and Saville continued distributing foreign films as before and handled the Nick Carter detective series but lost their profit by taking on some German cartoon films. They saw their best way of becoming producers was to start by creating advertising films or what we now call commercials. Through Sidney Bernstein (whose father owned a group of cinemas in suburban London that laid the foundations of the Granada chain of cinemas and later Granada TV), they won a bid to film a commercial with an oil company, marketed in the UK as Pratts. For the first time Saville was behind the camera and directed a film of a motorcar driving up to the first petrol pump in England to fill its tank with Pratt's petrol.

They had their eye on Herbert Wilcox's endeavours with Graham Cutts and when they became aware of Cutts' film *Cocaine*, they bought in a similar American film and retitled it as *The Cocaine Smugglers*. And, they watched as Graham-Wilcox brought over Mae Marsh and filmed *Flames of Passion* and *Paddy-The-Next-Best-Thing*. One thing was clear, the American market was vital if a big-budget British film was to become viable and it was necessary to engage a high-profile American star.

Woman to Woman

When Balcon-Saville-Freedman decided it was time to enter feature film production they engaged Graham Cutts, who was undoubtedly regarded at the time as the best director in London with vision and a great attention to detail. According to Michael Balcon, Cutts walked into their office one day and announced he had an option on the film rights to the play *Woman to Woman* by Michael Morton, staged in 1921 in the West End. Perhaps Saville and Balcon had already been in touch with him as the most likely candidate to give effect to their ideas, knowing he had already left Herbert Wilcox. Cutts suggested that they should produce *Woman to Woman* and he would direct. Recognising that they were fortunate to secure Cutts' services and that a good story was the basis of any good motion picture, they cut a deal. They all felt that the play was perfect screen material with the right kind of sentiment and both the author and director set about collaborating on the writing.

Although Cutts had made few pictures, every one of them had been well received and had made record figures for all concerned. Indeed the match with Cutts was perfect – 'His knowledge and an undoubted producing instinct have enabled him to become one of the foremost figures in British production in a comparatively short time: and his breadth of vision and courage make him beyond question one of the few Englishmen well fitted to challenge the American production field on its own scale of endeavour'.[3] His practical experiences as a showman in the film business were also seen as a huge advantage, which would 'stand him in good stead not only in giving the exhibitor just that kind of picture that his audience demands but also one that will provide plenty of scope for exploitation and presentation'.[4]

The company outlined its philosophy in stating that they would adhere to two principles: each production would be big in conception and execution and they would restrict the number of films to be made each year as they believed that 'in picture making mass production is not compatible with, and indeed is the enemy of quality'.[5] They also wanted to be highly competitive in setting their sights on the international market rather than just the domestic one. Like Herbert Wilcox, they sought to enhance the international value of their production in signing an American star.

Since the estimated budget was £40,000, the first step was to secure finance. They met Charles Woolf in a Soho café to explain their proposition and he listened with no reaction, knowing 'he was not a man of enthusiasms'.[6] They were surprised when he took out his wallet and laid on the table seven discount bills for £1,000 each and requested distribution rights. However, the terms of distribution promised little unless the film proved a smash hit. They visited others and raised more finance, with another backer being their old friend Oscar Deutsch from Birmingham.

The next thing they needed was a high-profile American star and so Victor Saville and his wife Phoebe travelled to America on a six-week trip, leaving for New York on 18th March 1923. They had their sights firmly set on Betty Compson, who was petite at just over five foot tall, with blonde curls and beautifully radiant features. She was a versatile performer and at the time was highly regarded for the success she had achieved in *The Miracle Man* (1919), *At the End of the World* (1921), *The Law and the Woman* (1922) and *The Green Temptation* (1922). Dainty and with a delicate femininity, she was adored as a 'jolly, effervescent and yet firmly practical young woman who puts on no airs and graces'.[7]

Leaving New York, the Savilles took the five-day train ride to Los Angeles and began socialising and networking. They enjoyed the various nightspots and spent a day on the stage with Charlie Chaplin, who was directing *A Woman in Paris* (1923). They also visited the Metro studio and met the famous director Rex Ingram. Saville's meeting with Betty Compson was productive as he sold the idea, the screenplay, their technical ability and their plans for wardrobe. Luckily, she was also at a loose end, having just refused to sign a new contract with FPL over pay. Since her early association with George Loane Tucker, Betty always wanted to visit England to see for herself the wonderful country about which Tucker never tired of telling her. She signed a two-picture contract with a salary of £1,000 per week, a rather huge sum that was believed to be a record for any film actress appearing in England, and arrived in the UK with the Savilles on 5th May 1923.

The issue of using American stars once again caused some consternation but it was observed that Cutts was 'the only director on this side who has worthily exploited an American star in good pictures. Cutts is not the only producer capable of doing so: but up to now he is the only one who has actually done so'.[8] It was also made clear that there was a good case for using American talent since they had fame and exposure which was of benefit in terms of creating success but also offered 'badly needed work for the British supporting cast to which is added the fine opportunity of appearing on American screens in real parts'.[9]

In Saville's absence, Balcon and Cutts began casting other players including the American Josephine Earle, who had made a name for herself in London and had been a star for Gaumont just after the war, the Scottish actor Henry Vibart and the British actress Marie Ault. The latter became the most famous British character actress playing mostly distinctive elderly parts and was to excel in many future brilliant screen performances. As their leading man they chose a rising new star called Clive Brook, who was smart and debonair. Following his war service Brook went on the stage but was then lured onto the screen by director Walter West. He was given the title 'One in a Million' because he had been very lucky and did not have to climb to the top from crowd work to bit parts; he started out as a leading man.

They also engaged Claude MacDonnell, who had worked for FPLBPL on *Dangerous Lies* (1922), *Beside the Bonnie Brier Bush* (1922) and George Pearson's *Love, Life and Laughter* (1923), to be cameraman, secured Dolly Tree, England's leading costume designer for the stage, to design all the gowns and costumes and signed Espinosa, the well-known choreographer to arrange all the dances. At the same time they visited the Islington studio, where Cutts had previously worked on the two Mae Marsh pictures and where Alfred Hitchcock and a core staff were still engaged. Most likely Cutts and Balcon visited the studio when George Pearson was filming Betty Balfour in *Love, Life and Laughter*, although perhaps Hitchcock was also working on *Always Tell Your Wife* – after all, there were two sizeable stages. They hired the studio to film *Woman to Woman* and began pre-production in mid- to late April before the arrival of Betty Compson.

Cutts presumably renewed his acquaintance with Hitchcock and recognising his enthusiasm and skill in many areas sought to introduce him into the production team. When Balcon encountered Hitchcock he viewed him as a 'handyman and draftsman, eager to do more'.[10] Plump and assertive, he looked younger than he was – despite a Charlie Chaplin moustache designed to make himself look more mature. Seeing a major opportunity, Hitchcock made himself indispensable and was asked to be assistant director.

It is a commonly held view that Hitchcock created the screenplay as suggested by Balcon, but Cutts and the author Michael Morton had already been working on it. Perhaps he may have been asked to add finishing touches or Balcon was mistaken and he was in fact referring to a different film. Indeed, in late April 1923, as production on *Woman to Woman* gathered pace, Cutts announced that Hitchcock was adapting the play *The Prude's Fall*, that was to be Betty Compson's second picture for Balcon-Saville-Freedman productions.

When the nominated art director (quite possibly Norman G. Arnold) decided he could not fulfill the task, Hitchcock volunteered to act in his place as well. Subsequently, when the team needed an editor and cutter, he recommended the titian-haired girl he had admired from afar and offered Alma Reville the job, a position she gladly accepted. Such enthusiasm was welcome as in the early 1920s studio working conditions were not easy and a crew had to multi-task.

For 1923 the story was considered daring, although from today's perspective it is somewhat naive and melodramatic. The screenplay, substantially different to the play, evolved into a simple tale of a British army officer (Clive Brook), who falls in love with Deloryse (Betty Compson), a French dancer at the Moulin Rouge. It is 1914 and he goes back to the trenches, where he is wounded, loses his memory and therefore fails to carry out his promise to marry the dancer. When the war is over, he returns to England and marries (Josephine Earle) and becomes a not-too-happily married man. In the meantime the dancer has borne his child and becomes internationally famous. Engaged to dance in England, she meets her old lover and his wife, the climax being a confrontation between the two women and the death of Deloryse.

The exterior of the Moulin Rouge set in *Woman to Woman* (1923)
Courtesy J.W. Mitchell Collection / Brian Twist

Cutts and Hitchcock went to Paris for a few days to do research for décor, as the film was to require some elaborate Parisian scenes. This was Hitchcock's first trip abroad and the first thing he did was to attend mass at the Madeleine but then became engrossed in the hedonistic atmosphere of the city by night. The pair toured Montmartre and visited all the sights to observe restaurants, street life, exhibitions and risqué nightclubs. They spent a longer time at the Moulin Rouge to gain inspiration, as they needed to create an exact replica of the famous cabaret that was to form a major scene in the film.

When Betty Compson arrived in London she was given a glittering reception by Balcon-Saville-Freedman at the Savoy Hotel on the evening of 7th May 1923, introducing her to all those involved in the production and key representatives of the literary and film world. Filming then proceeded smoothly and finished on schedule in June 1923.

Betty Compson in her ostrich-feather dress composed of
over 200 ostrich feather plumes and 1,000 pearls
in *Woman to Woman* (1923). Designed by Dolly Tree

The cabaret scene in *Woman to Woman* (1923)
Dresses designed by Dolly Tree
Courtesy J.W. Mitchell Collection / Brian Twist

Cutts liked music in the studio and was pleased that Betty was not just a tireless worker but also a wonderful violinist. She spent most of her time when she was not working playing the violin in a little orchestra, endeavouring to act as an inspiration to her director. The three-piece orchestra (piano, cello and violin) was there to aid Betty's acting for she was incapable of registering emotion without the aid of it. Throughout the production the orchestra would play specific tunes such as 'Mighty Like a Rose' and then she could cry. But it didn't go down well with Balcon, who would wince whenever he heard the tune thereafter!

One of the first scenes to be filmed was at the end of April, prior to Compson's arrival. It featured a life-sized reproduction of the exterior of the Moulin Rouge with showy electrical illumination of the frontage and the revolving sails of the mill itself. There was a length of pavement and a street, French taxis and adjoining cafés. The bohemian atmosphere of Montmartre was all-pervasive and the set populated by a mix of typical British Tommies, French *poilus*, artists, nondescript dilettantes, street urchins, gendarmes, sailors, waiters, flower sellers and of course delightful examples of Parisian femininity. Pedestrians strolled along the pavement, taxis dodged people crossing the road and the café tables were bustling with life. The manager of the Moulin Rouge stood outside the entrance and nodded to passing acquaintances as two street urchins bickered on the kerb. Clive Brook, the male lead, walked along the street, glanced at the entrance to the establishment and was ushered inside.

Many of the theatre scenes were filmed one afternoon at the Aldwych Theatre and in the final cabaret scene Betty Compson was carried in by four Nubian slaves played by the McLaglen brothers, all black of face. One such slave was Victor McLaglen, who was destined for stardom in Hollywood. A major scene with Compson took place at the end of May. Cutts had replaced the exterior of the Moulin Rouge with the interior for the great cabaret scene.

A large crowd of assorted picturesque Parisian types sat at tables and terraces with bohemian gaiety augmented by a large Negro orchestra. Betty emerged at the head of a sextette of dancers all scantily, but artistically decked out to perform their cabaret dance in beautiful dresses by Dolly Tree: 'a small fortune must have been spent for one dance number, with the star in an elaborate costume suggestive of those worn by Gaby Deslys'.[11]

Cutts, with the backing of Balcon and Saville, was clearly one of the few directors around who valued the art of the costume designer to add glamour and real class to his films. He had always been highly conscious of the importance of good costume since using Lucile to dress Mae Marsh in his earlier two films. It was reported that he had 'spent much time in getting every detail of costume' for *Woman to Woman* exactly as he wanted it.[12]

Dolly Tree would not only have dressed the principals but would have been responsible for ensuring the supporting cast were all suitably attired. Since she had also worked extensively in Paris, her knowledge of Parisian nightlife and culture would have been an asset. Her creations showed 'artistic merit and ingenuity'[13] and 'compared favourably with the best mannequin displays'[14] ranging from exotic cabaret costumes to appropriate contemporary fashions. The most praised creation was the ostrich-feather dress worn by Betty Compson towards the end of the film, which was composed of over 200 ostrich feather plumes and 1,000 pearls, and was described as 'one of the most extraordinary dresses that has ever been seen on the screen'. [15]

Perhaps Cutts had seen *Brighter London*, which was dressed by Dolly Tree, when launched at the Hippodrome in March 1923 and thought that Dolly Tree's talents would be perfect for his new film. Equally, Roy Moseley, who helped write Victor Saville's autobiography, [16] said that Dolly Tree was a friend of Phoebe Saville, a connection that may have aided her commission to design the costumes. Doubtless, Cutts would have been impressed to learn that she had worked extensively in Paris (she had contributed to the Folies Bergere in 1921, 1922 and 1923) and her obvious knowledge about Parisian nightlife and culture would have been an asset in the visual side of the production and presumably of help to Hitchcock in his role as art director.

The cabaret scene in the Moulin Rouge culminated in a representation of a stage show with the print being tinted to provide greater novelty value. Balcon and Saville had made a deal with the Casino de Paris to use one of their tableaux, 'L'Aquarium', replacing the female star with Betty Compson. It was not possible to film the tableaux in situ and so a stage set was built at Joinville, outside Paris, and the company and costumes transported after their performance on a Saturday, where they worked all night so the Sunday matinee could be resumed. Of course to appease the censor alterations had to be made to the costumes as no breasts could be exposed and so they employed a group of needlewomen to fit the chorus with brassières.

This scene made quite an impact – 'the producer has given his story beautiful and lavish settings, but never once does he allow these to overshadow or interfere with the action of the plot... rarely does one see so well staged a theatre scene as the one in this picture'.[17] *Variety* also admired this scene for its eccentric and flash costuming that 'will make the wise boys over here look the second time'.[18] It was acknowledged that Cutts had a greater latitude of treatment and an accompanying freedom in expenditure 'which few British directors have ever been able to experience... it is proof that money has been spent not only copiously but also intelligently… the gorgeous dance and stage settings are quite lavish – and as daring as any American efforts on the same lines'.[19]

Woman to Woman (1923) has been regarded as the most groundbreaking British films to be released in the 1920s and although the actual film is lost and therefore cannot be viewed, from the available commentary, reviews and remaining stills it was obviously a lavish and sophisticated production. A commercial success, both at home and in the US, it launched the careers of several men who would play major roles in the development of British cinema – Michael Balcon, Victor Saville and Alfred Hitchcock – and turned Graham Cutts into Britain's leading director.

When *Woman to Woman* was given a trade show in November 1923 (released 4th February 1924), it was adored by the critics with praise such as 'an outstanding British achievement',[20] 'a triumph'[21] and 'a film of exceptional artistic and dramatic interest'.[22] Perhaps most poignantly the film did 'one important thing astonishingly well – it forever blasts the delusion that a production, technically perfect, cannot come out of a British studio'.[23] From an American perspective it was regarded by *Variety* as 'an example of the better grade of work over there. It is unquestionably equal to a vast majority of the releases viewed in the first run houses over here'.[24] On seeing the finished film, Michael Morton, author of the play, was so impressed that he declared: 'America has her Griffith, we have Graham Cutts and with him your future is full of brilliant possibilities'.[25]

The principal actors were also greatly admired. It was thought that Betty Compson gave the best performance of her life: 'in the dramatic scenes she shows considerable power of emotion while her lighter moments are full of grace and charm'.[26] There was also praise for Josephine Earle in handling a difficult part with remarkable skill, for Marie Ault, who contributed a delightful character study of the maid and confidante Henriette, and for Clive Brook, who gave one of the finest performances of its kind on the screen.

After filming was complete, Michael Balcon made a ten-week trip to America, arriving in New York on 28th August 1923. He mirrored Saville's earlier visit and networked in New York before travelling to Los Angeles to visit all the major studios, studying American methods. However, his overriding ambition was to ensure distribution in the American market for *Woman to Woman* and future projects. At first he did not have much luck and was turned down by all the major American companies until at last he managed to strike a deal with the Selznick Select Company.

Given the circumstances involving the company at the time, it was a strange choice but presumably Balcon had little choice. With only one offer for American distribution he had to accept. The Selznick Select Company, part of the Selznick Picture Corporation, was owned and run by the Selznick family, led by Lewis J. Selznick and his three sons, Howard, Myron and David. The latter two were destined to become big names in Hollywood.

Originally in the jewellery business, Lewis J. Selznick had been involved in the film industry since 1914. Like so many other movie moguls his career had been turbulent but he had done well, acquiring a palatial Park Avenue apartment, servants, Rolls-Royces and control of several interdependent companies, all consolidated under the Selznick Corporation in 1920. Ruthless, grandiose, daring and optimistic, he had a genius for self-promotion. He loved battles and was mischievous in spending huge sums on advertising campaigns, sometimes employed merely to insult his rivals. As a result he made many enemies, most notably his competitors Adolph Zukor at FPL, William Fox and Louis B. Mayer. His son Myron went to Hollywood in late 1918 and formed the Selznick Pictures Corporation, signing the star Olive Thomas and making three pictures until, on her honeymoon in Paris with her husband, Jack Pickford, later in the same year, she died in mysterious circumstances.

Through the early 1920s the Selznicks had productions underway on both coasts, with thirty branch offices all over the US and offices in London, Paris and Australia. Seemingly, they were doing well. But Lewis J. Selznick had constant cash problems due to his lavish spending and increasingly Selznick pictures were not getting sufficient exposure on exhibition circuits dominated by the larger concerns. By early 1923 things were not good: as debts mounted, creditors became agitated and in February a petition for involuntary bankruptcy was filed against Select and the other companies. All the Selznicks were either removed or resigned and Selznick Distribution Corporation was thus formed as a new parent company for all previous debts and problems. A committee was set up to reorganise all affairs and continue trading. Although the Selznicks blamed their rivals for their demise they were really trying to evade responsibility. As David Thomson, biographer of David O. Selznick, wrote: 'There was no real evidence of malign conspiracies – rather the Selznicks had a business pattern of rapid legal maneuver, bluff and outright deceit, of throwing money around in the hope of attracting more and of being unable to compete in the more sophisticated picture business'.[27]

Although in receivership, Select and the Selznick Picture Corporation were still trading under the new company and struck a deal with Balcon. They secured distribution through the extensive Paramount chain and gained a New York premiere for *Woman to Woman* prior to the London release: the first British picture to date ever to premiere in New York.

Initially, there were censorship difficulties in America because of the illegitimate child, especially in New England and Boston in particular. Rather wisely, a second print had been made with a compromise that arranged for the hero and heroine to be married and this was screened on Sunday showings only.

The film was a big success, confirming Balcon's view that only good-quality British films with high production values could compete with Hollywood pictures at home and abroad. Sadly, the deal was not advantageous to Balcon-Saville-Freedman, who had to sign away most of their rights in order to get a foot in the door. As a result, little of the profit came their way.

Another success was in Germany when *Woman to Woman* was released through Mozart-Saal in early 1924. Although it did not meet with such a rapturous reception as in London, the magnificent sets and Betty Compson's dancing were generally acclaimed. It was hoped that this would be the first of many other distribution deals and indeed Walter West closed a deal for combined production and distribution.

Despite a further decline in British releases from ninety-five films in 1922 to just over seventy-five in 1923, the 1923 releases showed great optimism with tangible and demonstrable proof of an improvement in quality that could lead to expansion. *Woman to Woman* was singled out as an 'outstanding piece of production on the acting and producing sides and has certainly enhanced the technical prestige of the British Industry'.[28] Clearly, Balcon-Saville-Freedman had got it right.

The White Shadow

With *Woman to Woman* drawing to completion in the summer of 1923, and editing taking place towards the end of June, Balcon-Saville-Freedman began work on the second Betty Compson picture. The common view is that in their youthful haste, Balcon and his team had overlooked that Compson's contract called for two pictures, with the second to commence within two weeks of completion of the first and no preparations had been made. This is a fallacy since in late April, as they began preparations for *Woman to Woman*, Cutts revealed that the second Compson picture would be *The Prude's Fall* and Hitchcock was working on the scenario.

For whatever reason this did not happen and instead they decided to adapt an unpublished novel by Michael Morton called *Children of Chance*. No doubt in changing projects, things were done in haste, which in all likelihood caused problems. Whatever the complications, the scenario had been completed by the end of June since Graham Cutts, without a break or holiday, had already started on production work. Through the first part of July, he was filming exterior scenes in rural Devon, London and on the Continent in Paris, Switzerland and a Channel crossing, with the newly employed James Sloan as location and facilities manager. Sloan had been assistant manager to Major Bell at the FPLBPL studio in the early 1920s and had worked with many of the American directors operating in the studio before becoming advertising manager for *Motion Picture Studio* magazine.

The new picture was swiftly titled *The Awakening* and was billed as the same star and same production team as *Woman to Woman*. Thus, besides being directed by Graham Cutts (assisted by C.N. Russell), the photography was by Claude McDonnell, scenario by Alfred Hitchcock and there must have been a good possibility that Dolly Tree designed the gowns.

The story followed a man who fell in love with a woman who disappears but then her twin sister takes her place so that her sister's reputation may not suffer. She then sacrifices the love she begins to feel so that her now-repentant twin may be happy. The twin sisters (Nancy and Georgina Brent, played by Betty Compson) differed in temperament, character and disposition. Georgina was wistfully charming and self-sacrificing while the unrestrained Nancy was the devilishly fascinating idol of the Paris underworld. The implausible plot featured mysterious disappearances, mistaken identity, steamy cabarets, romance, chance meetings, madness and even the transmigration of souls.

Robin Field (Clive Brook) falls in love with Nancy Brent, coming over on the boat from Paris. Strong-willed and intemperate, she is like her father, but she has a twin, Georgina, who is entirely opposite. The existence of the sister is unknown to Field. One day, before her love for Robin matures, Nancy runs away from home to Paris, where she leads a wild life. Her drunken father (A.B. Imeson), beside himself with grief at the disappearance of his daughter, follows her to the city. No news comes through of either of them and prostrate with grief, the mother (Daisy Campbell), dies. Georgina inherits the estate, moves to London and presumably at this point has dealings with Herbert Barnes (Olaf Hytten), who plays a lawyer in a conventional stage villain manner. To save her sister's reputation she pretends to Robin that she is Nancy and finally falls in love with him.

One of Robin's friends, Paris art student Louis Chadwick (Henry Victor), sees Nancy in Paris and Robin begins to believe that Georgina is leading a double life. On hearing of this, Georgina goes to Paris, where she finds Nancy in a Paris cabaret and explains what has happened to her family. After this, thinking she has taken Robin's love under false pretences, Georgina breaks down and goes to a sanatorium in Switzerland. Finally, she persuades Nancy to take her place there and so when Robin follows, he finds the woman he first loved. Georgina dies and her soul passes into the body of her twin, thus altering Nancy's entire nature. Eventually, all ends happily after the deception is explained and Nancy's father is rediscovered and restored to sanity.

After finishing the exteriors, the bulk of the film was shot in the Islington studio through July–August 1923. In mid-August, with Michael Morton as an absorbed spectator, filming of the Montmartre cabaret scene took place, which was a big part of the picture and most likely the last scene to be filmed. The impressive set was striking but far from gorgeous, implying the cabaret was not meant to be one of the more salubrious Parisian venues, but most definitely one that was off the beaten track. It was a long gallery with plain stairs descending to the main floor, with a couple of refreshment bars in big alcoves beneath the gallery, unadorned boards on the floor and very ordinary furniture, fittings, mirrors and general décor.

Crowds of various types occupied chairs around many small tables, with Tom Waters as an ultra old bohemian artist, Harry Ashton in the guise of corpulent Frenchman and Dorine Beresford in a piquant dancing dress pirouetting by the piano for the delectation of the clients. The entire atmosphere was carefree and reckless, with everyone chatting and drinking. It presented a wonderful picture – 'the Gallic irresponsible, happy-go-lucky atmosphere had been wonderfully caught' – and the scene was regarded as being more Parisian than anything seen in Paris![29]

Cutts, with the energetic assistance of C.N. Russell, then directed some full-length shots. A harmless stranger (Bert Darley) entered from the street and descended the stairs. He shook off a woman sitting on the stairs, who gripped his foot but then a man stood up and noticed him. Soon all the crowd rose, yelling, 'Get out!'. The intruder fled and then another visitor – Louis Chadwick (Henry Victor) –arrived and the same thing happened, except he treated everything as a joke, shouted back something rude and was welcomed by the throng. This was a precursor for several close-up shots of Betty Compson in the cabaret itself.

Two scenes from *The White Shadow* (1923)
Courtesy J.W. Mitchell Collection / Brian Twist

On completion by the end of August, Compson appeared with Clive Brook in Maurice Elvey's *The Royal Oak* that was filmed before she returned to New York on 26th September. The studio was vacant again but in October 1924 George Pearson filmed part of *Squib's Honeymoon* and Walter Niebuhr directed *The Money Habit*.

The Awakening was re-christened *The Eternal Survivor* and then in early 1924 the title was changed once again to *The White Shadow*. When the film was given its trade show in February 1924 (released 13th October 1924), the reviews were all in accord. Although the central idea was a good one it was felt that the plot was confusing without any real plausibility and there had been no attempt at making the characters convincing. It was regarded as a rather ordinary production that fell short of the essential qualities of good story, sincerity and continuity since the treatment was careless to the extent that interest in the story practically ceased after the first two reels. Furthermore, it was observed that the picture had been indifferently edited and titled with stilted sentimentality and bad phraseology – 'When a production is made in this country with the pick of British stars and the added commercial and artistic presence of a pretty and clever American screen actress of great box office repute one is entitled to expect a better result than *The White Shadow*. If the picture had been the first effort of a modest little firm one could understand more readily some of the shortcomings and their causes'.[30]

Haste was deemed to be the culprit contributing to the picture's shortcomings in terms of the essential qualities of story and sincerity. Opportunities had been missed and the action instead of bringing character into play was mechanical and jerky: 'There is a complete lack of conviction in the way in which the sisters are mistaken for each other, and no attempt at a coherent and well-proportioned sequence of events. Everything happened in a haphazard sort of way as though the plot had been evolved as the production progressed'.[31]

Although Cutts started the story well, as soon as Nancy ran away to Paris the action proceeded in a disjointed way by moving in rapid succession to Paris, back to England, to Paris again, then to Switzerland and finally back to England. There was no attempt to evolve these changes carefully and realistically.

Claude McDonnell's photography was deemed to be even better than in *Woman to Woman* and the technique of double photography splendidly done. Although ingeniously contrived, it created a situation where it became tiresome trying to distinguish between the two characters and as a consequence there was in fact too much of Betty Compson on the screen. This monopoly by one artist gave the other actors little chance to develop. For example, Clive Brook as Robin Field has little to do except shake hands.

The idea of the twins being mistaken for each other by Field was not thought credible since so many characters had seen them together and they were so frequently in the same place that his ignorance became unconvincing. The father's madness was also affected in this quick-change manner. He disappears for the major part of the story and reappears by being knocked down by a car driven by his daughter and Robin; this occurs in a back slum so that the long arm of coincidence is palpably made to overreach itself.

Although it was felt there were numerous flaws, the productions values were highly praised and clearly no expense was spared in making an entertainment on a lavish scale. It was thought that Cutts was happiest when dealing with picturesque scenic backgrounds than in the handling of his artists: 'The best part of the production is the magnificent settings, photography and lighting which are worthy of a better plot. As a whole the *White Shadow* makes fair entertainment as a conventional melodrama, admirably staged (both in the lavish interiors and unusual continental exteriors) and featuring a well-known American star'.[32]

There was plenty of evidence in the picture of expenditure but it had not translated into something comparable to *Woman to Woman*. Despite this 'owing to the star's popularity, the producer's former successes and the excellence of the technical qualities' [33] it was believed it would prove a strong attraction despite the constraints of the story and construction.

The White Shadow was released in America as *White Shadows* via the Selznick organisation in May 1924, continuing the deal Balcon had made in the autumn of 1923. But it did not do well and Balcon and others referred to it as a box-office disaster, with the profits from *Woman to Woman* being swallowed up by this failure. However, watching the several reels that were found in New Zealand in 2012, I could not help being somewhat engrossed and enjoyed the footage. It was a shame that so many heralded this discovery as a 'lost Hitchcock' movie when Cutts directed it. Equally, with regard to the consensus that it was not a good film, one must not forget it was a team who made it and if the adaptation by Hitchcock was not right then it would have been flawed from the outset.

With the failure of *The White Shadow*, C.M. Woolf, who had distributed *Woman to Woman*, lost confidence and withdrew his backing for future projects. Patrick McGillan said that Woolf detested artistic film-making and blamed the failure of *The White Shadow* on too much artistry.[34] For Cutts it was a different story and he wondered if Hitchcock as assistant director was spreading himself too thinly and trying to do too much by also producing title cards, designing the sets, preparing the cast and supervising the costumes and props. Hitchcock had become Cutts protégé and must have learned a lot from him such as dealing with actors on and off the stage, getting the right story angles and much more. However, Hitchcock's desire to involve himself in everything may have become annoying. This was the start of Cutts' growing suspicion of Hitchcock and clearly Hitchcock's increasing dislike of Cutts. When Cutts discussed his concerns with Balcon there was no agreement and Balcon affirmed that he thought Hitchcock was a capable and cheerful asset.

Over time, Hitchcock and Alma Reville would not have any kinds words to say about Cutts and according to John Russell Taylor, perhaps repeating Hitchcock's words, Cutts 'was by all accounts not much of a director.'[35]

Interestingly, much later author Rachel Low would describe Cutts as having 'only a sketchy interest in film structure and he was, sadly, an uneven and unreliable filmmaker whose richness of imagination was not accompanied by discipline or control.'[36] Low's assessment is certainly one I do not share and it is worth stressing at this point in time he was London's leading director with considerable skill and vision because of his past experience as an exhibitor 'using his knowledge as a showman to get the "box office" angle'.[37]

Handsome and sociable, Cutts was pushing forty while the rest of the unit were all in their twenties. He also had a reputation as a womaniser, a partygoer and a drinker. Clearly he lived life to the full. The rumours about his activities have been perpetuated by John Russell Taylor and others who claimed that he always managed to keep attractive young women around him, playing small parts in films, and was famed for the feat of having two sisters in his dressing room in the course of one lunch break.[38] Donald Spoto added that he readily accepted both the attentions of established actresses and the admiration of young fans.[39] He was generally in the midst of some tempestuous affair, sometimes several at a time, and all were concealed from his so-called 'wife'. Cutts used friends and colleagues to pass communications between the latest mistress and his wife; there were subterfuges of double dinner parties, deceptive telephone calls and clandestine meetings, with Hitchcock making excuses to Mrs Cutts about late night shootings. Despite all of this Cutts was a 'shrewd packager, a fast talker and a good chap to have a good time with. He had energy and stamina – perfectly happy to party all night and turn up, more often than not, bright and fresh for work the next morning'.[40]

In the midst of filming *The White Shadow* an interesting experiment was underway in the autumn of 1923 in an attempt to help British film production. The 'All British Film Weeks' was a concept arranged by the British National Film League to stir up enthusiasm among exhibitors about British films. Access to the exhibition market was still an acute problem, while British producers complained that distributors' forward and block booking policies were preventing their films from being released. Starting in early 1924 'British film weeks' were organised to highlight this problem and to enable indigenous films to be seen more widely. To fund the enterprise exhibitors and renters agreed to pay 5% on the contract price for films shown.

At the opening night of British Film Week on 4th February 1924, the Kinema Club staged a colourful carnival at the Hotel Cecil in London. There was a midnight parade of characters from British films, in which all the best-known players appeared, headed by one of the most beautiful British stars as 'Britannia'. Despite all the good intentions it is doubtful if this strategy actually succeeded. Jeffrey Bernerd, managing director of the Stoll Film Company, thought that British Film Weeks did more harm than good. According to him exhibitors, critics and the general public were rightly focused on British pictures but some were not good enough to represent the standard of British production, some were not first class and some were not even new.

The Money Habit

After George Pearson filmed the big wedding scene for *Squibs Honeymoon* in early October 1923, another production unit rented the Islington studio to film *The Money Habit*. A new company called the Commonwealth Film Corporation had been registered with a capital of £10,000 in late 1923, led by Arthur Backner, the London manager of Grangers. The latter was a company that had been a renting organisation but had dabbled in film production and this was its latest incarnation. *The Money Habit* was its first, and only release under the Granger-Commonwealth banner, with a high-profile cast of leading British players, directed by Walter Niebuhr and assisted by James Sloan, who had only recently been working for Graham Cutts. Niebuhr was originally a lecturer and newspaper editor in America. In 1915 he was sent to Europe as a newspaper war correspondent and there he became interested in films. Back in America, he was put in charge of making government films for training troops. Later, he was involved with the American Cinema Corporation before arriving in Europe in late 1922.

The photography was by Baron Gaetano di Ventimiglia, who was born in Catanai in Sicily, Italy, around 1889 and descended from Italian nobility. In his younger years he excelled at football and later worked in America for the *Associated Press and Newark Times* before switching to film and photography in the early 1920s.

Adapted by Alicia Ramsay from a novel by Paul Potter, *The Money Habit* was a drama of love and finance about a trusting financier who is deceived by a treacherous employee. It was a vivid portrayal of wild, reckless youth and the foolish extravagance of those who have, or think they have, money to burn.

Richard Varian (Warwick Ward) is infatuated with Cecile D'Arcy (Annette Benson), an adventuress and persuades his employer, a wealthy young Englishman called Noel Jason (Clive Brook) to purchase an oil claim from Cecile that he knows to be worthless. Eventually the truth comes to light and Jason is faced with ruin. Varian leaves his employ and secretly marries Cecile in Paris. Jason devotes his energy to reorganising his business. Later, he finds a document disclosing Varian's treachery. He visits Varian and Cecile's mansion, where they are living on their ill-gotten gains, and forces them to pay back every single penny. Having paid his creditors in full and re-established his own financial position, Jason finds happiness in marriage to his fiancée Diane Hastings (Nina Vanna), who has remained faithful throughout.

At the trade show of *The Money Habit* in January 1924 (released 14th April 1924) the film was regarded as a first-rate production and received high praise: 'An outstanding piece of work'[41] and 'a really fine achievement'.[42] Described as elaborately mounted and well-acted, the story, however, was thought to be a little thin but had been skilfully disguised by Niebuhr's carefully naturalistic direction. For example, the dramatic conflict between Jason and his untrustworthy friend was well maintained and exploited. However, the appeal might have been improved had the psychological interest been emphasised in place of material action and the

Nina Vanna

Fred Rains and Clive Brook

Annette Benson and Warwick Ward.

Warwick Ward and Clive Brook

Clive Brook

Scenes from *The Money Habit* (1924)

sometimes over-direction that resulted in the artistes appearing somewhat mechanical.

With only a few exterior locations in London, the bulk of the film used office and mansion settings that were thought to be as good as any big American film and Baron Ventimiglia's photography was brilliantly clear, yet soft and pleasing.

Of the acting Clive Brook was natural and admired for giving a strong and effective performance, despite having little to do. Nina Vanna was distinctive and invested her role with grace and beauty, Eva Westlake gave a clever sketch of a duchess and Annette Benson and Warwick Ward were thought of as being just good.

6 A Passionate Adventure and The Formation of Gainsborough Pictures

On Michael Balcon's return from America on 9th November 1923 he began planning the next project with Graham Cutts but production stalled, due partly to the lukewarm reception to *The White Shadow* from C.M. Woolf and then the negative response at the trade show in February 1924. With Woolf removing his financial backing things were not good and when John Freedman, the third partner in the company, died tragically at an early age at the beginning of 1924, Balcon and Victor Saville decided to dissolve the Balcon-Saville-Freedman. Saville took over the advertising business of Crane Paget and later joined Gaumont.

Balcon would have been interested to learn more about the status of the FPLBPL operation that had remained dormant since 1922 and the plans for the Islington studio. In early February J.C. Graham, head of the FPL company in the UK, had just returned from one of his visits to America to participate in the annual convention and unveiled FPL's plans for 1924. He announced that FPL would not produce any films in Great Britain in 1924. Although he acknowledged that they had done pioneer work in the area of British production, in the opinion of the parent American company, 'the productions had failed to reach a quality comparable with those made in America and hence the determination not to proceed here'.[1] As a result a decision had been taken to drop film production in the Islington studio. However, he wanted to stress that the initial investors had received their full investment returned with interest at the rate of 6%.

The Passionate Adventure

Michael Balcon and Graham Cutts decided to continue production and formed Gainsborough Pictures with a capital of £100 in early 1924. Presumably the name of the new company was derived from Balcon's fondness for the paintings of Thomas Gainsborough and the use of 'Gainsborough' would impart the right note of Britishness and class.

Without the backing and distribution of C.M. Woolf, they sought a new arrangement and had a meeting with Colonel A.C. Bromhead and his brother Reginald, directors of Gaumont, to discuss financial backing and distribution and thankfully they agreed to support them. As a result the newly formed Gainsborough Pictures booked the Islington studio for a month with an option to continue for two weeks, if necessary and preparations went ahead. Alfred Hitchcock and Michael Morton created the scenario from a popular novel *The Passionate Adventure* by Frank Stayton about a frustrated husband in name only who finds escape in visits to the East End slums disguised as a derelict.

One of the major features of this production was the involvement of the Selznick organisation. As part of the deal that Balcon had secured the previous autumn, he was obliged to involve Myron Selznick in the production and bring him to London ostensibly to look after their investment as security. Myron was a 'short, barrel-chested man' with 'willpower and drive and a magnetic personality' and he 'knew how to make things happen'.[2] Insolently handsome, he had 'the belligerence to back his orders' and an 'innate depressive cynicism'[3] that looked smart and modish. He was also a heavy drinker but seemingly could handle his excesses.

Myron had already visited London and the Islington studio in early 1922 and shook hands with Alfred Hitchcock during that visit. This time they would work more closely together and begin a friendship that would endure for decades. Later, Myron formed one of the biggest and most important talent agencies called Joyce-Selznick Limited with Frank Coleman Joyce, the brother of Alice Joyce, and became Hitchcock's agent.

Through Myron Selznick, Balcon secured two major American stars – Marjorie Daw and Alice Joyce – to appear in the leading roles alongside other British players. In due course Selznick and Daw arrived in Southampton from New York on 13th March 1924 and settled into the Savoy Hotel, with Alice Joyce arriving on 29th March but staying at the Carlton Hotel.

Marjorie Daw was born Margaret House and her nickname was 'Piggy'. She was taken to Hollywood when she was a child and entered films at the age of fifteen. She played in nine of Douglas Fairbanks' films and several Universal productions, playing emotional roles with great sincerity and charm. On arrival in London she was married, although separated from the director Eddie Sutherland (they divorced in 1925) but was having an affair with Myron, whom she later married in 1929.

Tall, dark and exquisitely beautiful, Alice Joyce was the star of the picture. She had been a successful actress since 1910, excelled in parts of distinction and dignity and was dubbed 'The Madonna of the Screen'.[4]

Just before filming commenced, Marjorie Daw and Myron Selznick were seen at the Palace Theatre at the end of March for the opening performance of the film *Secrets* starring Norma Talmadge and she was greeted warmly. With youthful freshness she said she was thrilled to have the opportunity to visit London – 'it was such a wonderful opportunity to travel, I'd never been out of America before'[5] – and expressed her delight with England. It was also observed that Alice Joyce was showing off a new hairstyle since her hair had been shingled in a distinctive way for her part 'in quite a new fashion allowing her to preserve her beautiful dark tresses as a frame for her exquisitely chiselled features'.[6] She had also brought over from America some ultra-smart gowns and was spending time in both London and Paris acquiring further suitable creations.

In the midst of pre-production Balcon was in the throes of his own passionate adventure and was wooing a young lady from South Africa called Aileen Leatherman. They had met in early 1922 at a dance in Maidenhead, where he shared a weekend house with two bachelor friends. She had returned to South Africa but came back in late 1922 to continue her education in Paris and they met on one of her visits to Maidenhead to visit an aunt. Following a quarrel they had parted but Balcon was still keen. With the deal sorted through Gaumont, and feeling more secure, he went to see Aileen again and this time convinced her to become his wife. The pair were finally married on 10th April 1924. Since he was filming *The Passionate Adventure* while in the midst of his own romance, Balcon was relentlessly teased by friends and colleagues.

Graham Cutts began filming at the Islington studio on 31st March, with Claude McDonnell as cameraman and Alfred Hitchcock as art director and assistant director. Clive Brook was the male lead. Brook disclosed that due to his performance in *Woman to Woman* he had been made a tempting offer to appear in American films, which he had turned down because Cutts had engaged him for *The Passionate Adventure*. He said his part was even better than his previous roles and he was searching for suits among the most exclusive of tailors for his character, whom he described as 'exquisite'.[7] Two other significant cast additions were Lilian Hall-Davis, who Cutts had featured in *The Wonderful Story* (1922), and Victor McLaglen, who had appeared in *The White Shadow* (1924).

The Passionate Adventure had a contemporary setting with glimpses of the Great War and a glamorous mix of London high-life and dramatic low-life, showing contrasting scenes of opulence and slumdom. In essence the theme concerned intimate marital relations but an important feature dealt with the psychological changes produced in individuals during the war. Cutts created atmosphere by contrasting the locale of the various phases of the action in the story in using Mayfair and the East End Thames side.

When wealthy Adrian St Clair (Clive Brook) returns from the war he endeavours to break down the barrier of coldness between himself and his wife Drusilla (Alice Joyce), but ultimately finds his domestic life intolerable. Impulsively, and in disguise, he pays a secret visit to the East End to view real life. He protects Vickey (Marjorie Daw), a factory girl, from the savagery of Herb Harris (Victor McLaglen), a dangerous criminal. Assaulted by Harris, St Clair is nursed by Vickey in her room, where they live for some days before Harris is sent to jail. She falls in love with him but is ignorant of his true identity. Harris escapes from prison and attacks St Clair again but Vickey stabs Harris and apparently kills him, St Clair sends Vickey away and awaits the arrival of Sladen, a Scotland Yard detective and a personal friend. He offers an adroit excuse for his presence, professes ignorance of the crime and returns home. Meanwhile, Vickey has already discovered Adrian's address and visits his house, meeting Drusilla, who is deeply moved by her story. Later, Sladen arrives with the apparent intention of charging Adrian with the murder. To save him, Vickey says she will give herself up but then it is found that Harris is only suffering from superficial wounds. Impressed by her example and realising she has narrowly escaped losing her husband's love through her coldness, Drusilla promises that she will recognise her obligations as a wife in future.

One of the first big scenes was filmed at Waterloo station at the beginning of April, courtesy of the Southern Railway on a Saturday evening and well into

Sunday morning until 5am. The scene represented the arrival of troops coming home from France in the peace of 1919, depicting wild delirium from the huge crowd, with close-ups of Clive Brook. Other war scenes, for the beginning of the film, were necessary to explain the effects of the war on the hero (Brook). Cutts created some novel technical devices to depict the war with shadowgraphy. This treatment was most suggestive when the shadow of the crucifix was seen amidst the ruin of war.

Filming *The Passionate Adventure* (1924)
Left to Right; Cameraman Claude McDonnell, Alice Joyce,
Graham Cutts and Marjorie Daw
Courtesy J.W. Mitchell Collection / Brian Twist

When Alice Joyce and Marjorie Daw made their initial scenes in early April, both were nervous until they settled down. They found 'a wonderful atmosphere of quietness, politeness and consideration' in the studio, an atmosphere that they thought was 'quite foreign to many American studios'.[8] They also remarked on Cutts' 'quiet, persuasive and informative methods'[9] and were favourably impressed with the efficiency of the studio, believing wholeheartedly that a great future awaited picture enterprise in Britain.

There was an unexpected problem with Daw, who had not been in the best of health since her arrival, and she had to have a few days' rest, holding up production. Luckily, Gainsborough had taken the precaution of insuring against risk of illness or accident to the leading players. Otherwise Daw's condition, which did improve, might have been a serious inconvenience and could have brought the whole production to a standstill.

A big set was the hall in the Mayfair mansion that was seen many times and from many different angles; in fact it was created to give a minimum of 200 different camera angles. Another set was a beautiful billiard room with fine old timbered ceiling. One of the big dramatic scenes was staged on a Thames shoreline in the East End with buildings where a succession of fights took place, followed by a scream from Marjorie Daw as she came hurtling through a doorway to fall with a sickening thud on the cobbled roadway. Victor McLaglen was the miscreant who hovered menacingly. Clive Brook tried to interfere and was thumped by McLaglen in his best style with a force that threw him on his back, giving him bruises and shaking him up. The location was thought to intrigue Londoners – was it Wapping, or Wandsworth or Rotherhithe? It was in fact a rather magnificent set that Hitchcock created as a stretch of canal with houses beside it, all on one of the studio stages.

When Alice Joyce finished her scenes in mid-May, an informal dinner party was given for her at the studio to mark the end of 'happy days'. Joyce had been very popular with everyone and expressed the desire to come back. She openly discussed the opinion that Cutts was the best director she had ever worked with. Marjorie Daw stayed on as she was due to play for another company in *Human Desires* and was signed for the next Gainsborough picture, which was to be *Prude's Fall*, due to commence in July, which did not materialise.

Finally, production was complete at the end of May after six to seven weeks of strenuous work and the cutting, editing and titling began. However, since Cutts believed the perfect film should tell the story in its pictures not via titles, it was decided to use as few titles as possible.

For some reason the trade show of *The Passionate Adventure* was delayed several times from June to July and then finally it was staged on 14th August 1924 (released 3rd November 1924) at Shepherds Bush Pavilion. The trade reviews praised the film for its lavish production qualities, superb photography, fine acting, excellent costuming and clever treatment in direction but the story itself was considered far-fetched, unconvincing and lacked humour. It also suffered from an artificiality of action and development, with too many minor improbabilities and inconsistencies. Some of the flaws were clear. For example, there was no explanation given for the wife's coolness so the argument of the story was shrouded in a mist of vague, perhaps unpleasant implications. Equally, it was difficult to believe that an unhappy husband would seek solace for his domestic grief on the inspiration of a chance sentence in a book by lounging about the East End attired as a down and out. As a result the film became dull rather than daring and was a 'wholesome subject, which has been handled too timidly to possess even morbid sex interest'.[10] It could have been a more worthy story had the original been 'drastically modified towards plausibility'.[11]

Although the acting was admired, it was thought that the players were handicapped by the characterisation being too loosely drawn to the extent that the action sometimes reduced the players to the status of mere puppets. Alice Joyce as the passionless and childless Drusilla admirably did what she could to depict the contradictory qualities of the unwilling wife. Clive Brook made a striking figure as the melancholy husband but appeared to do everything under protest and seldom smiled. Marjorie Daw was decorative on conventional lines as the impassioned factory girl but far too immaculately groomed for the part. Lilian Hall-Davis's role as Pamela was that of a fluffy flapper floating about in an atmosphere of icebound passion in a somewhat obtrusive minor love story. The scenario described her as 'a philosophical flapper – a social Bolshevist, a curiously potent personality, modern, restless, picturesque, a trifle sudden in her manner'. Despite this she 'had very little to do except to look charmingly pretty'.[12]   The most effective performance was from Victor McLaglen in a brief, powerful and thoroughly humane role without emotional reservations, played with his usual fine sense of character.

However, despite the story's defects, it was firmly believed that the names of the stars would ensure its success. On viewing the film the Selznick Picture Corporation sent a cable saying 'consider *The Passionate Adventure* a wonderful picture which is proof that great American box-office production can be produced in England as satisfactory as Hollywood. Sure to be international success'.[13]

The Slump of 1924

When Jesse L. Lasky visited England again in June 1924 as part of his European tour, he made a point of looking over London theatres for new film stories and was searching for potential new blood since he believed there was a shortage of leading men in America who could wear clothes well and promising new actresses too. On visiting the Islington studio, presumably in the midst of shooting *Human Desires*, he was impressed by the high state of efficiency of the organisation and stated he wanted to make an occasional picture there: 'I am thinking on my return to the States of sending to England a director, a star and a couple of leading artistes to form a nucleus for production.'[14] This fuelled speculation that FPL was to at last resume production at the Islington studio. It was perhaps the uncertain future of the British film industry that prevented any such development.

Despite huge efforts to increase awareness of British pictures and aid the ailing film industry with initiatives such as British Film Week, there was a deepening crisis, with 1924 being not a good year. Even a plea from the Prince of Wales to take British films seriously had little effect. The number of films released dropped from seventy-five in 1923 to only fifty-six in 1924. An even more acute difficulty of marketing arose by the eclipse of a few independent renting units and the lengthening period between the trade show and general release. This slump also had an effect on British players and many were forced to seek work on the Continent. Some, like Clive Brook, Flora Le Breton and Victor McLaglen, left for America.

Equally, many companies were forced to cease production, with the most dramatic closure being that of Hepworth Picture Plays Limited, the oldest and most prestigious film company in the country. This was part of a bigger picture as many of the older directors and firms faded, all unable to keep pace with a new way of creating pictures. The new breed of film-makers like Balcon and Wilcox were paving the way with more modern business methods and styles of production and a more international view that encompassed continental Europe and America. In early 1925, for example, Balcon denounced the British film industry for its insularity and in pursuit of an international policy declared: 'making pictures "international" is an art in itself, which I and my colleagues have studied very closely. There is no doubt that British pictures with an international appeal will save British film production.'[15]

There was much debate about the reasons for the Depression and ideas about how to improve the situation. As before, much was made of the continued failure of exhibitors to support British films and various restrictive distribution practices. The celebrated actor and producer Henry Edwards offered his opinion by saying that the only thing that could save the industry was 'a more careful selection of subjects. It is no good going out to make films for the American market if we are to produce typically British pictures. I do not know that British pictures appeal at all to Americans if they are really British in sentiment. But provided that the stories are carefully chosen and the money is spent judiciously, good British films can still make money in this country if the public will give our best the encouragement they deserve. The English public have so long been served with the recherché dishes which are served out by American companies, that just plain roast beef is dull in comparison, although there are people who prefer it.'[16] Many were in agreement with Edwards that the average production was lacking in terms of story, scenario and treatment and what was needed was something interestingly told, well balanced and with a logical story.

Balcon added his firm conviction that it was necessary to stay positive: 'I am one of those who refuse to believe in the imminent extinction of British production and in my view considerable harm can be done by the prominence given lately to the strictures on English efforts made by prominent Americans – even if some of what they say has a justification in fact.'[17]

The winter months were usually less active but by late 1924 every British studio was idle and it was described as a record lull in home production. Creeping in were noises about legislation and more insular protective methods. Sidney Morgan, another well-known producer, although his influence was on the wane, suggested the need for import duty on foreign films, with Thomas Welsh of Welsh-Pearson advocating a voluntary reciprocal trading scheme.

Human Desires

As soon as Graham Cutts finished shooting *The Passionate Adventure* at the end of May 1924, Burton George stepped in to film *Human Desires* for the new concern of Anglia Films. Formed in September 1923 with a capital of £20,000, Anglia Films had been created by Archibold Nettlefold, who came from a Birmingham industrial family and was an heir to the Guest, Keen and Nettlefold's engineering firm (GKN). He had originally dabbled in stage production at the Ambassadors Theatre and at the Kingsway in 1922 before forming this new motion picture organisation.

The company's first film was a version of *The Fair Maid of Perth* directed by Edwin Greenwood, which was not released for several years, so technically *Human Desires* was its first feature release. Burton George was an American who had begun life as a bootblack at the age of eight and then started a career as a copy boy at the *New York Herald*. He worked his way up in American journalism and attained fame as a short story writer before succumbing to the lure of the screen, first as an assistant under D.W. Griffith and then as a producer himself.

George had arrived in Europe to make pictures for the Sascha film company in Vienna and Nettlefold brought him to England. It was George's own story, originally written for a newspaper, which Nettlefold decided to adapt and initiate the activities of the new firm. They must have had some clout as Nettlefold engaged a rather impressive cast including American actress Juliette Compton, Warwick Ward and significantly, Clive Brook and Marjorie Daw, who had both just finished work on *The Passionate Adventure*.

Myron Selznick was also involved in this production since Daw was the leading female star and he was an onlooker during filming. When leaving for America after filming at the end of July, Selznick took a negative of the film that was then released under the Selznick Picture Corporation banner.

Human Desires was described as a spectacular production of social and theatrical life about a young girl who rises to fame as a cabaret artiste and her complicated love affairs. French officer Pierre Brandon (Warwick Ward) takes an interest in Joan Thayer (Marjorie Daw), an English dancing girl whom he finds in a small French cabaret and introduces her to Georges Gauthier (Clive Brook), a theatrical manager. Gauthier launches her in a revue and she is a great success. He falls in love with her and out of gratitude she agrees to marry him, although she really loves Brandon. Gauthier dismisses his mistress Andree de Vigne (Juliette Compton), who then out of extreme jealousy contrives a detailed scheme to break them up. Brandon returns from abroad to find Joan famous and married and Andree manipulates a meeting between Brandon and Joan. Andree succeeds in arousing Gauthier's suspicions and planting the thought that Joan has been unfaithful, they quarrel and he tells Joan to leave. Later, he tries to win her back but she insists on a divorce, which leaves her free to accept the love that Brandon confesses. Repulsed by Andree, Gauthier moralises on his discovery that wealth cannot buy some women's love.

One of the first scenes filmed at Islington during June was the interior of a cabaret, where Brandon meets Joan. A huge set representing a subterranean cave cabaret in Paris had been constructed, where dozens of picturesque underworld types indulged in bursts of dancing and gaiety, with solo dancers adding piquancy to the atmosphere, distinctly blue with tobacco smoke. There was also an impressive theatrical stage set that featured two ballets, one of which had a huge typewriter with the keys manipulated by pretty girls, who were sitting on them. Since much of the film had a Paris setting Nettlefold, in a very thorough way, had the Parisian atmosphere supervised by Count Jean de Limur (who also appeared in the film) and had played a similar role for Charlie Chaplin's *A Woman of Paris* (1923). All the exteriors were taken in Paris during June, including some rather stunning scenes at Versailles, the Bois de Boulogne and the Auteuil Racecourse.

Human Desires was given a trade show in January 1925 and was seemingly given the title of *Love's Bargain* for the American market. The film was praised for its elaborate and magnificent settings and picturesque views of Paris, with its air of wealth and gaiety, good photography by Bert Cann and tasteful costuming. In *The Passionate Adventure* Marjorie Daw wore simple clothes most of the time and didn't need to concern herself about looking smart but in *Human Desires* she had to have twenty-two new outfits, which she bought in London.

The story itself was hackneyed with the age-old formula of a theatrical producer making a girl a star. It was stressed that Burton George 'relied on lavishness instead of story values'[18] and the plot was thought to be trite, confusing and the characters, despite their big names, totally lacking in conviction and sympathy.

In terms of the acting it was thought that none of the artistes were given the chance to shine. Marjorie Daw was hopelessly miscast because, although charming, she was hardly the type of woman to make a sensational success as a revue artist. Her personality was too sweet and gentle to flourish in the exotic atmosphere of a great Parisian music hall and her performance was therefore one of indifference. Clive Brook played his part with tact and discretion but equally lacked sparkle, while Warwick Ward had a colourless part and only Juliette Compton was viewed as being successful as the jealous vamp.

Oddly enough, despite all the criticism it was thought that 'the whole production is a credit to British enterprise'.[19] On its release in America in the spring of 1925, under the Selznick banner, it received a similar response to the UK trade press.

This was the last film that Clive Brook made before leaving England for America. He had been made numerous offers from big American film companies and finally accepted one from Thomas Ince. As soon as he finished filming *Human Desires* he went to America, arriving in New York on 15th July 1924. He had planned to stay for one picture but instead remained there for eleven years.

The Blackguard

In the summer of 1924 Michael Balcon was casting his eye towards the Continent and in June or July he went to Berlin, accompanied by Myron Selznick. Travelling first by boat to the Hook of Holland and then by train in the Kaiser Wilhelm coach for first-class travellers to Berlin and onto Potsdam, they visited the world-famous UFA studio at Neubabelsberg (New Babylon) near Potsdam. Here, they discussed collaboration with Erich Pommer, head of production. Their visit may well have deliberately coincided with that of Herbert Wilcox's unit, who were filming *Decameron Nights* at the time.

UFA was regarded as having the biggest and best-equipped studio in Europe, with multiple stages covering 200,000 square feet in contrast to Islington's just over 6,000 square feet. The studio had become renowned worldwide for its distinctive visual style and bizarre stories to date, such as the cinematic masterpieces of Robert Wiene's *The Cabinet of Dr. Caligari* (1920), Fritz Lang's *Dr. Mabuse the Gambler* (1922) and Lang's two-part epic *Die Nibelungen* (1924). Equally, Pommer was credited as being the great pioneer in German films. By keeping in touch with all aspects of the film industry 'he understood the new medium's special qualities and knew how to coordinate its commercial and artistic aspects'.[20] Pommer was clearly an important role model for Balcon and his methods and business style would have a significant influence.

Many continental production companies saw England as a closed market and were eager to find ways to gain access; co-production was an obvious answer. Herbert Wilcox had filmed *Chu Chin Chow* (1923) in Algiers and at the UFA studio but then made a deal with a Viennese company filming *Southern Love* (1924), starring Betty Blythe in Vienna in the autumn of 1923. It was not a good experience. Pommer had heard of Wilcox's near-disaster and invited him to make another film in Berlin, providing the screenplay, part of the cast and production facilities, plus 50% of the finance. Wilcox was to direct and bring in further British and American stars and the remaining 50% of the finance. He signed up the British star Ivy Duke and the Hollywood actor Lionel Barrymore. *Decameron Nights* (1924) was a lavish medieval love story based on the play derived from the tales of Giovanni Boccaccio and was seen as having wide international appeal.

Michael Balcon followed in Herbert Wilcox's footsteps and, with Myron Selznick as his American backer, made a deal with Pommer for co-production on the same terms as Wilcox, with Gainsborough undertaking to distribute through the English-speaking world. The first film was called *The Blackguard* (*Die Prinzessin und der Geiger*) and Graham Cutts was despatched as director, along with Alfred Hitchcock as assistant director and art director and Alma Reville was to look after continuity. They all arrived in Berlin in early September 1924, with production continuing through the autumn until Christmas.

The cameraman was Theodor Sparkhul, who had worked with Ernst Lubitsch, and there was a mainly German cast, with the British comic actor Frank Stanmore and the American star Jane Novak. A delicate, vulnerable, blonde beauty, Novak had begun her screen career in 1913, making many Westerns but also excelling in straight melodramas. She had starred with William S. Hart and Harold Lloyd. Although production started in the September, Novak, along with another actress, Gertrude Ryan, only arrived in Berlin from New York on 12th November 1924.

Adapted by Hitchcock from Raymond Paton's novel *The Blackguard*, the film was set in France and revolutionary Russia and concerned a violinist's tempestuous career as he is continually torn between his art and his love. Under Adrian Levinski's (Bernhard Goetzke) tuition, Michael Caviol, a child (Martin Hertzberg), brought up in sordid surroundings, becomes a gifted violinist and dedicates his life to music. On reaching manhood (then played by Walter Rilla), he achieves fame and happiness and falls in love with the beautiful Russian Princess Marie Idourska (Jane Novak) but finds himself dedicated to his art and resists the love he feels. She does not want to stand in the way of his career and leaves him so as not to hinder his ambition. Later, a revolution breaks out and in danger Marie sends for him. He finds the leader of the mob is Levinski, his old music master, and gets three passports in exchange for a violin. While the Princess escapes, Michael is found by Levinski and during a fight is wounded and hurled into the flames of a burning palace. Though injured, he escapes and is finally re-united with his princess.

A scene from *The Blackguard* (1925)
Courtesy J.W. Mitchell Collection / Brian Twist

The production featured grandiose set pieces, all spacious and artistically arranged, not least the Idouraka Palace, a symphony concert, a continental cabaret, the largest cathedral in Europe and a Russian town reproduced in the open for mob scenes of the Bolshevik revolution. One of the highlights of sheer imaginative filming was the vision caused by a blow to the head from a cognac bottle to the violinist. Depicting a dainty scene of dancing fairies and a spacious cathedral and castle interior as the realm of music, the hero ascends a vast celestial stairway to the throne of the God of Music.

Working at UFA was an interesting experience as Cutts and his unit were absorbed in the visual artistry of their German partners, learning new ideas and techniques regarding atmosphere, shadows, bizarre camera angles, extreme close ups and mobile camerawork. For example, F.W. Murnau was filming *The Last Laugh* (1924) on a neighbouring set. The film depicted every stage in the decline and fall of a grandly uniformed hotel doorman (Emil Jannings) and was designed to be the last word in visual story telling without titles. Hitchcock learned many useful ideas watching Murnau and gained an insight into the technique of set building and perspective. He also started to learn German and immersed himself in the work of Walter Röhrig and Robert Herlth, two of the UFA art directors.

Being in permissive and cosmopolitan Berlin must have been an exhilarating experience. In their limited spare time Cutts, Reville and Hitchcock must have had some chance to visit the cabarets, concerts, plays, museum shows, art galleries and not least, the big spectacular revue *Noch und Noch* at the Admiral Palast, a venue that rivalled the music-halls of Paris.

According to Patrick McGillan, they were one night taken out by the family of an UFA executive to a nightclub popularised by homosexuals. Berlin at the time was awash with over 160 such venues with evocative names like Cabaret of the Spider (Alte Jakobstraße), The Alexander-Palast (Landsbergstraße), Monte-Casino (Planufer) or the famous Eldorado (Kant-straße). At this venue men danced with men, and women with women; this may well have initially shocked Hitchcock, who had not witnessed things like this before. Even though he may have feigned innocence, having a curiosity in all forms of sexuality, he was entranced. The older, more worldy-wise Cutts, a nocturnal partygoer in London, almost certainly did not bat an eyelid. Here, they met two women who offered to take their group to a private party in a hotel. It is not clear exactly what happened but one story suggests the two women slipped into bed and started to have sex in front of the others. One member of the group – a young daughter of the UFA executive – put on her eyeglasses to see better. Later, Hitchcock suggested that this incident inspired a scene in *The Pleasure Garden* (1925), with sexual undertones between two girlfriends.[21]

Besides the daily filming there appears to have been a lot of behind-the-scenes shenanigans. Cutts, Hitchcock and Reville stayed in rented rooms; he had one room, Reville had a small room of her own and Hitchcock made do with a sofa in the living room. At some point Cutts acquired a 'girlfriend' who was a dancer and began an affair. But his so-called 'wife' arrived in Berlin and also stayed in the flat. To maintain his 'affair' but keep his wife happy, Cutts would make the age-old excuse of working late at the studio. Instead, he and his girlfriend, the cameraman Theodor Sparkuhl and his girlfriend, along with Alma Reville and Hitchcock, would visit the famous café Barberina (called the 'Palais des Westens') on Hardenbergstrasse, where they would eat, drink, dance and watch a variety of cabaret performers.

They undoubtedly visited another nearby popular venue called Kakadu (Cockatoo), which comprised a bar, restaurant, dance palace and cabaret, with parrots in cages over every table. Whenever a customer went to leave, they merely tapped the water glass with a knife, which acted as a signal for the parrots to squawk in a grating old man's voice, 'The bill! The bill!'

Above: The Café Barberina (called the 'Palais des Westens'), Berlin
Below: The Kakadu (Cockatoo), Berlin

Afterwards they drove home via Cutts' girlfriend's rooms in Dorotheenstrasse behind the Reichstag and here, he would disappear upstairs for a while, with Hitchcock and Reville sitting and waiting in the car. Eventually, they arrived back at their flat and 'Mrs Cutts' fed them a heavy typically English meal, which of course they could not refuse without arousing suspicion. Hitchcock got to the point of regularly excusing himself to throw up.

The antagonism between Hitchcock and Cutts that surfaced during filming of *The White Shadow* must have been exacerbated by this charade. Reville and Hitchcock claimed Cutts' behaviour became erratic and unpredictable, suggesting success had transformed him into a drinker and womaniser. However, these traits were not new and had been witnessed before in London: he did drink, he did party, and he did enjoy women. Cutts' professionalism on set was called into question, with suggestions that he procrastinated over specific details, found it increasingly difficult to handle technical problems and, neglecting his responsibilities due to his preoccupation with his girlfriend, left some of the decisions to Hitchcock.[22]

As assistant director, Hitchcock was used to handling incidental scenes, odd shots and scenes with extras but now he was sometimes left handling whole sequences. For example, it is claimed he directed the dream sequence in which the violinist sees himself ascending to heaven accompanied by welcoming angel hosts, which utilised the idea of forced perspective with the angels graded in size.[23] For some, Cutts' filming technique gave the impression of being inhibited by the UFA environment since he preferred to cut clumsily within set-ups rather than move the camera.[24] Perhaps this was the fault of the cameraman, not Cutts, but also, perhaps like Hitchcock, he was learning new methods and a few months later, when filming *The Rat* (1925), he had acquired the use of a small trolley on rails, called a 'dolly', and had developed more sweeping, fluid camerawork as a result.

If we are to believe the account, the tale then takes a remarkable twist for towards the end of filming Cutts fled Berlin with the girlfriend, leaving the few remaining scenes for Hitchcock to complete. Presumably 'Mrs Cutts' had already returned to London. At Calais the girl could not enter England with her existing papers. Frantic, Cutts sent telegrams to Balcon and others, threatening suicide or that he would go off to South America and become a professional tango dancer, if they did not get entry papers and a work permit for her.[25] Cutts remained in Calais as Hitchcock and Reville returned to England just before Christmas on the overnight boat from Kiel. It was a stormy crossing but this did not deter Hitch from proposing marriage to Reville. She accepted.

Back in London, as production progressed on *The Blackguard* and when *The Passionate Adventure* did well, C.M. Woolf after realising his mistake came back to Balcon with an offer for W&F to act as distributor once again. Balcon accepted. According to John Russell Taylor, Balcon and his team were always scratching around for money and facilities and as a result it was scarcely possible to plan more than one picture at a time. There was also no specific contract with W&F and instead Balcon had to renegotiate terms for each project, effectively giving Woolf control over what was made.[26] However, if this was a true assessment, things were changing and Balcon and Gainsborough would soon begin steps to expand as their fortunes improved.

After the trade show of *The Blackguard* at the Royal Albert Hall on 29th April 1925 (released 26th October 1925), a well-known film critic said that it 'is the best British film I've ever seen because it is so German… a noteworthy contribution by a Britisher to the art of making films.'[27] This set the tone for further praise, with phrases like 'worthwhile', 'beautiful', 'imaginative' and a 'masterpiece'.[28]

It was thought that a film about music and musicians was a difficult theme and unfortunately the story was somewhat cumbersome with improbabilities and loose ends. Despite these shortcomings it was finely produced by Cutts, who had clearly infused many of the best characteristics of German production into his work, illustrating the benefits of a European collaboration but for some this was too much: 'the mixture of international styles, though not without technical interest, tends to produce a confused effect'.[29] With many novel features it was vividly presented with imagination and breadth of atmosphere and as a result, the keynotes were brilliant acting, beautiful and artistic sets and imaginative directing – 'no British picture has succeeded so happily in combining these three essentials'.[30]

The characterisation was excellent and the cast well directed but the heroine, Jane Novak, was rather colourless and obscured by the brilliance of the rest. The dominant figures were the teacher-turned-revolutionary (Bernhard Goetzke), the hero's besotted grandmother (Rosa Valetti), a powerful, though sinister character, the boy Michael (Martin Hertzberg), who had a natural genius, the dreamy hero in later life (Walter Rilla), played with grace and dignity, and Frank Stanmore, who supplied the lighter touches.

9   THE HITCH-CUTTS DIVIDE

After a dire 1924, 1925 began to look more positive. There were bold statements that British studios were far from extinct and signs of a welcome revival: 'In view of the unstable conditions which cramp native effort more than ever, it is impossible to withhold cordial encouragement to those who are doing their best to maintain the standard of our screen product and giving much work to players who have experienced the worst winter in the annals of the British studio'.[1] However, it was not all rosy and only forty-five films were finally released, a continued reduction on previous years.

The Prude's Fall

The second Gainsborough picture was announced as *The Prude's Fall*. A subject that had been gestating for some time, beginning life as Betty Compson's second picture following *Woman to Woman* in late 1923, it was abandoned in favour of *The White Shadow*. It was also intended to follow *The Passionate Adventure* but was again sidelined to make *The Blackguard*. Hitchcock had originally adapted the play by Rudolf Besier and May Edginton that had been given a successful run at Wyndham's Theatre in 1920, starring Sir Gerald du Maurier. Michael Balcon must have felt it was time to resurrect the project and bring it to fruition, getting Alfred Hitchcock to polish the screenplay.

According to the official record, Graham Cutts returned to London from Berlin after finishing work on *The Blackguard* in late January 1925. If we are to believe John Russell Taylor, derived from Hitchcock himself, Cutts did not return to London but had left Berlin in December and was 'fuming and fretting'[2] in Calais with his girlfriend and with no one knowing what was to happen with the next film. Hitchcock wrote a screenplay and sent the first draft to Cutts in Calais. Revisions and alterations were made until it was ready. Finally, it was decided to visit continental locations and Hitchcock and Alma Reville went to meet Cutts in Paris.

John Russell Taylor's account does not really add up and I wonder if only part is a reflection of true events. Firstly, perhaps Cutts did finish *The Blackguard* and stayed on in Berlin to cut and edit the film, but he did get held up at Calais, trying to gain entry to England for the girlfriend. However, to suggest Cutts did not return to London in light of accounts to the contrary in the trade press sounds odd. What is also misleading is that Hitchcock had already been working on a screenplay since late 1923 and plans for filming *The Prude's Fall* were clear from the outset as Jane Novak had been brought over on a two-picture deal and it was not a good idea to keep her idle. She had also left Berlin for London and planned to take a look around England before commencing work. Production plans, casting and other details must have been finalised between Cutts and Balcon in London and so Cutts must have left the girlfriend at Calais.

The screenplay originally specified filming in various glamorous parts of Western Europe and Balcon made it clear that the screen version of *The Prude's Fall* offered 'many opportunities for varied exterior locations'.[3] As a result, the trade press announced that the entire company of cast and crew were going to the Continent to film exteriors in St Moritz, Venice and the Italian Lakes. Cutts and a unit comprising Alfred Hitchcock as art director and assistant director with Alma Reville as editor, cameraman Hal Young and some of the key players set out for Europe in early February. Perhaps not the best time for filming exteriors.

Hal Young was a new cameraman for Cutts. He had worked for FPL in America before becoming the principal cameraman for FPLBPL from the inception of production in 1920 and was adept at both location and studio work. When FPLBPL ceased production, Young worked for Guy Newall on *Fox Farm* (1922). He was 'a tough and cynical character noted for his habit of reading the racing reports while he cranked the camera with his free hand'[4] and became an important member of Cutts' crew.

In addition to Jane Novak, Balcon and Cutts secured the glamorous American Julanne Johnston, famous for playing opposite Douglas Fairbanks in *The Thief of Bagdad* (1924). The rest of the cast was British, including Warwick Ward, Hugh Miller, Henry Vibart, Gladys Jennings, Miles Mander, Edith Craig (daughter of Ellen Terry) and Marie Ault.

Again, John Russell Taylor's account of what happened on the continental trip is generally accepted. He claims that Cutts travelled from Calais and met his crew in Paris with the girlfriend. She liked Paris and so Cutts stayed and sent his unit to St Moritz, he himself arrived a week later. The girlfriend liked St Moritz and so Cutts sent the unit to Venice. On arrival the girlfriend didn't like Venice, thinking the water was unhealthy and lugubrious. They all moved on to Lake Como but when they arrived, there was a storm (which the girlfriend didn't like) and so Cutts announced that the weather was impossible and they all moved back to St Moritz. However, an avalanche blocked the railway line and so they finally abandoned the trip and returned to London.

After travelling around Europe at great expense, John Russell Taylor said they had 'shot not a single foot of film.'[5] The implication was that Cutts was far too distracted with the girlfriend and had acted unprofessionally. Despite all of this, on his return it was reported that 'Cutts has had a strenuous time in three different continental countries utilising many striking actual locations for scenes which go beyond the scope of the original play'.[6]

Blaming Cutts and his obsession with the girlfriend is a convenient way to account for the fact that on returning to London they had, what Taylor claimed, was little usable footage. Although an amusing story, it does paint Cutts in a rather bad light and was symptomatic of Hitchcock and Reville's later dislike for him. Both believed that it was through their efforts that Cutts' films were successful and Reville actually said that Cutts 'wasn't a really pleasant man, he knew very little, so we literally carried him.'[7] It was this feeling that punctuated their observations of Cutts and the filming of *The Prude's Fall*. Needless to say, once

Hitchcock moved on to direct on his own films, Cutts carried on with new team members and continued to produce further successes, including *The Rat*, *The Triumph of The Rat* and *The Sea Urchin*, which in my opinion negates their assessment of his abilities but not his behaviour and actions.

I seriously wonder about the validity of Taylor's account of the continental trip. Even if the girlfriend proved a distraction, could there be another story where weather conditions and other logistical problems prevented a satisfactory outcome? After all, the trip was hastily arranged, short in duration, at a bad time of year and expectations ran high. What happened to the girlfriend is not known, but, once again, Gainsborough Pictures leased the Islington studio and Cutts arrived back with his company and began filming interiors on 23rd February 1925.

It has been suggested that Hitchcock revamped the script and came up with ideas about how they could film *The Prude's Fall* without the exotic locations. None of which really helped proceedings. Sadly, since only part of the film has survived, it is not possible to assess whether exterior foreign locations were used. Whatever the truth, filming was rather swift and completed by the end of March. Several big scenes featured a hotel ballroom scene, a huge cathedral set on the ground floor and a bridal scene, with Julanne Johnston carrying a beautiful bouquet refreshed exactly each day. Filming was noted as being conducted perfectly: 'Cutts' calmness, the almost inaudible camera of Hal Young and the absence of din so noticeable in some studios, all created a sense of tranquillity'.[8] By mid-March *The Prude's Fall* was nearing completion. Julanne Johnston completed all of her scenes and left for New York, arriving 24th March and followed by Jane Novak, who arrived back in New York on 1st April 1925.

The Prude's Fall was a much-involved story about a French captain who persuades a rich widow in a Cathedral town to become his mistress but it is only a scheme to test her love. Beatrice Audley (Jane Novak), a cold English maid, is engaged to hot-blooded Frenchman Andre le Briquet (Warwick Ward) but repels his affection. To test him, she asks a friend, Sonia (Julanne Johnston), who is her opposite in type, to visit when Andre returns home from a trip. Beatrice tells him she has decided to call off their engagement and at the opportune moment, Sonia, the girl friend, walks in. The fiancé falls for her and soon they are engaged. However, Sonia is acting as a decoy for a gambling den in London. She has disclosed this in a letter to Andre that was to be handed to him prior to the ceremony by his former fiancée but she does not deliver the letter until after the ceremony. The fiancé thinks it is a trick by the girl who discarded him and he also turns on his bride. While still in her wedding finery the bride commits suicide and the cheated groom swears vengeance.

Two years later he returns to England after spending time in North Africa. He again lays suit to Beatrice, who reciprocates his seeming affection. There is no necessity for marriage, he argues, and Beatrice practically consents to become his mistress. She discloses that she didn't intend to trick him but retained the letter to shield her friend. In the end, Andre proves irresistible with his French ways and all ends well.

A scene from *The Prude's Fall* (1925)
Left to Right: Jane Novak, Warwick Ward and Julanne Johnson
Courtesy J.W. Mitchell Collection / Brian Twist

The film was another disaster, following a similar pattern to *The White Shadow*. Filming was rushed and the screenplay and story were really not up to scratch; Cutts did the best he could with the material at his disposal. No trade show was given to *The Prude's Fall*, suggesting all concerned did not deem it worthy of a trade screening. It was finally released in the UK on 23rd November 1925, with an announcement that well-known artists were featured and the 'title, cast and story all present good exploitation angles. Graham Cutts the director is a name beginning to mean something to picturegoers'.[9]

It was released in America in November 1926 under the title of *Dangerous Virtue*. *Variety* was not impressed and declared it was atrociously cast and acted. Although they thought the best performance came from Julanne Johnson, in their view Jane Novak never got started and Warwick Ward would never find a spot before a camera in America. They concluded that *The Prude's Fall* was 'one of the striking examples of why British-made films are not acceptable to American audiences – just a piece of junk – the New York audience laughed at it and practically hooted it from the screen in derision.'[10]

The Prude's Fall experience highlighted the continued souring of the relationship between Hitchcock and Cutts; indeed each was dissatisfied with the other. Cutts was annoyed by Hitchcock's influence and perhaps his annoying habit of wanting to do everything, tinged with jealousy for his ability and youthful quest for knowledge and experience. He was also increasingly resentful of the implication that Hitchcock was getting too much credit for the overall effect of his films. Hitchcock was unnerved by the growing hostility and resentment from Cutts. It was no surprise some insults and bad mouthing occurred on both sides. The situation was made worse by the cameraman Hal Young, who was Cutts' ally and, for whatever reason, did not like Hitchcock and 'delighted to poison Cutts's mind against him'.[11]

Due to this ongoing antagonism, Michael Balcon decided it was time to separate them. It was no doubt a delicate issue that required carefully handling. Balcon could not afford to lose his top director but equally could see great potential in Hitchcock. Luckily, he found a solution.

Balcon must have been disappointed that his deal with Erich Pommer at UFA fell through. The reasons for this are not clear but most likely reflect the precarious state of affairs that UFA was going through in the mid-1920s. Pommer and Fritz Lang visited America for the premiere of *The Nibelungs* in late 1924 and travelled to Hollywood, hoping to improve the sale of German films and learn from the Americans. Their networking paid off but not in terms that they originally envisaged. By early 1925 UFA was in deep financial crisis. Their 'aggressive strategy of expansion that had brought it dominance during the inflationary period gradually led to its undoing'.[12] UFA had accumulated considerable losses and could not get out of their financial trouble without outside help. Ultimately, in late 1925 UFA was forced to capitulate to American interests and in lieu of considerable financial aid, signed restrictive contracts with MGM, Paramount and Universal to distribute their product in Germany. The last straw came in early 1926 when Erich Pommer left UFA for Paramount.

With the UFA deal in disarray, Balcon sought a new partner in Germany and signed a five-picture deal with Emelka, a Munich-based competitor of UFA in the late spring of 1925. Munchener Lichtspielkunst was known phonetically as MLK or Em-el-ka and had been formed in 1918 by producer Peter Ostermayr as a distinctly Bavarian alternative to Berlin's dominance with a studio in Geiselgasteig. In March 1925, Emelka had signalled its intention to move towards co-operation with British film-makers in doing a deal with Frank Tilley, former editor of *Kinematograph Weekly*. Their first project had been *Venetian Lovers* (1925), which Tilley co-directed with Walter Niebuhr.

As Balcon and Cutts made preparations for the next Gainsborough production it is likely that Cutts said he did not want Hitchcock as part of his team. At a meeting with Hitchcock, Balcon told him that he was not to work on it. With signs that Gainsborough were expanding with the Emelka deal, and further arrangements on the horizon, it became clear to Balcon that Cutts could not direct all their films. Balcon liked Hitchcock and was impressed by him. He knew he could direct and had the necessary experience, having learned every aspect of film-making from being so intricately involved in many previous Cutts' productions. It was an easier, cheaper option to get Hitchcock to direct rather than employ someone new.

Despite later denials to the contrary, Hitchcock must have also made it obvious he wanted to direct – after all, it was the logical outcome to his career progression. Balcon's problem was how to get Hitchcock to direct, since C.M. Woolf would not be prepared to finance a homegrown project directed by an unknown as this would be far too risky. The Emelka deal provided the solution and a few weeks after their initial chat, Balcon asked Hitchcock to go to Munich to direct two films – 'I had to arrange to have these two subjects made in Germany because of the resistance to his becoming director,' he wrote later.[13] If successful, Balcon would have an important new talent: Hitchcock finally had his chance.

The Rat

In mid-April 1925, Graham Cutts announced that his next picture would be the screen adaptation of *The Rat* starring Ivor Novello and with the welcome return of Mae Marsh. He engaged Leslie S. Hiscott as his new assistant director, along with Hal Young as cameraman. Previously Hiscott had worked at the FPLBPL studio and for George Pearson and effectively replaced Alfred Hitchcock. There was also a new art director called Charles Wilfred Arnold, brother of Norman G. Arnold.

Adrian Brunel

The Rat, a sensational story of Parisian low life, was written by Novello with Constance Collier in late 1923 as a film-play and had been optioned by Adrian Brunel as a follow-up to his Atlas-Biocraft feature, *The Man Without Desire* (1923). None of the distributors showed any interest and Brunel failed to gain funding so the rights reverted. Novello and Collier then turned it into a play, which enjoyed a successful tour in the regions and then the West End in June 1924.

Incredibly versatile and multi-talented, Adrian Brunel was born in Brighton in 1892 and educated at Harrow. His mother was a drama teacher and he too succumbed to the arts and trained as an opera singer, having an amazing tenor voice. However, he was equally fascinated by cinema, developed his writing and acting skills and became a talented photographer and keen traveller. Rejected for war service, he gained a job in distribution for the Moss Empire and then the Ministry of Information's Film Department. After the Great War Brunel immersed himself in the art of film-making, doing almost everything before finally directing. Starting with a series of short comedies released through Minerva Films, he then directed *Broken Sands* in late 1921, filmed in North Africa and released as *Lovers in Araby* (1924). His most prominent project was *The Man Without Desire* (1923), an unusual time-travelling period piece with atmospheric visuals, starring Ivor Novello and Nina Vanna.

Sometime in 1924, Leila and Alex Stewart (the latter was the famous photographer simply called 'Sasha') invited Brunel to dinner with Michael Balcon and his wife Aileen (Leila Stewart thought that they might be useful for each other). Balcon would have known about Brunel's previous film work and this meeting would be a constructive one leading to various collaborative efforts in the future. It is not inconceivable that Brunel encouraged Balcon to secure the film rights to *The Rat*. Already Balcon was a great fan of Novello and had seen all of his earlier films and it was after seeing the stage play of *The Rat* that he decided to secure the film rights.

Novello was a man of many talents, much like Adrian Brunel. Remembered with affection for his later romantic musical plays he was also an actor, composer, lyric writer, playwright and actor-manager. Born plain David Davies in Cardiff in 1893, one of the most important influences in his life was his eccentric mother Clara, who became an internationally renowned singing teacher and choral conductor. Novello was educated at Oxford and given his family background it was no surprise that he began publishing songs, with his first big hit 'Keep the Home Fires Burning' becoming one of the most popular songs of the First World War.

Novello's first play, *Theodore & Co*, was staged in 1916 and his first acting role was in a film. The French director Louis Mercanton was in London casting *The Call of the Blood* (1920), to be filmed in Sicily, and visited Novello's agent. There he saw Novello's photograph and because he looked vaguely Sicilian with dark romantic looks, Mercanton insisted on casting him in the lead role despite the fact that Novello had never acted before. More films followed, including *Carnival* (1921) and *The Bohemian Girl* (1922) from the abortive Alliance film studio, both of which secured good notices. He then made his stage debut in *Deburau* (1921).

Spotted by the legendary American director D.W. Griffith, largely because of his classical good looks he was taken to Hollywood and appeared with Mae Marsh in *The White Rose* (1923) without making much of an impression. At the time Novello was writing *The Rat*, and created the part of Odile especially for Marsh. His next film with Gladys Cooper, *Bonnie Prince Charlie* (1924), fared better. Though surrounded by some of the most beautiful women of the time, Novello was more interested in fellow actor Bobbie Andrews. Their lifestyle was certainly rather hedonistic and both had many other 'flings' despite living together.

Novello was a great party giver and his legendary flat over the Strand Theatre in the Aldwych was the centre of a gay and interesting social set. Any number of stars of film and stage went there for countless evenings of fun and frivolity. He also launched the 50-50 Club in Wardour Street for those connected with the arts in October 1924, which, despite making little money, became very popular. Funny and charming, he was also a tough, practical businessman. Balcon described him as 'a gentle, kindly man of infinite, sincere charm'[14] and although no newcomer to the film world it was his role in *The Rat* under Gainsborough that made his name and established him as a huge box-office draw.

Filming of *The Rat* took place from May to July 1925, with interiors taken first at the leased Islington studio and then exteriors in Paris in late June. This included some spectacular scenes from the latest Folies Bergere show, *Un Soir de Folie*. Mae Marsh arrived with her mother on 9th May 1925 and returned to America on 10th June and so Cutts filmed her scenes first. However, on arrival she was unwell and discovered she was in fact pregnant and so Balcon had to set up what amounted to hospital facilities in the studio to nurse her through the production.

One important feature of filming included the introduction of a small trolley on rails for cameraman Hal Young and Cutts. This was a new device that Cutts himself had designed and had sought a patent for. The track eliminated jumping from longshots to close-ups and enabled artists to play continuous scenes without a break in a semi-close shot. Previously, a long shot and a close-up had to be posed separately but Cutts did not like the break in the action and so invented this moveable platform to run a long shot into a close-up at will. Cameraman Hal Young said, 'it spares a whole heap of time and a lot of footage too.'[15] It quickly became a ubiquitous piece of film-making equipment and the technique of the moving camera was highly admired as an intriguing new development. In fact this device – a 'Dolly' or 'track' – had been around for a while and was pioneered by the Russian director Yevgeni Bauer and the Italian director Giovanni Pastrone. Cutts may have learned about it or seen it in action at UFA when filming *The Blackguard*.

By mid-May Cutts was filming the main scenes of the Parisian underworld with the wonderful set of the White Coffin Club. The entrance was through a coffin-shaped door and then down steps into a cellar that had purple walls, over which the inmates and the lights cast weird green shadows. Madame Colline (Marie Ault), proprietress, was behind the counter of the bar in truly wonderful make-up and costume. A reporter from *Picturegoer* was on the set and marvelled at Isabel Jeans in her first big movie part. Novello said: 'Isabel is something we needed very badly, a British screen vamp,' and added that he was working on a new play, a sequel to *The Rat* called *The King of Shadows*.[16]

Renie Morrison, Cutts' continuity lady, recalled some interesting moments on the set of *The Rat*. For example, there was the matter of Ivor Novello's tie. He arrived at the studio to continue a scene in a spotted tie but the previous day it had been striped one; he also had a different shirt and socks. Luckily, she was at hand to rectify and correct his attire.

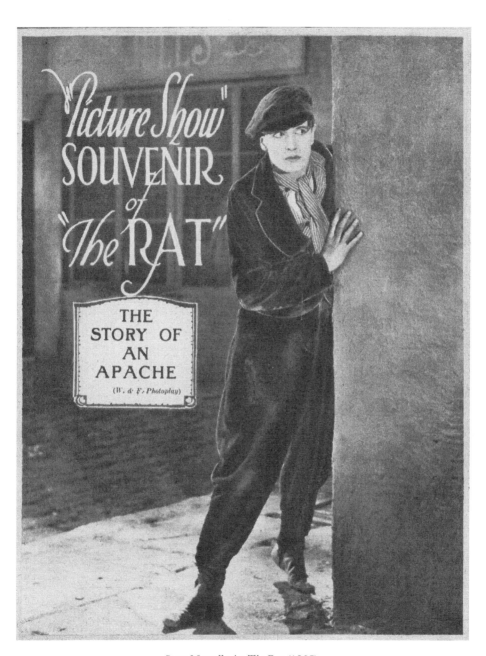

Ivor Novello in *The Rat* (1925)

Ivor Novello and Isabel Jeans in *The Rat* (1925)

Another time Morrison noticed that six people in a crowd scene had disregarded orders and adopted different costumes from their previous appearance before the camera. As the crowd numbered over 200 this was not too serious but she kept the six offenders in the background. She also noted that Isabel Jeans needed a lot of attention because she was a screen vamp and wore a profusion of jewellery. The problem of which rings and how many ropes of pearls she should wear in each sequence was a constant issue.

Morrison observed that a continuity writer's task was not all straightforward. There were subtler points to remember 'such as the angle of the camera, the position of the player's head, feet and hands', all of which were 'of vital importance' in 'matching up' scenes' that were shot over a period of time.[17] It did not look good if in a finished film there was a long shot of an artist with her head in her hands and immediately afterwards a close-up with her hands in her lap. One of the hardest matching tasks was with the scenes in the White Coffin Café. When these scenes were begun, Ivor Novello was not at liberty and so to shoot they had to imagine his presence, take his actions later on and dovetail the different takes, matching everything precisely.

The Rat was a good old-fashioned melodrama, with a simple plot about a good-looking Apache who falls in love with a beautiful Parisian aristocrat but returns to his faithful sweetheart. The story follows Zelie de Channet (Isabel Jeans), a prosperous but bored demi-mondaine of Paris who becomes infatuated with Pierre Boucheron, called 'the Rat' (Ivor Novello), a handsome young apache, who she meets in the underground cabaret called The White Coffin.

Zelie's protector, the corrupt and sinister Herman Stetz (Robert Scholtz), renounces her and pursues Odile (Mae Marsh), a quiet, domesticated girl who mothers the Rat. Stetz lures the Rat to Zelie's flat by means of a forged note and while Zelie mesmerises him, he gains admittance to Odile's attic, where he attempts to take her by force. The Rat returns and interrupts the struggle, then stabs and kills Stetz. To save her lover, Odile surrenders to the police, declaring she committed the murder despite the Rat's protestations. At the trial Odile pleads justifiable homicide and is acquitted, returning to the Rat, who realises his love for her.

The trade show of *The Rat* was on 6th September 1925 (released 1st February 1925), and although Ivor Novello was on tour with the stage version, he was present to witness 'a triumph for the British film industry'.[18] *The London Opinion* had summed up the play well 'as a work of art, the value of *The Rat* is about nine pence, but as a box office attraction it ranks at about £1,500 a week.'[19] The same sentiment permeated all reviews of the film. Perhaps some thought it both 'nasty' and 'morbid' but it was nothing of the sort and welcomed by the majority as 'thoroughly good, clean entertainment'.[20]

It was thrilling and fun and therein lay the attraction. For many it was an introduction to the idea of 'slumming' – the idea of going places and experiencing things that were usually totally off limits, out of bounds and below one's social standing. In showing the seedier side of life in the Parisian underworld on the stage or film audiences were presented with something they would never dare experience themselves but were all the same eager to see. But *The Rat* was not the only view of the Parisian underworld on offer as Adelqui Millar's *The Apache*, (1925) another romantic story showing all aspects of Parisian life, was also released at the same time.

Scenes from *The Rat* (1925)

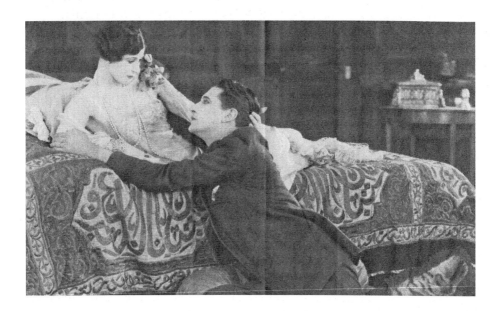

The Rat was hailed as 'a really fine piece of work giving a vivid impression of the abandoned, passionate life of the Parisian criminal scene'[21] and described as 'a first class picture. Excellent acting and polished, interesting technique combine in putting over a fine version of the successful play….A strong general attraction and a British picture that will do much to encourage the future of British effort'.[22]

Cutts was applauded for his brilliant technique in translating the successful play into a first rate British Picture of a standard that 'transcends the quite theatrical quality of the ultra-romantic story'.[23] It was viewed as being magnificently staged and the underworld Parisian atmosphere was truly spectacular. The cabaret scenes were full of vitality and packed with thrilling incidents, such as the fight between two infuriated female rivals for the love of the scornful apache, intoxicating underworld dances and the brazen criminal exploits of the dexterous thieving hero.

The acting of the main players was hugely admired. *Picturegoer* observed that Ivor Novello had not been lucky in his past screen roles but 'at last he has found something that suits him – as the swaggering, ultra romantic hero of the Gallic underworld and makes the most of a role that offers much to the right man'.[24] Indeed, he portrayed the handsome, unscrupulous and somewhat unsavoury character of the Apache in such a sympathetic and attractive light that one naturally cannot help but like him. Thankfully his bearing and looks were thought to be free of any effeminacy and his semi-brutal swagger was effective without appearing bounderish. He had become one of the world's supreme young men of the screen.

Mae Marsh was thought to have little to do but made the most of her opportunities and gave a typically wistful and human study of Odile that fitted her frail personality. Isabel Jeans, as the naughty little vamp responsible for most of the thrills and all the trouble, was a striking study and a gave a cleverly played performance.

One interesting addition to the cast was the young brunette Julie Suedo. She had been admired as a London cabaret artist and given small parts in a series of films from Stoll, with characters ranging from 'oriental languor to Latin frenzy'. Her exotic beauty was partly attributable to her Spanish mother. It was noted that Cutts, 'whose cabaret complex'[25] was so pronounced, gave her a big break in *The Rat*, where her fiery little role as one of the fighting girls of the Paris underworld made an instant impression. Clearly, Suedo was one of Cutts' protégées and also perhaps one of those actresses who had caught his eye.

The Rat scored a big reaction in America and the review from *Harrison's Report*, a New York based film trade journal, was exceptional: 'If the majority of the pictures that are made in Great Britain are as well directed and acted and the plot is as well constructed as in that of *The Rat*, the American exhibitors need not worry about shortage of good pictures. All that will be necessary for the British producers to do then will be to create a demand for their product among the American public and they will find the American exhibitor a ready buyer. From the point of view of production *The Rat* is distinctive. The scenarist has shown unusual intelligence in the development of his plot: he has taken so good a care to do the characterising that when the heroine offers to sacrifice her life to shield the man she loves, one takes such a sacrifice as natural. The plot unfolds smoothly: the direction is skilful, the acting particularly of the principal characters is extremely artistic. Miss Marsh appears winsome and Mr Novello a he-man. It is a picture that no first rate theatre need be ashamed to show.'[26]

During this time Michael Balcon became friendly with Sam Eckman Jr, who had been sent over from America to head MGM's British company. Eckman advised Louis B. Mayer, head of MGM, that they should become associated with British production in some way. As a result he was authorised to do a deal with Balcon to finance a series of films starring Ivor Novello. Balcon and other British producers had battled to gain distribution for their pictures in America and had succeeded in some instances but one key advantage was to have American-financed British pictures.

It was an interesting proposition and MGM agreed to guarantee a return of £30,000 net to Gainsborough Pictures from North and South American revenues alone. If they failed to produce the equivalent net revenue then MGM would still pay the sum stated. Balcon procrastinated for days and in the end decided that the financial control of British films needed to remain in British hands and so he turned the offer down.

The Pleasure Garden

As Graham Cutts was in the midst of filming *The Rat* in the summer of 1925, Alfred Hitchcock and Alma Reville left London, arriving in Munich on 5th June 1925 to film *The Pleasure Garden*. They were accompanied by cameraman Baron Ventimiglia, who had previously worked for Walter Niebuhr on *The Money Habit* (1924), *Venetian Lovers* (1925) and *The City of Temptation* (1925) and British actor Miles Mander, who Cutts had used in *The Prude's Fall*.

Adapted by Elliot Stannard from a melodramatic novel by Oliver Sandys (the nom de plume of Marguerite Florence Barclay), *The Pleasure Garden* was about the contrasting temperaments and fates of two chorus girls and the men in their lives. The story was of British people set in England and the Far East, but the leading ladies were American and it was filmed in Italy and Germany.

Instead of going directly to the Emelka studio at Geiselgasteig, just outside Munich, they divided into two groups. Hitchcock, with Mander and Baron Ventimiglia, went south to Italy to film exteriors while Alma travelled to Cherbourg to meet the two American leading ladies, Virginia Valli and Carmelita Geraghty, who were arriving on the liner *Aquitania* from New York.

The petite Virginia Valli was Universal's stunning brunette leading lady and she was married to New York businessman George Lamson. She had started her career as a dancer on the stage before joining the old Essanay Studio in Chicago in 1915 and subsequently found fame with Fox, Metro and then Universal and was known for her cheery practicality. David Spoto thought that Valli 'had an unusually affecting screen presence and a porcelain innocence that, with her dark hair and distracted, almost sad eyes, gave her the look of an ingénue saint.'[27] The equally petite Carmelita

Geraghty was the daughter of former FPL story editor Tom Geraghty and a good friend of Valli's. She started as an extra in the early 1920s before getting bigger parts including some leads for a variety of different companies. David Spoto said that Geraghty's 'pert blond sassiness was a perfect counterpoint'[28] to Valli's appearance.

Hitchcock's train left Munich on Saturday, 6th June at 8am, arriving before dawn on the Monday. Things started off badly when shortly before the train was due to leave Mander realised he had left his make-up kit either in the taxi or waiting room. He ran off to retrieve it as Hitchcock shouted instructions to him about how to get to Genoa the next day. Luckily, the train was late and Mander jumped aboard at the last minute but this set the tone for the whole trip. As they approached the border Ventimiglia said they must smuggle the camera through customs because it was liable for duty. The camera had been placed under Hitchcock's seat and he was in a state of anxiety. Although the police did not find the camera, they confiscated 10,000 feet of film because it had not been declared so when they arrived in Genoa, they had no film to start shooting. All available money was changed into Lira to cover all other expenses and Hitchcock sent another cameraman to Milan to get more film at great expense.

When they returned to their hotel from dinner that night Hitchcock discovered he had been robbed of all the cash he had unwisely left in his luggage. At the same time, the hotel manager said the police and customs officials had arrived with the confiscated film stock and a demand for duty. Hitchcock was forced to wire Munich for an advance to cover the cost. The next day at noon they filmed a Lloyd Triestino liner leaving for South America, with shots taken from the pier showing the departing ship and then shots from the deck with the shore receding. The latter scenes involved an expensive transfer by tug from the liner back to shore.

From Genoa, Hitchcock and crew travelled to San Remo for two days to film several exotic beach scenes, with the Mediterranean being a substitute for the tropical seas of the Far East. After lunch at the Bristol hotel they got ready to shoot the scene involving the drowning of a native girl, but there was a commotion when the girl said she could not go in water because she had her period. Extraordinary as it might seem it was Hitchcock's introduction to such matters. The girl was summarily dismissed and they had to find a substitute at short notice.

From San Remo Hitchcock and crew moved to Lake Como to meet Reville and the two American stars, and filmed the picturesque honeymoon scenes at the Villa d'Este on the shores of the lake. However, on arrival Reville had no money left since both actresses had arrived with tons of luggage and expected the big star treatment. The gowns and costumes for the film that she bought for them in Paris cost more than was expected and all attempts to get both actresses into the modest but comfortable Hotel Westminster on the rue de la Paix were brushed aside: they had to stay in the Hotel Claridge. Despite wired advances, hotel bills were mounting, there were motorboats to hire and various other expenses. Over and above financial concerns Hitchcock was also anxious and agitated, hoping the Hollywood stars would not know this was his first big feature.

Hitchcock cajoled Reville to borrow $200 from Virginia Valli and so managed to keep the budget afloat. This enabled them to return to Munich by train via Belgrade, Vienna and Zurich and to pay the excess baggage charge on the voluminous luggage belonging to the Hollywood starlets. But further mishaps followed, including missing the connection in Vienna and having to stay overnight and accidentally smashing a window while trying to move the film equipment. In late July Hitchcock arrived back in Munich penniless.

Joined here by the second male lead, the young British actor John Stuart, they began filming the interiors in sets that had been constructed for them while in Italy. One of these was the nightclub dancing sequence filmed in a glass-roofed studio in the searing summer heat, which proved almost unbearable. Their evenings were spent preparing for the next day of shooting with usually Hitchcock drafting story boards for Ventimiglia and Alma coming up with suggestions for improving the script and looking after the delicate issue of finance. The Hollywood ladies 'had a breezy confidence, a certain elegant haughtiness, and money' and tended not to socialise with Hitchcock and the rest of the crew.[2]

Carmelita Geraghty and Karl Falkenberg in a scene from *The Pleasure Garden* (1925)
Courtesy J.W. Mitchell Collection / Brian Twist

By mid-August filming was complete and as the Hollywood ladies made their way home, Hitchcock did some judicious editing to tighten things up and rearranged the footage and improved the pace. When Michael Balcon arrived at the end of August to review the film, he was very pleased and thought that it did not look like a German film and that its lighting and cutting style appeared completely American, which was necessary if it was to have international sales potential. Hitchcock reminded Balcon that his earlier training had been with Americans in an American-built studio. Today it is viewed as having both American and German technical qualities.

Described as a strong, dramatic story, clearly and logically constructed, it was in essence a romantic melodrama. Patsy Brand (Virginia Valli) is a chorus girl in the Pleasure Garden music hall. She befriends a newcomer, Jill Cheyne (Carmelita Geraghty), who is engaged to Hugh Fielding (John Stuart). Hugh travels to the Far East and in his absence Jill pursues Prince Ivan (Karl Falkenberg) and follows a fast life in the London theatrical scene, leaving Patsy's care. Patsy marries Levet (Miles Mander), but he too goes East. She borrows money and goes to visit only to find him drunk and in the embrace of a native girl. Patsy realises that she married a worthless man. Hugh meanwhile has fever, having learnt that Jill will marry the Prince and Patsy goes to nurse him. Levet murders the native girl and drags Patsy off to his bungalow, where he attempts to kill her. He is shot by Hugh, who rescues Patsy, and they find consolation in each other.

At the trade show of *The Pleasure Garden*, in March 1926 (released 24th January 1927), it was greatly admired and hailed as a 'masterly production... a film of outstanding merit'[30] and 'it is something out of the ordinary and if the reports are correct, then Hitchcock is a discovery'.[31]

The sets were thought to have unusual beauty and the intimate shots of life behind the scenes of a big musical comedy show and the nightlife of London were well staged. Equally, the exteriors, particularly on Lake Como, were delightful. Baron Ventimiglia's photography was also greatly admired for its 'artistic sympathy'.[32] However, for some it was unpleasant and rambling and the story a weak edition of *White Cargo*, 'but Hitchcock had done marvels with it. There is nothing conventional about his methods and he holds interest with clever detail and suggestive touches. He keeps the continuity smooth and well developed'.[33]

Virginia Valli was thought to give a very sympathetic and charming picture of Patsy, being equally effective in her lighter moods and under the stress of emotion. Carmelita Geraghty was well suited as the selfish and materially successful Jill. John Stuart had little to do as Hugh, but did it well. The most powerful performance came from Miles Mander, who was convincing as the polished man of society and the degraded victim of drink and despair in the final scenes.

Despite the overall praise things were not all rosy and at the time much internal politics at Gainsborough Pictures led to complications for Hitchcock that held up the national release. When he and Reville arrived back in London for a short period in September 1925, before returning to Munich to make a second picture, many interesting changes were afoot at Gainsborough.

Changes at Gainsborough

In the autumn of 1925 major developments took place as Michael Balcon and Graham Cutts took on more staff and increased production. The first appointment in late August was that of Charles Lapworth to become editorial director. Lapworth was a cosmopolitan Englishman born in 1878, who had lived in Paris, Rome, Berlin and America. In his early years he was a socialist activist and he became a journalist working on the *Daily Herald* and *Daily Mail* before visiting America and finally editing the *Los Angeles Times Graphic*. Formerly personal representative for Charlie Chaplin, for over three years he was agent for Samuel Goldwyn in London. He had just returned from two years in Hollywood, where he had been associated with Victor Seastom and Donald Crisp. Lapworth's views about the state of the British film industry matched Balcon's. His speeches at the resumed conference of the Cinematograph Exhibitors Association, where he discussed the question of British production, created a good impression, as did a series of articles for *Kinematograph Weekly* drawing on his recent transatlantic experiences. Not only were his writing skills useful but his connections in America and his wide knowledge and experience of the business were invaluable. It was felt that his appointment would 'inspire exhibitors to look with confidence for even bigger successes from Gainsborough in the future'.[34] His first assignments were working on screenplays for the next two Gainsborough pictures, *The Cabaret Kid* and *Fear O'God*.

Next, Balcon appointed George A. Hopton as general manager of Gainsborough Pictures. Hopton was another Englishman with American experience who had began his career with Thomas A. Edison and subsequently joined the Film Service, a renting company in London. When Pathe Freres took over in 1913, Hopton opened up branches in all regional cities. Eventually, he settled down in Birmingham and later joined the Fox Film Company as Birmingham manager. Within one year he was promoted to general sales managerfor the UK, a position he held for two years before joining Gainsborough. In mid-October it was announced that negotiations had been completed for an association with Carlyle Blackwell, the well-known American actor and producer. Blackwell was born in 1888 and made his film debut in 1910 for Vitagraph in John Stuart Blackton's *Uncle Tom's Cabin*. He went on to appear in numerous films, started directing in 1914 and became known as America's most handsome actor. Neat, well tailored and polished in his manners he was attractive and snappy, with the dark brown eyes, black hair and olive skin of an Italian. Indeed he could have been an extremely well-bred Italian count.

Blackwell arrived in London in May 1922 to star in *Bulldog Drummond* (1922) and then J. Stuart Blackton's *The Virgin Queen* (1923) but stayed longer than expected. While in London, in late 1922, his divorce to his first wife, Ruth, became final. Blackwell liked London so much that he created his own producing unit in 1923, releasing *The Beloved Vagabond* (1923) but further productions, including an epic set in India called *The Idol of Jallunga*, stalled. He then appeared in a few more British films, including Samuelson's *She* (1925) alongside Betty Blythe, and with Betty Balfour in *Monte Carlo* (1925). Some time in 1924 he met and fell in love with Mrs Leah Haxton, a married woman who was called 'The Queen of Diamonds', being the heiress to the deceased Barney Barnato, South African diamond millionaire, and they married in July 1925.

Balcon wanted Blackwell to make a series of films to be released through Gainsborough Pictures. It cannot be amiss to notice that Blackwell had just married a millionairess and one cannot

Carlyle Blackwell

help but wonder if he brought a financial incentive to the table. The first of these projects was *The Four Warriors*, based on an original photoplay by Charles Lapworth. It was described as one of the strongest and most powerful stories designed for the screen based upon the Great War. There were four lead characters and negotiations were being conducted with four of the greatest names on the world screen to star in the picture that was to be set in England, France, Germany and America. Even before going into production, Balcon had received offers for the American exploitation of the film.

Another significant event in October 1925 was the inauguration of the London Film Society, an organisation conceived by Ivor Montagu and the actor Hugh Miller. The two men had met on a train travelling back to London from Berlin and found they had a lot in common. Montagu had been visiting the UFA studio for *The Times* newspaper and Miller had appeared in two pictures for Walter Niebuhr filmed in Germany. Both wanted to increase awareness in continental films, particularly in London. Modelled on the Stage Society set up in 1899, the aim of the Film Society, which was a members-only group, was to promote film as an art form and a medium of communication by screening films of artistic and technical interest which the trade had deemed uncommercial or which the censor had refused to classify.

Ivor Montagu was an intriguing character. Born in 1904, he was the son of the eminent banker Lord Swaythling and was brought up in splendour in Kensington. After Cambridge he studied Zoology, became a writer, left-wing intellectual and table tennis champion. In early 1925 he met Adrian Brunel and together they formed a company to edit films. Their cutting rooms were regarded as a film university of sorts because many brilliant young aspiring workers passed through their doors. Montagu was a socialist when he began the Film Society after a life-altering trip to the Soviet Union in 1925 and his motivation was to introduce and promote films that had been censored for political reasons by the reactionary British Board of Film Censors. He later joined the Communist Party and went on to become president and a successful soviet spy (code name 'nobility').[35]

Montagu and Miller canvassed many people in the industry and gained thirty founder members before setting up an organising council that comprised Iris Barry (film critic), Sidney Bernstein (film exhibitor), Frank Dobson (sculptor), Walter Mycroft (film critic), Adrian Brunel, Hugh Miller and Ivor Montagu. On 25th October 1925 the society launched the first of its Sunday afternoon screenings at the New Gallery Kinema in Regent Street. The house was packed with film people, intellectuals, arty-types and the beau monde of Bohemia to see Paul Leni's *Waxworks* (1924) and other short films including Adrian Brunel's *The Typical Budget* (1925) and Charlie Chaplin's *The Champion* (1915). The society thrived and meetings were genial, but sometimes there were politically radicalised exchanges with vigorous debates.

Despite the society raising the profile of both British and foreign-made films the film industry remained mostly hostile and suspicious, believing, like some of the press, that it was elitist and had a communist agenda. Indeed, there was a strange vendetta against the Society from the press, who maintained it was 'high brow' and an evil influence, being an agent of Moscow because it showed Russian films.

Michael Balcon and Alfred Hitchcock were members of the society which had some impact on Gainsborough Pictures through its championing of many continental styles of film-making. Balcon also began to utilise the talents of Brunel and Montagu and so they too had an influence on later Gainsborough product.

Gainsborough Pictures were now being called 'A British firm which sells to America'[36] and Cutts was being courted by American film companies. There had been a previous attempt to lure him over the Atlantic and then came a second offer with an even more tempting figure for a long-term contract: 'Cutts' recent triumph with *The Rat* confirmed his position in the eyes of the film trade as a sure-fire maker of box office attractions which not only are successful at home but receive substantial recognition in America and the rest of the world'.[37] However, Cutts refused the offer after deciding to stay with Gainsborough and help to aid the revival in British production. Balcon and Cutts must surely have gained gratification in the bid that showed their worth and proved their productions had found a market and made an impression in America.

In the midst of all these new developments Herbert Wilcox booked the Islington studio to film *Nell Gwyn* with Dorothy Gish, Hitchcock returned to

Munich to film *Fear O'God* (re-titled *The Mountain Eagle*) and Cutts started pre-production on *The Cabaret Kid* (re-titled *The Sea Urchin*). Since Wilcox had booked the Islington studio, Balcon and Cutts were forced to find an alternative and so they booked the old Alliance studio in Twickenham to film *The Cabaret Kid*.

The Sea Urchin

At the beginning of September 1925 Graham Cutts was preparing to film *The Cabaret Kid*, the title given at first to Charles Lapworth's adaptation of the play *The Sea Urchin* from John Hastings Turner. The star of the film was Betty Balfour and Cutts made no secret of the fact that he had longed to work with her. Filming started at various outdoor British locations in early October and then exteriors in Paris were taken before settling down in the St Margaret's, Twickenham studio at the beginning of November, with completion by early December. Once again Cutts' team included Hal Young as first cameraman, Leslie Hiscott as assistant director and Charles Wilfred Arnold as art director.

Playing opposite Balfour was the American actor George Hackathorne, who had been chosen for the role of Sid Sawyer by Mary Pickford in *Tom Sawyer* (1917) and *Huck and Tom* (1918) and then gained a fine reputation with success in such films as *The Merry Go Round* (1923) and *Capital Punishment* (1925).

A good popular farce on lavish lines, *The Sea Urchin* was a perfect role for Balfour, being full of adventure, humour and romance. She first appeared as the orphan Fay Wynchebec – mischievous, irresponsible and utterly charming. Fay lives her young life within the grim walls of a French orphanage. Sullivan (Clifford Heatherley) is the proprietor of the Café Caucasian, a notorious cabaret in Paris, who receives a dying wish from an old acquaintance asking him to deliver his daughter Fay Wynchebec from the orphanage to her aunts in Cornwall. Sullivan decides the girl would be more useful as an attendant in his cabaret and so pretending to be her father, takes her to his cabaret, where she is given a Russian costume and made to dispense cigarettes to the customers. An elaborate cabaret scene is featured with the New Princes Frivolities girls from the New Princes Restaurant in London.

The hero Jack Trebarrow (George Hackathorne) lives on his father's estate adjoining the Wynchebec home in Cornwall and he is an amateur airman. He decides to fly to Paris on a whim but makes a forced landing in a fruit market, causing a real commotion and providing the biggest laugh from the havoc wrought on the skirts of certain fair Parisiennes by the aeroplane propeller. Jack bumps into Fay, who by sheer coincidence is in the market. They retire to a café, where he discovers her identity. He decides he must take her to visit her aunts in Cornwall. The next day Fay goes to meet Jack but is followed by Rivoli, a man who has pestered her with unsavoury attentions. Jack bribes one of the crew of a trading steamer to let them hide in the hold. Rivoli follows Fay to the ship and tells the captain about the stowaways. The captain seizes Jack and locks him up. His attentions to Fay create a situation but Rivoli intercedes and fights the captain until he is overpowered by the crew and thrown overboard.

Betty Balfour in *The Sea Urchin* (1926)

Two scenes of Betty Balfour in *The Sea Urchin* (1926)

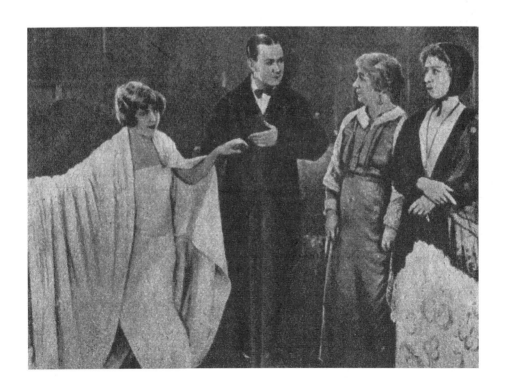

Jack escapes and with Fay jumps into the sea. Ultimately all is well and they arrive in Cornwall, near Jack's house. Fay is re-united at the Wynchebec home with her two sweet maiden aunts and weds Jack.

The Sea Urchin was given a trade show in February 1926 (released 1st November 1926) and the overwhelming comment was that Cutts had 'presented an ideal vehicle for the talents of a most popular artist'.[38] Produced on a lavish scale, the picture was a major attraction due to Betty Balfour's popular appeal and her own spirited brand of humour. It was thought to be 'more worthy than anything since *Reveille*'[39] and Betty simply carried proceedings with her tricks of expression and general sprightliness.

The film was admirably designed to show off Balfour in the 'type of sparkling and sophisticated comedy in which she has few equals. She romps with fellow orphans, is cheeky with the habitués of the cabaret or playing a game of make believe with her boy lover in the hold of the steamer. She is always bright and merry and attractive'.[40] Although Betty dominated the screen, she was admirably supported by an excellent supporting cast: George Hackathorne as Jack Trebarrow was the best foil for Betty for some time and was natural and polished, giving an assured if somewhat coy performance. And Clifford Heatherley as Sullivan gave one of the film's best performances as the engaging villain while the rest of the cast was extremely capable.

A convoluted and improbable storyline, which in the end followed the original play very slightly, faded into insignificance due to the excellent acting, farcical incidents and quite humorous irrelevances. The pace was brisk and there was a smoothness to the shots, including the moving camerawork that was used more sparingly than in *The Rat*. However, for some the film relied far too much on cabaret glitter and Cutts was criticised for his fetish for cabaret footage that was thought to be excessive.

Nell Gwyn

Like Michael Balcon at Gainsborough Pictures, Herbert Wilcox was also gaining momentum. After filming *Decameron Nights* at UFA in 1924, he had left Graham-Wilcox Productions in the hands of Sol Soloman and in March 1925 formed Herbert Wilcox Productions. His first production was *The Only Way* (1925), adapted from the stage show based on *A Tale of Two Cities* by Charles Dickens and filmed at the St Margaret's studio at a cost of £24,000. It was taken up for distribution by the British arm of First National Pictures with a cash guarantee of £12,500, which initiated their British programme with a commitment to encouraging British production.

Wilcox was thinking of the next project and saw a theatre bill headlining Dolly Elsworthy, whom he had seen performing at the Camberwell Palace doing her famous 'Orange Girl' sketch. This gave him the idea to film *Nell Gwyn* but he needed a bright and vivacious actress to play the lead. He decided this should be the American star Dorothy Gish. A cable was sent and, since her career was in a bit of lull, she was keen to visit England and play Nell Gwyn and so immediately accepted the offer, receiving a salary of £1,000 per week. Secure with the distribution deal from First National, Wilcox booked the Islington studio, forcing Balcon and Cutts to find another studio to film *The Sea Urchin*.

Dorothy Gish, along with her older sister Lillian, had started her career in vaudeville before being introduced to director D.W. Griffith by their friend Mary Pickford and from 1912 went on to appear in countless movies. After leaving Griffith in 1917 she joined Paramount/Aircraft, making a series of comedies, but in 1921 appeared with Lillian in Griffith's epic *The Orphans of the Storm*. Short at five feet tall, she was bright and vivacious but was forced to become a brunette to differentiate her from her blonde sister, who overshadowed her. She was a brilliant comedienne, with a wonderful sense of humour and quick wit. Griffith once described her as 'pert and saucy.'[41] Her utter lack of pretension, gregarious behaviour and great sense of fun made her a joy to be with. However, she was restricted and frustrated being in her sister's shadow, which is probably why she jumped at Wilcox's offer. On meeting her, Wilcox described Dorothy as 'extremely intelligent and wildly humorous, never bitchy but biting to a degree.'[42]

Instead of adapting a play such as *Our Nell*, which had been a big success with Jose Collins in 1924, Wilcox bought the film rights to a new historical novel called *Mistress Nell Gwyn* by Marjorie Bowen and wrote the screenplay himself. A spectacular period romp of Nell Gwyn's association with Charles II and the rivalry of Lady Castlemaine, it was essentially a romantic comedy.

For the purpose of the story Nell is introduced to the King Charles II (Randle Ayrton) while she is selling oranges at the doors of the Drury Lane Theatre and is entertained at supper by the merry monarch and his rather melancholy brother James, Duke of York (Gibb McLaughlin). Since neither has a penny, Nell has to pay. Nell gives imitations of popular actresses and expresses her desire to go on the stage.

The King pays handsomely for his supper with the present of a pair of silk stockings and an introduction to the theatrical manager Charles Hart (Forrester Harvey). Soon Nell moves from her bathtub in Drury Lane to a silver four-poster in St James as the King's mistress and her rivalry and conflict with the Duchess of Castlemaine (Juliette Compton) provides much entertainment. The film ends with the death of Charles and Nell's refusal to transfer her allegiance to his brother James.

Wilcox, with assistant Arthur Barnes, started production with a budget of £14,000 at the leased Islington studio in mid-September 1925. He began by sorting costumes and discussing sets with Norman G. Arnold, which included the reconstruction of historic buildings and the selection of a supporting cast. Tom Heslewood, an expert in the Stuart period, was engaged to advise on settings, costumes and customs and Doris Zinkeisen, famous for being C.B. Cochran's costume designer, was engaged to design all the gowns worn by the court ladies.

Dorothy Gish in *Nell Gwyn* (1926)

Dorothy Gish and Randle Ayrton in *Nell Gwyn* (1926)

When Dorothy Gish and her mother arrived in Southampton from New York on 25th September 1925, along with cameraman Roy Overbaugh, who had previously worked for FPL on several pictures, everything was in place. By the end of September, despite the enemy fog they were in full swing filming a huge set representing the old Drury Lane theatre interior by night. There was a picturesque mob of 1663 in sharp contrast to the smart set, who arrived at the playhouse in sedan chairs escorted by linkmen with flaming torches. Norman G. Arnold designed a fine replica of this romantic corner of old London based on careful research with novel lighting effects, cobbled stones, timbered houses and leaning posts. At the edge of the set was an imposing group of cavaliers clustered around Charles II, including his sinister brother the Duke of York (later James II) and the saturnine Earl of Shaftesbury (Fred Rains), who all advance in state to the classic theatre door. By mid-November there was another set which was a fine reproduction of Charles II's Palace at Whitehall and the arrival at Court of Nell, the orange girl and a quaint hobby horse display at a state banquet. The famous oranges had to be made up with greasepaint and powder to avoid their photographing black in their natural colour.

As filming progressed, the money ran out and Wilcox had to edit the film himself but then out of the blue he was saved. Wilcox had met the American film magnate J.D. Williams who was forming a new British company and in mid-October he had been an observer on the set of *Nell Gwyn* at the Islington studio. On 15th December 1925 Wilcox was having lunch at Ciro's club in Orange Street with his bank manager, trying to raise more cash when he was called to the telephone. It was J.D.Williams with an amazing offer: he offered to buy world rights, giving him 50% profit plus production costs, meaning £14,000 costs and about £7,000 profit. Wilcox accepted immediately, presumably side-stepping his previous deal with First National.

The American James Dixon Williams was a tenacious character whose business dealings crossed continents. He started his career as a travelling picture showman in Northwest America and then moved his activities to Sydney, Australia, in 1909. Within a short period of time he had established an empire of picture theatres but the business was full of cut-throat competition, constant manoeuvring to undermine rivals and to advance and maintain one's own position. He didn't survive and soon he was gone, resurfacing in America, where he co-founded First National Exhibitors Circuit with Thomas L. Tally in 1917, challenging the mighty moguls of Hollywood. Subsequently, it developed into a production and exhibition combined and made the first million-dollar deal with Mary Pickford and Charlie Chaplin. Once again, boardroom intrigue resulted in Williams being removed in 1922 and this time he resurfaced in London in 1925, forming British National Pictures (BNP). With a capital of £50,000 he began building a huge new studio complex at Elstree with the intent to secure a competitive advantage for large-scale British film production. His first acquisition was *Nell Gwyn* and Herbert Wilcox.

Wilcox and Williams left London for New York in early January with a print of *Nell Gwyn*, which was given a special presentation at the Ritz-Carlton Hotel on 25th January 1926. It was a knockout and the reviews outstanding: 'the first British picture that seems to have a chance in the best houses in America'.[43] As Williams enthused that it was the 'finest picture ever made in England and one of the best ever made anywhere',[44] Adolph Zukor of Paramount secured the American rights. But it didn't end there: Zukor gave Williams a contract, worth $1 million, to make three more films with Dorothy Gish, all to be directed by Wilcox. Back in London, *Nell Gwyn* was given its first UK showing to inaugurate the Paramount Plaza Theatre in Regent Street on 22th February 1926.

The reaction in the UK was more measured, with some criticism that the historical accuracy and story values were weak and that Wilcox had missed the real charm of the period. It was thought that the main appeal rested on Gish's performance and the artistic sets and costumes conveyed an effective atmosphere of the period. Wilcox had transformed Dorothy Gish into a vivacious blonde with sex appeal galore: 'she found scope for uninhibited expression and she positively radiated with the joy of life'.[45] It was thought that here at last was a part that really gave her a chance to show what she could do. Gish was 'her charming self seen to the best advantage and is triumphantly successful in her presentation of humour and vivacity'.[46] She revelled in the character and carried the film, although there were criticisms that she did not reproduce the airs of the seventeenth century. The rest of the cast was deemed adequate but special praise was given to Juliette Compton as Lady Castlemaine, who acted with dignity, distinction and conviction.

With such a huge success in both America and at home and big plans for BNP Balcon at Gainsborough may not have been too envious by these developments as he had his own surprises rising to fruition.

The Mountain Eagle

As Graham Cutts began preparations for *The Sea Urchin* and Herbert Wilcox began work on *Nell Gwyn*, Hitchcock and Reville were working with Eliot Stannard, who was creating the scenario from Charles Lapworth's story called *Fear O'God*. Finally, they both returned to Munich, along with cameraman Baron Ventimiglia, arriving late September 1925 to start work on this second Emelka picture that became *The Mountain Eagle*.

Balcon was clearly paving the way for Hitchcock to become an accepted figure in the British film industry and in mid-October stories appeared in the trade press announcing his discovery as a new and talented young director. His background and varied career that included training as an artist, then working alongside many American directors and being assistant director to Cutts, was made clear. Indeed Balcon was so confident of his capacity and his growth that he predicted 'his name as a director will soon be known the world over'.[47]

At the same time Reville was being described as the only woman assistant director in the trade, who was a 'clever and experienced little lady' and 'a striking example of these important assistant film-makers upon whom the limelight of publicity seldom, if ever, blazes'.[48] Calm and efficient and always smiling, her critical faculties were highly admired. It was noted that women subjected films to a 'swift and unerring scrutiny and spot many things' and so a film director could not 'escape the lash of feminine criticism unless he has a superwoman assistant whose eye is sharper than an eagle, with huge patience'. Alma Reville was 'nothing like as unsophisticated as she looks as some tough film guys have discovered to their cost'.[49]

Filming in Germany, there was a clear incongruity with the locale of the story being set in Kentucky. Hitchcock thought that the Tyrol would be a good substitute. On arrival in October he was looking for locations to take exterior shots and after seeing a painting of a village in a shop window, he was told it was Obergurgl in the Urz valley, the highest village in the Austrian Tyrol. It was a two-hour train journey and then a five-hour road trip away. In October 1925 Hitchcock and crew went to shoot background scenes, some with snow and some without. They were told that the first heavy snows came in November but there was an unprecedented snowfall a month early and so they had to reshuffle the shooting schedule.

Behind the scenes, Balcon signed the famous British actor Malcolm Keen for the lead male role. He had just completed a successful performance as the bigoted clergyman in W. Somerset Maugham's *Rain* (1925). Cable negotiations were also going on with a well-known American screen actress to play opposite Keen, along with John F. Hamilton, the juvenile star, and Bernhard Goetzke who had been in *The Blackguard.*

Finally, Nita Naldi was engaged to play the lead female role, playing against type as a straight, unsophisticated heroine. Naldi had been typecast in the past as a femme fatale vamp and had made her name with John Barrymore in *Dr Jekyll and Mr Hyde* (1920) and then with Rudolph Valentino in *Blood and Sand* (1922) and DeMille's *Ten Commandments* (1923). At the time she was taking an extended vacation in Paris with her companion, the wealthy James Searle Barclay, Jr, who was twenty-four years her senior and whom she would later marry.

When Naldi arrived she was dark, Latin, slinky and glamorous, with four-foot heels and long nails. Dressed in black with a black dog to match, she called the elderly Barclay 'papa'. She was also 'cynical, irreverent, bawdy, often undisciplined, and far more intelligent than she let on and she never took herself too seriously'.[50] Hitchcock found her to be an amusing woman, bizarrely at odds with her statuesque screen presence and despite her protests transformed her to match the demure and plain character she was to play.

In November the entire cast and crew returned to film exteriors in Obergurgl, where they spent two weeks. From there they returned to Munich, filming interiors at the Orbis Studio, where Willy Reiber (who had created the London settings for *The Pleasure Garden*) had designed and constructed a replica mountain town. After playing the heroine in the somewhat dowdy attire of a schoolmistress all day, Naldi changed for the evening into a low-backed dress and with her oriental face make-up and the inevitable elongated cigarette holder could be seen seated in a nearby cabaret. By Christmas filming was finished.

The Mountain Eagle was described as a strong, moving and human-appeal story about a feud between two men and a schoolteacher in old Kentucky. She escapes the clutches of one and hides out with the other, whom she eventually marries. Pettigrew (Bernhard Goetzke), Justice of the Peace and owner of the village stores in a small mountain village, hates John Fulton (Malcolm Keen), a lonely mountain dweller, known as 'Fearogod', as much as he loves his son Edward (John F. Hamilton), who was born a cripple as his mother, whom Fulton also loved, has died. Beatrice Talbot (Nita Naldi), the village schoolmistress, incurs the enmity of Pettigrew because he believes that she encourages the attentions of his son Edward, who takes evening lessons. While questioning Beatrice and in an attempt to reprove her, Pettigrew is influenced by her charm and attempts liberties, which she strongly resents. The son sees this and leaves the village. Pettigrew is furious at the rebuff and proclaims her a wanton and the other inhabitants drive her from the village. Beatrice is saved their fury by the mysterious stranger known as Fearogod, who lives a solitary life in a cabin, to which he takes her.

Pettigrew sees the chance to arrest Fearogod for abduction and Beatrice as a wanton. But Fearogod forestalls him by coming back and demanding that Pettigrew marries them. The pair then fall in love, but Pettigrew, incandescent with rage, has Fearogod arrested and thrown into prison on a charge of murdering his son, who has not returned. Fearogod has been kept in prison for over a year when he decides to escape. He finds his wife has had a baby and with them he runs off to the mountains. When the child is taken ill, Fearogod goes back to the village to find a doctor, where he sees Pettigrew.

There is doubt as to which man is going to strike first but then an onlooker fires a gun, wounding Pettigrew in the shoulder. The sudden return of his son Edward convinces the old man of the futility of proceeding with his accusations of murder, so he makes the best of matters by shaking hands with the man he has persecuted and all is supposed to end happily.

The trade show of *The Mountain Eagle* was in October 1926 (released 23rd May 1927) and the reviews were broadly in agreement that the undoubted artistic merits, skilful direction and good acting should compensate for the weakness of the story that was seen to lack conviction with 'an air of unreality'.[51] Hitchcock's direction was described as being 'thoroughly imaginative'[52] and many of the scenes were cleverly handled with dramatic force. Although all the exterior mountain settings were greatly admired, they were thought to be unplaced geographically and the English named characters appeared incongruous with their surroundings. As for the acting, Naldi was viewed as achieving success in a part with fewer opportunities than she usually faced. Goetzke gave a fine performance so that you could almost feel the train of his thoughts by his expressions and Malcolm Keen was equally admirable.

Alfred Hitchcock shows Nita Naldi how to hold a gun during
filming of *The Mountain Eagle* (1926)

10   GAINSBOROUGH'S PROGRESS

Throughout 1925 the Board of Trade, the Federation of British Industries and the Cinema Exhibitors' Association were studying the plight of the British film industry. Attempting to ascertain the reasons for the severe decline in British production, they particularly examined the practices of block, blind and advance booking. It was even discussed by Parliament in May 1925 with the consensus that something must be done, but what? The debate was fierce and varied, with a range of possible solutions that had been discussed for several years. It was an endless cycle because of the deep divisions among the parties concerned, all with different agendas. Eventually in mid-October 1925, the FBI and the CEA reported their findings and made the recommendations that included the introduction of a quota system to increase the number of British-made films shown and the abolition of block booking. But this proved to be the beginning of another long period of discussion and much behind-the-scenes machination from the various interested parties.

In the midst of this debate, in early November 1925, Gainsborough made an announcement with the headline 'British Films for America'.[1] This was claimed to be the most important event ever made with regard to British production and placing British pictures on the American screen. After lengthy negotiations, Gainsborough's representatives in New York had signed a contract with Lawson-Harris Productions Inc., representing a new group of American financiers from the West and East coasts. The deal was for Gainsborough to produce six features as from 1st February 1926, which were to be distributed in North and South America by the Lee-Bradford Corporation, later renamed the AmerAnglo Corporation following the death of F. G. Bradford in 1925. Although not one of the bigger distributors, it helped that the President, Arthur A. Lee, liked British films and had concentrated on dealing with better-quality British productions in the past. Lee also did a deal with Gaumont and claimed that the output of both companies was sufficient to meet the requirements of his corporation.

The contract called for the inclusion of one well-known American star in each picture and for the collaboration on suitable story material, direction and budgeting. Liberal finance was to be guaranteed, ensuring the pictures would be of a first-class character. Lawson-Harris Productions were to pay their share of the picture cost before each production commenced. It was noted that earlier productions from Graham Cutts and Michael Balcon, such as *Woman to Woman* and *The Rat*, had been successful all over the world as the best of the American product, and so there was confidence that the new product, to be shown in America and every market worldwide open to American pictures, would compete on terms of merit.

Balcon explained the deal: 'Ourselves and others have talked a great deal about reciprocity between the British and American branches of the industry, and we are glad to say that we have been able to accomplish more than talk. This is reciprocity of a most practical character. There is no question of spending more money on a British picture than we can get out of the English market, and hoping that America will be kind enough to take the film, or of contracting to give an American concern the right to a film subject to viewing. Based upon actual experience with Gainsborough Pictures, the Americans have enough confidence in us to put up their cash before production.'[2]

He made it clear that each picture made by Gainsborough had been placed in the United States, thanks to the excellence of Graham Cutts' work, 'and now we are extending our activities we hope to mobilise the best picture talent in the country and demonstrate to our American colleagues that their faith in us has been well placed. We are ambitious and confident in our aim to lead the revival of the British film-making industry and have set our faces against any compromise in the matter of cheapness or skimpy finances which will militate against British pictures taking a proud place on the screens of the world. We think it good business, observing the popularity of the better American pictures in Great Britain, to assume that the box office is the best guide as to what we shall do. We hope to give both the American and the British public the kind of picture they like. We are aiming at a continuity of output, which will still enable us to attract the best brains of the country, to develop the talent we know exists in Great Britain and retain it so that it is not attracted abroad. The cheap and sporadic nature of much of the British productions heretofore has discouraged the discovery of talent. We believe the best way to build a permanent organisation is to make the best pictures – but beforehand, to assure ourselves of our market, and that there is no limit to that market.'[3]

Later, in mid-November, Gainsborough engaged W.J. O'Bryen to handle the selection of stories. Bill O'Bryen was one of Balcon's oldest friends, who knew his brother, 'Shan' Chandos, as they had been in the war together. In 1914 Bill and Shan had attended the Oratory, the well-known Roman Catholic school in Birmingham. Bill then deceived the army about his age and was only sixteen when he enlisted. Shan Balcon became a member of the Officers Training Corps, gaining a commission in the Royal Warwickshire Regiment, and Bill followed. Bill got three military crosses, including a Légion d'Honneur and a Croix de Guerre. After the war Bill joined the literary agency of Curtis Brown and soon took over their film department. For eighteen months he worked for them in America, selling important film subjects to Hollywood and Broadway. Back in London he was associated with the Atlantic Union production of *Owd Bob* (1924) for Henry Edwards as production manager before joining Gainsborough, where he later took on publicity and casting.

With confidence in his growing team and the American deal, Balcon placed an impressive advertisement in the trade press. It was simple and most effective, with the large letter 'G' and text inside reading 'Gainsborough are putting British Productions on the screens of the whole world'.[4] At the same time it was announced that Gainsborough Pictures were contemplating an ambitious

Gainsborough
are putting
British Productions
on the screens of the
whole world

Gainsborough Pictures Ltd
From Bioscope 7th January 1926

programme of at least nine features for 1926, all of which would compete with American productions on equal terms. All of these films would be seen in America and all were being made largely with American capital. This investment in British films was seen as 'the first practical sign of American confidence in the ability of British producers and expresses a real confidence in the Gainsborough unit'.[5] We must remember that at the same time, Herbert Wilcox was moving forward with a similar deal via J.D. Williams at BNP and Adolph Zukor of Paramount.

Of these nine films, three had just been completed and were waiting to be released: *The Sea Urchin*, *The Pleasure Garden* and *The Mountain Eagle*. Of the remaining five projects, two stories had been acquired for early production: *The Lodger* by Mrs Belloc Lowndes and *Hunting Tower* by John Buchan (a big offer had been made by Douglas Fairbanks but Buchan preferred to accept the British offer from Gainsborough). Negotiations were in progress with other well-known British authors to purchase further film rights.

In order to fulfil these obligations and keep pace with the planned production activity Balcon needed his own studio space and so to this end he decided to restructure his activities and formed two new companies, Piccadilly Pictures Limited and Piccadilly Studios Limited in January 1926. Through the latter company he immediately began negotiations to acquire the Islington studio. The studio had not been used by FPL since 1922 and for the past four years had been used by a several independent production units, although Balcon's team had been predominant and this was an obvious choice for Balcon to make (he may also have heard on the grapevine that FPL were willing to relinquish ownership). With his accountant, Reginald Baker, he went to see J.C. Graham, head of European activities for FPL/Paramount. According to Balcon the negotiations had an *Alice in Wonderland* quality:

Graham: Yes, I am willing to sell the studio. I want £100,000.
Baker: We have a surprise for you, Mr Graham. We can only raise £14,000.
Graham: Well, I have an even bigger surprise for you – I am going to accept your offer.
Baker: Today is full of surprises, Mr Graham. We shall have to spread our payments and give you £2,000 a year for seven years.[6]

J.C. Graham accepted their terms. Balcon and Gainsborough Pictures now owned their own studio and two important members of staff retrained from the old FPLBPL staff nucleus were Harold Granville Boxall (storekeeper, who became studio manager) and George Gunn (electrician). However, although everyone knew unofficially about this acquisition, it was not until July 1926 that it was officially recognised, along with fuller details of the company restructuring.

As Balcon arranged to purchase the Islington studio, J.D. Williams with Herbert Wilcox embarked on the mammoth task of building what they called the biggest and the best studio ever seen in the UK, at Boreham Wood, Elstree. Work started 4th January 1926 and completion was sought for July, with the intent of forming the nucleus of a British Hollywood to revive the rapidly declining industry in England.

But before Gainsborough began production of its programme of features for 1926, it released two series of short films that were titled *Brunel Burlesques* and *Stephen Donoghue Racing Dramas*, both of which were launched in January 1926.

Brunel Burlesques

Adrian Brunel had been on good terms with Michael Balcon since their meeting in 1924 and had produced a few short films before releasing *Crossing the Great Saraganda* (1924) and *The Pathetic Gazette* (1924). Both cost £90 to produce and were distributed by Brunel's own company, Novello-Atlas. *The Pathetic Gazette* (1924) was a satire on the popular newsreel and magazine film series. Both films were shown at the Tivoli Theatre, London and then at the Film Society, where they were highly admired and successful.

A spoof on the popular travelogue films of the day, *Crossing the Great Saraganda* comprising one third titles, one third shots of various travel films and a final third of original footage, it was quirky and full of playful visual wit. Intrepid explorers set sail for Sagrada, sailing via the Bay of Biscay. They trek through tropical rainforests, paddle in a canoe up the Salamander River and ride on camels across a vast desert. Eventually they reach their goal. As they wearily make their way homeward, one by one they drop down dead in the desert.

Brunel cleverly exposed the conventions and absurdities of the travelogue genre of the time and highlighted the inherent dishonesty with incongruous intertitles, such as tagging a view of an African mud-hut village as Wapping and a sequence of the heroes struggling across a desert landscape as Blackpool Beach. According to Jamie Sexton on BFI Screenonline, the film's surreal humour prefigured that of later innovative British comedy, such as *Monty Python's Flying Circus*.[7]

The manager of the Tivoli arranged for C.M. Woolf to see *Crossing the Great Saraganda* at a private screening. He liked it and as a result, Balcon offered to produce a series and so they signed a contract for Brunel to make five one-reel British comedies lampooning fads or institutions of the day. Seemingly filmed some time in 1925 at the small Bushey studio in Hertfordshire, the five films were:

A Typical Budget (a satire on the topical film with items that included Daylight Saving, Economy in the Household, The Art of Self Protection and Paris Fashions For Men); *Cut It Out* (a slap towards the over-zealous censor); *Battling Bruisers* (a burlesque of boxing pictures); *So This is Jolly Good* (a lament on the position of British film and its general ineptitude in comparison with its American counterpart) and *The Blunderland of Big Game* (not a single wild animal appeared!). The latter was a parody of the usual big-game picture and concerned the great travellers Mr and Mrs Sherry Keating, Mr Forsita Fords and their native guide, Oompapa, as they ascend Mount Undervest.

Stephen Donoghue Racing Dramas

In late 1925, C.M. Woolf persuaded Michael Balcon to produce a series of six two-reel racing pictures starring Stephen Donoghue, the most celebrated champion jockey of his day. The obvious director to engage to film this series was Walter West, who had made his name at Broadwest in the early 1920s creating numerous racing dramas. According to West, Donoghue took to the medium of film like a duck to water and was not in the least bit camera conscious or awkward.

Stephen Donoghue and Madge Stuart in *A Knight of the Saddle* (1926)

The first film was *Riding for a King*, which featured Carlyle Blackwell, Miles Mander and the pretty actress June Tripp (simply called June). Filming began with preliminary shots at Newmarket in early November 1925 before moving to the Islington studio. It was turned around very fast and screened in January 1926 to an appreciative audience who regarded the series as 'a sure fire showman's proposition'.[8] The story was slight, concerning Lady Betty Raleigh (June), who secretly marries Harry Swindon (Carlyle Blackwell), who has backed his horse Boneventure far more heavily than he can afford at the Lincolnshire Handicap. To save Swindon from ruin, Betty asks her friend Stephen Baxter (Donoghue) to ride the horse. Baxter is in Paris to ride for an unknown king but flies over, landing on the racecourse just in time to ride to victory.

Although lacking a little in creative snap, the picture's chief purpose was 'providing a full-length study of Donoghue's personality in private life and on the racecourse'[9] and he was seen as a charming little man, with an evident sense of humour. Needless to say, the race climax was the best part of the film. Another five pictures were filmed in the first few months of 1926 and released thereafter: *Dark Horses*, *A Knight of the Saddle* (with Carlyle Blackwell and Madge Stuart), *Beating the Book* (with Carlyle Blackwell and Violet Hopson), *The Stolen Favourite* and *The Golden Spurs* (with Irene Russell).

The Lodger

Alfred Hitchcock and Alma Reville returned to London from Munich after filming *The Mountain Eagle* in early 1926. Before they arrived back it had already been announced in December 1925 that Hitchcock's next film would be *The Lodger*, the third production for Gainsborough, with a budget of £12,000. Hitchcock also become involved with the newly formed Film Society and began socialising with those who like him had a passion for film and its development as an art form, including founder member Sidney Bernstein, the director Adrian Brunel, film critic Iris Barry and the writers Angus MacPhail and Ivor Montagu.

The early part of 1926 was quiet and production everywhere was at a standstill due to weather conditions except for Gainsborough's activity on the Donoghue racing series. In this lull various deals were done and pre-production for *The Lodger* commenced.

A major initiative by Balcon was to secure Ivor Novello, who had excelled in *The Rat* and really proved his box-office worth. He was signed to a long-term contract with Gainsborough at the beginning of February with the view that he would play the lead in *The Lodger*, due to start filming at the beginning of March. At the same time, and in anticipation of an expansion of production, Balcon announced the appointment of another director. George A. Cooper had previously been a director for Quality Films and Gaumont and had worked on the much-applauded *Claude Duval* (1923) before making a big splash with *Somebody's Darling* (1925), starring Betty Balfour for Gaumont. Preparations for his first film project, *The Beautiful White Devil*, a thrilling tale of piracy on the high seas were underway. However, nothing much happened and by April it was announced that the film had been indefinitely postponed. It was in fact scrapped and Cooper left Gainsborough.

In addition to projects already announced in the press, it was revealed that Gainsborough also planned to film a biographical picture depicting the brilliant and romantic life of King Edward VII, called *Edward the Peacemaker*. It was assumed that practical aid and counsel from the highest quarters was being sought in order to create a balanced and acceptable screenplay. A huge advertisement was placed in *Kinematograph Weekly*[10] stating that the film was in 'active preparation' in association with Jeffrey Bernerd, who had been managing director of Stoll Pictures until his appointment as general manager of W&F distributors in 1926. This was an interesting connection since W&F were Gainsborough's UK distributor but this project also evaporated.

In mid-March 1926 Michael Balcon, Charles Lapworth and Arthur Rawlins (financial director) travelled to New York to accomplish business deals and discuss forthcoming Gainsborough projects with Lawson-Harris Productions and Lee-Bradford. They also hoped to add a little to the campaign to 'sell the idea of more British pictures' to the exhibitors and public of America.[11] Although they were lunched and dined by various industry bodies the climate was less than receptive due to the comments of Will H. Hays, head of MPPDA (Motion Picture Producers and Distributors of America) and widely dubbed the tsar of the America film industry. He had voiced his alarm in the press at the encroaching threat of European films and plans to aid native film industries with subsidies or quotas that constituted 'a serious menace to the continued maintenance of our foreign film trade'. Back home these comments were viewed as 'an avowal of America's private intention to stifle her competitors at all costs'.[12] In light of the unease and hostility from some quarters, it was clearly an advantage that Gainsborough already had a good reciprocal American deal in place.

During this trip Balcon was also courted by First National Pictures and had meetings with their foreign manager, E. Bruce Johnson, who offered to finance a number of pictures to be directed by Graham Cutts and distributed by First National worldwide, saying 'we had seen Cutts' work and we are convinced that this director can make pictures.' Johnson added that they had already partly financed Herbert Wilcox's *The Only Way* (1925) and also funded *Nell Gwyn* and were willing to finance production with any reputable British concern that could show a record for making good British films up to 50% of the negative cost. But the deal never came off because Johnson believed Balcon was unable to change arrangements made with a British renter but actually this must have been due to the existing deal with Lee-Bradford.[13]

During pre-production of *The Lodger* in the early part of 1926 Hitchcock was involved in story conferences with Eliot Stannard, who was adapting the 1913 mystery novel by Mrs Belloc Lowndes based on the notorious crimes committed by Jack the Ripper. Regarding the adaptation of the book, Hitchcock believed that it is 'nearly always impossible to translate a novel into the technique of the screen exactly as it stands.'[14] One of the contentious issues was the ending. Hitchcock wanted an ambiguous conclusion but was forced to make it clear that Ivor's character was innocent, indicating interference from Balcon or Woolf. Novello simply could not be seen as villain.

Hitchcock had read the book and had seen the play called *Who is He?* adapted from the novel by Horace Annesley Vachell and staged at the Haymarket Theatre in 1916. Later, he said that he chose *The Lodger* from the studio's available properties but it would appear Balcon allocated the project to Hitchcock because he thought that the director's strong sense of character and narrative would balance the mystery aspects of the story. Hitchcock's familiarity with the book and play were seen as an advantage.

Once the scenario was underway, Hitchcock began recruiting other cast members and by mid-February 1926 had engaged Malcolm Keen, Alfred Chesney, Marie Ault and June. The latter had impressed everyone in her role in the Stephen Donoghue racing drama *Riding For King* and was thought perfect for the role of Daisy Bunting although originally her part was to be filled by a high-profile American actress.

Starting her career as a dancer, June had trained under Pavlova with her first appearance on the stage at the age of ten in Anna Pavlova's *Snowflakes*. Before long she was appearing regularly in the West End under Charles B. Cochran and then Jack Buchanan and became a highly popular musical comedy performer. Together, June and Ivor Novello had their first screen tests for the Ideal Film Company and were told they were hopeless and would never work on the screen. Despite this she did appear in two of their films and then rejected an offer from Hollywood, before being sought by Gainsborough Pictures.

At the time June had made a sudden exit from *Mercenary Mary* at the Hippodrome to undergo an appendix operation and was recuperating in the South of France for a month. She got a wire from Ivor Novello asking her to play opposite him in *The Lodger*. He told her that there was 'no dancing required. You will act beautifully and we shall have fun.' Although still a little weak (and she had also been forbidden to dance for a few months), June agreed, which was somewhat premature as she later had a relapse.[15]

June described Hitchcock as 'a short, corpulent young man, who spoke in a curious mixture of cockney and North country accents with a laboured stress on elusive aitches. His humour was salty or subtle, according to his mercurial moods and his brilliance was patent.' She added that after his Berlin experience the director 'was being hailed as the Great White Hope of the lagging British motion picture industry. I have heard it said that he was largely responsible for dragging it out of its superannuated swaddling clothes and putting it into long trousers.'[16]

The Lodger was a thriller about a Jack-the-Ripper type criminal who enjoyed killing fair-haired girls on foggy nights, near London Bridge. As the murderer terrorises London he leaves a calling card with a triangle and the word 'avenger' printed on it near his victims.

Ivor Novello in *The Lodger* 1926)

Mr and Mrs Bunting (Arthur Chesney and Marie Ault) and their pretty fair-haired daughter Daisy (June) live in a house in Bloomsbury. A mysterious stranger comes to Mrs Bunting's lodgings one foggy night in search of lodgings. He takes rooms and behaves strangely. Joe Chandler (Malcolm Keen), a young detective who is placed in charge of the Avenger case, is a frequent visitor to the Buntings and he is also in love with Daisy. He views with alarm the growing interest Daisy has in the lodger. Mrs Bunting grows suspicious of the lodger, thinking he might be the Avenger but does not express her fears although she forbids Daisy to go out with him.

The lodger and Daisy fall in love, much to Chandler's chagrin when he finds them embracing. Chandler also becomes suspicious and secures a search warrant for the lodger's rooms, where he finds a map plan of the murder, a revolver and the photograph of the Avenger's first victim. The lodger protests innocence and insists the murdered girl was his sister. He is arrested but manages to escape into the night. Daisy follows and finds him. He tells her that murdered girl was his sister and how he has promised his mother to avenge her death. But the lodger is hounded down by a mad mob. At the last minute Chandler learns that the real Avenger has been arrested and is in time to save the lodger. He then takes Daisy in his arms.

At the beginning of March Hitchcock began filming exteriors with Baron Ventimiglia once again as cameraman, Alma Reville as assistant director and Charles Wilfred Arnold as art director, along with his assistant, newcomer Bertram Evans. The first scenes of *The Lodger* were taken near Westminster Bridge on the Embankment at midnight, with Ivor Novello in a grim sequence about the finding of a body in the black waters of the Thames. Much time was taken to get the lighting right and in finding the spot for the enactment of the tragedy; work was not completed until 6am.

Every corner of the studio was stamped with Bloomsbury and the sets included a three-sided house with narrow walls and low ceilings to resemble a typical middle-class home. Camerawork was conducted in this small space by tracking or suspension, especially to follow the staircase that was three storeys high. A front door inscribed with the sinister number twelve led into a neat linoleum-covered hall with a wooden hat-stand on the right. The staircase ran up straight ahead to a landing and a doorway, twisted to the left to another landing, and another doorway then up another flight. There were difficulties in lighting since usually most sets were built with two sides left open and this only had one small opening on the left of the entrance hall and the staircase boasted not only walls but a ceiling too. Upstairs was a shabby, sitting room with a piano, covered with the usual family portraits. Everything was staged with painstaking attention to detail, such as the Victorian ornaments on the mantelpiece to lend the right atmosphere.

One clever interior scene was taken in the evening. It was necessary to show the lights of the passing traffic flashing past the curtains at the window. Hitchcock thought of a simple but clever solution of passing a small arc light mounted on a trolley backwards and forwards in front of the window at intervals to achieve the desired effect.

Since June's character Daisy Bunting worked in a couture establishment, one of the important scenes was a spectacular view of a mannequin parade in a dressmaker's salon, a gorgeous and glittering affair. All the gowns were supplied by Peron Couture and the clothes on show were estimated to cost in excess of £10,000. Since Dolly Tree, who had dressed *Woman to Woman* in 1923, was sole designer for Peron, it is possible that perhaps some of these clothes were from her designs.

Ivor Novello and June in *The Lodger* 1926)

Filming carried on through to mid-April and one of the last scenes was in a public bar, where the lodger, handcuffed wrists hidden by his cloak, was dramatically detected and then chased by a mob.

June observed that Hitchcock had been highly influenced by his stay in Berlin and 'was imbued with the value of unusual camera angles and lighting effects with which to create and sustain dramatic suspense that often a scene which would not run for more than three minutes on the screen would take an entire morning to shoot.' She described the filming of one particular scene where she had to carry an iron tray of breakfast dishes up a long flight of stairs, 'but by the time Hitch was satisfied with the expression of fear on my face and the atmosphere established by lights and shadows, I must have made the trek twenty times, the tray seeming to grow heavier every passing minute.'[17]

Another observation about getting things right came from Renie Morrison, Cutts' continuity lady, who was working on *The Lodger*. She said that Marie Ault as Mrs Bunting, 'could not reveal suspicion of her lodger before a certain scene.'[18] Before this she had to have an innocent expression and thereafter one of unmistaken suspicion. This had to be carefully choreographed.

During filming a carefully placed and worded feature about Hitchcock appeared in *The Picturegoer* magazine, titled rather pompously 'Alfred the Great'. He was described as 'an unassuming and delightful personality' with 'such a complete grasp of all the different branches of film technique that he is able to take far more complete control of his production than the average director of four times his experience. The fact is that he has crammed twenty years of experience into five years of practise, while his youth is a tremendous asset toward freshness of treatment'.[19] Interestingly, the feature was written by Cedric Belfrage, who was on the staff at Gainsborough Pictures. He had started out as an assistant in the days of Balcon-Saville-Freedman and may now have progressed to working on publicity for the company and was orchestrating a major corporate PR coup. In conclusion Belfrage wrote, 'it would be difficult to say what successes the future still holds in store for Alfred Hitchcock, who at the age of twenty-six has already produced two films, all who have seen which, declare to be almost perfect in their technical and artistic perfection'.[20]

In contrast, Hitchcock's fellow director Adrian Brunel said 'he was not a good director in those days, but his work was interesting and his methods of publicising it were intelligent and thorough.'[21] Brunel thought that every picture he made had some amusing and original twists or angles of treatment and that Hitchcock was shrewd enough to always bring these to the notice of the press since he had the ability to exploit his personality and to inspire belief in his gifts. Hitchcock was intelligent and resourceful and had he not campaigned for himself as he did, he would not have received the recognition to enable him to progress in the industry as he did.

Hitchcock himself outlined his views on film production, stating that he believed 'in drawing out character, so that the people on the screen are real and not the colourless puppets of so many pictures.' Since he had been through every branch of film production he attributed 'the failure of many directors to the fact that they haven't sufficient technical knowledge.'[22]

During Michael Balcon's absence in New York, and while Alfred Hitchcock was filming *The Lodger*, *The Pleasure Garden* was given its trade show at the end of March 1926. Even though the reviews were all positive, things did not go well. C.M. Woolf was not happy with the result – he thought the film would confuse and upset audiences because of the strange camera shots that included overhead views of a spiral staircase, odd angles and shadows, high contrast in lighting and low-angle shots of the chorus girls' legs. Simply put, the way Hitchcock and Ventimiglia had created atmosphere with light and shadow and striking camera angles was far too Germanic. Woolf believed that British audiences were more accustomed to the simpler techniques shown in American or British films, despite Balcon's view that the film was more American than German. Woolf's taste lay more in the productions by Cutts and one must question how much influence Cutts had on Woolf. He was adamant that circulating the film would endanger future bookings for other Gainsborough projects and so the project was shelved. Whatever discussions occurred this must have come as a severe disappointment to Hitchcock.

Behind the scenes there was a lot of tension. When Ivor Novello was assigned to the project Cutts was not happy seeing the actor he considered to be his star given to Hitchcock and made his views clear to Balcon. But it didn't end there. Cutts was not actually directing at the time and would have been an onlooker when studio interiors began. According to Donald Spoto, Hitchcock felt awkward filming so close to his former superior, who referred to him as 'that boy on the set'.[23] As filming progressed, Cutts dropped by several times and spread rumours about the incomprehensibility of the film. He told everybody that Gainsborough 'had a disaster on our hands'[24] and C.M. Woolf listened to him. Woolf was equally negative for he had not liked *The Pleasure Garden*.

Because of Hitchcock's association with the Film Society and its members, word spread that they had influenced him too much and he was going too arty or that his German experience had become overwhelming. One day he had a floor built of one-inch thick plate glass about six foot square, put a camera underneath and was photographing Ivor Novello walking on it, thus filming his feet. Many were mystified by this and other things he was doing. Still busy sniping, Cutts declared, 'I don't know what he is doing.'[25] In fact, this was one of Hitchcock's rather clever ideas to show the lodger pacing his room.

When Balcon arrived back from New York at the end of April 1926, Hitchcock had already completed six weeks of filming by mid-April and had cut and assembled the film ready for private viewing by Balcon and others. He was presumably distressed by Cutts' behaviour and equally disturbed by Woolf's decision about *The Pleasure Garden*. At the same time he was presented with a storm of protestations from Cutts. According to Balcon, *The Lodger* produced a delicate and trying situation 'for Cutts was not at all well disposed to Hitch. He had been perfectly happy with Hitch the young handyman and even as his assistant director. Hitch could not understand what he had done to offend Cutts and I had to explain to him that he had done nothing wrong; it was only that Cutts was jealous. Hitch was rising too fast for Cutts's taste and he resented him as a rival director in the same studio.'[26]

When *The Lodger* was given a private screening for Woolf, the crew and potential exhibitors in the summer of 1926, Woolf did not understand it. According to Donald Spoto, Woolf, who had the ultimate veto in terms of distribution, told Hitchcock, 'Your picture is so dreadful that we're just going to put it on the shelf and forget about it.'[27]

For Balcon this was naturally a disaster as he had expended a great deal of time, effort and money on the three Hitchcock projects. *The Lodger* had cost £12,000 and Woolf was also holding up the two earlier Hitchcock films as he considered them also unmarketable. Meanwhile, Gainsborough needed more product to follow the success of *The Rat* and *The Sea Urchin* and in his opinion *The Lodger* was a good proposition because of its star, Ivor Novello. He also needed to fulfil his obligations with his American partners Lawson-Harris Productions and Lee-Bradford.

Balcon decided to cancel the existing trade show date for *The Lodger* and talked to Adrian Brunel about using Ivor Montagu to revise the footage. He had heard about Montagu's critical faculties and of his excellent work with Brunel translating and re-editing foreign films; he also knew that he was acquainted with Hitchcock via the Film Society. Montagu and Balcon duly met for lunch at the Monaco restaurant to discuss what could be done to improve *The Lodger* and re-edit it into a more presentable form to sway Woolf's opinion. He then gave him a screening at which Montagu was impressed, saying it was technically and artistically ahead of its time, the narrative compelling, the design innovative and images haunting.

When Montagu began discussions with Hitchcock he found him to be resentful and unshakeable in his confidence about his own technical judgement. But Montagu persuaded him that his ideas would improve the film. In August they worked together re-editing and re-shooting part of the final chase sequence. They also reduced the titles to a bare minimum and made them more punchy. Montagu employed the American poster artist E. McKnight Kauffer to draw sinister title backgrounds that would highlight the film's triangular structure and thematic design (the triangle was the shape of the notepaper left by the murder but also a symbol of the film's three-way love interest). But Hitchcock never acknowledged Montagu's contribution: 'it was the first clear example of an ungenerous streak in Hitchcock's nature…he cherished the illusion that every element of success was his own'[28] even though Montagu was brought in as as supervising editor on the next two Hitchcock movies.

The significantly improved film was finally given a trade show in mid-September 1926 (released 14th February 1927) and was an instant success with amazing press coverage: 'Perhaps the most polished and brilliant of British productions yet seen and one that grips the interest'[29] and 'It is possible that this film is the finest British production ever made' were two of the many superlative notices.[30] Overwhelmingly, *The Lodger* was viewed as a milestone, the most imaginative picture produced to date and pictorially expressive and magnificently photographed. Hitchcock's unconventional treatment illustrated many clever touches that showed care and skill throughout. The lodging-house setting and the general atmosphere of fog and mystery encircled the characters and heightened the mystery of the story. Equally, the way in which the scenes were filmed with shadows, unusual camera angles and quirky compositions were gripping and helped convey a sense of unease and tension.

The way in which Hitchcock kept the tension going, the ongoing mystery of the identity of the Avenger, the gripping nature of the scenes and the fact that the actual crimes were shown with a minimum of footage were all regarded as skilfully done. The fact that the plot was advanced by clever visualisation rather than an abundance of subtitles was also admired. Every glance, every gesture, every step, every inanimate object and every character was significant in building up the story and contributed to the impression the audience was meant to receive. Several gems of continuity were noted as being exemplary, including the scene when the police mark a map with the locations of the crimes, which then dissolves into another scene shot over the shoulder of the lodger doing exactly the same.

All the players were highly admired. Novello was thought to play his part in a restrained and interesting manner that admirably conveyed the impression of a sinister and mysterious man hiding a subtle secret. June in her blonde wig was charming and gave a dainty and appealing performance, skilfully depicting her fascination with the lodger. Marie Ault gave an extraordinary fine piece of work, which was the biggest character role of her career and showed what a truly great artist she was. She presented a perfect study of a middle-aged, good-natured London landlady and 'her clothes, her expressions, the way in which her growing suspicion and fear are shown by almost imperceptible changes of expression, her few gestures, the very position her body falls into, belong to the woman she is portraying'.[31] Arthur Chesney was equally delightful and Malcolm Keen an admirable foil for Novello.

The glowing reaction must have annoyed Cutts and embarrassed Woolf but validated Balcon. This changed everything and *The Mountain Eagle* was given a trade show the following month. Woolf also condescended to give national release dates for all three Hitchcock films set for early 1927.

The Triumph of the Rat

After languishing for several months, Graham Cutts began preparations to film the sequel to *The Rat*, called *The Triumph of the Rat*, with a scenario prepared by Reginald Fogwell and a team that included Hal Young as cameraman, Bertram Evans as art director and two assistants, Leslie Hiscott and Jimmy Kelly. Following the disruption of the General Strike at the beginning of May 1926, Cutts left

London at the end of May to film exteriors in Paris that included the opening sequence in the fashionable society rendezvous of the Château Madrid in the Bois de Boulogne. By the middle of June, filming was in full swing, with interiors at the Islington studio on both floors that included various sequences set in the White Coffin cabaret, a plush apartment, a fashionable café and restaurant and a fancy-dress ball with some garden settings. For the ball, Jimmy Kelly secured a suitably dressed Parisian crowd of 500 people overnight.

Perhaps to appease Cutts over his aggravation with Hitchcock and the filming of *The Lodger*, his new film was described as being 'destined to be the greatest thing the company has undertaken'[32] and then on completion as Gainsborough's 'biggest effort to date'.[33]

Once again the star of *The Triumph of the Rat* was to be Ivor Novello, ably assisted by the glamorous Isabel Jeans. Despite the fact that Novello was signed to a long-term contract with Gainsborough at the beginning of February, Balcon made it clear in June 1926, as filming commenced, that Gainsborough were to retain his services throughout the whole of 1927.

As the Rat abandoned his old Parisian haunts for a cottage in the country with the innocent Odile in the last scenes of *The Rat*, it was a foregone conclusion that this idyll would not last. After all, a life of crime and the attraction of the White Coffin cabaret would be hard to give up for a simple life. In the new episode Odile has gone and Pierre Boucheron, the famous Apache (Ivor Novello), goes back to Paris after some years and succumbs to Zelia de Chaumet's (Isabel Jeans) charms with a promise to make a gentleman of him. He becomes the idol of Parisian society and kept by Zelie, who in turn is kept by Henri Mercereau.

Pierre meets the Comtesse Madeleine de L'Orme (Nina Vanna) and immediately falls for her. Zelie taunts him, so he wagers that within a month he will win Madeleine's love. The Rat wins the wager but falls in love with Madeleine, who claims him from the dazzling heights of society to which he has climbed and rouses his better instincts again. Zelie sees that her foolish taunt has driven Pierre away and is determined to use her influence to ruin the Rat and send him back to the gutter. Zelie meets Madeleine and tells her the story of the wager. Horrified, Madeleine will not listen to Pierre's explanations so his progress on the downward path commences. Later, he becomes potman at the White Coffin, where once he reigned as king. But Zelie is not content: she engineers a plot by which the Rat seems to have betrayed his own comrades and at the end we see him friendless and alone. Starving, he is turned away from his old haunts and only one girl expresses her sadness.

In the second week of August final exteriors were chosen at Boulogne but suddenly they were not available and so new ones had to be hurriedly found at Dieppe. Perhaps these formed the exteriors for the garden party sequence in the grounds of a grand château. Ivor Novello worked all day on Sunday and Monday morning and then dashed by car to a convenient point and crossed by aeroplane in time to appear at the matinee of *Downhill* at the Princes Theatre. Finally, as Cutts began cutting and editing, Roland Pertwee (a novelist and short story writer) was engaged to write the titles.

Ivor Novello and Nina Vanna in *The Triumph of the Rat* 1926)

The Triumph of the Rat was given a quick turnaround with a trade show in September 1926 (released 21st March 1927) and was a sure-fire hit, greatly admired for its fine and efficient acting, magnificent settings, excellent photography and splendid touches. Although the story itself was viewed as being thin or even negligible, it was seen as Cutts' best work to date, with many ingenious effects and well-directed scenes. Some original shots included seeing a mass of balloons that gradually parted to reveal the fancy-dress ball in progress and the overhead shot of people looking at a newspaper feature about the Rat.

Ivor Novello and Isabel Jeans in *The Triumph of the Rat* 1926)

It was felt that Ivor Novello had never done better work, playing with a fine sense of dramatic values. Isabel Jeans looked beautiful and gave an excellent performance, acting with distinction despite having a part with little scope. Nina Vanna was sweet and appealing but although her characterisation was good, she displayed a somewhat limited range of expression. As ever, Marie Ault provided her usual superb characterisation. Julie Suedo, the girl of the underworld, gave the best feminine performance, being thorough and full of feeling, and it was noted she needed to be given a real chance. Cutts had also introduced Gabriel Rosca, a French dancer and genuine habitué of the Parisian underworld, brought over to supply atmosphere. He behaved like a true Apache and provided a true touch of reality. Needless to say, the leisurely development of the very slight story and a climax that just fizzled out was designed to make way for a sequel.

During filming of *The Triumph of the Rat*, Graham Cutts was interviewed for *The Picturegoer* magazine and provided a feature titled 'Secrets of a film director'[34] in which he disclosed some interesting details concerning his views on film production. This was perhaps engineered by Balcon as another form of appeasement following the feature on Hitchcock in an earlier issue of the magazine.

Cutts observed that the film director's most difficult and absorbing task was conceiving and directing feminine roles. As the job of the director involved deciding how people would behave in dramatic circumstances and then to get his artists to behave accordingly, it was important to study women in every conceivable mood to further this objective. He believed that the main difference between the sexes in dramatic circumstances was that a man could endure emotional tension for hours and more or less control himself but a woman nearly always broke down and collapsed in tears, hysterical laughter or even fainted. A director should be able to project himself into a 'hysterical state of mind' in order to grasp just what an actress should do, depending on the character developed. However, sometimes the right emotion simply would not come, in which case the director must assist the actress so that she achieves the required state of mind through straight talking or by using less obvious tactics. For example, Isabel Jeans was doing a scene to be inserted into *The Triumph of the Rat*. She was sitting in a car beside Ivor Novello, her lover in the picture, who was badgering her and she had to let her eyes fill with tears.

The scene was being taken during the day, outside with artificial light and without the usual soft music to assist. But no tears came. Indeed, nothing happened. So, Cutts, knowing how harsh words can often unleash a woman's grief, shouted a sentence couched in quite unparliamentary language and at once her eyes swam with tears.

Cutts explained that a director played far many more roles in his career than the most versatile actor 'not so much because he must "live" in every part in every film … but because he is so often acting at his players.'[35]

As a result he described the cunning wiles of achieving emotion in some female players. If he wanted an actress to look open, candid, trusting and later to close up sharply in suspicion or indignation, he would first charm her gently and lead her deprecatingly, knowing all the time that soon he was going to rap out an order with the express intention of wounding her feelings – 'It is sometimes an essential method of getting the right expressions.'[36]

In June 1926, Balcon once again reiterated Gainsborough's ambitious programme of between eight to ten films for 1926 and revealed that Cutts' next project was to be *The Silent Warrior*, adapted from an original story by Reginald Fogwell (who wrote the scenario for *The Triumph of the Rat*), and would star Carlyle Blackwell. Originally, this picture was to be filmed by Hitchcock but he had refused and it was then agreed that he would start work on a film version of John Buchan's novel called *Hunting Tower*, with a strong 'boy-scout' flavour and was to star Carlyle Blackwell. Neither project came to fruition, but *Hunting Tower* did resurface in 1928 as a Welsh-Pearson picture.

11   THE RESTRUCTURING OF GAINSBOROUGH

Although everyone in the film world had known unofficially for six months, Michael Balcon only unveiled the restructuring of Gainsborough Pictures in late June 1926, announcing both the formation of Piccadilly Pictures and the purchase of the Islington studio. New German and American equipment had recently been installed in the studio, along with a new plaster shop where clever craftsmen were now able to add much to the artistry of the sets. It was recognised that the studios were 'now better prepared than ever to contribute to the production of British films on a scale which will enable them to compete with the products of any other country in the world'.[1]

Piccadilly Pictures was formed in partnership with Carlyle Blackwell and had acquired all of Gainsborough Pictures' shares in becoming the controlling company of Gainsborough Pictures and Piccadilly Studios Limited, which held the lease on Islington.[2] All actual business would in future be carried out with this name under the Gainsborough trademark. C.M. Woolf of the W&F Film Service Limited was made chairman, with Balcon and Blackwell as joint managing directors on the commercial and production side. Woolf's stature within the industry and Gainsborough was re-affirmed by stressing that through his efforts at least twenty first-class British pictures had been made and distributed in the leanest years of British production. The financial director was Arthur Rawlins and R.P. Baker was secretary. Graham Cutts retired from the directorate, allegedly to devote his time more closely to the demand for increased production, although given the circumstances of his previous antics one wonders if there were other considerations in this move. Charles Lapworth also relinquished his position as editorial director of the company.

This may be when Angus MacPhail joined the company to take over some of Lapworth's duties in the story department. MacPhail became one of Balcon's faithful friends and counsellor and eventually story supervisor at Gainsborough. Brilliant, resourceful and entertaining, he was educated at Westminster and Trinity Hall, Cambridge and was one of the founders of the Cambridge University Kinema Club. Adrian Brunel and Ivor Montagu had initiated him into the art of screenwriting at their film editing business and may have introduced him into the Gainsborough fold.

Patrick McGillan observed that[3] Alfred Hitchcock did not view the reorganisation and expansion plans in a positive light. He believed Gainsborough was in mounting disarray, losing money, and there was a battle for the control of production between Balcon and Woolf, which was as disruptive as his 'feud' with Cutts. More than likely this negativity stemmed from his frustration at all the politics surrounding the release of his first three films. Despite reservations he did sign a new contract with Gainsborough but then shortly afterwards he was made an offer by J.D. Williams to join his new concern of BNP with Herbert Wilcox. Clearly, Williams and Wilcox saw that Hitchcock was a rising star and would be an invaluable addition to their growing concern and so they lured him away with the promise of new freedom and bigger budgets. With a multi-picture deal and a contract for £13,000 per year, Hitchcock accepted on the understanding he would not be available until his contract with Gainsborough ran out in early 1927.

Described as a 'genuinely creative artist', it was clear that *The Lodger* established Hitchcock as a new force in British film-making and that he had worked hard to achieve such accolades – 'it is worth noting that Hitchcock's success is the result of studio experience from the humblest job upwards coupled with thoughtful study of details'.[4] He made it known that his future lay with BNP, that he was busy with preparations for his first subjects for them and that one project at least would be a striking departure on unusual lines.

Hitchcock's decision to leave Gainsborough and presumably a disgruntled Cutts, who may also have discussed quitting the firm, would have been problematic for Balcon since he had just secured the finance and support to expand the company's activities. Undoubtedly, he would have been looking to recruit new, good-quality directors.

In the summer of 1926 there were more discussions about the problems of British film production and the ongoing plans for legislation: 'the present situation has not arisen because British companies have lacked skill or enterprise but solely because in present conditions the regular production of films is inherently and fundamentally an unsound business proposition'.[5] It was the issue of available markets and competitive conditions that made it almost impossible for the British film industry to flourish – 'Export markets are the key to success and the only market that really counts is the American one'.[6] Once again the schemes of introducing a quota or following the idea of reciprocity were raised. It was also recognised that the only effective way to ensure that British pictures were given American distribution was to employ a well-known Hollywood star. Significantly, both Michael Balcon and Herbert Wilcox had already been using American stars for some time and had also been following the idea of reciprocity to some degree but had taken things further by securing financial involvement in their productions, ensuring American distribution.

The actual number of films produced in 1926 dropped to thirty-seven from forty-five in 1925, but the decline slowed and there appeared to be an upturn in production. This provided some optimism that there were signs of a revival for 1927: 'British picture production is speeding up and films are being made with British stars and British money and the faith is coming back'.[7]

Michael Balcon confirmed that Gainsborough was to increase output: 'We are going to make more pictures than ever next year.'[8] He added that the 1927 programme would include three films starring Ivor Novello, with a contract being signed at the end of December 1926 covering the period 1st January 1927 to 1st September 1927.[9] When Balcon's American distributor, Arthur A. Lee of the Lee-Bradford Corporation, arrived for a visit to London in late September, he said that Ivor Novello 'was becoming popular and it has been whispered that he might easily take the place of Valentino in the public's affections.'[10]

The Rolling Road

In mid-August 1926 Graham Cutts started work on a production called *Shanghaied* from an original story by Boyd Cable, with plans to direct another movie with Ivor Novello immediately afterwards. From the outset there was confusion over the title that erroneously evoked a Chinese background so it was swiftly re-titled *The Rolling Road*.

A drama and romance of the sea, it was adapted from Cable's story by Mrs David Powell, widow of the late, noted screen actor David Powell, who had died in April 1925 of pneumonia at the age of forty-two. He had been a prominent actor in the early days of FPLBPL and had appeared in several of their films made at Islington. The lead male role of the sailor hero was specifically written for Carlyle Blackwell and this was his first starring role at Piccadilly Pictures. His co-star was the delicate beauty Flora Le Breton. Cutts had already used her before in one of his earliest films *Cocaine* (1922) and she had appeared in several other films before visiting America in late 1923. Le Breton had appeared in some American pictures and stage shows before returning home at the beginning of August. She had made no secret of her preference to appear on the British screen and within forty-eight hours of landing, she was signed by Gainsborough to co-star with Blackwell.

Set mainly aboard a big sailing vessel, the story concerned two young lovers who, after being separated by their enemies, find themselves marooned on a desert island and at last sail home to happiness. Tom Forty (Carlyle Blackwell), a young sailor who has saved a bit of money, falls in love with Nell (Flora Le Breton), the ward of a boat-builder, who promises to marry him if he will give up the sea. Tom agrees and a wedding day is fixed. Nell is the ward of her uncle John Ogilvie (Clifford Heatherley), a boat builder, and he is anxious for her to marry Christobel (A.V. Bramble), a well-to-do ship chandler and owner of a sailing ship. They concoct a letter from Tom purporting to break the engagement and have him shanghaied and put on a boat called *The Gleam*. Thinking Tom no longer cares for her, Nell agrees to marry Christobel. Tom escapes and travels back to the village only to find Nell married, so he goes off in despair and signs on as deck hand, back on *The Gleam*. Without his knowledge, Nell follows him to escape from her home and husband and is tempted by the captain (Benson Kleve) to go as a passenger on *The Gleam*, where she is re-united with Tom. But they are caught by a ship's mate (Cameron Carr) and Tom is marooned on a desert island by the captain. Not wanting to be without him, Nell hides in the boat and shares his exile. When Christobel hears that his wife and Tom are alone on the same island he makes the captain of *The Gleam* take him in pursuit. On the island they knock Tom out and forceably remove Nell to the ship, but Tom follows. During a tremendous storm Christobel and the captain are washed overboard but after braving the elements, Tom is miraculously swept aboard, takes command and sails home with Nell to safety and happiness.

Flora Le Breton and Carlyle Blackwell in *The Rolling Road* (1927)

With Hal Young as cameraman and Robert James Cullen as chief assistant, Graham Cutts began exteriors in Porthleven, Cornwall, followed by interiors at the Islington studio in September. This included an intimate scene in a Cornish cottage, where Flora Le Breton was in full bridal array, and a recreation of a realistic desert island by art director Bertram Evans, with a real waterfall, a running stream, sand, palm trees and waves breaking on the beach and Flora Le Breton in charming, primitive garb. Further exteriors were taken in October at North Beach, Great Yarmouth, using the three masted Norwegian clipper ship called *The Shakespeare*.

There were some tough scenes taken at sea, but the actual storm scene aboard *The Gleam* was filmed back at Islington in November in studio No. 1, with the benefit of the large water tank. It was a massive undertaking, with a reproduction of the deck of the boat itself complete with rails, hatchways, skylights and ropes, and a simulation of a fearsome hurricane force storm. On command from Cutts, by means of a loud whistle, the ship began to roll and plunge. Rain swept the decks, driven by an aeroplane propeller. Then came another whistle and 24,000 gallons of water were released down a chute to break like a tremendous sea or wave on the ship and as the energy of the waves was spent, the body of a man was seen lying on the deck as the hero had been washed aboard.

By mid-November *The Rolling Road* was complete and went for editing and cutting. Even before its release, it was noted that Cutts had worked on a subject differing widely from his customary style. There were no cabarets, feverish revelry or spectacle, just a love story of the sea. It was thought to be a reversion to the simpler intimacy of his first film, *The Wonderful Story*.

The trade show of *The Rolling Road* was in May 1927 (released 19th September 1927) but the reaction was lukewarm. Although applauded as a story full of adventure, adequately played and produced with marvellous sets and action, the plot was regarded as unrealistic and contrived, the expedients for bringing characters together artificial and far-fetched.   The strong cast of well-known favourites was admired. Carlyle Blackwell played with strength and sincerity and made a pleasing and athletic hero. The dainty Flora Le Breton was rather doll-like and although her performance was sincere, it was never sensational and sometimes a little artificial. However, their parts were of the ordinary hero and heroine type. Of the supporting cast Clifford Heatherley gave a vigorous interpretation of the scheming uncle and Marie Ault as a toothless dame of the Cornish village was, as ever, a delight, but it was felt she ought to have been able to infuse more humour to alleviate some of the more drawn-out scenes.

Overall, Cutts treated the melodrama in a straightforward style and rarely indulged in anything imaginative, suggesting this was 'below the director's usual standard, showing little of the art that generally marks his work'.[11]

Blighty

When Alfred Hitchcock decided to leave Gainsborough in the summer of 1926 it was no surprise that Michael Balcon swiftly began grooming a new director in the form of Adrian Brunel. He had previously appointed George A. Cooper in the spring of 1926 but for some reason this had not worked out. However, Brunel was a perfect choice to join Gainsborough since he had already been involved with the company with his series of *Brunel Burlesques* that were released in late 1925 and he knew Balcon well.

In September 1926 Balcon discussed the idea of Brunel directing a film provisionally called *Après la guerre*, based on an Ivor Montagu story. The title of the film was a phrase strongly embedded in general speech and was to deal with peace and the war's aftermath. Brunel was not keen on war films because he felt that nearly every one was based on the chivalry, bravery and the sacrifice of men and was inevitably pro-war, and the public was sick of them. But he liked this story as it 'fulfilled the requirements of a popular patriotic picture' showing an 'English family behaving decently',[12] while resolute in what they believed to be right and just. The war was never shown but rather the reactions to it on the Home Front. It was an anti-war picture rather than a pro-war picture and the title was swiftly changed to *Blighty*.

A month later, in October, the deal was announced and pre-production commenced immediately. The story was adapted for the screen by Elliot Stannard with help from Brunel and Montagu. By November casting was complete with Ellaline Terriss, the wife of the actor Seymour Hicks in her first screen appearance, Lilian Hall-Davis, Jameson Thomas, Nadia Sibirskaya (or Sibirskaia) and Godfrey Winn, with small parts for Seymour Hicks, Wally Patch, Dino Galvani and the Houston sisters. The latter lent their unique comedy gifts to the parts of typists in a city office on the day that Armistice was declared.

Blighty was a modest, inexpensive production with a simple story that touched on many patterns of behaviour at the time, including the realisation that the outbreak of World War I was the end of an era and perhaps most importantly, that it accelerated the breakdown of class barriers. Essentially, it highlighted the impact of the war on ordinary English characters and painted a truthful picture of the chief events, as seen from the Home Front.

At the outbreak of war the family of Sir Francis and Lady Villiers (Annesley Healy and Ellaline Terriss) and their friends refuse to believe that Britain will be drawn into the conflict, or if it does happen that their lives will not be disrupted too much. However, gradually they become involved.

The chauffeur, David Marshall (Jameson Thomas), joins up and then their only son, Robin Villiers (Godfrey Winn), also enlists. They go the Front, while those at home do what they can to help in the general cause. Robin meets a girl (Nadia Sibirskaya) in France, marries her, but then meets his death a few months later. When the chauffeur (Marshall) returns to England on leave, he falls in love with the Villiers' daughter Ann (Lillian Hall-Davis). He finally returns home wounded as Robin's wife arrives as a refugee. She finds the Villiers and introduces them to their grandchild, which gives some consolation for the loss of their son. Following the Armistice Robin's wife at first feels overwhelmed and out of place, while Marshall and Ann Villiers have to overcome class-based prejudice before they can marry. Eventually everything is resolved and the family becomes reconciled

Filming began at the Islington studio at the end of November 1926 and carried on into early 1927, with a crew that comprised cameraman Jack Cox, assistant director Norman Walker and with art direction by Bertram Evans. There were a great many interesting sets that included the interiors of a London house, a French café, a Zeppelin raid, some battle scenes at the Front and Armistice scenes in London.

A scene from *Blighty* (1927)
Courtesy J.W. Mitchell Collection / Brian Twist

One big scene was the set of a library in a London mansion. Richly solid furniture and decorative effects, including a coat of arms over the fireplace, described a setting of exclusivity and a family with a long line of antiquity. The British atmosphere of the household was accentuated by a delightful bulldog lying in front of the hearth, who upholds the traditions of his country in refusing to be seriously disturbed by anything. Beside a piano a small group of people sing old wartime songs with patriotic fervour. A dignified, elderly gentleman with wonderful white hair (Francis Villiers, the father) sits at his desk, looking more picturesquely aristocratic than the majority of aristocrats. His emotion is effectively conveyed as the others sing 'Keep the Homes Fires Burning'.

Blighty was given a trade show in March 1927 (released 6th February 1928) and it was regarded as sincere and popular: 'Brunel has taken a heart interest story and interpreted it with imagination and minute attention to detail'.[13] The slight story had no real plot development, being a simple chronicle of the war without the battle scenes, showing the everyday record of events as it affected the average family in England. The call of freedom affects the whole family: the only son and the chauffeur who join the army, the house being given up to wounded men nursed by the mother and the daughter, the head of the house doing duty as 'a special', the problems confronting those who are anxious to fight but are unsuitable for service. There are the more domestic details of food and fuel rations too.

The cast was an interesting collection of artists, who all received praise. Ellaline Terriss gave a remarkably sincere performance and brought her personal charm to the screen. During filming she observed, 'Mr Brunel is most kind and encouraging and I really feel that it will be easy to work for him. I have long wanted to do some picture work and was more than delighted when Mr Balcon offered me this opportunity, more particularly because it is a part to which I think I am well suited. I am and always have been tremendously interested in British films and am a firm believer that we can and will make them just as well as America.'[14]

Jameson Thomas who played the chauffeur hero, who becomes an officer, was an actor who combined experience and ability. He first came to prominence on the stage just after the war, playing his first screen role in *Chu Chin Chow* (1922), and had appeared in many more films leading up to this role. Nadia Sibirskaya played the part of the French wife with great charm. Brunel had seen her in a Film Society importation of *Ménilmontant* and thought she was a great little artist. Despite the Russian-sounding name she was in fact French and married to the director Dimitri Kirsanoff. However, on arrival her exhibitions of temperament from the start were unfortunate and it was decided to pay her off and send her back to France. She sobbed, apologised to everyone and after giving an assurance that she would behave was allowed to stay.

Godfrey Winn, who played Robin, gave a pleasant picture of the boy. At the time he was nineteen years old and it was his first film role, although he had appeared in some stage productions from the age of seventeen and was due to go to Oxford and then into his father's business. Spotted by Eddie Marsh, an influential patron of the arts, he was introduced to Ivor Novello and others, which is perhaps how he came to Balcon's attention. As a result of his performance Winn's stage career was assured and a new career in film looked promising but instead he became an outstanding journalist.

Lilian Hall-Davis made the most of a rather colourless part. She was admired for wearing a remarkably natural blonde wig over her own dark hair, its silken tresses arranged in becoming coils in keeping with the period. This was in contrast to many other actresses in war pictures, where producers made the mistake of allowing them to appear with shingled hair at a time when the shingle was relatively unknown.

Downhill

Since completing *The Lodger* in the summer of 1926, Alfred Hitchcock had not worked for several months. His forthcoming contract with BNP and his annoyance with Gainsborough perhaps made him reticent to agree to direct anything new. He had turned down directing *The Silent Warrior* to star Carlyle Blackwell, which never came to fruition and he was also assigned *Hunting Tower* but this stalled. Nevertheless, he was clearly optimistic about the new BNP deal as he and Alma Reville were married on 2nd December 1926, and as Adrian Brunel filmed *Blighty* and over in Berlin Graham Cutts filmed *The Queen Was in the Parlour*, the couple took a few weeks off over Christmas for their honeymoon. They took the boat train to Paris and met up with the American actress Nita Naldi, who they had befriended while filming *The Mountain Eagle*, and her companion, James Searle Barclay, Jr., before relaxing at the Palace Hotel in St Moritz. This was the beginning of their annual trip to the place they loved most.

In mid-December 1926 Michael Balcon announced that Gainsborough's next production would be an adaptation of Ivor Novello's play *Downhill*, with Novello as star. The idea certainly resonated with the trade press: 'Piccadilly Pictures are certainly the most active and enterprising British producers we have and Michael Balcon who directs their energies is to be congratulated upon his splendid judgement in choosing subjects which not only make money at the box office but which do an enormous amount of good to British film in general'.[15]

Balcon had the film and the star, but no director. When Hitchcock returned to London in early 1927, he was under contract to BNP but not in a position to do much. Balcon asked him if he was interested in directing *Downhill*. Hitchcock was reticent for he did not particularly like the play, thinking it was poor, and also believed the major difficulty was that Novello was in his thirties and was to portray a young man still at school as part of the film. Nevertheless, it was a shrewd move to follow up *The Lodger* with another Hitchcock-Novello vehicle as Novello was regarded as 'undoubtedly one of the biggest box office names today'.[16] It was also better for Hitchcock to do something rather than nothing. In the end Balcon's persuasiveness succeeded and he negotiated with BNP so that Hitchcock could return to Gainsborough, effectively being loaned for a period of time.

Meanwhile, all was not good at BNP, which explains Hitchcock's predicament. With his autocratic style J.D. Williams had managed to alienate his business partners, including I.W. Schlesinger from South Africa, who had provided most of the finance, and there was considerable discord. Into the fray stepped John Maxwell. A Glasgow solicitor, Maxwell had entered the film business as an exhibitor in 1912, acquired a chain of picture theatres and became chairman of Wardour Films in 1923. By early 1927, he had secured control of BNP, ousted Williams at the end of 1926 and went on to reorganise the company into British International Pictures in March 1927, taking over BNP assets and the new studio complex at Elstree. Hitchcock's deal transferred to BIP and a little later in July 1927, Herbert Wilcox left the new company, founding British and Dominion Films (B&D).

Back at the Islington studio, Eliot Stannard had already created the script for *Downhill* and after story conferences, Hitchcock began filming on 17th January 1927, with a crew comprising Frank Mills as assistant director, art director

Bertram Evans and cameraman Claude McDonnell. Ivor Montagu also acted as a script consultant and editor, as he had done on *The Lodger*. Seen as a modern 'Rake's Progress' it was the tale of two schoolboys who made a pact of loyalty, which one of them keeps at a price that leads to his downfall.

Ian Hunter and Isabel Jeans in *Downhill* (1927)

Roddy Warwick (Ivor Novello) is in his last term at public school and has the promise of a brilliant career. But Mabel, the scheming vamp (Annette Benson) who runs the village teashop and confectioners called Ye Olde Bunne Shoppe, makes wrongful accusations towards his friend Tim Wakely (Robin Irvine). Because the boy is the son of a parson and the disgrace would kill his father,

Roddy takes the blame. After a scene in the headmaster's study where Mabel accuses Roddy of 'not doing the right thing by her'[17] in a spirited and fiery manner, with the boy looking innocent and guileless, he is eventually expelled. His father (Norman McKinnnell) casts him adrift without listening to his defence. Roddy enjoys various adventures earning his own living and becomes a chorus boy. He then receives a legacy from his godfather and marries Julia, an actress (Isabel Jeans), who with the assistance of a gentleman friend called Archie (Ian Hunter), manages to spend his money. Roddy becomes a dancer and gradually goes down the social scale until in the docks at Marseilles his health breaks down. Hoping for a reward, some sailors agree to transport him back to England. On arrival he gets away and instinctively goes home to find that during his absence his name has been cleared and having uncovered the truth, his father asks for his pardon.

The play and the film was episodic and so it was necessary to have three groups of players to conform to the three sections of the unfolding drama: the school (with Annette Benson, Robin Irvine and Roddy's parents, played by Lilian Braithwaite and Norman McKinnnell); the exile working in the theatre (Isabel Jeans and Robin Irvine) and the finale of Roddy's complete fall from grace in Marseilles and his ultimate return home. Each episode contained a 'descent' of some kind, representing the degradation and the gradual degeneration of the central character.

Filming began with the public school and village scenes, followed by Mabel's outburst in the college rooms, the scenes in Ye Olde Bunne Shoppe and the theatre scenes. The fight scene between Roddy (Ivor Novello) and Archie (Ian Hunter) begins with Archie paying too much attention to Roddy's wife Julia (Isabel Jeans). Although waged in all seriousness it is relieved with subtle humorous touches because as Hitchcock said: 'You can't treat two men fighting in a flat in lounge suits seriously. The scene must be funny.'[18] Julia watches the fight anxiously, though not out of concern for either man but because she is worried about her possessions. As the battle develops, her furniture suffers and she becomes agitated and implores them to stop, not wishing her home to be wrecked. But they ignore her and so she collects her most cherished vases and ornaments, removing them from the danger zone. Finally, after downing Archie, Roddy leaves his apartment, recently signed over to his wife, and takes the lift.

Hitchcock then filmed the hall after a college football match with dozens of boys of different ages all in uniform, along with various guests with a mix of considerable underlying tension and joviality. Next came the scene of a cheerless, bleak Marseilles garret with a setting of artistic squalor. One of the most memorable scenes follows Roddy descending the escalator at Maida Vale Tube station (taken early one Sunday morning after the trains had stopped running). Roddy is shown leaving his home dejected and he wanders off to the nearest station, takes a ticket without caring about his destination and steps onto the moving staircase as the camera films his gradually receding figure.

Above : Ivor Novello and Annette Benson in *Downhill* (1927)
Courtesy J.W. Mitchell Collection / Brian Twist

Below: Ivor Novello and Isabel Jeans in *Downhill* (1927)

A subtle documentary on the alleged wildness of youth forms one of the last interior scenes to be completed, which was a Parisian nightclub set, though not the average nightclub with wild flappers and jazz-mad youths but a skit on nightclub life in general. It was full of subtle humour. Filled with over 200 people past their prime, the young Roddy (now a gigolo dancer), was one of the main attractions. When a man chokes and faints, the windows are opened to let some air in and the light radiates the grim reality, shattering the illusion and artificiality of the place and its occupants. For this scene the studio carpenters refused to make Hitchcock a coffin on superstitious grounds.

The final scenes of *Downhill* were taken by Hitchcock on a Sunday at Ashridge Park estate in late March to simulate a great British school and surroundings using two full teams of Oxford undergraduates for a school rugby match.

During filming Basil Dean, the famous theatrical producer, who had staged many of Noël Coward's plays, was a visitor at the Islington studio and spent some time watching Hitchcock work. Soon it became a well-founded rumour that there was a distinct possibility he would enter film production.

Towards mid-March, when the final interior shots were complete, there was a fabulous party. It had been noted as a rule trade functions were not usually enjoyable but this was solved when Gainsborough started to give impromptu parties in the studio. This was the second event, indicating there had been a similar party on completion of Adrian Brunel's *Blighty*. They retained the nightclub set, which had been the last interior to be filmed, and so the atmosphere was perfect. The party got going at midnight and went on until 4am and featured W. Tytol's band from the Astoria with a cabaret show provided by Ed Lowry, Ben Blue, the dancers Delys and Clark, and many others. Those attending provided a veritable who's who of British cinema and stage including Alfred Hitchcock, Adrian Brunel, Constance Collier, Ivor Novello, Isabel Jeans, Marjorie Hume, Lilian Hall-Davis, Phyllis Monkman, Ian Hunter, Flora Le Breton, Dorothy Seacombe, Dorothy Batley and many more.

The trade show of *Downhill* (released 24th October 1927) was in May 1927 and it was received well. It was thought to be another personal success for Hitchcock and the general view was that he had created a production of great interest. Through his efforts the film had actually been turned around into something tangible and watchable. His excellent direction and imaginative treatment got the most out of what was regarded as a weak and rather sordid simple tale of conventional morality. He was almost playful in some scenes, deliberately done to lighten the darker elements, and his use of symbolism was given full play with the dramatic power of Roddy descending the Tube escalator and the lift to accentuate his downward spiral of despair. Towards the end of the film his depiction of the delirium that Roddy endures achieved some wonderfully clever effects. However, for some the plot was barely plausible and there were elements of inconsistency. It was felt that a youth full of brilliant promise could not be expelled and cast adrift on the unsupported word of a girl, with no real effort to prove the truth. The father's transition to repentance was also not clearly explained – how did he discover his son's innocence?

Although one reviewer thought the film unworthy of the remarkable cast,[19] most believed the cast was of unusual strength, with Novello carrying the production and giving an outstanding performance that shone in contrast to a lot of very unpleasant people. Isabel Jeans played the errant wife with excellent effect, but the best performance was thought to come from Annette Benson as the girl who lands the hero in trouble.

At the time Hitchcock explained a little of his philosophy of film-making in saying that he believed in attempting to satisfy all portions of the public, if possible. He realised that the average 'highbrow' picture was seldom a good box-office proposition because the story was often above the heads of the average picturegoer and he himself preferred to take a 'lowbrow' story and give it the 'highbrow' treatment so everybody ought to be satisfied.[20]

Michael Balcon overlooking Ivor Novello as he signs one of his many contracts with Gainsborough Pictures

12   COWARD'S WIT

Amidst all the other developments in the summer of 1926, it was also revealed that Gainsborough actively sought original stories written specially for the screen by prominent British authors. Michael Balcon elaborated by saying that out of the hundreds of novels which he had read only a few possessed any screen possibilities, and of these various American producers were offering fabulous sums for the film rights. With regard to acquiring the rights to stage plays, he added that British dramatists were keener to sell to America and were giving good deals solely to American producers and making it impossible for British film producers to compete. It was partly these difficulties that made him realise that he should focus on obtaining original stories. He also thought that the filming of plays and novels was a compromise, with one medium of expression being adapted to another. He believed that 'the story specially written for the screen will come into its own' and with time, screen dramatists would 'rank equally with playwrights and novelists'.[1]

Noel Coward

As part of this process he was in negotiations with the celebrated playwright Noël Coward, whom he admired greatly, to discuss taking the film rights to his plays. The talented and fashionable Coward was cheeky, but chic and riding a tide of popularity. In 1925 he had four successful shows in the West End: *The Vortex*, *Fallen Angels*, *Hay Fever* and *On With the Dance*. *Easy Virtue* had been first staged in New York and then in London in June 1926, followed by *The Queen Was in the Parlour*, which opened in August 1926.

In the face of American competition, an announcement was made in late August 1926 that Gainsborough had secured the film rights to Coward's plays and were encouraging him to write specifically for the screen. At first they acquired Coward's current play, *Easy Virtue*, with the plan that

Graham Cutts would direct and although Coward would not actually write the scenario he would actively collaborate on the adaptation. For the leading role created in London by Jane Cowl, Gainsborough were in the process of selecting a very prominent screen actress, later confirmed as Isabel Jeans. This was a significant move and widely applauded – 'the combination of Coward and Cutts is a strong one'.[2]

In the meantime, Coward took the role of Lewis Dodd in Basil Dean's production of *The Constant Nymph*, which opened in September. It proved to be demanding and Coward subsequently suffered a breakdown and withdrew after a few weeks; his understudy, John Gielgud, took his place. Coward went away for a few months to rest, travelling to New York, San Francisco and Honolulu during the winter of 1926.

At the beginning of December 1926, Gainsborough finalised the purchase of the world screen rights to two more Noel Coward plays: *The Queen Was in the Parlour* and *The Vortex*. All three of Coward's plays secured by Balcon were planned to go into production in 1927.

As Balcon embarked on his mission to acquire the film rights of various properties, this 'behind the scenes' activity was seen as a positive development and a real revival in studio activity – 'This is a good sign. For any projected increase in output must mean acquiring its subjects months ahead. The story and its treatment are not only the most important ingredients of a successful film, they are the cheapest. Yet, in spite of years of experience, it is the incredible lack of due attention to this vital aspect of picture making that has caused more and bigger flops to production firms than any other single cause'.[3]

Later, Balcon expressed some regret about the deal, arguing that they had been 'mentally stagebound' and looked too eagerly to the theatre for much screen material: 'It was no doubt wrong of us to seek to bask in the reflected glory of people like Noël Coward; we followed trends and did not try to make them. It was doubly a mistake to lean on stage plays because we were making silent films, so the plays were deprived of their very essence, the words!'[4] Balcon wanted Coward to write directly for the screen and, at some point, he did write a story called *Concerto*, but the script needed the spoken word and music and simply would not work as a silent film. Eventually, the deal would be terminated and *Concerto* became the stage play, *Bitter Sweet*.

The Queen Was in the Parlour

Although it had been stated that Cutts was to direct another film with Ivor Novello and was also to be assigned Coward's *Easy Virtue*, neither came off and instead he was assigned to direct *The Queen Was in the Parlour*. Rumours that he would direct the film and that the continental actress Lili Damita would be the star surfaced in August 1926 but it was not until mid-December that the production was publicly confirmed. During the interim period all details were being finalised and it was decided to once again move production to Berlin, through new business partners Felsom Films, which was run by Josef Somlo and Hermann Fellner. Somlo was a Hungarian film producer, who had studied law in Budapest but became managing director of Viennese-based film companies in 1908. From 1919–22 he was head of UFA's foreign department before founding his own production company with Fellner. At the time little was made of this arrangement and it wasn't until April 1927 that it was announced and formalised.

The glamorously attractive Lili (or Lily) Damita was born Liliane Marie Madeleine Carre in France in 1904 and at fourteen she was enrolled as a dancer at the Opéra de Paris. Two years later, as Lily Deslys, she was performing in popular music halls, eventually appearing in several shows at the Casino de Paris during 1924. She was also frequently used as a photographer's model and in 1921 won a magazine beauty contest, the prize being a role in the film *Maman Pierre* (1922) for Pathé Frères. Further small parts followed before she gained her first starring role in *Red Heels* (*Das Spielzeug von Paris*, 1925), directed by the Hungarian Michael Curtiz, whom she married but they divorced a year later. She then made two films for Germany's leading director, G.W. Pabst.

Cutts arrived in Berlin before Christmas and began preparing the script with Fanny Carlsen before filming began in mid-January 1927 at UFA's Babelsberg studio with cameraman Otto Kanturek. Some spectacular opportunities were provided by Court ceremonials and an elaborate carnival, all designed by art director Oscar Friedrich Werndorff. Later, some exteriors were taken in Engelberg, Switzerland, and then filming was complete, with Cutts arriving back from Berlin in early March 1927.

Both the play and the film had an imaginary 'Ruritanian' setting of a fictional country in central Europe. Ruritania was a mythical kingdom created by Anthony Hope for his novels and then adapted by many others, including Noël Coward and Ivor Novello for some of their plays. It became a favoured model for a variety of films in the late 1920s, which muddled cultural identity but found an appreciative market in both America and the Continent.

With a theme of lovers being trapped between love and duty, this was a dramatic and tragic romance. Nadya (Lili Damita) is married to the dissolute Prince of Krayia and is thoroughly disillusioned. After his sudden death she leads a hectic life in Paris, finally meeting a young writer called Sabien Pascal (Paul Richter), with whom she falls madly in love and promises to marry. On the day of the wedding Nadya learns that the King has been assassinated and she is in the line of succession. She is finally persuaded to go, leaving Sabien heartbroken. On her return to Krayia she is compelled to renounce the idea of happiness and for her country's sake agrees to marry Prince Keri of Zalgar (Harry Liedtke). The night before the state wedding a revolutionist tries to assassinate her but is prevented by a man in the crowd. She sends for the man to thank him and sees it is Sabien. He begs for a final interview, which she grants him. Meanwhile, a revolt is stirring and revolutionists surround the palace. The Queen's life is in danger and Prince Keri and her ministers urge Nadya to flee. Instead she faces the crowd from her balcony and calls on them to shoot her. Awed by her spirit and daring, the crowd disperses. As she turns to the Prince a shot is heard from her room and she knows that Sabien has committed suicide. The Prince understands and explains to the household that a revolutionist has been shot while attempting to enter the Queen's apartment. He then turns to her and promises friendship and understanding.

Harry Liedtke and Lili Damita in *The Queen Was in the Parlour* (1927)

The trade show of *The Queen Was in the Parlour* (released 27th February 1928) was in April 1927 and it was admired for its excellent production, direction, camerawork and acting: 'Graham Cutts has produced nothing more finished or well directed as this'.[5]

Despite being considered a 'brilliant adaptation'[6] of Noël Coward's play, it was observed that the play without the dialogue left only a skeleton plot and a paucity of action. And yet the situations were gripping and interest never diminished. Perhaps this was because although it was a passionate and romantic story, genuine human feelings were portrayed that resonated with the audience, accentuated by perfect interpretations by first-rate artistes.

The characters were thought to be well-drawn with polished and natural performances. Lili Damita was exceptional and an ideal representation of the Queen, possessing youth, beauty, regal dignity and dramatic power. The suave and handsome Paul Richter was a sympathetic hero, playing naturally with great panache. However, when screened in America as *Forbidden Love*, the critics were less kind. Even though Lili Damita was described as a European sensation it was thought that she would not prove a sensation across the pond. Despite having class she was not the type that American fans would rave over – strange then that shortly afterwards she was snapped up by Samuel Goldwyn, who brought her to Hollywood.

In transferring the play to the screen Cutts had filmed it with a 'typically heavy British hand' and without the crisp and sparkling dialogue of the play, it was somewhat flat with 'oodles of titles that clutter up the footage'.[7] Although thought to be 'good entertainment' that 'attained a high standard of excellence… thoroughly interesting, well acted, mounted and produced',[8] because it was made in Germany, it was disappointing. This was to become a conundrum for Balcon and his team in the future. On the one hand he wanted to continue building working relationships with American and continental partners but on the other the difficulties of the British film industry created some protectionist thinking. The movement towards legislation and the idea of a quota system was also meant to restrict foreign-made films.

In mid-January 1927, when Cutts was beginning to film in Berlin, it was made known that he had severed his connection with Gainsborough. The reasons for him not being assigned the next Ivor Novello picture and *Easy Virtue* were thus made clear but on the surface his reasons for leaving are perplexing. His main gripe would have been the presence of Alfred Hitchcock but since Hitchcock had also announced his departure from Gainsborough to join BNP, why did Cutts also find it necessary to leave? Perhaps he was not happy at being removed from the board of Gainsborough, thought his stature within the company was not being recognised and that Balcon had let him down through 1926. However, the real reason stems from Balcon's visit to New York in the summer of 1926, when First National had made overtures to finance a series of pictures made by Cutts. The deal had never materialised but clearly, First National wanted Cutts and so by-passed Balcon and entered into negotiations with him directly.

By March 1927, it was announced that Cutts had joined First National Pictures and had been in negotiations with J. Frank Brockliss, managing director of First National, and Richard A. Rowland, general and production manager in London, before his departure for Berlin.

Cutts' achievements were under scrutiny but he was genuinely admired: 'the majority of his pictures are inclined to lean a little too much toward American methods in ornate extravagance but there is no doubt as to their entertainment value'.[9]

First National's history was embedded, as we have seen earlier, with J.D. Williams, who had been ousted from the American board in 1922 and moved to England to form BNP. Like other American concerns viewing the advent of legislation and the quota, First National sought to begin British production and were also planning to finance a programme of film production in Germany under the supervision of Ray Rockett.

Upon arrival in Berlin, E. Bruce Johnson, general foreign manager of First National, drafted a contract with Cutts on behalf of the New York executive of his company. It was announced that upon completion of *The Queen Was in the Parlour*, Cutts was to visit the First National studio in Burbank, California, in May, where it was planned that he would make one picture prior to returning to London in order to make pictures there in September for First National. This was seen as giving him a unique experience in America, adding to those already gained in the UK and Germany. His broad experience and track record was highly admired: 'Cutts already evinces remarkable ability to register his stories in a manner that creates international appeal'.[10] It was also made clear that he wrote all his own scenarios and has 'considerable practise in the art of giving an English story an essentially British atmosphere, an adjunct which is greatly sought after by exhibitors'.[11]

Easy Virtue

Immediately following *Downhill*, Alfred Hitchcock was asked by Michael Balcon to direct an adaptation of Noël Coward's *Easy Virtue*. Originally allocated to Graham Cutts, the play had been staged in New York in December 1925 and in London in June 1926. As plans were being made, it was revealed that almost concurrent with *Easy Virtue* would be a production of *The Constant Nymph* and Basil Dean and Margaret Kennedy, who were responsible for the novel and part-authors of the play, were collaborating on the treatment with the important questions of casting being left until this was complete.

Coward took an interest in the filming of *Easy Virtue* and, having just returned from his extensive trip to recover from a breakdown, stopped by the Islington studio to confer with Hitchcock as he was filming the final scenes of *Downhill*. Hitchcock gained his approval of both the adaptation and the cast. Eliot Stannard was writing the scenario, having already been responsible for Hitchcock's previous scripts. He was regarded as the most experienced and prolific of British screen authors, with no less than 300 scenarios to his credit. The crew was to be the same as *Downhill*, with Claude L. McDonnell in charge of photography, Frank Mills as assistant director and Ivor Montagu as creative consultant and editor.

A major new addition to the Gainsborough team was Clifford Pember as art director. Pember was born c.1882 and was educated at Winchester, then went to Oxford and afterwards trained as an architect before graduating to film and stage decor. He was articled to the firm of architects Basil Champneys but went to Canada in 1909 and then on to New York, where he contracted typhoid. In 1911 he went to Boston to recover, stayed and became art director for the Toy Theatre. Returning to New York in 1916, he was engaged by the celebrated actress Alla Nazimova to design for her stage productions and various other shows. He also worked on several films as an art director, including D.W. Griffith's *Way Down East* (1920). finally, he returned to London in early 1924, working for Archibald De Bear on his revues and cabarets, but by 1927 film work became more prominent. Bert Evans remained as scenic artist and worked in conjunction with Pember.

Above : Robert Irvine and Isabel Jeans in *Easy Virtue* (1927)
Courtesy J.W. Mitchell Collection / Brian Twist
Below: Isabel Jeans in *Easy Virtue* (1927)

Casting was conducted quickly, with Isabel Jeans taking the wonderful leading role. Jeans had been justly regarded as one of most enticing stage vamps but here she played her first sympathetic role as a wife brought home by a 'boy' husband to his critical family. Appearing in every scene she was the heroine in this matrimonial disaster and one of Coward's most clever characterisations. Violet Fairbrother was allocated to play the hard, cold, matter-of-fact, supercilious mother and Robin Irvine was the young, impressionable husband.

A social drama dealing with the complexities of divorce, it was a bitter indictment against the divorce courts and the stiff-necked attitudes adopted by conventional members of good society towards those who had the misfortune to end up there. Larita Filton (Isabel Jeans) gains notoriety by her divorce, in which she is the innocent victim of her drunken husband's (Franklin Dyall) jealousy and the ill-advised chivalry of a young artist. Larita goes abroad and meets John Whittaker (Robin Irvine), from a country family. They fall in love and marry, even though John knows nothing of her past and his family resent her. The mother's (Violet Fairbrother) resentment increases when she discovers her daughter-in-law has figured in a notorious divorce case. Larita decides to live up to the lurid impression John's mother has of her and attends a ball in a very low-cut evening dress. She depends on her husband to stand by her but he is weak and has already realised the disadvantages of an unconventional alliance. Larita's only resource is therefore an undefended appearance in the divorce court.

Hitchcock began filming towards the end of March 1927, taking racecourse scenes before leaving for the South of France to shoot exteriors around Nice and Monte Carlo. He also took some final shots for *Downhill* with Ivor Novello, who had arrived grandly at the Hotel de Paris in Nice for one night, gave a lot of interviews in his suite and then relocated to a humble pension. Hitchcock had to film Novello walking dejectedly past an English backdrop, suggesting his return to England from the Continent, so they did this on the flat roof of the pension with a couple of men holding a painted backdrop of the London Docks while Novello walked or staggered on the spot in front of it in the bright sunshine. Meanwhile the locals looked on incredulously, wondering what the crazy Englishmen were doing.

The Riviera sequences were done in a leisurely ten days, with Isabel Jeans and Robin Irvine joining Hitchcock for part of the time, and by early April they were back in London to film the interiors. One of the first scenes to be completed was the opening sequence in the divorce courts. Pember designed and built a remarkable replica of the Divorce Courts and went to admirable lengths to suggest age with the solid, well-worn panelling and fittings. Numerous small-part actors and actresses and extras were employed in the crowd scenes to great effect. By mid-May, Hitchcock shot the final scenes at Roehampton polo ground, where his simple and direct methods of direction were seen as both artistic and commercial: 'He knows what he wants, just how to get it and wastes no time – the happiest of combinations'.[12]

Easy Virtue was given a trade show in August 1927 (released 5th March 1927) and was greatly admired: 'Hitchcock renews his claim to be the cleverest director in British studios with this adaptation' and he showed 'decided ingenuity in handling situations and a sound knowledge of technique'.[13] The main issue was seen as the difficulty in translating Coward's brilliant wit and subtle characterisation to the screen and adapting a play that was entirely based on the importance of smart dialogue. It was thought that Eliot Stannard and Hitchcock did convey something of this to the screen. For example, Stannard had to anticipate the action of the play by showing Larita meeting John and the evidence at the divorce court. Here, Hitchcock's direction was noticeable as he introduced his characters and used flashbacks with the action by means of clever symbolism and variation of shots.

There was some criticism of the development of the plot that showed weaknesses not apparent in the original play. It was difficult to imagine how Larita, by merely changing her name to Grey, could escape recognition as the much-photographed subject of a notorious divorce case until some time after her second marriage. It was also thought the Whittaker family were not so aristocratic as they professed to be and the characters introduced at the Whittaker home were far too exaggerated.

The cast was applauded, with considerable praise bestowed on Isabel Jeans as Lydia, who played her with a measure of skill and attractiveness and got everything possible out of the part, securing the full sympathy of the audience. Franklin Dyall excelled as the husband, but Robin Irvine as John Whittaker was thought to be colourless, making it incredulous that he became Larita's second marital venture. Violet Fairbrother as Mrs Whittaker looked handsome but the part prevented her from showing the distinction of country birth essential to the character. The other ladies looked charming in very uninteresting parts and Benita Hume was given her first chance in a brief scene as a telephone operator. Through her changes of expression as she listened in on the switchboard she had to get over an acceptance and proposal of marriage by two unknown persons. Her performance was noticed and applauded. Later, she would become an important star and a lifelong friend of Hitchcock.

On finishing *Easy Virtue*, Hitchcock's days at Gainsborough were over and he left for BIP and began filming *The Ring*. For Balcon and Gainsborough this was the dawn of a new era with the loss of his original star director Graham Cutts and the new rising star of Alfred Hitchcock.

The Vortex

At the end of April 1927 Gainsborough announced that Adrian Brunel was to follow up *Blighty* with Noël Coward's *The Vortex*. The play was adapted by Eliot Stannard and Brunel's unit comprised cameraman James Wilson, art director Clifford Pember, assistant director 'Shan' Balcon (Michael Balcon's brother) with assistance from Ivor Montagu. Brunel starting shooting on 1st June even though the cast was not complete, starting with all the interiors at Islington and then completing the film in mid-July with some exteriors. He had seen the play and although he thought it was excellent entertainment, he was not too happy about adapting it for the screen as the story was too slight for a silent film and 'because I very much doubted if I would be allowed to make anything but a bowdlerised version of it'.[14] Michael Balcon shared his reservations but it had to be done.

Coward's clever study of modern degenerate society, seen as a vivid study of post-war psychology, concerned a mother who has a lover and a son who takes drugs, so before production commenced they had to ascertain what the Board of Film Censors thought. Needless to say, they were not happy with the subject matter and decided that although the film could go ahead, the mother could not have a lover and the son must not take drugs. A new story had to be written based on these constraints and when Coward read it, he let out a torrent of criticism. After much discussion a script was finally created but it was substantially different to the play and contained little of the powerful drama.

Because the heart out of the play had been removed, Brunel decided to borrow some of Alfred Hitchcock's tactics in attempting to embellish the script with a display of technical devices that might divert attention of the critics who wanted to see Coward's *The Vortex* on the screen. So each day he thought out some little twists, intriguing camera angles, effective close-ups and unexpected shots.

For the leading parts, Ivor Novello took Coward's original role but it was a difficult task assigning the mother, originally played by Lilian Braithwaite. Over forty actresses were considered for the part and finally they secured the pretty and youthful American stage actress Willette Kershaw, who had created the stage role of *Woman to Woman*. This was to be her first screen role, along with Frances Doble, who played Bunty Mainwaring.

The story follows Florence Lancaster (Willette Kershaw), who clings to her youth. She is horrified at the idea of growing old, indulges in every modern society distraction even to the extent of getting herself talked about in connection with a young idler, Tom Veryan (Alan Hollis), who consents to act as her constant attendant in return for pocket money. Her son Nicky (Ivor Novello), who is a musical genius, falls in love with Bunty Mainwaring (Frances Doble) and brings her down to his father's country house. Tom has been a former admirer of Bunty and Nicky falls into a jealous rage when he sees them in the garden together. Florence is also furious and jealous of Bunty. Bunty breaks off her engagement and is discovered being forcibly kissed by Tom. Florence loses control of herself and disgusts Nicky. That night, mother and son have a heart-to-heart talk, which brings the former to her senses. Bunty makes it up with Nicky and they are reunited.

On completion, Brunel was supposed to edit the film, which was a jigsaw, but he had to go off to Germany to work on *The Constant Nymph* and therefore could not supervise the assembly and editing. For him the result was a disappointment.

The trade show of *The Vortex* was in March 1928 (released 23rd April 1928) and it was mostly considered to be a well-presented adaption of Coward's play, well directed and produced: 'Considering the difficulties of the story which is hardly

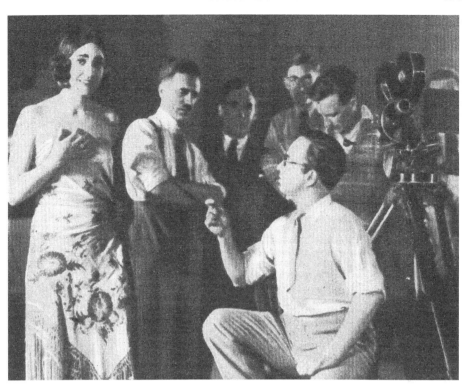

Above : Adrian Brunel filming *The Vortex* (1927)
Below: Ivor Novello and Frances Doble in *The Vortex* (1927)

suitable for screen purposes, Adrian Brunel has done very well'.[15] The photography and settings of country and town house interiors with pretty garden exteriors were greatly admired. Although there was much character in the production, with smooth continuity and some well-handled dramatic moments, the action was slow and missing in action and Coward's brilliant dialogue: 'It is an excellent production but proves that the most successful of stage plays is not necessarily a fit subject for the screen'.[16]

However, *Theatre World* was not impressed calling it 'tedious' by losing all of its 'gripping intensity and satire.' Coward's plays, they thought, did not make for good screen entertainment since 'all that constitutes Noel Coward's gift as a dramatist - the wit, the technique and unerring sense of the stage and the sparkling dialogue - go for nothing when translated into cinematic terms.' [17]

None of the characters succeeded in arousing much interest. Willette Kershaw expressed the foibles of the character well with an avoidance of the unpleasantness of the original but was essentially colourless. Ivor Novello did not convince with his sincerity and France Doble was gracefully ineffective.

As *The Vortex* was being filmed Noël Coward gave an interview in which he outlined his views about film in general. Firstly, he discussed the alleged rivalry between stage and screen that he called nonsense: 'I believe there are still some theatrical people who regard contemptuously everything connected with film. I am not one of them.' He believed that films were not an offshoot of the stage but a totally different medium. Both had different limitations and one limitation of film was dialogue: 'You lose the actor's voice on the screen but then you don't hear the voice of a character in a novel either.' Also, some actors and actresses might be excellent in one medium and ineffective in the other, or good in both, or bad in both. However, Isabel Jeans in the screen version of *Easy Virtue* was an example of complete success in both.

In contradiction to Balcon's desire to commission more original stories for the screen, Coward insisted he would not write original scenarios for the screen: 'I am not interested in writing scenarios at all – I want to write words, not stage directions. I don't want to cast any slur on scenario work and I readily admit that it is a highly expert business but as a dramatist, dialogue and its psychology are practically my sole concern. You will notice that in the published versions of my plays the stage directions are cut down to an absolute minimum.' Overall he felt that British producers should be honest with themselves and do their best without reference to what the public were supposed to demand: 'Let British film-makers talk less about what the box office is supposed to want,' he concluded.

Despite the fact that many in the film industry regarded the acquisition of Coward's plays as something of a feat by the 'go-head organization'[18] of Gainsborough, Michael Balcon would later admit that the filmed versions of *Easy Virtue* and *The Vortex* were both financial failures.

13   THE GAUMONT-BRITISH COMBINE

As Alfred Hitchcock completed *Downhill* the Cinematograph Films Bill, based on the quota system, was presented to the House of Commons in March 1927 after years of wrangling. The Bill was seen as far from perfect and it was recognised that it would go through some changes during its passage. Even at this early stage it had an immediate effect on production: 'very soon indeed the British producer, player, cameraman and scenario writer will pinch themselves unable to realize that the "boom" the coming of which "next year" had been a tragic joke since 1921 has indeed arrived'.[1] With increased production on the cards it wasn't long before properly equipped floor space was in great demand. It was predicted that demand would soon outstrip capacity and some films would have to be made in foreign studios or delayed.

The downside was that although it was recognised that there were fine studio personnel in the UK, unfortunately there were also some 'duds' who would rely on the film bill to 'get away with it' and make sub-standard product: 'The trade must do everything possible to protect the investor from the undesirable and incompetent. It is infinitely less risky to invest in a solid and well-known firm than to take producers at their own valuation'.[2]

Provocatively called 'a declaration of war on America' by Thomas Welsh of Welsh-Pearson, Michael Balcon said more moderately: 'Legislation was inevitable for we must admit the Trade's failure to solve its own problems unaided. Gainsborough Pictures have gone on very well without a quota; but it certainly means greater confidence and expansion all round'.[3]

With the idea of the implementation of the quota moving forward, and as a result of greater market security, there were many changes in the industry in anticipation of legislation and this included the formation of the Gaumont-British combine that had significant implications for Balcon and Gainsborough.

British Gaumont had been started in London, in 1898, by two brothers, Colonel A.C. and Reginald C. Bromhead, with the purpose of distributing films made by Gaumont in France. Renting and distribution was the core of the business but later they opened a small studio in Shepherd's Bush and went into production. In 1922 the Bromheads bought out the French interests and there was a flurry of post-war activity, but production slowed between 1923–25. Then, in 1926, some bigger features were made following the appointment of the celebrated director Maurice Elvey. Formerly with Stoll, he had made several films for Fox in America and on his return to the UK became an independent director and had a big success with *The Flag Lieutenant* (1926). Elvey was part of a production team with Victor Saville as producer and V. Gareth Gundrey in charge of scripts. A big forward programme was announced and the first release, *Mademoiselle from Armentieres* (1926), with the new star, Estelle Brody, proved to be a big hit, followed by *Hindlewakes* (1927). Other big features were underway, with Betty Balfour in *Little Devil May Care* (1927), *Quinneys* (1927), *Roses of Picardy*

(1927), *The Arcadians* (1927) and *The Glad Eye* (1927). In order to fund their expansion and desire to enlarge and renovate their studio, the Bromheads turned to the Ostrer brothers, the merchant bankers, for finance.

There were five Ostrer brothers but Maurice, Isidore and Mark ran the Ostrer Brothers Merchant Bank, set up in 1921, which had been responsible for the flotation of several companies and had come into the industry by investing in cinemas. In March 1927 they floated the Gaumont-British Picture Corporation (GBPC) with a huge capital of £2,500,000. The company acquired the Bromheads' Gaumont company, with its old production and renting business and the large studio at Shepherd's Bush, the renting firm of Ideal and twenty-one cinemas. These included the Bicolour Circuit (London and regional cinemas) and four London cinemas owned by the Davis family. The Ostrers also acquired C.M. Woolf's renting firm of W&F, which handled all of the Gainsborough output. The Bromheads, Simon Rowson of Ideal and Woolf were to be on the new board but all three companies would continue to be run under a separate board of directors.

The merger was thought to ensure greater economy, both in the buying and in the distribution of films, which would greatly improve their marketing prospects in the UK and abroad. It also laid the foundation for a new, large combine with production, distribution and exhibition functions, which would take advantage of the forthcoming quota legislation.

Balcon knew the Ostrer brothers and was aware of their plans in late 1926, including their intent to acquire W&F, a plan that made him apprehensive. Initially, Woolf denied he had any intention of selling but subsequently acquiesced. He assured Balcon that as soon as the details of the merger were completed they would do something about the capitalisation of Gainsborough, an idea that Woolf championed. In effect, Gainsborough was no longer totally independent but locked into the new organisation, even so, at the time, it was recognised as being preeminent within the industry: 'Gainsborough is the most progressive organisation and has reached the top of the ladder in a remarkably short space of time'.[4]

Meanwhile Balcon was busy planning a project called *One of the Best*, which was intended to be Ivor Novello's next picture for Gainsborough, which would incorporate the famous historical incident of the charge of the Light Brigade. But there were problems gaining the necessary facilities and backing from the War Office and the film was eventually made without Novello or the famous charge. Novello was Gainsborough's major asset and he was secured with another contract in April 1927 covering the period between 1st January 1928 and 31st December 1928.[5] Balcon also acquired the rights to Captain Reginald Berkeley's war play, *The White Chateau*, which had been produced at The Everyman and St Martin's Theatre, and commissioned Michael Morton to make a sequel to *Woman to Woman*.

One of the immediate effects of the Cinematograph Films Bill, which was going through Parliament during the summer of 1927, was a much-needed buoyancy in confidence resulting in plans for expansion by many firms: 'Things have not been so good for some years in the British picture industry as they are today and there is every prospect of the improvement continuing'.[6] The downside was that for those without their own studio, there was suddenly, as predicted, a shortage of studio space. The studios at Cricklewood, Islington, St Margaret's and Shepherd's Bush were all booked indefinitely and there were limited opportunities at Isleworth, Bushey and Beaconsfield. Many of the bigger studios were being renovated and enlarged. Finally, Elstree (now owned by BIP) was ready in May 1927. It was ironic that British production should find its own expansion an obstacle. Equally, there was a discussion about an alleged famine of reliable producers and stars since many had fled to America and the Continent to gain work, but Maurice Elvey and Michael Balcon were convinced there was the talent to keep pace with the expected demand.

At the time Balcon was solely intent on building an industry on a firm basis, giving employment, increasing the technical talent available, providing a profitable investment and making a living. He was regarded as highly influential: 'There is no more dynamic personality in the industry, no man with a greater number of friends and none more quick to decision'.[7] The secret of his success was thought to be because he had been commercially trained and while he had an artistic sense, which was illustrated by the quality of his output, he never allowed 'art for art's sake' to dim his vision or the artistic to outweigh the commercial aspects of film production and so he managed to maintain a record of sound, commercial, money-making pictures.

Balcon's attitude towards finance had been one of painstaking shrewdness during the lean years. Despite talk of the millions that American are supposed to have had at their disposal he felt it wrong to assume money maketh the picture and vulgar to boast about mere costliness. He firmly believed that it was foolish to think that big money was a guarantee of a 'big' picture. Despite the necessity to strive for the world market, his overriding belief had been to base film costing on the home market, since not all British pictures made for the world market and based on world market costings would reach the world market. He also thought it was important not to put all of one's eggs in one basket and so costings based on the British Empire was a very good first objective. Risks had to be taken to capture world markets but it was always difficult to decide which project was going to be worth the investment and effort, therefore it was better to be cautious and, by 'improving our standards of production without necessarily increasing our budgets, we can make a profit within the home market. Better an assured small profit on a steady flow of pictures than the gambling risk upon a few costly high fliers'.[8]

The Ghost Train

Filmed under the aegis of Gainsborough Pictures in co-operation with Fellner & Somlo in Germany, *The Ghost Train* was a curious film because the story was a mix of the supernatural, horror and comedy and the details of the production were seemingly deliberately disguised. Jeffrey Bernerd and C.M. Woolf of W&F had secured the rights to *The Ghost Train*, a long-running play by Arnold Ridley (later famous as Private Godfrey in *Dad's Army*) in February 1927. The play had been a big success and ran for 600 performances after its launch in November 1925.

It was to be directed by the Hungarian director Géza von Bolváry and would star the British actor Guy Newall. At first it was stated that it was to be put into production at the Islington studio but in the end it was filmed in Berlin during April and May 1927. This was on a similar basis to *The Queen Was in the Parlour*, directed by Graham Cutts in Berlin a few months earlier, but the film, on release the film was not described as a Gainsborough Picture, simply a W&F release, which was strange. Equally interesting was the fact that some of the names of the German cast were changed to sound less foreign – for example, Hertha von Walther became Rosa Walter.

The reason for downplaying the fact that the picture was filmed in Germany with a largely German cast and crew appears to be the advent of the Cinematograph Films Act. One of the primary features was to establish a quota system requiring renters to show a percentage of British films. It was the emerging criteria of defining a British film that would become important and perhaps the reason for a hesitancy in divulging too much publicly about the production. Previously, Balcon had arranged to film several Gainsborough Pictures in Germany but this would become a thing of the past.

Géza von Bolváry (Géza Maria von Bolváry-Zahn) had attended the Imperial Military Academy in Budapest and served in the Hungarian army during the Great War. Afterwards he became an actor and then progressed to directing, working for Emelka in Munich before joining Fellner & Somlo in Berlin, in 1926.

Guy Newall had been a leading light in the British film industry immediately after the war. He had considerable stage experience and entered films via small roles and writing scenarios before becoming part of George Clark Productions and making a steady flow of pictures with Ivy Duke, whom he married in 1922. But with the downturn in production from 1923 onwards, he focused more on his stage appearances and this was his big return to the screen.

The elaborate railway scenes, including the vivid train smash, were filmed in the UK by an undisclosed director, in the first half of April 1927 over five nights, in co-operation with Southern Railways, utilising a powerful engine, two trains and a full station staff. Then Newall went to Berlin to film the bulk of the picture at the Staaken studio. Formerly the Zeppelin manufacturing hangars, they had been converted into Filmwerke Staaken in 1923, becoming the largest film studio in the world with a floor area of nearly 18,000 square metres.

The premise of the film was that several train passengers become stranded on the platform at Hellbridge Junction late at night, and are told by the stationmaster (Louis Ralph) to beware of the phantom 'ghost train' that was said to haunt the station. The passengers include a newly married couple (John Manners and Hilde Jennings), a more mature couple (Ernest Verebes and Agnes Korolenko) and a vehement temperance reformer (Ilse Bois). They are stranded because a foolish man called Teddy Deakin (Guy Newall) pulls the emergency cord as his hat has blown on the line. There was no connection until 7am, the nearest farm being five miles away, and a storm was blowing.

The stationmaster tells them the story of the train that crashed on an open viaduct and then eerie tales of the subsequent ghostly train that passes through the station. The temperance reformer gets drunk on Deakin's brandy and retires to the waiting room. Complications arise when a distraught young woman (Rosa Walter) arrives and wishes to see the ghost train, followed by her self-styled doctor and brother, who declare she is mad. The train arrives but it is a real one smuggling arms. It turns out Deakin is a detective and he arrests the distraught young lady, her brother, the doctor and the driver of the train. Deakin explains how he tracked down the smugglers and the mystery is cleared.

The Ghost Train was given a trade show in September 1927 (released 19th March 1928) and was greatly admired for being a clever, effective and spectacular version of the play: 'A definite triumph for its director …excellent comedy, extremely well worked up thrills and general entertainment value'.[9] It was thought that Bolváry's brilliant direction was the making of the picture since he neither followed the play nor the story but succeeded in making proceedings scary and at the same time introducing humorous elements through clever handling. His 'scare' climax when the ghost train arrived was very well conceived. Clever camerawork by Otto Kanturek added to the mystery, with brilliant angles and intriguing dissolving shots, while the simple sets of the lonely railway station on a rainy and windy night were well constructed by Oscar Friedrich Werndorff.

The supporting cast were all well-characterised and there was huge praise for Guy Newall, who gave a polished and vivacious performance as the astute detective who conceals his vigilance behind a mask of simplicity, posing as the stupid man. The most telling remark came from *Kinematograph Weekly*, who said, 'One of the most amusing thrill-cum-comedy made in this country and equal to anything from abroad,'[10] clearly thinking the film had in fact been made in the UK. The subterfuge must have worked.

Land of Hope and Glory

As Adrian Brunel finished work on *The Vortex*, the Islington studio was leased out for a few weeks to Glory Productions and Napoleon Films, both offshoots of G.B. Samuelson, one of the early pioneers of British film production. Harley Knowles had been engaged to direct *Land of Hope and Glory*, adapted by Valentine Williams and Adrian Brunel from Edward Elgar's work, 'Anthem of Empire', and his song of the same name.

The story started well, evoking pride of Empire and country, but progressed to a feeble spy melodrama. Blacksmith Roger Whiteford (Lyn Harding) and his wife (Ellaline Terriss) are at a loss to know what to do with their five sons, unemployed a year after Armistice. Sir John Maxeter (Henry Vibart) suggests he sends them to the Colonies and offers to employ one, Ben (Robin Irvine), in his aircraft factory. The other boys go off to South Africa, Australia and Canada and one of them, Matt (Arthur Pusey), elects to go wandering on his own. Ben does well and perfects an aeroplane stabiliser, which Sir John hopes the

British Government will adopt. It is turned down but a foreign government agency has its eyes on the device and sends Myra Almanzov (Ruby Miller) to Sir John's home (she pretends that her late husband tried to save Sir John's son in the war). She is welcomed and attempts to influence Ben. Fresh from his wanderings, Matt turns up and recognises Myra as a crook but she steals the plans. He helps Ben to make an arrest and recover the plans and finally there is a reunion of all the sons at the Whiteford's house on his wife's 60th birthday.

Knowles began filming at Samuelson's small studio at Worton Hall, Isleworth, in June 1927, where he covered many of the dramatic sequences, including some clever exterior work of a reproduction of an English village and surroundings with huge crowd scenes. There were also special daring aerial stunts filmed at Hendon before moving to Islington in July to do interiors for several weeks and finally, more exteriors in September before completion; all the sets were created by art director Hugh Gee and his assistant, John F. Mead. Back at Worton Hall various segments were shot showing historical episodes dealing with Empire heroes. This was staged when Ben viewed the Trooping The Colour and was inspired by the lives of great Englishmen, including a scene where Nelson breathes his last on the cockpit of *The Victory*, with the players grouped according to A.W. Davis's famous painting, a glimpse of the Siege of Quebec with Gerald Wolfe's fall in the hour of victory, the planting of the British flag on the shores of Australia by Captain Cook and Captain Scott, the Antarctic hero.

Land of Hope and Glory was given a trade show in November 1927 (released 15th October 1928) and although thought to be topical, it had lost its way and become tedious and contrived. The production and direction were on orthodox lines and the cast suffered a lack of direction, with little use made of Lyn Harding and Ellaline Terriss as the parents. The main attraction was in the patriotic but sentimental opening before it degenerated into a somewhat silly and crude spy melodrama. Had they stuck to the core story and followed the fortunes of the five boys as four of them travelled to the Colonies perhaps the outcome might have been different.

One of the Best

In the summer of 1927 Michael Balcon continued his mission to acquire properties. It was observed that there were few studios in the country like Islington, where so many successful all-British pictures had been made. Gainsborough was thriving and had a good selection of subjects scheduled for production, mostly adaptations of successful plays and novels: *The Constant Nymph, One of the Best, The White Chateau, Our Betters, Those Common People, A South Sea Bubble, Riceyman Steps* and a sequel to *Woman to Woman*. Several of these options were not exercised: *The White Chateau, Our Betters, Riceyman Steps* and the sequel to *Woman to Woman*. Balcon also hoped to buy an original story by Ivor Novello, which had a Ruritanian setting and a sophisticated atmosphere, to star both Novello and Isabel Jeans. By July 1927, he announced that Gainsborough would have three subjects concurrently in production: *One of the Best*, *The Constant Nymph* and *A South Sea Bubble*. Although the former two were filmed at roughly the same time, the latter was somewhat delayed until the end of the year.

With production plans intensifying, Balcon centralised all casting for Gainsborough in the hands of Bill O'Bryen, publicity manager, with the assurance that this new arrangement would not interfere with O'Bryen's existing activities.

In early July Balcon appointed the American Thomas Hayes Hunter to direct *One of the Best*. Born in Philadelphia, Hunter was educated at the University of Pennsylvania. He started off acting in a stock company, and in three years rose to become a stage-director. Migrating to New York, he become stage manager for Daniel Frohman's Lyceum Theater and later, produced plays for David Belasco, Klaw and Erlanger, Cohan and Harris, and the Shubert organisation. Switching to movies, he then worked for the Frohman Amusement Corporation before becoming associated with the Goldwyn Pictures Corporation. He had a reputation as a good commercial director of modest budget films, including *Earthbound* (1920), *Recoil* (1924), *Wildfire* (1925) and *The Sky Raider* (1925). Wonderful company, with a constant smile, Hunter was gentle as a Labrador, tall, square-shouldered, with almost white hair; everyone loved working with him. It was no surprise that he was called 'Happy Hunter' because he was 'one of those transparently sincere and genial personalities who radiate friendship by sheer sunniness of disposition'.[11]

With his attractive wife Millicent, who had given up a successful Broadway stage career at its peak, they visited Europe for a six-week holiday and on arrival in London, Balcon engaged him. During their stay they became one of the most popular couples in London. Meanwhile Balcon said that Hayes Hunter was not a great film director and part of his charm was that he knew it.

Balcon had secured the screen rights to the military melodrama based on the famous Dreyfus trail called *One of the Best*, a fine, full-blooded story of army life, written by Seymour Hicks and George Edwardes and originally produced on the stage at the Adelphi Theatre in 1895 and twice revived.

Hunter's unit comprised Jimmy Kelly as assistant director, Clifford Pember as art director, Tom Heslewood (who supervised all the costuming), James Wilson as cameraman, P.L. Mannock (a regular correspondent to the trade magazine *Kinematograph Weekly*) who created the scenario and Colonel Ewart (Boyd Cable), who vigilantly supervised all the military detail. Carlyle Blackwell, who had just arrived back from a vacation in Rio De Janeiro, was secured to play one of the main roles of the central villain.

The story was a simple one of an officer falsely accused of treason and then rescued by the woman he loves. Philip Ellsworth (Carlyle Blackwell) compromises Esther (Pauline Johnson), niece of Colonel Gentry (James Carew) of the regiment. He goes to town and is persuaded by Claire Melville (Julie Suedo) to gamble with Maurice de Gruchy (James Lindsay). After losing all his money, he gives a note for £5,000 but when the note is due he is still unable to pay. De Gruchy tells him that he can get it cancelled if he will obtain fortress plans from the barracks. Esther tells Ellsworth where they are hidden. At the same time Lieutenant Dudley Keppel (Walter Butler) of his Majesty's 144th is in love with Mary Penrose (Eve Gray), another niece of the Colonel.

On the night of the annual military ball, Keppel is detained in his room, working on the regimental estimates. To please Mary, the Colonel himself goes to free Keppel from his task. Ellsworth breaks into the safe and surprising him, the Colonel is knocked down. Keppel rushes in on hearing the noise to find the Colonel lying unconscious, the safe open and valuable documents scattered about. More people arrive to find Keppel stooping over the prostrate figure. Keppel is arrested and accused of treason. At a court martial he is sentenced to dismissal. Meanwhile, Mary learns from Esther that Ellsworth attempted the theft and she forces him at gunpoint to write a confession. Armed with this, she rushes onto the parade ground and Keppel is released. While attempting to leave the country Ellsworth is then killed by de Gruchy.

There was a lot of debate surrounding the context of the film. Should they preserve the original setting of the 1890s, should the story be modernised and set in the present of 1927, or should they introduce the Great War or indeed any war?

The play was thought riddled with military errors and what was acceptable on the stage was not necessarily agreeable for the screen as
usually such errors were subject to ruthless criticism. Compromise was always necessary but accuracy for its own sake could be quite dull: 'If one happens to have a story sense as well as a knowledge of technical detail, it is often possible to strain a point of accuracy a little for dramatic ends'.[12] This was why Balcon decided to engage Colonel E.A. Ewart (Boyd Cable) to provide advice and to supervise the numerous details of uniform, equipment, drill, deportment and gesture. Previously he had been called in to advise on other British military films and had written the story for *The Rolling Road*, filmed in 1926. P.L. Mannock, the scenario writer, demanded exhaustive detail and supported the suggestion that Colonel Ewart should be on the studio floor during filming, as well as at the barrack square for the elaborate routine of an officer's degradation. Equally, Hunter had an insistent reliance on Ewart's advice on every detail.

At first it was decided to anchor the story in 1885, then in the end, after careful consideration, Gainsborough placed the setting in the post-Waterloo period of the 1820s, which from a standpoint of uniforms was a most picturesque one, even though the cost of the production was considerably enhanced due to the costuming. Production started in mid-July 1927, with interiors of fine Georgian sets, including a representation of Archer's, a big gaming house of the period. In mid-August Hunter was filming close-ups and long shots of the court martial scene in which the heroine (Eve Gray) makes an appeal to the General (Randle Ayrton) on behalf of her soldier lover (Walter Butler). This was followed by one of the most picturesque moments in the film, the ball scenes of a regimental dance. The gallant gentlemen with varied British army uniforms and ladies with bewitching curls and high waists lent colour and life to a most

Above: A scene from *One of the Best* (1927) with Walter Butler and Eve Grey in centre
Courtesy Townly Cooke Collection
Below: Walter Butler in *One of the Best* (1927)

attractive setting. The set was not a lavish, glittering one as it had a quaint realism of a drill-ball with bunting and flags; palms were not used as decoration as their incorrectness for the period had been established by a horticultural authority. A regimental orchestra played music and the company went through the Waltz (a German importation regarded as scandalously immoral by the matrons of the day) and a Polka.

In one scene there was a fierce fight between the two villains played by Carlyle Blackwell as the plotting gambler and a foreign emissary (James Lindsay). Apparently, the set was wrecked in the process and Lindsay was out of action for a week as a result of the ruthless realism. Hunter and Balcon also decided to introduce the novel scene of a cricket match and engaged Mr P. F. (Plum) Warner, the famous English cricket captain, to stage the game and to be responsible for the faithful and accurate reproduction in 1820.

By early September, Hunter was nearing completion as he filmed the climax on a parade ground for the dismissal sequence at Hounslow Barracks, where the buildings were admirably of the period 1820, although some alterations and camouflage were sanctioned. A battalion of 300 real soldiers, all in period uniform, were specially rehearsed and drilled by the Hounslow Command under Captain Oakes-Jones for the public drumming out from the British Army of the traitor officer. Correct down to the rifles and officers' medals, the troops looked magnificent. A rhythmic symphony in grey, white and red, they were headed by a drum major and a fife band of the Scots and Irish Guards played 'The Rogue's March'. They marched on the ground and relapsed into the old-fashioned stand easy while the General and Colonel (Randle Ayrton and James Carew) joined them and the prisoner, Lieutenant Keppel (Walter Butler), was marched on to hear the adjutant read out the court martial's sentence: 'Expelled from the Army with Ignominy'. The impressive ceremony continued with a public degradation as the hapless officer's epaulettes, hat, sash and decorations were wrenched from his tunic and flung on the ground, his sword broken in half across his head. The prisoner was then slowly marched round, hatless and disgraced, finally being escorted off by all ranks with the drums beating.

Throughout filming, all observers thought that *One of the Best* had all the ingredients of a box-office success. Hunter also made a big impression on everyone and all the cast hugely admired him – 'his methods are transparently effective, yet he seems to possess a half-hypnotic persuasiveness, coupled with a marvellous absorption in his control of the players'.[13] All Gainsborough staff were also impressed by the magnificent manner in which he handled the story and his professionalism with the entire production. He started filming each time with the expression 'Smile, Happiness, Happiness- camera!' and was thought to be so persuasive and magnetic that he had the team in the palm of his hand. His sincerity and charm plus his 'golden patience and a benevolent domination'[14] inspired everyone.

The trade show of *One of the Best* was in November 1927 (released 10th December 1928) and it was viewed favourably for recreating the essentially

English atmosphere of the Regency period, the careful attention to military detail, clever direction, good, clear photography, accomplished acting and effective settings. Overall, it was admired for being 'a faithful, colourful reconstruction'.[15] The scenario was well planned and the somewhat conventional story flowed evenly with no real subtlety as the main themes of trickery, treachery and villainy were unashamedly and scarcely disguised. Hunter had brought his great experience and painstaking ability to the production. It was a straightforward, workmanlike piece, characteristic of his work.

The acting was regarded as admirable and all thoroughly in period. A new find in the form of the young Walter Butler, who played the wrongfully accused Lieutenant Keppel in a soldierly and natural manner, was thought to be a great new discovery. The leading ladies, Eve Gray and Pauline Johnson, were deemed to be effective and charming and looked exquisite in their high waists and poke bonnets. By far the biggest praise went to the robust villains, represented by Carlyle Blackwell and James Lindsay, who stalked through the story with deadly intent. Blackwell gave a clever performance on melodramatic lines, whereas Lindsay played with polished ease and a sense of atmosphere. The film was significant for the screen debut of Elsa Lanchester.

For the premiere in December 1928, a special Marble Arch Pavilion charity show was given, which turned into a big royal event with the attendance of David, Prince of Wales.

After filming there were rumours that T. Hayes Hunter would join Gaumont and then more rumours still that he would stay with Gainsborough to direct *A South Sea Bubble*, due to go into production immediately after completion of *The Constant Nymph*.

The Constant Nymph

Pre-production of *The Constant Nymph* had begun in the spring of 1927, when it was announced that Basil Dean and Margaret Kennedy, who co-wrote the play, were working on the screen treatment. It was also decided to film exteriors first of all in the Austrian Tyrol, followed by interiors at the Islington studio. The big issue was casting, which was seen from the outset as difficult, especially for the part of Tessa. Eventually it was confirmed in May 1927 that Dorothy Gish would play the role, despite murmurings of discontent about using an American star.

Crisp and business-like, Basil Dean, the brilliant stage producer, had been keen to get into pictures and had been an onlooker at the Islington studio in March 1927 when Alfred Hitchcock was filming *Downhill*. As a result, it was rumoured that he would direct *The Constant Nymph*. In the end Adrian Brunel was allocated as director to work in association with Basil Dean in accordance with their joint ideas. Clearly treading on eggshells, Michael Balcon announced that Dean had secured the co-operation of Adrian Brunel, 'a young man of vision and great artistic ability',[16] as his choice of director. When Brunel joined the unit already a lot of work had been done with the script and casting.

Ivor Novello and Mabel Poulton in *The Constant Nymph* (1927)

Basil Dean

Although Dean had the reputation of being instinctively aloof, if not coldly pontifical, he was usually communicative and courteous. Nevertheless, Brunel did not relish the idea of working with a supervising stage director and decided to be tactful and accommodating yet firm, when needed. Clearly, in order to realise the film, it was necessary for a great deal of tact and diplomacy to accommodate Dean's ambition and ego.

The production was delayed when it was learned that Dorothy Gish would not be available until July and then suddenly she pulled out and there was a dilemma as to who would fit the part. Dean, Brunel and Balcon began looking for a suitable British actress. What was needed was a girl 'with the face of an angel, the figure of a child of fifteen and the intensity of thought and ability of a really great actress'.[17] Exhaustive tests were conducted but the right actress proved elusive. Brunel suggested Mabel Poulton but was laughed at. Everyone had heard of her, but she had not done anything startling because it was thought that she had never had a real opportunity. Brunel affirmed that she was a promising little artiste, had been under contract to Abel Glance in Paris and had already made her mark in several films. Meanwhile, Poulton herself bought the book and saw the play and was determined to become Tessa. Brunel had some tests of her taken in Paris that attested to her suitability since she was Tessa in appearance, thought and mentality. Balcon and Dean relented and in early August she got the part. Described as being a clever little actress and 'long regarded as a potential supreme film comedienne',[18] Balcon had to negotiate with Archibold Nettlefold (who had her under contract), his old friend Victor Saville and Gaumont, who had also secured her to play in *The Arcadians* (1927) but generously released her so that she could appear in *The Constant Nymph*.

Gainsborough also utilised several recent acquisitions for the other important female parts, placing the charming young English actresses Benita Hume, Dorothy Boyd and Yvonne Thomas as Tessa's sisters and Francis Doble (the beautiful young Canadian actress), who was given the opportunity to characterise Florence, Lewis Dodd's wife. Boyd had been given her first big chance in *Easy Virtue*, Hume had also played in *Easy Virtue*, while Doble had proved successful in *The Vortex*.

Finally, Ivor Novello was given the lead role of Lewis Dodd. Novello had seen the brilliant characterisation of Lewis Dodd on the stage and when first approached to play the character on the screen he thought he was nothing like Dodd and turned it down. But Basil Dean was persuasive and after many tests Novello became satisfied that he was right to play 'a pure character study in pictures'.[19]

The adaptation had been worked into a suitable screenplay by Alma Reville and was episodic because the book contained so many varied characters and was divided into three parts: The Sangers' home in the Tyrol, Florence and Lewis's London home and Lewis's revolt and flight to Brussels. Among the mountains of the Austrian Tyrol, Sanger, an erratic musical genius, dies suddenly, leaving his three daughters and his latest wife to the mercy of the world. Robert Churchill (J.H. Roberts), a distant and respectable relative of the dead man, arrives in Austria with his pretty niece, Florence (Frances Doble), to make provision for two of the children, Tessa (Mabel Poulton) and Paulina (Dorothy Boyd), to be sent to school in England. The other daughter, Toni (Benita Hume), marries. Lewis Dodd (Ivor Novello), a brilliant young musician and an old friend of the Sanger family, is also a guest and Tessa adores him but he impulsively proposes to Florence, who eagerly accepts his hand.

Back in London, Lewis is now a bohemian and married to Florence. He is already unhappy at the respectability of their Chiswick home and Florence's musical friends and rebels at her attempts to run him musically. Tessa and Paulina are unable to endure the discipline of school life and seek refuge with Lewis. The discord between Lewis and Florence, who is vaguely jealous of Tessa, widens. Gradually Dodd discovers that he loves Tessa and, unable to endure matrimony with Florence any longer, announces his intention of going abroad after a concert at which he is to conduct Sanger's works. At first Tessa refuses to go with him but after a quarrel with Florence, she changes her mind. When the concert is over, the two leave for Belgium but their happiness is short-lived. On reaching Brussels, Tessa falls ill and before Lewis realises that her condition is serious, the frail child dies.

With the casting finalised and a budget of £30,000, production commenced in mid-August 1927 with Dean, Brunel, cameraman David W. Gobbett and George Harris (Dean's friend, adviser and art director) leaving London for the Austrian Tyrol via Munich to secure locations. At the Dutch frontier a railway accident was narrowly averted when a coupling gave way but they finally arrived on the shores of Lake Achensee, north of Jenbach, and based themselves in a modest lakeside hotel. At first, rain delayed work but a short time later, after the rest of the crew and cast arrived, they had glimpses of sunshine. Miles from comfortable hotels and motoring roads, and hundreds of feet above sea level, they had a wonderful background of snow-topped Alps and fir-clad slopes and the gleams of sunshine were eagerly taken advantage of to film lakes, mountains, pines and snow. At the outset Kenneth Kent, who played Ike, the husband of Toni, suddenly contracted mumps and had to be replaced by Evan Thomas.

The unit initially fractured into two camps: the film contingent with Brunel and the stage contingent with Dean. Although there was some friction at the beginning things settled down. George Harris's 'gentle and tolerant wisdom'[20] was helpful and calming, keeping various temperaments under control.

Scenes from *The Constant Nymph* (1927)

At the same time the lovely surroundings, sunshine, fresh air and good food made for a pleasant stay that mitigated any strife. It became a glorious holiday and great fun aided by Gobbett, who was a constant source of amusement with his wise-cracking, and Francis Doble with her attractive quality of allowing people to laugh at her.

However, Gobbett did take a professional objection to Dean because as a Hollywood cameraman he resented 'theatrical interlopers'. Dean's constant phrase when he wanted to get something done – 'this is what Miss Kennedy had in mind' – became a joke, although at first it grated. The difficulty of having two directors with different backgrounds was evident when Dean mapped out a particular scene that no camera could encompass and could only have been evolved on the stage with great difficulty.

Brunel knew it was impossible to shoot but decided to let Dean work that out for himself unaided and to let him make as many mistakes as possible so that he would learn quickly and could then see how the scene could be filmed. When this process was finished Dean said, 'That's roughly the idea, Adrian. What d'you think about it?'

Towards the end of August, the unit moved to the Emelka Studios at Geiselgasteig, near Munich, to film some interiors – perhaps because Hayes Hunter was still filming *One of the Best* at the Islington studio. Studio life was less intimate than on location and less communal as they stayed at the vast Hotel Bayerischer Hof. The actors had their own dressing rooms, travelled at different times and in different cars between Munich and the studio, although there was some outside fun with parties to the opera. By mid-September sets were being assembled by Bertram Evans at Islington in readiness for the unit's arrival from Munich at the end of September.

Scenes filmed in October were the delightfully satirical and finely composed sequence of Lewis Dodd's musical soirée with its odd muster of highbrow guests, a girls' high school dormitory and a high school recreation room, with an attractive crowd of girls. One of the really big scenes was staged at the Queen's Hall Roof, with fifty-four scenes being shot from 11pm on Saturday through to 4am on the Monday. This was for the amazing spectacle of a specially staged concert in which Lewis Dodd (Ivor Novello) conducted his own symphony orchestra, with a large audience and many of the key principals.

Novello was painstakingly coached to make the correct movements as a conductor but not a note of music could be heard. The filming was the result of a series of long and patient negotiations on the part of Balcon and his team. Dean arranged a meeting with the board of directors of the Queen's Hall Roof and secured the services of the London Symphony Orchestra, who appeared after their concert at the Albert Hall on Sunday afternoon. Dean orchestrated the crowd scenes and proved a grand pageant master, with these scenes being some of the best of his many fine contributions. Despite the silence of the orchestra, he did engage Eugene Goossens to compose a special score, which was seen as a new and far-reaching departure in British screen methods, not to mention a sensational coup.

Scenes from *The Constant Nymph* (1927)

On completion, spirits were high and the early consensus was that *The Constant Nymph* would be 'the greatest British screen success ever made'[21] and Mabel Poulton was 'expected to create a furore'.[22]

The Constant Nymph was given its trade show at the Marble Arch Pavilion on 20th February 1928 and proved to be a huge success: 'A triumph of acting as well as of production ... There is a charm and sincerity running through the whole picture that augers a great success... as a film it stands pre-eminent among British productions'[23] and 'this is another British picture that bears comparison with any American feature and is an augury for the future and for Gainsborough'.[24]

It was thought that the script was well constructed and the spirit well maintained in a good picturisation of the novel and play, which was a delicate piece of work. However, there was some criticism of the actual adaption. It was acknowledged that in preparing a film version of a widely known novel or play the adaptor is confronted with the dual consideration of making an accurate translation and creating an effective screenplay. In the case of *The Constant Nymph* it was felt that screen values were overlooked in order to reproduce the novel and play as fully and closely as possible. In effect the difficulty of having two directors, both with a different agenda and vision (Dean from a stage perspective, Brunel from the screen), was manifest. Brunel's direction, though meticulous in detail, was lacking in originality, perhaps due to the overbearing supervision of Dean, who clearly erred on attempting accuracy rather than seeking to recreate the spirit of the story in a new form. As a result the film was regarded by *The Bioscope* as impressive but 'as a workmanlike, if uninspired piece of picture making,'[25] and *Theatre World* as a disappointment due to no new insights and as a mere 'picturisation of the play, following the latter in detail that is almost too faithful.'[26]

There was huge praise for the cast, who were all thought to be well-drawn, but none more so than Mabel Poulton, who gave an outstanding performance that was charmingly unaffected and simple-hearted: 'at one stroke Miss Poulton takes a front-rank place among the international stars'.[27] Everyone agreed that she lived as Tessa and no one could have filled the part more sympathetically but *Theatre World* believed that although she was Tessa to perfection 'the passion proved to be beyond her.'[28] Balcon later observed that Poulton 'possessed that inner something which enabled a few silent-screen actresses to convey emotion without the power of speech.'[29]

Ivor Novello also gave a clever performance and was thought to have never appeared to better advantage. The beautiful Florence Doble characterised Florence extremely well as capable, generous, but too strict-minded, but succeeded in getting sympathy out of a rather unsympathetic character. Benita Hume was fascinating in her brief appearances as Toni, while Elsa Lanchester was thought to be outstanding as a friend of Florence and clearly brought much gaiety to proceedings.

Basil Dean much later observed 'from a director's practical point of view... the secret of a successful film story and the key to its making lies almost wholly in the detailed scenario without which the director can no more proceed properly than the stage producer can manage without the dramatists work.'[30]

14 AN INTERLUDE WITH CUTTS

Chance the Idol

When Graham Cutts left Gainsborough in the spring of 1927 for First National,[1] they had problems securing studio space to begin work on their first feature and, as options were discussed, he was loaned to W&F to make *Chance the Idol*. Eventually, like others, First National were compelled to make their pictures on the Continent.

Chance the Idol (also known as *Die Spielerin* or *The Gambling Woman*) was another curious production similar to *The Ghost Train*, adapted by the German Curt J. Braun from a play by Henry Arthur Jones. It was produced by the Romanian Harry R. Sokal for H.R. Sokal Film and W&F, with cameraman Theodor Sparkuhl and art directors Andrej Andrejew and Alexander Ferenczy. Filmed between May to July 1927, on location on the Riviera and in Berlin, there was a continental cast that included Agnes Esterhazy, Jack Trevor, Harry Leidtke, Eberhardt Lietoff and Dene Morel.

A Monte Carlo gambling story, the film follows Ellen Farndon (Agnes Esterhazy), who is deserted by her lover, Alan Leversage (Dene Morel). She borrows money and goes to Monte Carlo to find him. When she inherits £2,000, she agrees to pay his debts and bring him back for the sake of their child. Envious of the money won at the tables she becomes a victim of chance and wins large sums. She pays off Alan's debts and is on the high road to affluence when luck deserts her and she loses everything, including the father of her child. However, she meets another suitor, Ernest Ryan (Harry Leidtke), and falls in love and is then truly happy.

Given a trade show in September 1927 (released 6th May 1929), *Chance the Idol* was viewed as being a well-constructed version of the play with good direction, fine individual characterisation and lavish settings, including wonderful exterior shots of Monte Carlo and interior scenes of the casino gaming rooms and a cabaret performance.

Confetti

In late summer of 1927, preparations were finally complete for Graham Cutts to begin work on *Confetti*, his first film for First National. A Riviera setting was needed and so he left London for Rex Ingram's studio in Nice, France, in August 1927.

Cutts, with his unit comprising production manager Harry Ham, art director Norman G. Arnold and cameraman Roy Overbaugh, began filming at the beginning of September, with the talented cast of Sydney Fairbrother, Jack Buchanan, Robin Irvine and Annette Benson. Cutts had also discovered a new leading lady called Andree Sayre, who was just seventeen. She was a shining illustration of the possibility of finding stars among crowd players. Blue-eyed, golden-haired, with delicate, clear-cut features and vivacity and intelligence, she had trained to be a dancer and had been engaged in small parts in a couple of London pantomimes. Cutts was impressed 'less by her beauty and photographic qualities than by her unusual intelligence and lack of camera consciousness'.[2]

Another major addition to his team was the American designer Gordon Conway[3], who costumed the film. Famed for her stunning artwork gracing magazines and posters, Conway had also built up a reputation as one of London's leading costume designers for stage and cabaret. Cutts had undoubtedly met her in late 1925 when he was filming *The Sea Urchin* with Betty Balfour. There was an elaborate cabaret scene in which the Princes Frivolities girls from the New Princes Restaurant in London were featured. Conway had been the designer for Percy Athos's New Princes Frivolities throughout most of its incarnations and would no doubt have taken an active interest and participated in the filming at the time.

Discussing her philosophy of dressing the movies, Conway said that first she considered the story itself carefully before designing anything. Overall she believed 'that clothes can and do tell the story and express its spirit' and she explained: 'I try my best by means of line and drapery and materials to express that story in terms of clothes.'[4] For *Confetti* she tried to have the costumes (like the settings) express the theme of a 'Mediterranean Night's Dream', which is what they all called the film.

Gordon Conway and Annette Benson (1927)

Scenes from *Confetti* (1927)

The idea and manuscript for *Confetti* was from Reginald Fogwell and Douglas Furber and the former had been involved in the writing of the scenario of *The Triumph of the Rat* (1926). Both were part of the crew enjoying the Riviera. Seen as devoid of any real plot, the story was set during carnival time in Nice, when an old Countess (Sydney Fairbrother), disappointed in love, maliciously diverts her nephew's (Jack Buchanan) affections from Dolores (Annette Benson), a woman of thirty, to Roxane (Audree Sayre), a young girl. The nephew soon sees the impossibility of the match and returns to his old love, while the girl finds love with an unsophisticated young man (Robin Irvine).

Although most of the cast and crew stayed at the Negresco hotel, Cutts rented a villa where everyone congregated and through seven weeks until early November, the unit savoured the summer heat, capturing some amazing sequences including a recreation of the famed 'Battle of the Flowers' parade with 300 extras in carnival attire on a gigantic open-air set, an outdoor dance floor in an open-air café and the ballroom of a Southern Plazzo with 100 extras, featuring the dancing of Jack Buchanan. There were also several sequences taken at the famed Chateau Fielding, one of the showplaces of the Riviera and a magnificent white villa with terraced gardens overlooking the Mediterranean. Despite the rigours of filming, everyone found time for nocturnal outings with dining and dancing at Biffi's, the Grand Blue, Ambassadeurs and the Perroquet.

At the trade show in December 1927 (released 15th October 1928), *Confetti* received mixed notices. It was felt that Cutts had excelled himself in the technical side of the production with a shrewd eye to the glitter and glamour of the carnival spirit, but with one exception of the old countess (Sydney Fairbrother), failed to make his other characters believable. Jack Buchanan was thought to be badly miscast in his more serious role: 'Here is a comedian of brilliant versatility condemned to moon about in a nebulous tale without a vestige of redeeming humour' [5]

The big deficiencies in the story were also seen as a major handicap for Cutts, who was 'directing a story overlaid with misplaced symbolism and meretricious cleverness and equally so devoid of plot that I doubt anyone could have made more of it'.[6]

God's Clay

On his return from the Riviera, Graham Cutts began preparations for his second film for First National. Originally this was to be *Petticoat Lane* but instead it was decided to film *God's Clay* with the same crew as *Confetti* (including Gordon Conway as costume designer). Filming took place at Elstree studio from February to March 1928 with the slight, slender and fair Anny Ondra. Ondra was an accomplished star of Czechoslovakian and German silent comedies but her career in the UK proved short-lived because with the advent of sound her accent was not appreciated. She began her career on the stage in Prague and in 1919 appeared in her first film, *Palimpsest* (1919), opposite Carl Lamac, who became her frequent co-star, primary director and eventually her husband.

An adaptation of the novel by Claude and Alice Askew by Maclean Rogers, the somewhat sordid story was about Angela Clifford (Anny Ondra), a respectable woman in society and social worker, who takes in the wife of Geoffrey Vance (Haddon Mason) after a serious motoring accident. Angela then falls in love with Geoffrey. Geoffrey takes his wife to Cornwall, affording some Cornish seaside locations and a studio recreation of a storm on a cliff top, and continues to see Angela. Meanwhile Angela opens a welfare club at a factory owned by Geoffrey and appoints Horace Newton (Franklyn Bellamy) as secretary, who turns out to be a unpleasant chap. Clearly a philanderer, already he has betrayed one factory girl and makes Poppy (Trilby Clark) his mistress. Here, there were some exteriors of the modern factory of Keystone Knitting Mills, and interiors showing life in a stocking factory. Despite Poppy, Newton aspires to marry Angela for her money but is repulsed by her and after finding out about her affair with Geoffrey seeks revenge. He blackmails Angela but is eventually murdered by Poppy. When his wife dies, Geoffrey proposes to Angela.

At the trade show of *God's Clay*, given in August 1928 (released 11th November 1928), the film did not receive a good reception. Regarded as an old-fashioned melodrama in modern dress, with a thoroughly unpleasant and weak story that was not an attractive theme for the screen, it was sadly not 'redeemed by skillful acting and direction'.[7] Although mostly the result of an inadequate script, Cutts' direction was thought uninspired and he revealed neither imagination nor dramatic instinct, with too many incidents that were clumsy and contrived. He also had great difficulty in giving any semblance of life or reality to his characters, whose performances were simply wooden.

Eileen of the Trees

On completion of *God's Clay*, Graham Cutts went into immediate production with *Eileen of the Trees* (released as *Glorious Youth*) with a new production manager, James Sloan (who had worked with him before on *The White Shadow*), and once again with cameraman Roy Overbaugh. He also engaged Marcelle de Saint Martin, previously costume designer for FPLBPL in the early 1920s, to supervise all the women's costumes.

Based on the novel by Henry De Vere Stacpoole, it was the story of Eileen (Anny Ondra), who has been left a ward by her deceased father to a garage proprietor and acts as a nursemaid but she is ill-treated. A young aristocrat – Lord Patrick Spence (William Freshman) – visits the garage, where his car is stored, meets Eileen and falls in love with her. To prevent further ill-treatment, Patrick effectively abducts her to his country estate and proposes marriage, but the Earl – his uncle – arrives, together with an uncle of Eileen, recently in the country from Australia. The uncle has believed her to be in good hands and is anxious to see her. Upon learning of their arrival Patrick and Eileen mistakenly believe there will be objections to their betrothel and flee with the idea of being married in

Scotland. A car chase through London ensues but when their car hits a gate they are captured although everything ends in happiness with both uncles expressing no objection to the marriage.

William Freshman and Anny Ondra in *Eileen of the Trees* (1929)

All interiors were taken at Elstree Studios and exteriors were filmed near Minehead, in Somerset, in April, followed by further exteriors of a long chase through the London streets passing many famous landmarks including Tower Bridge, the Houses of Parliament, Trafalgar Square and various parks.

Eileen of the Trees was given a trade show in April 1929 (released 20th January 1930) and although the story was seen as slight, convoluted and lacking any dramatic punch it was also regarded as a pleasant and pretty enough picture. Cutts directed with skill and ingenuity, holding interest with his excellent characterisation, the use of beautiful country scenes and the magnificent car chase, producing a popular entertainment with a typically British atmosphere.

At the time there were changes afoot as John Maxwell of BIP took part in the merger of First National and Pathe in December 1927 and later, in August 1928, it was confirmed that Maxwell and BIP had bought a 51% share in the company, stating that BIP would perhaps produce future films for First National-Pathe. Perhaps these changes prompted Cutts' contract with First National to come to an end in May 1928 as he was filming *Eileen of the Trees*, even though he was under contract to make one more picture. Staying in a hotel in London, he was visited by his friend P.L. Mannock, from *The Picturegoer* magazine, and the American director Denison Clift. Cutts was described as 'a remarkable man inasmuch as he says exactly what he thinks at all times – a rare trait in the industry – and will talk to you under any circumstances without interrupting himself'.[8]

A few months later, in July 1928, Cutts was involved in an abortive venture called the Allied British Film Producers Limited, formed with a capital of $1,500,000. The board of directors included Victor Sheridan as managing director, Rhys Williams and Herman Millakowsky, with Graham Cutts, Denison Clift, Reginald Fogwell and Victor Sheridan on the production council. Sheridan was the guiding genius of the new Wembley Motion Picture Studio and presumably the intent was to produce films at Wembley directed by Cutts and Clift, but nothing appears to have happened and eventually Sheridan sold out to British Talking Pictures.

Cutts was out of a job.

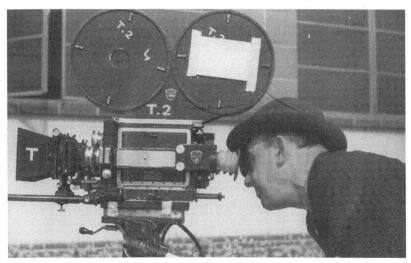

Graham Cutts in front of the camera
Courtesy Nick Baker Findlay

15 WALTER WEST'S FLUTTERS

Walter West

After a lengthy career as a pioneer of British films, Walter West, famed for his racing dramas with Violet Hopson, resurfaced in 1927. Previously, he had been invited by Michael Balcon to direct the Stephen Donoghue racing dramas in late 1925 and then went through a quieter spell. In 1927 he formed Q.T.S. with a capital of £4,000, which was raised to £20,000 in August 1927 with the backing of Harry Rowson as producer. Harry and his brother Simon were both directors of the Ideal Film Company, recently incorporated into the new Gaumont-British combine that included Gainsborough.

Maria Marten

By 1927 it was announced that Walter West was to direct the full-blooded old murder melodrama *Maria Marten* or The Murder in the Red Barn. It was based on a notorious murder case from 1827, when William Corder killed his lover, Maria Marten. The story had become a national sensation with a succession of songs and plays that thrilled audiences for decades. At the time the play was enjoying huge success at the Elephant and Castle Theatre in London.

For his leading lady, West snapped up a newcomer called Trilby Clark, an Australian actress. Beautiful and vivacious, with Titian hair, a fair complexion and only five feet four in height, she was a delightful character. Born in Adelaide in 1903, she had won a beauty contest, thereafter being known as Australia's Golden Apple Girl, before embarking on a stage career. She also appeared in the Australian film *The Breaking of the Drought* (1920), before visiting America. In New York she joined the cast of the *Greenwich Village Follies* in 1921 and then got a screen test, leaving for Hollywood and working first at Fox and then for Hunt Stromberg Productions. When her sister moved to London she followed and her film experience proved to be an asset. She was engaged first by Dinah Shurey for *Brittania's Carry On* (1927) and then by Walter West, when she took the lead role opposite Warwick Ward.

William Corder (Warwick Ward), a handsome young country squire, lives extravagantly with the intent of marrying a woman of wealth. He kills the gipsy father of a girl he has betrayed and then proceeds to betray another, Maria Marten (Trilby Clark). Corder needs to get her out of the way to make room for his marriage to a rich heiress, Lady Dorringham (Margot Armand). On the pretence of an elopement to London, he lures her to the Red Barn on his estate, where he kills her and then buries her body. Months pass and due to the disturbance caused by Maria's disappearance the crime is traced to Corder by the gipsy's son (James Knight). Corder is tried for murder, sentenced to death and duly hanged.

West decided to place the picture fifty to sixty years prior to the original events, during the Georgian period, presumably to give every advantage to greater picturesque detail in the matter of dresses and scenic effects. It also gave Corder a position in the world of elegance and fashion, rather than as a tenant farmer, which accentuated the depravity and heartlessness of the villainous hero.

The first interior scenes were taken in the Islington studio in mid-October, followed by exteriors in Alfriston, Sussex, during November 1927, filming old English garden settings and winding lanes. Forty local Eastbourne men and women were used as extras for a picturesque crowd scene of the arrival at the old 'Star' Inn of the London-Ipswich four-horse coach, with a full load of passengers in cocked hats, frock coats of the period and buckled shoes. Among them was Maria's brother-in-law (Charles Ashton), who has been to interview the wicked Squire Corder (Warwick Ward) in London, recently married to a society wife since murdering Maria in the Red Barn. Rapid progress was made with more interiors, including the big murder scene. Amidst a realistic reproduction of the barn itself, created by art director Bert Evans, with straw-thatched roof and half-timbered walls, the heinous crime was committed during a raging thunderstorm. The storm was a superb piece of realism with a tropical downpour and almost a whirlwind, admirably recreated by an aeroplane propeller. During one day of filming Trilby Clarke was murdered several times before and after lunch in various re-takes. As they neared the end of filming in early December, another big sequence was taken of a ball in the town house of the society lady who Corder (Warwick Ward) is courting. A pretty Olde English atmosphere was created and a large company danced the Minuet. There was also a realistic set of a foxhound meet and elaborate scenes of fashionable society life, as well as more sombre and well-conceived incidents of the trial and execution of Corder.

After the trade show of *Marie Marten* in March 1928 (released 11th March 1929) the reaction was lukewarm: 'It is a very ordinary, harmless entertainment and could have been better if more imagination was used'.[1] However there was huge praise for the Georgian period sets and costumes, with all the necessary airs and graces that made a highly picturesque and pleasing picture. But what the film gained in pictorial effect masked a lack of thrills and elements of melodrama: 'It is a good sound melodrama and has many beautiful settings but the realism necessary to melodrama is obscured by the camouflage of powder and patches'.[2] West's direction was viewed as being very strict when it came to the actual facts of the crime but he did not capture the necessary melodramatic spirit. He also missed other points of the stage production – for example, the omission of the vision or ghost scene that led to the murderous squire's undoing was considered a flaw.

Of the cast, Trilby Clark was thought to be reasonable playing a conventional part on conventional lines but conveyed no idea of rural innocence and beauty. Warwick Ward was suave, distinguished and debonair, showing appropriate melodramatic action but he could hardly be described as a cold-blooded murderer. All the supporting cast members were well rendered. James Knight as the avenging gipsy who becomes a sheriff's officer and volunteer hangman acts well but was thought to look like a comic opera figure. Charles Ashton and Vesta Sylva supplied the love interest as the son of the local innkeeper and Maria's sister.

Sweeney Todd

Once *Maria Marten* was complete in December 1927, Walter West began preparations for a second film, the hair-raising classic, *Sweeney Todd*. The character actor George Thomas Moore-Marriott was cast to play the part of the villainous barber alongside the talented young actress Iris Darbyshire, in her first screen role.

An adaptation of the famous Elephant and Castle Theatre melodrama by George Dibdin-Pitt, founded on the legend of the demon barber of Fleet Street, West's version concerned a man (Moore Marriott) who returns home and reads an account of the villainous career of Sweeney Todd. He falls asleep and dreams that he is the infamous criminal and his crimes unfold. In his greed he adopts the idea of trapping and murdering his wealthy customers and his alliance with Mrs Amelia Lovett (Iris Darbyshire), the pie-shop keeper next door. He attempts to kill a young sea captain (Charles Ashton) but the captain's sweetheart Joanna (Zoe Palmer) unmasks him. Following his arrest, the sleeper wakes and is relieved it was only a dream, although he does not relish pie for supper!

By mid-February 1928 plans were afoot to construct an extensive outdoor set of Fleet Street from Temple Bar to Ludgate Circus as it existed 200 years ago in the Georgian period of 1760, complete with the demon barber's sinister shop and the adjoining pie shop. This was to be constructed on a plot of land near the old Ideal studio at Borehamwood and exteriors were filmed there before transferring to the Islington studio for interiors, commencing 9th April 1928.

The last shot was taken in mid-May, with a set of a Hogarthian bedroom as Moore-Marriott (a truly fearsome Sweeney) was engaged in strangling Mark Ingestre (Charles Ashton) on a bed with venomous fury and maniacal snarls. The police arrive at the right moment (Philip Hewland) and the raving villain is borne out and down the stairs, struggling, while Joanna (Zoe Palmer) watches.

Sweeney Todd was given a trade show in September 1928 and was considered better than *Maria Marten*. 'A first rate adaptation of a good old fashioned melodrama'.[3] It was thought that West gave the play an original touch in treating the picture as a dream: 'This helps to disarm criticism and enables one to take the picture as a thoroughly entertaining joke rather than blood-curdling melodrama'.[4] Indeed, it was felt that treating the subject as a burlesque, with touches of natural comedy, tempered the full-blooded action very successfully so that taken in the spirit of fun, it was good, popular entertainment.

Throughout West preserved the atmosphere of the times and there were few dull moments and ingenious staging as he wasted no time in plunging into the hair-raising spectacle of the victims being polished off, one by one. Moore Marriott was viewed as giving an excellent impersonation of the barber with truly demoniac expressions.

Sadly, Walter West's days were perhaps numbered. Given his background, his two new films were a strange choice and being of the old school he was not adventurous in his film-making techniques, such as intriguing photographic devices that might have added more panache. Although he visited Hollywood in late 1929 and was described as having a great picture instinct and being 'a first-rate maker of films'[5] he was unable to adapt to the new style of film-making nor indeed to the advent of the talkies. After returning to familiar turf in the racing drama *Warned Off* (1929) for Herbert Wilcox at B&D, which was not well received, his output faded.

16 The Bubble Breaks with the "Quota Act" and British Lion Growls

The Tinkling of Sound to the 'Quota Act'

Perhaps no one in the British Film world was too concerned when the premiere of *The Jazz Singer* at Warner Brothers flagship theatre in New York took place on 6th October 1927. It has been regarded as the first part-talkie feature and the film that paved the way for future talkie pictures. In fact the first Warner Brothers sound feature was *Don Juan* (1926), but this had only a synchronised score and sound effects. Since Warners controlled the Vitaphone Corporation it was natural for them to use and exploit the Vitaphone system that was based on a phonographic record or disc being made alongside the film. For Al Jolson's first feature film there were synchronised singing sequences and some synchronised speech that included his famous catchphrase 'wait a minute, wait a minute, you ain't heard nothin' yet'. It was a sensation followed up by *The Singing Fool* (1928) and by the first all-talking feature, *Lights of New York* (1928).

But this was not an isolated incident and there had been many previous attempts to emulate sound, as we have seen with the experiments of Claude Hamilton Verity and Harry Grindell Matthews in 1921.[1] The British had been ahead of the game all along and in July 1923, the British rights to De Forest's Phonofilm system were acquired by C.F. Elwell, who registered a company in that name with a capital of £50,000 to make British sound pictures. In late 1924 De Forest and Elwell gave a demonstration of Phonofilm before the Royal Society of Arts. This system actually photographed the sound on the negative so that synchronisation was automatic and therefore more practical than the Vitaphone and other systems. Throughout the next few years the company was experimenting at the Clapham studio in Cranmer Court and finally released an extensive programme of shorts in 1926 and 1927, with a range of directors including G.A. Cooper, Thomas Bentley and Miles Mander. Many of these shorts featured British vaudeville artists, including one with Billy Merson that was screened in September 1926, but there was also a marital comedy by Mander called *As We Lie* (1927), where a husband teaches his wife a lesson by feigning an affair with another woman on the telephone. The company even fitted the system in forty cinemas at a cost of £300 each in the summer of 1928 and screened its sound shorts featuring bands, entertainers and sketches, including one with music-hall star George Robey doing his turn, The Barrister. The synchronisation was viewed as being perfect, but resistance continued, for example: 'I am of the opinion that it is not going to put the silent screen out of business. In the first place the silent film is universal in its appeal, it needs no knowledge of language'.[2]

Despite progress with sound film in the UK, *The Jazz Singer* is still accorded prominence. Not long after its release many of the other Hollywood studios were realising the importance of the talkies and began adapting to the new technology. But in Britain, even with the efforts of Phonofilm and others, it was still regarded as experimental and largely a fad that would run its course. Neither the exhibitors nor the producing companies wanted to invest in all the new equipment. Besides, everyone was too caught up in the progress of the film bill and all the major developments that continued to emerge as a result.

There was a new air of optimism as the autumn of 1927 was considered to be the busiest for at least six years, with over fourteen productions in progress despite the usual fog and mist. Congestion was regarded as inevitable as new producing units were formed and studio space became increasingly limited despite the various new studio-building projects. It was also a concern that some of the bigger American film companies would embark upon English-made films on a colossal scale, possibly dwarfing British activity.

The Cinematograph Films bill, known as the Quota Act, passed its third reading in November and was then debated in the House of Lords in December and finally became law on 1st January 1928. Its overall aim was to secure some protection for the British film industry. All films had to be registered with the Board of Trade and the practice of blind and advanced booking was effectively made illegal. Distributors and exhibitors were required to show a proportion of British films starting at 7.5% and 5% respectively in 1928 and then rising to 20% in 1936. Defining a British film, it was specified that any given film had to be produced by a British person or British registered company, filmed in a British studio and 75% of salaries and payments for wages had to be made to British subjects. The definition of British was extended to include the British Empire.

Reaction was mixed and polarised, as it had been during all the years of debate and as the bill passed through Parliament. But it was significant because the British Government had become vitally aware of the importance of film as a 'factor in the education of all classes of the community in the spread of national culture and in presenting national ideas and customs to the world'.[3] There was alarm that the downside of the 'Quota Act' would mean an increasing output of badly made films as 'Quota Quickies' and warnings were given that British producers should be mindful of their own reputations and refuse to make cheap and shoddy pictures.

On a more positive note British production did become healthier and resulted in a mass of better-made pictures and increased production. From only thirty-seven features being shown in 1926, the number rose to forty-five in 1927, then seventy-two in 1928. Some exhibitors had thought only bad quota films would be produced after legislation but they soon realised that their fears were entirely without foundation – 'many now see that the quota is not a hardship but a blessing'.[4]

Besides lack of studio space another consequence of the 'Quota Act' was a lack of good performers. Bill O'Bryen, casting director at Gainsborough, observed that in the lean years prior to legislation there were plenty of artists of ability and experience to fill any part, three to four times over, and there were no restrictions on using foreign artists. With new circumstances and increased production there were not enough good actors to go around. O'Bryen believed it was not simply a matter of creating new talent by using good-looking men and beautiful women and placing them in lead roles. Any aspiring and promising performer had to be trained slowly, surely and carefully, graduating from crowd work to small parts and then ultimately, if they blossomed, into the right kind of roles that might lead to stardom. The journey, in most instances, was a long and bitter struggle. At last, some crowd artists, who had been around for a few years with obvious and definite talent, might now get their chance. Dorothy Boyd had been a crowd artist but had made a sudden leap to fame in being fortunate enough to secure the right sort of part to suit her unique personality and ability in *Easy Virtue* (1927) and *The Constant Nymph* (1928).

O'Bryen thought there was 'a lack of screen ingénues of proven ability'[5] and observed that in casting *A South Sea Bubble* they could not find a girl of requisite experience to undertake a big role. In the end Benita Hume had to be brought back to London from America, where she had been for only ten days, in order to play the part. The only alternative was to engage a high-priced American or continental stars to fill parts but they were invariably too pricey to warrant the extra expenditure.

Another effect of the Quota Act was that suddenly British studios became the focus of national interest and all sections of society were talking about the prospects and imminent growth of native-made films. Many misguided people thought they could also 'get into films' with little or no experience. Half of Debretts were obsessed with the desire to enter the industry – 'many bright young things in society have been visiting studios just for the fun of it with their furs and latest Parisian models, parking their limousines outside and taking weary producers and their secretaries out for dinners or country weekends'.[6] At the same time, film folk were now to be found in many smart society drawing rooms and 'usually invited from motives entirely unconnected with their own intrinsic personal charm or social qualities'.[7]

As the 'Quota Act' became law there were three developments that became significant for Gainsborough in a broader sense, echoing a synergy in thought and action, relating to Herbert Wilcox, Victor Saville and George Pearson. In January 1928 Herbert Wilcox launched big plans for his new company, British and Dominion,(B&D) with a flotation and a public issue of £300,000. When Wilcox left John Maxwell's nascent British International Pictures, which had evolved from BNP, he formed B&D in July 1927, in association with his brother Charles and the popular musical comedy star, Nelson Keys, with a capital of £55,000. His proven track record with such pictures as the *Only Way* (1925), *Nell Gwyn* (1926), *Mumsie* (1927) and the three Dorothy Gish vehicles, *London* (1927), *Madame Pompadeur* (1928) and *Tip Toes* (1928), were invaluable assets and a clear indication of his worth. He signed a distribution deal with Charles Woolf at W&F, planned to build a new studio and like Balcon, was acquiring a range of new subjects. At the same time he was becoming aware that a film did not need to be spectacular to be big and went on to to make *Dawn* (1928) and *The Woman in White* (1929), both modest in outlook but well received.

Victor Saville, who had been a member of the well-known Gaumont production trio with Maurice Elvey and Gareth Gundrey, decided to leave Gaumont and launch his own production unit, Burlington Films, with a capital of £105,000 in January 1928. John Maxwell of BIP was appointed chairman, indicating Saville's films would be an invaluable asset to BIP, with the departure of Wilcox, and his first films, *Tesha* (1928) and *Kitty* (1929), proved successful.

Throughout 1927, Welsh-Pearson's activity was minimal as they went through a period of debate, criticism and self-analysis. Thomas Welsh visited America in search of inspiration to make bigger and better pictures, while George Pearson worked on a forward programme and looked at new talent. Though admired as a leader in the industry Pearson's recent output, including two films with Betty Balfour, *Little People* (1926) and *Blinkeyes* (1926), were regarded as poor. In early 1927 Pearson secured the rights to Sir John Buchan's *Hunting Tower*, taking up Gainsborough's lapsed option, and cast Harry Lauder as star, with backing from Paramount in America. But in February 1928, with another flotation, the company was reorganised as Welsh-Pearson Elder Films. On the board beside George Pearson were Thomas Welsh and T.C. Elder as joint managing directors and R.C. Buchanan was chairman. Subsequently marginalised, Pearson became a fierce advocate of the possibilities of sound but the board chose to ignore him and instead embarked on an expensive and unimaginative programme of silent films that resulted in considerable losses. However, he later went on to make *Auld Lang Syne* (1929) with Harry Lauder and managed to get the songs synchronised, which proved a shrewd move.

Number 17

At the end of 1927 the Gaumont-British combine, associated with W&F and Ideal, formed an alliance with UFA in Berlin. Under this deal UFA would distribute a proportion of British films in Germany and Gaumont-British would handle German films in the UK. This was to complement the existing deal that Gainsborough and W&F were forming with Fellner & Somlo, also in Berlin. Previously they had jointly filmed *The Ghost Train* with Guy Newall in mid-1927, and in early 1928 Newall once again left for Berlin to appear in two more films in association with Fellner & Somlo titled *Number 17* and *The Butterfly on the Wheel*. Given the conditions of the 'Quota Act' this was a strange move since both films would have found distribution in the UK difficult, given the criteria of legislation.

Number 17 (*Haus Nummer 17*), directed by Géza von Bolváry who had directed *The Ghost Train*, was a mystery thriller based on a play by Joseph Jefferson Farjeon, which had a successful West End run in 1926. The story featured a criminal called Shelldrake (Fritz Greiner), who breaks out of prison and shelters in a sinister London house used as a shelter for other criminals called *Number 17*. A mysterious down-and-out cockney sailor called Ben (Guy Newall), a man of simplicity and superstition, also goes there but is innocent of any evil intent. The mysterious house fills him with alarm. Shelldrake has concealed a diamond necklace there. As the place is being watched by the police, who have their suspicions, ultimately he is recaptured and the necklace recovered.

Given a trade show in early 1929 (released 25th November 1929), the film was thought to be a good adaptation of the play, with Bolváry capturing the eerie atmosphere but it was a little bewildering in places. Though well produced and acted, it lacked a strong love interest. Guy Newall's performance was thought to be a 'remarkable study'[8] and was the chief asset.

The Butterfly on the Wheel was directed by Robert Wiene, starred Lili Damita and was given a trade show in July 1928 (released 25th February 1929 and renamed *A Scandal in Paris* for America). Because it was based on a British play, it must have been the original plan to include Newall in the lead opposite Damita to add gravitas and reinforce the essential British character of the film, but this did not happen. Described as an impressive drama, Damita gave an outstanding performance but *Variety* did not understand that she was in fact the French wife of a British politician, and thought she was somewhat out of place as a sedate English wife.[9]

A South Sea Bubble

In late 1927 Gainsborough secured the rights to Lord Dunsany's play *If*, a fantastic melodrama staged at the Ambassadors in 1921, with Gladys Cooper and Henry Ainley. Adapted by Alma Reville and Angus MacPhail, the story was of a young man bored of his routine existence at home and at a crossroads in his life who plunges into the exotic atmosphere of an Eastern romance. It was the perfect role for Ivor Novello and originally one of the lead female parts was assigned to Dorothy Boyd but then given to Annette Benson, who had excelled in *Downhill* (1927) and gained enormous success in her subsequent work in *Confetti* (1927) and *Shooting Stars* (1928). T. Hayes Hunter was assigned to direct with filming set to begin on 12th December and with the additional casting of Isabel Jeans. It was announced that some of the cast of *If* would be carried forward to appear in *A South Sea Bubble*, which would commence filming immediately afterwards and would be the first of Gainsborough's pictures for 1928. However, by early December the production was postponed due to unforeseen circumstances and *A South Sea Bubble* brought forward instead.

Gainsborough had bought the rights to Roland Pertwee's adventure story *A South Sea Bubble* in May 1927 and originally Adrian Brunel was assigned as director in August 1927, with production due to commence in the September. Perhaps because Brunel was busy on *The Constant Nymph*, Michael Balcon changed his mind and asked T. Hayes Hunter to direct instead even though production did not start until December, which was after the completion of *The Constant Nymph*.

Principal roles were assigned to Ivor Novello and Annette Benson with the addition of Benita Hume, Alma Taylor and the husband-and-wife team of Gerald

Ames and Mary Dibley. Since much of the action took place at sea and in semi-tropical places various locations were being sought and at first it was thought filming might take place on Madeira or somewhere in the Canaries. The scenario was created by Alma Reville, Jim (James Graham) Kelly was assistant producer and Walter Blakely and Jimmy (James) Wilson were appointed as cameramen. Balcon also engaged Gordon Conway to design all the costumes following the success of her work for Graham Cutts on *Confetti* (1927).

Above: the cast in *A South Sea Bubble* (1928)
Below: Ivor Novello and Benita Hume *A South Sea Bubble* (1928)

The story, a blend of romance, comedy and drama, followed the romantic adventures of a company of people on the hunt for buried treasure on a South Sea island, with characterisation a strong factor of the plot. Vernon Winslow (Ivor Novello) has fallen on hard times, but possesses an incomplete chart to buried treasure passed down to him by an ancestor who was a pirate. He forges the rest of the chart and advertises for six adventurers to help search for the treasure. Three men and three women are persuaded to put up the money but at the last minute an eccentric millionaire called Isinglass (Ben Field) enters the picture, offers his yacht and spoils Vernon's swindle. But Vernon carries on and adds Isinglass and a female press reporter, Averil Rochester (Benita Hume), who has her suspicions about Vernon's authenticity, to the party. The men fall in love with the girls and Vernon falls for Averil. Frank Sullivan (S.J. Warmington), a former fiancé of the reporter and a friend of Vernon's, tries to expose the swindle by becoming a stowaway. He is made to work at the boat's furnaces but does everything he can to wreck Vernon's scheme. On the island Isinglass plants a chest of treasure that he has brought with him to save the expectant adventurers from disappointment but they find the real treasure. Escaping from the boat Sullivan appears and is mad with jealousy. After a struggle with Vernon, he seizes Averil and the jewels and attempts to escape by boat. Vernon rescues Averil but in the process Sullivan falls overboard with the jewels and drowns. The remainder of the party realise they have found greater happiness than wealth can bring.

Filming started in mid-December and over several weeks various interior shots were filmed at the Islington studio, including a Fleet Street scene outside the offices of the *Daily Mail* and a big ballroom set in a Columbo hotel. Here the cast are on the dance floor but behind curtains a baccarat party is in progress. An exuberant Hunter is heard to shout 'Now, ladies and gentleman, don't go and die on my hands!'[10] in an attempt to cheer his dancing crowd on to get the desired joie de vivre. Finally, the top-floor studio at Islington was the scene of an interior of a cabin in a private yacht featuring Winslow (Ivor Novello) and Lydia la Rue (Annette Benson). Benson is doing the Charleston to a gramophone record when Novello enters and turns it off with evident annoyance. In vain she attempts to coax him out of his disapproval for he brushes her aside and strides brusquely from the cabin.

At last it was decided to film all the tropical and desert exteriors in North Africa and Hunter and his company, along with assistant producer 'Shan' Balcon, left London for Algiers on Thursday, 2nd February 1928, on Southern Railway's Southampton boat train. Michael Balcon and a big crowd went to Waterloo to say au revoir, along with Mrs Balcon, Roland Pertwee, Bill O'Bryen and a host of relations and friends. At 6pm the party sailed on the *Jan Pieterszoon Coen* of the Nederland Royal Mail Line. More than eighty important scenes were shot onboard during the five-day voyage before arrival in Algiers on 7th February. Bad weather greeted the party for the first three days, but eventually they took the eighteen-hour train journey to Biskra, an oasis of date palms in the Sahara Desert, via El Guerrah, where the buried treasure scenes were taken over a two-week period.

One set was a palm hut in the centre of a lovely plantation built by J. Skelly, the clever chief property master, and another set was an oasis of beautiful date palms with shallow pools of clear water here and there, great clusters of cacti and a green carpet of tangled weed basking under a deep blue sky and a bright sun. Here was a love scene between Ivor Novello and Benita Hume, with a vista of the oasis between the trunks of two large palm trees.

The company arrived back in London on 9th March 1928 and a month later, T. Hayes Hunter gave a party at his flat in Queen's Gate to celebrate the completion of the picture. Everyone was there, including Michael Balcon, George Hopton, Bill O'Bryen, Arthur A. Lee (on a visit from America), film cutter Arthur Tavares, Mrs Hayes Hunter, Roland Pertwee (author), and the full cast and crew. Pertwee gave a speech and said that although the cast thought Hunter was a slave driver of the worst possible description, they still managed to retain some sort of maudlin affection for him and as a token of this affection presented him with a gold cigarette case inscribed 'To Happy Hunter' from a bunch of English boys and girls who helped him to make a good picture, *A South Sea Bubble*, 1928'.[11] He was immediately loaned to Herbert Wilcox to direct *The Triumph of the Scarlet Pimpernel* (1928) for B&D starring Matheson Lang, but no more directorial assignments were forthcoming from Gainsborough.

A South Sea Bubble was given a trade show in July 1928 (released 18th March 1929) and was greeted with a mixed, lukewarm reaction. It was thought to be an intriguing story combining melodrama, sentiment, a love interest, an adventure element, comedy and a touch of fantasy but although there were pleasing moments it was dramatically unsound and did not hold the interest continuously. The main difficulty was that the story could never decide whether it was a comedy, drama or fantasy – so that it was viewed as 'a hotchpotch of crude comedy and melodramatic incident, the whole being without punch or sincerity'.[12]

The picturesque settings on a well-appointed yacht and seaports were all admired but there were issues with the tropical island, which might as well have been Southport, where the sandhills and rocks looked good, and with the addition of a few palm trees would have been just as realistic as the scenes filmed in North Africa. The acting was 'more or less apathetic, unconvincing and negligible'[13] and Hunter appeared to let his artistes get out of hand so that they all overacted.

The moustachioed Novello was the main box-office attraction but was thought to be miscast and hardly suited the part of a naval man and a descendant of a pirate because his performance followed his usual attractive manner of well-bred immobility, which was somewhat at odds with his character's devious and mean streak yet his repentance and the manner in which his character was reformed was applauded. Benita Hume and Annette Benson were charming, Alma Taylor graceful and attractive, S.J. Warmington as Frank Sullivan was strong and forceful, but the fine character actor Ben Field as Isinglass gave the best individual performance as the benevolent millionaire.

Later, Michael Balcon was reported to have said of the production: 'It was really a load of nonsense, indifferently directed by Hayes Hunter. In fact, it was a failure.'[14]

Chick

Another company formed during the evolution of the 'Quota Act' to take advantage of legislation was British Lion Film Corporation, a small concern registered in November 1927 with a capital of over £200,000. Founded by Canadian Sam W. Smith (managing director), a deal was struck with the author Edgar Wallace to adapt his work for the screen and he was duly made chairman. Percy Nash, a respected veteran of the film industry, was made production manager and the Canadian Sidney Olcott was brought over from America as studio head. They bought the derelict Beaconsfield studio from George Clark for £52,000 and started a complete renovation and modernisation.

The first production was to be *The Ringer*, about a notorious vigilante who assassinates evildoers clever enough to escape the law. Because the Beaconsfield studio was not ready, the Islington studio was leased and production was due to start on 13th February 1928 with a cast that included Leslie Faber and Annette Benson (dressed by Gordon Conway). However, Olcott suddenly disappeared. Later, he sued British Lion on the grounds that *The Ringer* was not suitable as a superfilm, which his contract stated, and so he had left (his place was taken by Arthur Maude). The shenanigans meant a delay and in the end although many of the sets had been constructed at Islington, production was moved to the completed studio at Beaconsfield, with filming taking place in April. When finished, *The Ringer* (1928) was applauded as being an excellent adaptation, with good direction and acting.

The second British Lion feature was *Chick* and since production on *The Ringer* had been deferred, it was decided to bring production forward and film *Chick* at Islington instead. *Chick* was a romantic comedy with a dash of drama about a clerk who inherits a peerage and makes an impressive entry into the House of Lords. It featured the Australian actress Trilby Clark (who had already appeared in *Maria Marten* and *Confetti*) and a young stage actor called Bramwell Fletcher as principals.

Chick (Bramwell Fletcher) is a kind but shrewd cockney youth who is a poor and not too efficient clerk living in a cheap boarding house in Bloomsbury. He forms a friendship with Mrs Gwenda Maynard (Trilby Clark), a pretty actress with a small child. One night he is suddenly awoken by reporters, who break the news to him that on the death of his eccentric uncle he has become the Marquis of Pelborough. But there is no money so he has to stay employed. Mr Jarviss (John Cromer), an unscrupulous company promoter, decides to exploit Chick and starts off by making him a director of a bogus oil company. Jarviss's daughter Minnie (Chili Bouchier) sees the title 'My Lady' and so she goes all out for him, throwing modesty aside in the hope of one day becoming a peeress. After being turned down by Chick, she denounces the bogus company and its founder.

On the day that Chick takes his seat in the House of Lords there is a debate following a Child Welfare Bill, which he supports with such eloquence that he becomes the hero of the day and establishes his reputation as an able politician, much sought after by company promotors. An excursion into high society follows and he saves a distinguished nobleman from a gang of crooks but soon Chick becomes disillusioned and frees himself of his city entanglements. He saves a friend from being cheated in a gaming house and on his return to his Bloomsbury rooms rescues the little actress from being ill treated by a blackmailing brute. Chick then discovers that the child is really her sister's, wife of the blackmailer, but happiness follows and he decides to devote himself to her.

At the end of February 1928 A.V. Bramble began filming for a month with the assistance of Bert Evans of Gainsborough, creating some rather inventive sets. The first was a section of a London street with basement area, railings, paving and roadway, showing Chick's Bloomsbury boarding house; three houses were built, complete with curtained windows. Here, various episodes were shot, dealing with Chick's accession to the peerage, and a batch of reporters swarm the steps, eager for an interview. Another set was a Lyons teashop opposite the House of Lords but the most impressive one was a replica of the interior of the House of Lords built over a month, complete with carved panels, seating and candelabra, all accurately reproduced from photographs. For this major scene, A.V. Bramble gained the willing assistance of Westminster officials in obtaining full details of the procedure as to how a new peer would take the oath and in the process his seat.

A scene from *Chick* (1928)

While directing *Shooting Stars* (1928) in 1927, A.V. Bramble cast seventeen-year-old Chili Bouchier as a bathing beauty and had declared 'that girl's clever', promising her another part. She was cast in the role of what she called the 'baby vamp' and while shooting a ballroom scene, noticed on the call sheet 'Lounge Lizard Harry Milton'. After taking one look at this tall, dark and handsome man, she fell in love. She was to dance and flirt with him outrageously but because she was so smitten, A.V. Bramble kept shouting 'Cut!' over and over again as she tried in vain to do what was asked of her.[15] The pair later married.

Chick was given a trade show in August 1928 and was hailed as being amusing light entertainment: 'bright, lively, novel, funny, romantic and based on a rattling good essentially English story'.[16] Yet, despite the praise, Bramble's direction was thought to be unremarkable and the story patchy in places. One of the difficulties was translating the author's dialogue into screen terms because stories of low and high life can be more effectively described than picturised. Equally, the humour was inconsistent and vacillated between straight, broad and slapstick and was sometimes good, sometimes bad.

Of the acting, the two feminine leads came in for some criticism. Trilby Clark was disappointing and thought to be miscast, being perceived as too old to play the heroine. Since it was hard to believe she was the object of boyish adoration all interest and sympathy was lost. Chili Bouchier, as the daughter of the millionaire profiteer, gave an admirable performance but was thought to be too artificial to make an effective and convincing coquette.

The main attraction was the acting of Bramwell Fletcher in his first screen appearance and he who presented Chick as a thoroughly lovable young fellow. Although the part demanded an actor of long experience as a comedian he was outstanding and excelled in the remarkably fine scenes of magnificent ceremonial in the House of Lords. Fletcher's discovery proved he was a young man with real possibilities and a personality to be reckoned with due to his youth, good looks, easiness and a sense of quiet comedy.

British Lion continued to turn out more films based on Edgar Wallace's work and all distributed through Ideal, part of the Gaumont-British combine. After *The Ringer* and *Chick* came A.V. Bramble's *The Man Who Changed His Name* (1928), G.B. Samuelson's *The Forger* (1928), *The Valley of the Ghosts* (1928), Arthur Maude's *The Clue of The New Pin* (1929) and *The Flying Squad* (1929). However, all three directors were considered to be of the old school and the films somewhat lacking, so that in the first year British Lion experienced heavy losses.

17   THE REORGANISATION OF GAINSBOROUGH AND A LAST GASP OF SILENTS

About a year after the formation of the Gaumont-British combine in March 1927, Gainsborough Pictures (1928) Limited was registered as a public company on 27th April 1928. C.M. Woolf had kept his word that after the merger was successfully completed he would turn his attention to the capitalisation of Gainsborough.

The capital of Gainsborough Pictures (1928) Limited was £262,500 and the flotation issue consisted of 200,000 ordinary shares of £1 each and 1,250,00 deferred shares at 1s to be made available on 9th May 1928. The new company adopted all agreements with Gainsborough Pictures and Piccadilly Studios Limited and a new board of directors was duly appointed consisting of C.M. Woolf, Michael Balcon and Maurice Ostrer. Gaumont-British also retained the right to nominate two further directors. Balcon was made managing director for a five-year term, while C.M. Woolf was made chairman. From 1st May, Balcon received £2,500 per annum and 7.5% commission on net profits after providing for the fixed dividend of 8% on the ordinary shares. Effectively, Gainsborough Pictures became a wholly owned subsidiary of Gaumont-British.

The Islington studio was seen as one of the most central and self-contained features of British film production and the hub of Gainsborough's activities. On taking over the studio in early 1926, Balcon had utilised the existing internal framework and structure but reorganised everything into a smooth film-making machine. The intermediate between the studio and the head office based in Wardour

Street was the general manager, George Hopton, who applied his wide experience of business to inter-office affairs and studio co-operation. Under the aegis and direct control of Balcon, studio manager Harold Granville Boxall had supervised the running of the studio that had reached a stage of remarkable efficiency.

There were twelve spacious offices and administrative rooms and the restaurant was still thriving. Each section of the business was neatly divided into departments. The Publicity and Editorial (scenario) departments were for a long time controlled by Bill O'Bryen but gradually Angus MacPhail took charge of the script factory and literary clearing house while O'Bryen, retaining his position looking after Publicity, also took charge of casting. The intricate business of production schedules was undertaken by production manager 'Shan' Balcon, who besides being the brother of Michael Balcon, possessed wide experience of the industry and had previously assisted Graham Cutts, Alfred Hitchcock, Adrian Brunel and T. Hayes Hunter. The art department and set dressing was under the direction of Bert Evans and Allan McNab. Carpentry and plaster modelling were housed in large, well-equipped shops with access to all floors by an elevator. Electrical and engineering equipment was in the charge of George Gunn. The lighting department was sustained by a constant adoption of fresh standards in the system and had an exceptionally mobile outfit of some 115 units comprising six sun-arcs, fifty-two floodlights, fourteen Cooper-Hewitt mercury banks, three simpex domes and a variety of scoops, incandescent spots and a 70kw portable generating unit for exterior work. In the later stages of construction the picture passed through the hands of Arthur Tavares, the cutting supervisor, assisted by Ian Dalrymple and Miss Dicker, in a well-appointed department equipped with all the latest apparatus. The camera equipment consisted of the finest and most up-to-date brands available, including Bell and Howell and Debrie. Finally, the stockroom was run by Mr Pleace and the wardrobe department by Miss Bainton.

As part of the new reorganisation, Balcon also created a new logo that was placed on letterheads, advertising material and at the beginning of each film released after spring 1928. The company had been named after the famous painter Thomas Gainsborough and to reinforce this association, he chose an image of a beautiful woman in eighteenth-century finery and a large feathered picture hat set in an ornate oval frame. It was seen to be suggestive of 'art and gentility and class'.[1] On film, the woman was seen smiling and nodding slightly to the camera. Later known simply as 'The Gainsborough Lady', the inspiration for this image came from Gainsborough's famous portraits of Sarah Siddons, an outstanding tragic actress of her time, and Georgiana, Duchess of Devonshire. Who exactly featured in the original filmed sequence is not known but later representations have been identified as being the actress Glennis Lorimer.

Balcon was regarded as being among the 'most progressive of the younger powers behind British films today. His sound commercial perception has identified him with post-war British film activity in both distributing and producing'.[2] Under his expert guidance Gainsborough Pictures had traded with marked success and the brand was a particularly good one. Gainsborough was seen as being one of the few British film companies that consistently made a profit but was advantaged by its agreement with W & F, a company that had achieved considerable success as a distributor of films and particularly British releases. It was estimated that the new company's share of the bookings and sales of the five films forming the 1927 production of the old company would show a profit of £20,000. With new investment, Balcon was contemplating the production of at least twelve films annually, with an estimated profit of £75,000 per year – equivalent of 3% and 70% respectively on the ordinary and deferred capital. The total sum involved in the cost of the purchase of the films and the lease of the studio was £134,644 and the actual purchase price payable for the business was £145,960.

At the same time the working arrangement with Fellner & Somlo of Berlin was ratified following the co-production on several films, including *The Queen Was in the Parlour* (1927), *The Ghost Train* (1927) and *Number 17* (1929). In future it was stated that all Gainsborough films would be made in conjunction with this enterprising continental house but in the main production would be based at the Islington studio. A month later, Fellner & Somlo secured the old established Bruckmann renting organisation in order to distribute their own and Gainsborough's product throughout Germany.

The first co-production was to be *The Fortune Hunter* featuring Ivor Novello but this was to be filmed on the Continent. Michael Balcon also secured the film rights of Arnold Ridley's railway thriller *The Wrecker* and was in discussion with Lili Damita, star of *The Queen Was in the Parlour* (1927), to begin a production to be filmed at Islington. There were also plans to engage the American director Harry Lachman to film *The Brethern*, a film to be based on H. Rider Haggard's spectacular story of the Crusades and to star Ivor Novello. Neither the Damita project nor the Lachman film materialised.

At the same time Balcon negotiated a deal with the newly formed United Motion Picture Producers Limited in America. This was J.D. Williams' new company with backing from an influential City group. The new concern had been formed for the purpose of distributing selected films from British production companies to the US and Canada, aiming at the 15,000 independent cinema theatres in America, in particular. Williams purchased the rights to *Downhill, East Virtue, The Constant Nymph* and *A South Sea Bubble* with the intent of taking all of Gainsborough's future work. Since it was the policy of the company to open up the American market for all worthwhile British productions, he also signed Herbert Wilcox's newly formed B&D. His intent was to be financially interested in future British productions by advancing capital on selected propositions.

With all these deals in place and the flotation of Gainsborough underway, Balcon was in a strong position and believed that his association with Gaumont-British was not controlling and that he still retained some freedom. For the first time he had the cash resources and distribution network to expand his production activities and did not have to scratch around to finance each project but what he and his fellow directors failed to appreciate was the advent of the talkies.

A Light Woman

After completing *The Constant Nymph* in late 1927, Adrian Brunel missed the boat with *The South Bubble* when it was allotted to T. Hayes Hunter. When Michael Balcon offered him a three-picture contract he started looking for a new property to film in the spring of 1928. Brunel had about ten possible stories and issued analysis forms to readers and each story was carefully considered. One of these – *A Light Woman* – was in fact written by Dale Laurence, the pseudonym for Mde Adey Brunel, Adrian Brunel's mother. It was ironically enough considered the best story and went into pre-production.

The atmosphere of the story was interestingly British, but had a daring, almost French flavour and much of the action took place on the French Riviera. It was about an attractive, retired British general who is something of a merry widower and his equally attractive and determined daughter. Part of the theme was 'like father, like daughter'. But for some unknown reason C.M. Woolf instructed Balcon to change the background of the film to Spain – 'He wants all the characters to be Spanish and all the action to take place in Spain,' Balcon told Brunel. As a result, Brunel worked with Angus Macphail on translating the script to a Spanish setting during a few weeks spent in Eastbourne.[3]

With a first draft 'Shan' Balcon went to Spain to scout for locations as Balcon and Macphail polished the script and began casting. The leads were allotted to Gerald Ames, who had been in *A South Sea Bubble*, and Benita Hume, who had shown what she could do in *The Constant Nymph* and *A South Sea Bubble*. Balcon had signed her to a contract with Gainsborough, who claimed that they had 'discovered, trained and will shortly establish a real British screen star of international value'.[4]

The story was essentially about a young girl's wilfulness and her two loves. Dolores (Benita Hume) is the daughter of an old rake, the Marquis de Vargas (C.M. Hallard). She is being educated at a convent but her conduct shocks the nuns and she is duly expelled. At home her father is living with a mistress and proves an unreliable guide. Ramiro (Donald Macardie), her sweetheart, offers marriage, but she spurns him and flirts with a friend, Don Andres (Gerald Ames), a famous explorer, as she dances in the street with the peasants and visits a shady nightclub. To save his friend from marriage to this 'Light Woman', Don Andres encourages her but when marriage is suggested he turns her down, arousing her indignation. Later, the father realises how his conduct is affecting his daughter's career and reforms. However, Ramiro thinks she loves Don Andres and quarrels with him. He attempts to climb a dangerous mountain and when Andres finds out, he goes after him and they are reconciled. He falls and dies, but Ramiro comes down to find that Dolores has realised her faithful lover's worth and the pair at last find happiness.

With a budget of £17,000, Brunel assembled his unit with 'Shan' Balcon as assistant director, Claude McDonnell as cameraman and Anna Newnham looking after continuity. Before he left for Spain with his cast at the beginning of April

1928, Brunel threw a party for the whole crew and various friends and colleagues. At the Spanish frontier they met 'Shan' Balcon and made their way to Madrid. He assured them that he had found some wonderful locations and had been promised all permits and facilities. As they waited for the permits in Madrid they killed time loitering in an enormous and gloomy café near the hotel (which they nicknamed 'Café Dreary'), ready to dash off to the southern sunshine. They also went to bullfights, which precipitated a heated debate: was it picturesque, dangerous and exciting, or cruel and brutal? Someone suggested that it was hypocritical to criticise the Spanish since Britain was the home of blood sports.

Gerald Ames and other male members of the cast had grown their side whiskers because they thought it would make them look Spanish but found that whiskers are regarded as being typically English and are always worn on the stage by Spanish actors playing English parts. They were all alarmed at the vast quantities of food given in the hotel, with six to seven courses for lunch and more for dinner.

Despite firing off telegrams nothing happened so Brunel moved his unit to Seville. The weather was not good but they began work in the garden of a private house. The son of the owner welcomed them until he found out that they were going to film a love scene. He told them his mother hoped that nothing 'improper' was going to take place and after being reassured, allowed the camera to be set up. All was going well until the owner arrived. He took a quick look at Benita Hume in an evening frock and said politely that he regretted he could not allow anything of that sort in his grounds!

The cameraman Claude McDonnell did not like any of the other chosen settings, saying 'I can't photograph people against white houses'[5] and so they moved to Malaga, where 'Shan' Balcon had been promised some locations and where there were fewer white houses. On arrival Brunel met a lieutenant of the Bourbon regiment, who was also an art critic and film reviewer for the local paper, and he became their guide and interpreter, lending authority with his uniform when handling crowds. He took Brunel to a perfect, nearby picturesque little town called Pizarra and did most of the valuable scenes there and found them authentic gipsy dancers and guitarists.

Benita Hume's stunning good looks caused a riot among the local men. Dukes and marquesses with shining racing cars, all eager to take her out, frequented the hotel regularly at night. She was very skilful in accepting two invitations for the same time, thus securing a chaperone. Anna Newnham, Brunel's continuity girl, was blonde and attractive and therefore also a target.

In Pizarra they staged a fiesta and the whole village turned out to participate. One shot featured Gerald Ames and Donald Macardle making a tour of the village in a mule cart surrounded by a galloping cavalcade of Caballeros mounted on horses and mules, many in sombreros. Benita Hume gave a dance inside a ring of locals to the accompaniment of a guitar, with stamping and clapping from the outlookers. When she did a few steps of the Charleston between shots, everyone roared with laughter.

One of the scenes involved a car being driven madly around a mountain path. Everything was set, the road was cleared, the camera turned, the car sped along the narrow path when suddenly out of nowhere a flock of goats, two mules, a bullock cart and other vehicles emerged from a side turning to cover the entire path. The artists in the car escaped with their lives, missing all the animals and charged on, just missing the crew with the vehicle turning over on its side and stopping 200 yards up the mountain slope – but they got the shot!

When the Malaga and Pizarra scenes were done, they moved to Granada in a cavalcade of open cars, followed by a lorry with all the equipment, and filmed through the Andalusian countryside, stopping for refreshment in one quaint and attractive town after another. Reaching Granada, they boarded the perilous mountain railway to visit a hotel in the Sierra Nevada for the mountain sequences. There was then a perilous horse ride up an insecure road to the somewhat luxurious hotel at the end but the views were magnificent. On the way home they stopped for the night in Madrid and Brunel took Señor Alvarez, their prospective Spanish distributor and his charming wife, out to dinner at the smartest Madrid nightclub but there he made a faux pas in asking the Señora to dance. She refused, saying only prostitutes and foreign women danced in public.

By the end of May Brunel and his unit were back in London and began filming interiors at Islington throughout June 1928. The brilliant young artist Alan MacNab was making his debut in art direction, with striking sets that included a chic dressmaker's establishment and a Spanish nightclub. The latter was a vivid colourful spectacle, full of gaiety and life. Music was provided by Billy Trytel's band and an Argentinian orchestra in Spanish national costume; a crowd of 150 people drinking, dancing and eating, with some tables set in attractive alcoves running around the semi-circular walling of the set.

The trade show of *A Light Woman* was in December 1928 but the reaction was lukewarm. It was admired as a pretty picture, beautifully produced and photographed with wonderful Spanish settings, but the story was thought to be slight and weak. The title suggested entertainment value through delicate situations, subtle characterisations and emotional acting of a high order but some of those qualities were absent and some scenes fell flat and the characterisation was deemed ordinary. Brunel's direction was regarded as poor and hardly comparable to his work on *The Constant Nymph*. He had done little to put life into the plot and characters – 'it has a weak construction, aimless theme and negligible character drawing'.[6]

The acting was thought to be adequate but not exceptional. Benita Hume, although showing promise for the future, was merely pleasing and did not rise to the occasion but did as much as possible with a part that offered little opportunity. Donald Macardle was very weak as Ramiro, while Gerald Ames was stilted as Don Andres with a big moustache that did not suit him. Only C.M. Hallard, as the father, was praised as being the only real living character in the picture.

The film was released some time in 1929 just as the talkies were taking hold and silent films were not being favourably viewed, so more than likely faded quickly.

The Gallant Hussar

Ivor Novello's last silent picture, originally titled *Fortune Hunter* and renamed *The Gallant Hussar (Der fesche Husar)*, was to meet a similar fate to *A Light Woman*. Described as a charming love story set against a background of Hungarian military life, it starred Novello and Evelyn Holt, an artiste of great continental reputation, and was made by Gainsborough in association with Fellner & Somlo and filmed in Berlin, with exteriors taken in Budapest during April and May 1928.

Ivor Novello in *The Gallant Hussar* (1928)

Based on an original scenario by Hungarians Artur Bardos and Margarete Langen, it was another combination of strange cultural mixes in a typical 'Ruritanian' setting directed by Géza von Bolváry. Novello played an Austro-Hungarian army officer with the unlikely name of Lieutenant Stephen Alrik, who has become a drunkard, gambler and a rake. A difficulty with a money-lender brings matters to a head and he is hauled up before his colonel and given a warning. Fortunately his father and the Colonel are friends and Alrik is sent to his sister's fiancé's farm to think over his misdemeanours. Before leaving, he catches a glimpse of a girl with whom he promptly falls in love and sends her flowers. She is Mary Wentworth (Evelyn Holt), daughter of a rich American millionaire. At the farm he learns that the millionaire has arrived with his daughter and has taken a nearby mansion. In his capacity as farm hand he meets the daughter again, incognito at a village fair, and gradually wins her love. But then she learns who he is and also that he knows her identity so she sends him away. Reformed, he is recalled to his regiment and sends her flowers again – forget-me-nots. She relents, convinced his love is true and not about her father's money and the pair marry.

Towards the end of filming in early June 1928, Michael Balcon went to Berlin to see the final stages and on his return, perhaps somewhat predictably, said that he thought it was the best Novello film to date. Given a trade show in September 1928 at the London Hippodrome, *The Gallant Hussar* was described as a bright and sparkling entertainment, with much comedy and luxurious settings. Although the storyline was simple and far too sentimental, Bolváry's treatment was charming, so minimising the weaknesses in the plot and enabling him to create a film that was 'delicate and extremely well produced with strong feminine appeal'.[7]

Of course Ivor Novello (retaining his recent moustache) dominated the picture and would please the fans with his portrayal of the dashing romantic lover. Gainsborough were clearly 'determined to milk his Valentino image to the last drop'.[8] His performance never forfeited sympathy as he was 'endowed with a personality suggesting innocent irresponsibility rather than ingrained wickedness'.[9]

Being classified as a foreign film by the 'Quota Act', *The Gallant Hussar* received only a limited release in the UK. Because it was also a silent film like *A Light Woman* it was therefore not given a real chance to perform.

Ivor Novello in *The Gallant Hussar* (1928)

The First Born

Miles Mander's book *Oasis* and play, *Those Common People*, were optioned by Michael Balcon in early 1928, when it was announced that Mander would not just star in the movie but would also make his debut as a feature director.

Miles Mander

Mander was a colourful character who had been in musical comedy and then travelled the world, getting involved in boxing promotion, aviation, sheep farming and eventually writing for magazines and creating film scenarios. Clever and ingenious, 'he was a thin, elegant man with the eyes of a ferret, a curly moustache, and a mannered way of speaking that suggested a cavalry colonel'.[10] During a break in his war service he dabbled in film crowd work and after the Great War decided to take up a career in the movies. Essentially, he became a male vamp playing villains, English gentlemen and upper-crust cads. A great friend of Adrian Brunel, he formed the Atlas-Bioscope Film Company with him and Ivor Novello in 1922. He had also appeared in several previous Gainsborough pictures:

The Prude's Fall (1925), *The Pleasure Garden* (1926) and *Riding For a King* (1926) and directed a few sound shorts for Phonofilm.

For his leading lady, Mander chose Madeleine Carroll. Destined for stardom, the exquisite-looking Carroll was a French language teacher and hat model before she made her stage debut as a French maid in the 1927 West End production of *The Lash*. Known for her confident air, poise and sophisticated allure, she won a film beauty competition that started her film career and was first glimpsed by audiences in Sinclair Hill's *The Guns of Loos* (1928) for Stoll, followed by Edwin Greenwood's *What Money Can Buy* (1928) for Gaumont-British.

Filming *The First Born* (1928)

Alma Reville, who had been involved with Mander on two previous collaborations, was engaged to create the adaptation with him. A provocative society melodrama about the double standards of the upper classes, the film had it all – deceit, adultery, jealousy, secrecy and a smattering of political intrigue. Sir Hugo Boycott (Miles Mander) and his beautiful young wife Madeleine (Madeleine Carroll) have frequent quarrels, partly due to her jealousy and because he has no son to inherit. After one such quarrel Hugo leaves for Africa, where he has a mistress and child. Because she still loves him Madeleine adopts the unwanted child of her manicurist and lets her husband believe that the child is his. Delighted, Hugo returns and stands for Parliament. Two years later Madeleine has a son of her own but all Hugo's affection is given to the adopted child Stephen (played by Theodore Mander, Mander's son). Two days before the election Hugo goes to town and Madeleine's jealousy is roused once again when she discovers that he is visiting Nina (Ella Atherton), her friend who suggested the adoption. Madeleine is moved to accept advances from Lord David Harborough (John Loder), who provides more devotion and a fidelity that she has failed to find in her husband. On being discovered and to save herself, Nina arouses Hugo's suspicions as to the legitimacy of his first born. There is a furious scene where he refuses to believe Madeleine's story that she adopted the boy and he returns to Nina on election night. But after a quarrel with her, Hugo goes missing and it is later reported that he has died after falling down a lift shaft. Madeleine tries to remain loyal to his memory but later learns that Stephen was Hugo's illegitimate son. She concludes that she has wasted her devotion on something that never existed and marries Harborough, who has provided sympathetic support through all her troubles.

Filming was scheduled to take place at the Islington studio between May and June 1928 but due to the unforeseen extended occupation by the Walter West's *Sweeney Todd* unit, at the last minute space had to be found at the British International Pictures studio in Elstree. Mander's unit comprised cameraman Walter Blakeley, art director Charles Wilfred Arnold and assistant director Lionel Rich.

Gossip has suggested that during filming Miles Mander had an affair with Madeleine Carroll and, allegedly, Mander's wife turned up on the set to demand an explanation. A young Michael Powell, who was a stills photographer during filming at Elstree, took suggestions even further, claiming Mander's treatment of Carroll was appalling, if not sadistic and that he had no sense of shame. Seemingly he delighted in humiliating her in public, taking advantage of her innocence in explicit bathroom and bedroom sequences.[11]

Given a trade show in December 1928 (released 14th October 1929), *The First Born* was admired for its skilful direction, admirable acting and clever technical details but was thought to leave a 'nasty taste in the mouth'[12] through the unconvincing and sordid story that would not appeal to the general public – 'As a stage play it would attract a certain class who hunger for sensational sex stuff but as a screen play it fails to approach the category of good popular entertainment'.[13] However, it was thought to be 'well suited for continental trade'.[14] These collective puritanical comments condemned the picture to be of passing interest only in the UK, whereas in America it was described as 'a remarkable tour de force'.[15]

Miles Mander was thought to give a clever character study but lacked a personal attraction and qualities that could arouse the interest and sympathy of the audience. In portraying his unpleasant character he seemingly abandoned restraint with the result that his behaviour became unconvincing. Madeleine Carroll was regarded as the only redeeming feature. She had a most difficult emotional role to portray, one that did not always provoke sympathy, particularly when it came to her unwavering loyalty to her villainous husband and yet her charming personality enabled her to play the part with grace and genuine sincerity.

In 1930 there was a tribute by Paul Rotha in the book *The Film Till Now*. It was revealed that the picture had been poorly assembled and mounted by a cutter without the control of Mander, with the result that much of his original conception was not realised. The film had been conceived as a light commentary of married life flavoured by semi-political domestication with a subtlety of wit and Mander was seen as having a shrewd knowledge of feminine mentality, as seen in his expert handling of Madeleine Carroll. Rotha believed that had the film been well assembled to the original manuscript it would have been 'a unique instance of an English domestic tragi-comedy in the cinema.'[16]

With the BFI's restoration of the film in 2011, a new evaluation emerged and despite reservations made about the cutting and assembly in Rotha's earlier assessment, it was hailed as sophisticated, compelling, mesmerising and masterly. Full of stylistic flourishes, visual wit and clever photographic touches, Mander's skill was recognised as being because he thought cinematically and grouped and lit his characters, props and settings 'with an intelligent eye for telling design and emotional resonance'.[17] In one impressive and atmospheric setting various characters are introduced at a dinner table, each of them isolated by the surrounding dark but punctuated by the beautiful lighting of two lamps. The camera peers at each guest, dissolves and retreats, giving visual dynamism to dialogue without the use of endless intertitles. If his ingenuity illustrated what has been called from a modern perspective 'Hitchcock-like elements', could this have had more to do with Mander's own artistic creativity than any instruction derived from Alma Reville's influence on his directorial methods? Indeed, the film provided a fantastic showcase for his talents: 'Mander was arguably ahead of Hitchcock artistically by 1928 and who knows, given the right opportunities, could have been one of the great British directors'.[18]

18   GAINSBOROUGH'S HYBRID SILENT - TALKIES

During the spring of 1928, following the flotation of Gainsborough, and after producing four silent pictures: *A Light Woman*, *A South Sea Bubble*, *First Born* and *The Gallant Hussar*, Michael Balcon decided to introduce sound effects to subsequent productions illustrating his awareness of the growing interest in sound film production.

Gaumont-British, which now encompassed Gainsborough, had already made a bold move in the direction of encompassing sound technology before the impact of *The Jazz Singer*. In late 1926 they had formed a subsidiary company called British Acoustic, designed to explore and implement a provision for sound films using the synchronisation system of the Danish engineers Arnold Poulson Axel Peterson. Much experimentation had then followed at the Gaumont studio at Shepherd's Bush.

The system consisted of a simple attachment by means of which a separate sound film strip was run alongside the film, thus synchronising sound and picture. The sound recording device gave greater scope in pictorial production but also in photographing of tonal vibrations, securing greater volume for individual sounds recorded simultaneously. Rather prematurely, it was announced that the invention was foolproof and it was claimed to be 'potentially a most powerful contribution to the lower-priced sound film inventions'.[1]

One of the first public tests was used in the stage production of *Marigold*, produced at the Kingsway Theatre in April 1927. This was the first time that a sound film had been used for effects in a stage play. A delightful and delicate love story set in the early days of the young Queen Victoria, part of the story had a Scottish theme and here was inserted a British Acoustic soundtrack of a military band called the Buffs and the bagpipes of the Highland Light infantry, all recorded at Aldershot. It was a highly effective and not regarded as an obvious gramophone sound but extraordinary real and rich.

Through 1927 and 1928 more experimentation was being done and work began on providing synchronised sound effects for several 1928 Gainsborough productions, namely *The Wrecker*, *Balaclava*, *Lady of the Lake* and *The Crooked Billet*. At the same time British Acoustic projection apparatus was installed at the Capitol Theatre, the Shepherd's Bush Pavilion, Marble Arch Pavilion, the Palladium and Avenue Pavilion, along with fifteen regional cinemas. By the middle of 1930 they had installed their equipment in over 250 further theatres.

It was not plain sailing and numerous problems surfaced which delayed the release of the films earmarked for synchronisation. One reason was that the British Acoustic sound system used a separate film for the sound, which ran faster than the actual film and did not prove satisfactory. Eventually,

Gainsborough abandoned British Acoustic and opted for the Radio Corporation of America's (RCA) Photophone system which used sound on film but this delay meant that many of the 1928 films were not given a trade show until 1929 or even 1930.

The Wrecker

Michael Balcon had secured the film rights to Arnold Ridley's play, a railway thriller called *The Wrecker*, in April 1928. It was playing at the New Theatre in the West End at the time. A sequel to *The Ghost Train*, it was made as part of Gainsborough's arrangement with Fellner & Somlo in Berlin, but this time Michael Balcon brought over the German team of director Géza von Bolváry, cameraman Otto Kanturek and art director Oscar Friedrich Werndorff.

With leading players Carlyle Blackwell, Benita Hume and Gordon Harker, filming took place from July to August 1928, with interiors at the Islington studio and exteriors taken with the co-operation of one of the major railway companies. Harker was regarded as the finest character actor of his type and had come into films via Alfred Hitchcock's *The Ring* and *The Farmer's Wife* made at BIP, where he established himself as a real screen comedian and was then signed by Gainsborough. Significantly, a big feature of the production was the use of sound effects created by using the facilities of British Acoustic Films Limited.

Prepared by Angus McPhail, the script dealt with the competition between the rail and coach industries. The country is alarmed by many dreadful accidents and the public is transferring its patronage to road coaches. Sir Gervaise Bartlett (Winter Hall), director of the United Coast Railways, gets his nephew, the young official Roger Doyle (Joseph Striker) and his secretary, Mary Shelton (Benita Hume), to investigate. They are drawn together during this process and Mary – 'a sensible woman' – has aspirations of being a detective. Ambrose Barney (Carlyle Blackwell), the general manager, shows no sympathy with their investigations. The mysterious disasters continue and their unknown perpetrator becomes popularly known as 'The Wrecker'.

It is noted that following an accident the coach company always starts a nearby service. Sir Gervaise Bartlett suspects Ambrose Barney and his accomplice, Beryl Matchley (Pauline Johnson). In a dramatic shooting Barney has him murdered. Barney then tries to get Mary and Roger to travel on the *Rainbow Express* since he has arranged for it to be wrecked, but the girl goes alone, with Roger missing the train. Roger is warned by Beryl that the train will be wrecked. He rushes by motorcar to a signal box and manages to avert disaster. Beryl then reveals the identity of The Wrecker and the young couple gain sufficient evidence to convict him. Confronted, Barney bolts for a train marked for disaster. He is overpowered and the calamity averted but he throws himself out of the train and is killed.

Above: a scene from *The Wrecker* (1929)
Below and left: the nightclub scene from *The Wrecker* (1929) in the Islington Studio

Filming began on some of the interiors for *The Wrecker* in mid-July 1928 at the Islington studio, including a striking light-coloured drawing room and a vestibule set designed by Alan McNab, followed by an elaborate nightclub scene.

By mid-August the impressive exterior shots of the actual railway collision began. It took over a week's work involving 100 men and cost in excess of £6,000. For many years British Railways had refused to grant facilities to film-makers but Southern Railways finally relented and provided a mile or so of their track, a 4-4-0 express locomotive, four coaches and assistance in all areas, including interior shots of carriages, the interior of a London Bridge signal box and shots at Cliddesden and Waterloo stations.

The collision took place on Sunday, 19th August at Salter's Ash crossing on the Basingstoke to Alton branch line and the huge operation was co-ordinated by assistant director 'Shan' Balcon. Over 200 people arrived in cars and congregated in a specially erected marquee near Lasham Hill Farm, near Basingstoke, with views of the crossing below. Allegedly, twenty-two cameras, some concealed, filmed proceedings as an express train hurtled along at fifty miles an hour down a gradient towards a heavy lorry laden with sand bags, stuck in the middle of a level crossing. Driver and fireman James Brown had opened the throttle and jumped. With a deafening crash the train dashed through the gates, hit the lorry, demolished it, derailed and fell on its side, 100 yards further on, with the carriages jamming together at odd angles. A gush of flame from the fire box, volumes of steam and the wreck was complete. Several scenes were then taken of passengers escaping and after a while the carriages were sprinkled with paraffin and set on fire. A camera had been placed on the front of the buffer of the engine on automatic and was recovered and found intact with some perfect footage.

Filming was complete by late August 1928 and a trade show expected before the end of the year but in fact it was not until July 1929 that it was finally shown. The reason for this delay was simple: the British Acoustic sound system used a separate film for the sound effects, which ran faster than the actual film and did not prove satisfactory. Eventually, Gainsborough were forced to abandon the system and *The Wrecker* was synchronised by RCA in New York.[2]

When the trade show was finally given, *The Wrecker* was hailed as extraordinarily spectacular, thrilling and 'the most sensational outdoor film scene yet made',[3] containing some of the finest railway atmosphere seen on the screen. The synchronised sound effects were also thought excellent. However, the story was described as weak, complicated, banal and absurd –, melodramatic hotch-potch lacking in conviction and full of ridiculous incredibilities.

Over the years there had been many unkind criticisms of Southern Railway's shortcomings and its antiquated carriages but the company's directors had clearly seen this opportunity as a major PR exercise and the well-appointed internal accommodation was seen to great advantage.

Amusingly, in terms of the cast, it was thought that the star was the British railway system.[4] It was clear that few of the players carried any conviction, which was more to do with the fact that Bolváry had not been able to make more of the story. Joseph Striker as the young hero and Benita Hume as the girl secretary were both pleasing but the latter somewhat dull in comparison to Pauline Johnson, who looked markedly attractive and far more effective. Carlyle Blackwell as the villain gave a straightforward performance but over-emphasised his part and never suggested a man leading a kind of Jekyll and Hyde existence.

Shortly after filming had begun on *The Wrecker*, the entire company had a day out at the seaside for Gainsborough's second annual staff outing to Margate: 'I know of no studio where a cordial spirit between employers and employed exists to a greater degree than Gainsborough'.[5] Led by the company's leading lights – Michael Balcon, Carlyle Blackwell, George Hopton, Harold Boxall, Bill O'Bryen, Arthur Tavares, Otto Kanturek and a Berlin contingent presided over by George Gunn – nearly 100 people were transferred by coach from London and taken to the Grand Hotel, where lunch was served.

The Lady of the Lake

In August 1928 Gainsborough decided to work on a joint production with the American James A. Fitzpatrick, who was to direct *The Lady of the Lake* based on Walter Scott's 1810 poem. At first this association might appear strange but it must have been an attempt by Michael Balcon to ensure Gainsborough had another foot in the door with the developing interest in sound film-making.

Fitzpatrick had started his film career making comedy shorts for children in 1916, worked for Charles Urban creating more shorts, and then did the same under his own banner specialising in music history and travel documentaries. Previously he had created *The Famous Music Master Series*, which had met with success in the US and UK and was considered to be one of the foremost American directors of sound pictures and the pioneer producer of music films. In early 1928 he repeated this success with a series titled *Schubert's Centennial Series* (five shorts), based on the life of Franz Schubert, seemingly screened as a feature in Europe. He had used the sound on disc method for the Schubert series but *In a Music Shoppe* (1928) for Fox Movietone he used a sound on film system. In August 1928 he returned to Europe to make some of the first of twelve in a series of short *Music Travelogue* pictures, all with sound for Paramount. The aim was to record the sound during the photographing of action at old world landmarks and locales that inspired great masters to create musical masterpieces. *The Lady of the Lake* was another major project regarded as the first in a series of 'super-sound features'.[6]

A simple costume romantic drama, the screenplay was created by Angus Macphail and the story, set in the early part of the fifteenth century, concerned the feud between King James V and the family of Douglas. While hunting incognito in the Grampian Mountains, King James of Scotland (Percy Marmont) becomes separated from his fellow hunters and accepts the hospitality of Ellen Douglas, the lady of the lake (Benita Hume), claiming he is merely a lost nobleman. She takes him to the island retreat where her father (Douglas Payne) is hiding with a group of people exiled by the King in a colony headed by the powerful outlaw Rhoderick Dhu (Lawson Butt). When Dhu's men take the nobleman prisoner, the girl rescues him and he in turn presents her with a ring, which he says the King will recognise to grant her any wish in return for her service. The outlaw leader tries to force her father to consent to their marriage and when her fiancé, Malcolm Graeme (Haddon Mason), objects, he is banished from the colony and then captured by the King's men and taken to Stirling Castle. The girl's father offers to give himself up if the youth is released but the King's men decide to kill both of them. The girl goes to the castle to claim the favour of the ring and soon realises that the nobleman she has befriended is King James; he releases her father and the fiancé.

A scene from *The Lady of the Lake* (1931)

Fitzpatrick and his crew, consisting of cameramen Bert Dawley and Leslie Rowson along with the cast, left for Scotland in late August and were filming through September 1928, using the British Acoustic system for the sound effect recordings. The unit was based around Loch Katrine, not far from Sterling, and locations were chosen to display the native wildness of the country as it must have been in the period depicted by the original poem.

When Fitzpatrick completed his other activities he returned to New York in February 1929 with a final cut of the picture and began the task of synchronising the sound effects and music at the Victor studio, Camden, New Jersey. There was no spoken dialogue but the added sound accompaniment featured Nathaniel Shilkret's Victor Concert Orchestra playing typical Scottish melodies, along with a chorus of forty male voices and a troupe of bagpipe players. But something went wrong, presumably with the sound system, and by late 1929 the final editing, cutting and synchronisation was completed at the RCA Gramercy studio. However, more inexplicable delays continued and it was not until November 1930 that the film was finally released in the US and then in May 1931 in the UK.

Reaction in America was amazingly positive, describing it as well done, sincere, noteworthy and a fine production. There was huge praise for the beautiful scenery, sound effects and the excellent direction that was simple and direct, enhancing the charm of the idyllic story. The costumes, sets and photography were combined to make a film of real beauty and cinematic charm with a clear and smooth narrative showing 'dignity, restraint and beauty that the subject deserves'.[7] For some it was difficult to assess and categorise because 'nothing like it has ever been done before'[8] but overall it was believed that it would appeal to lovers of literature and children and class audiences. Benita Hume was thought to dominate the picture and was described as 'a beautiful heroine of real ability'.[9]

For UK critics although the story was presented adequately, it was thought to have little dramatic strength or punch, development was painfully slow, technique dated and the actors had few opportunities to excel but there was 'much to please and nothing to displease'.[10] Compensation came with the romanticism, picturesque scenery, well-chosen captions from Scott's poem and an appropriate and excellent musical score that produced an alluring 'freshness and delicacy'[11]. Percy Marmont was regarded as admirably suited as King James, playing with quiet dignity and kingly condescension but Benita Hume was seen as being far too theatrical.

It was a piece of art for its time but from a modern perspective *Lady of the Lake* does appear dated, dull and somewhat tedious with very lack-lustre performances from the whole cast, which not even the much-hailed Scottish scenery could redeem.

Balaclava

The next big Gainsborough production after *The Wrecker* was to be *Balaclava*. For several years this had been a project on many people's minds – in late 1927, for example, the American director Denison Clift had been suggesting that he would make a film with a British company (presumably Gainsborough) from an original story based on Tennyson's poem, *The Charge of the Light Brigade*. In January 1928 it was announced that Gainsborough would film a story by Boyd Cable, which would embody as its high spot the charge of the Light Brigade, but there was no mention of Denison Clift. Months dragged on and in July it was revealed that there had been postponements in production due to the Army training season and the requisite facilities would not be available until the autumn.

At last, in September 1928, *Balaclava* went into production with Maurice Elvey as director. Elvey had made his long-cherished ambition to produce this Crimea subject clear and was loaned to Gainsborough from Gaumont, ousting any previous arrangement with Clift. Like George Pearson, Elvey was one of the leading lights of the British film industry and had arrived in films via the stage, acting and directing in late 1913. He moved rapidly from one company to another, from Motography to B&C, the London Film Company, Ideal, Stoll and finally, Gaumont, where he had made some landmark British pictures with a flair for 'understanding the cinema public's taste'.[12]

Balaclava went through numerous name changes and became *The Jaws of Hell*, *The Charge of the Light Brigade* and *The Valley of Death* before reverting to the original *Balaclava*. Surprisingly, filming began in mid-September at Gaumont's studio in Lime Grove, Shepherd's Bush. Elvey's unit consisted of art directors Andrew Mazzei and Alex Vetchinsky, cameramen Percy Strong and James Wilson and assistant director David Lean. He also engaged Captain Oakes-Jones, a War Office authority on military pageantry, to advise on getting all aspects of military detail as authentic as possible. In addition to the actual filming, sound was also being recorded using the British Acoustic process and following the pattern of *The Wrecker* and *The Lady of the Lake*.

Elvey must have insisted that V. Gareth Gundrey (also working at Gaumont) should draft the script from Boyd Cable's big historical war story, said at the time to show that in some cases truth is stranger than fiction. Lt John Kennedy of the 93rd Highlanders (Cyril McLaglen) quarrels with Captain Gardener of the 14th Hussars (Miles Mander) over a question of discipline and the pair decide to settle their quarrel on the field of honour. A duel is arranged and Kennedy fires in the air but mysteriously, Gardener is mortally wounded in the back in such circumstances that incriminate Kennedy. Kennedy is falsely accused of the shooting by a rival officer, court-martialled for duelling and then dishonourably discharged from his regiment. Later, he joins the 17th Lancers (or the Glory Boys) as Trooper Kent and is posted as a cavalryman to the siege of Sebastopol during the Crimean War. While reconnoitering with a friend, he discovers a small farm and falls in love with a charming Scottish girl, Jean (Benita Hume), who is living there with her father. The intrusion of a Russian spy masquerading as a British soldier, whom he captures, enables Kennedy to pass on information of a surprise Russian attack and events lead up to the historic charge of the Light Brigade to take the Balaclava Heights. Kennedy is badly wounded but he is fortunate to survive and is proved innocent of Gardener's death by the confession of the actual murderer.

Beside his lead characters, Elvey cast appropriate incidental characters to be featured, such as Czar Nicholas I of Russia (Boris Ranevsky), Emperor Napoleon III of France, Queen Victoria (Marian Drada), Albert, the Prince Consort (Eugene Leahy), Lord Palmerston (Wallace Bosco), Lord Raglan (J. Fisher White), the Sultan of Turkey and the Earl of Cardigan. It was thought that the famous charge would be re-created at Aldershot.

Meanwhile it was reported that Elvey was having the time of his life directing this ambitious and spectacular story and some of the early scenes were an ornate set representing the Imperial Palace at St Petersburgh in 1854 and a Crimean town of great variety and animation, full of cosmopolitan inhabitants. In mid-October Elvey's unit moved to Salisbury Plain, where the military authorities had granted unique facilities for making some of the big battle scenes. In early November they moved to the 'Long Valley' at Aldershot for the filming of a reconstruction of the charge of the Light Brigade since this was deemed a fair representation of the Crimean battlefield itself. With considerable co-operation from the Army Council they employed up to 600 men from the 1st (King's) Dragoon Guards, the King's Own Yorkshire Light Infantry and the Royal Artillery, dressed in the richest variety of uniform of the period supplied by the costumier Willie Clarkson.

The battle proved a triumph of logistics and mounting and was filmed at the end of November. Captain Nolan (Harold Huth) was the only actor in the big charge; he was prevented from getting to Lord Cardigan with countermanding orders by a shell explosion that killed him soon after the charge began.

A scene from *Balaclava* (1930) showing Lord Regan (third from left) with his staff watching the famous battle of Balaclava. On left is Captain Nolan of the Hussars who gave the fatal order for the charge of the Light Brigade and next to him is General Airey
Courtesy Townly Cooke Collection

On the slopes a Russian ambushing army with archaic cannon waited patiently. The signal for the charge was given and the gallant horsemen, led by a convincing Earl of Cardigan, broke into a gallop. At the same time instant guns on the hillside flashed a cross-fire bombardment. Jets of flame appeared everywhere; the illusion of exploding shells complete, streams of grey-green smoke met the advancing brigade. Finally, to secure the aftermath there followed a bustle of khaki-clad Tommies, who dotted the course with uniformed dummy corpses and horses.

By the end of December Elvey had finished cutting and assembling, but like other productions this one was held up, presumably once again due to the British Acoustic sound effects.

Through 1929 reports continued to emerge that the film was to be altered and changed. Finally, in early 1930, dialogue and sound effects were added using the RCA Photophone system with some colour sequences, all under the direction of Milton Rosmer and a trade show was hastily given in April 1930. The reviews were overwhelming complimentary, full of praise for the stirring battle scenes, inspiring military pageant, good characterisation, lavish sets, period detail and dramatic story that combined to create 'a full-blooded patriotic melodrama crammed with popular interest',[13] which was a 'distinguished contribution to British film production'.[14]

The characterisation was thought to be excellent and Cyril McLaglen as Kennedy gave a strong portrayal that was breezy and effective. Miles Mander played the overpowering Gardener with venom and Benita Hume, who had only a small role as the heroine, nevertheless invested it with charm. One of the most important features of the film was the brilliant record of the immortal charge, which was described as thrilling and realistic and represented 'one of the finest spectacles yet seen on the screen'.[15] The dialogue was clear and decisive while the realistic sound effects and incidental music helped to create atmosphere and greatly added to the authenticity.

The Crooked Billet

In the summer of 1928 negotiations were in progress for Gainsborough to acquire the screen rights of the West End stage success *The Crooked Billet* by Dion Titheradge, which was to be the subject of Adrian Brunel's next film. Production started with casting at the end of September and Brunel explained that he 'was blessed with Madeleine Carroll's beauty, Carlyle's competence and generosity and Gordon Harker's great skill and good company.'[16] The project was also interesting in that it featured Miles Mander alongside Madeleine Carroll following their escapades together during the making of *The First Born*. Filming began in early October at the Islington studio, running through November with a unit that comprised cameraman Claude MacDonnell. Once again there were to be undisclosed British Acoustic sound effects.

Scenes from *The Crooked Billet* (1930)
Courtesy J.W. Mitchell Collection / Brian Twist

Described as a conventional comedy, crook melodrama, *The Crooked Billet* was adapted for the screen by Angus MacPhail and told the story of Sir William Easton (Frank Goldsmith), the head of CID, who conceals valuable documents in a village inn called The Crooked Billet. Dietrich Hebburn (Carlyle Blackwell), an international crook, is determined to secure the documents and carries Easton off to the Inn. He also seizes his daughter Joan (Madeleine Carroll) and his son Philip (Kim Peacock). Guy Merrow (Miles Mander), a young detective and intelligent member of the CID who is in love with Joan, arrives on the scene and a fierce battle of wits ensues between Merrow and Hebburn. Of course the Law triumphs and Hebburn makes a dramatic exit from a life of crime in an exciting underground duel.

Brunel took some striking scenes included a realistic eerie-looking old inn and an elaborate set of a smart nightclub called The Chez Maurice. Here, an amusing scene was enacted as 100 people danced to the Billy Trytel orchestra, the maître d'hotel appeared and spluttered in broken English that the police had arrived and everyone rushed to the exits but they were all pushed back by policemen.

Shortly after the picture was finished, in late 1928 Adrian Brunel's year-long contract with Gainsborough was over. Another picture was owing to him as it was a three-picture deal but he only got paid per picture and was not paid for a third. Brunel was short of money and so engaged a solicitor and there was an exchange of letters with Gainsborough. Eventually Michael Balcon settled out of court and paid all of Brunel's expenses. In the meantime Carlyle Blackwell (a director of Gainsborough) lent him money to see him through but there were repercussions and as a result, Brunel did not work for almost a year.

Like *The Wrecker, The Lady of the Lake* and *Balaclava* there were delays in completing *The Crooked Billet* due to the complexities of adding sound effects via British Acoustics and eventually dialogue was added to part of the film via the RCA system. Finally, a trade show was given in March 1930, with the film being released through Ideal rather than W&F, but nevertheless all part of the new Gaumont-British family. It was admired as good entertainment, with a good tempo, splendid acting, charming love interest, rich humour and 'a full measure of thrills and excitement',[17] including hand-to-hand fighting, drugged drink, an abducted girl and various exciting clashes. However, the direction was thought to be a little laboured at times, with the result that some of the more sensational scenes were unduly prolonged.

Despite the fact that it lacked 'the briskness and smoothness of American pictures of this type', it was 'refreshingly English in atmosphere'.[18] Carlyle Blackwell was true to the tradition of old melodrama and made a convincing and first-rate villain. Madeleine Carroll was charming, while the suave Miles Mander acted with ease and conviction but the acting honours went to Gordon Harker, who gave an amusing study of the villain's cockney henchman.

The opening reel was silent but 75% of the picture featured sound dialogue, which was strange. Had the film had been released as a 100% talkie it was thought that it would have been a far better booking proposition. Even so, the dialogue element was seen as clearly delivered and recorded.

The Return of the Rat

To the great delight of many, it was announced in August 1928 that Graham Cutts would return to Gainsborough to start work on a third Rat film at the beginning of October. The idea for the story was drafted by Ivor Novello and then adapted for the screen by Angus MacPhail, with Edgar C. Middleton. Called *The Return of the Rat*, it followed the wild adventures of the Rat among the Demi-Monde and the Parisian underworld and once again featured the old favourites, Zelia and Mere Colline.

Having married the famous beauty Zelie (Isabel Jeans), the Rat Pierre (Ivor Novello) has deserted his old haunts. He visits the famous Longchamp races with his wife who despises him and she flirts with Henri de Verrat (Bernard Nedell), a wealthy race horse owner who has been blackmailed by the glamorous Yvonne (Gladys Frazin). Zelia loses a big bet and is unable to repay Henri but agrees to visit him in his apartment. Pierre decides to visit his former friends of the Underworld at the White Coffin Café. It is now ruled by Morel (Gordon Harker), who covets Lisette (Mabel Poulton), a protégé of Mère Colline (Marie Ault), owner of the White Coffin. Lisette falls in love with Pierre and he fights the bully. Later, Pierre discovers his wife in Henri's arms and in a duel he is dangerously wounded and then taken to the café and tended by Lisette. He determines to disappear from society by allowing a report to circulate that he is dead. When Zelie's engagement is announced to Henri, Pierre decides to visit the masked ball in celebration to once again confront Henri. Morel is jealous of Pierre's popularity and also decides to go to the ball with the intention of killing him. During a fight the lights are switched off and Zelie is wounded. Pierre is suspected and forced to flee. Lisette is prepared to save him from the police by sacrificing herself to Morel but at the last moment the guilt is brought home to Morel.

Cutts' unit consisted of cameraman Roy Overbaugh, assistant director L.B. Lestocq, art director Alan MacNab and costume designer Gordon Conway. Conway worked in conjunction with production head 'Shan' Balcon and the rest of the team. She was already familiar with Cutts' style but watched the previous two films before her designs evolved. Besides creating all the outfits for the key players, the gowns had to follow the smartest Paris fashions and she also helped to cast mannequins and extras for all the other spectacular scenes. She worked closely with Bill O'Bryen, publicity manager, who was known for his clever promotional schemes and he peppered press releases with costume tid-bits and stories about Conway herself. For example, in a big feature in the *The Bioscope*[19] she outlined various key elements concerning the role of the designer and her own objectives, stressing the importance of considering the appropriateness of clothes expressing correct character and the complexities of using colour and particular fabrics as there was a vast difference in the effect obtained by the camera when photographing certain colours and materials.

Filming commenced at the beginning of October with Cutts and his crew visiting Paris to take appropriate exteriors at the Longchamp races and scenes in

Montmartre outside the Moulin Rouge. By the beginning of November, he was back in London and filming interiors at the Islington studio well into January 1929, starting with a huge set representing the lawn and grand stand at Longchamp, complete with paddock, track and stables. The Grand Stand was the centre of action, where Zelie flirted with Henri and lost a big bet, placing herself in his power. In early December they were shooting the big duelling scene and both Ivor Novello and Bernard Nedell were shown the moves and trained by a duelling expert. While rehearsing, Novello suffered a minor wound. Slightly later, Cutts filmed various scenes at the White Coffin Café. One of the women engaged in the crowd scenes asked if she could take an hour off at lunchtime so she could get married! Cutts and the crew arranged to shoot the scenes so there was a bigger interval than usual and had a very attractive wedding present ready when she returned.

Ivor Novello in *The Return of the Rat* (1929)

In mid-December, Cutts was filming some unique comedy scenes with Harry Terry and Scotch Kelly playing a couple of cockney tourists in Paris. Knock-kneed and cheeky, Scotch did everything wrong and Terry spent all his time putting him right, in an almost typical routine made famous by Laurel and Hardy. The typically British humour was reminiscent of the old Fred Karno School and Harry Terry had been a member of the troupe with Charlie and Syd Chaplin.

Top: filming *The Return of the Rat* (1929) as Graham Cutts inspects the chorus girls

Bottom: a scene from *The Return of the Rat* (1929) with
Ivor Novello and Mabel Poulton at left

At the beginning of January, Cutts began work on the big masked ball sequence that began with a troupe of dancers emerging through showers of bubbles in charming and effectively simple costumes. They wore headdresses of black and white ostrich plumes, breastplates and trunks of dazzling sequins; patterns were painted in black on their bare flesh. Gordon Conway described how the 'costumes' were conceived. Originally the patterns were to be painted with gold paint on the body but they could not find a non-toxic gold or silver paint so they had to use greasepaint and simplified the design. Dressed in smocks and armed with plenty of brushes, Conway and Alan McNab, the art director, set to work and laboriously painted the girls one by one before the scene commenced.

Cutts followed this sequence with the set of a jolly little side street in Montmartre with a newspaper shop on the corner, a florist, second-hand art dealer and confectioners and opposite a drab-looking pension, electrical supply shop and the Café Doree. Outside the café were groups of people seated and drinking. Shopkeepers leaned in their doorways, a cyclist tinkling his bell swerved around the corner, an errand boy dodged in and out and there was a scrap between a couple of dogs. A Renault pulled up outside the White Coffin Café and a cloaked figure stepped out and disappeared down the steps into the café. Then a police inspector and four gendarmes descended and a crowd gathered. Shortly afterwards Novello emerged, struggling in the arms of the police, while behind him his friends surged, shouting and gesticulating until they made a mad rush and overpowered the gendarmes, enabling the Rat to escape. They gave a cheer and vanished for none were anxious to incur the wrath of the Law. The props for the window displays were all authentic and had been brought from Paris when they did the exterior shots – 'such details cannot possibly be all noticed on the screen, yet Cutts insists on them for they create atmosphere'.[20]

By mid-January filming was complete and the trade show for *The Return of the Rat* was given in May 1929 (released 24th February 1930). It was received with lukewarm enthusiasm and was seen as following closely in the style of the previous Rat stories being 'equally sugary and impossible'.[21] Although there were some exciting adventures Cutts was hindered by a very slight story that was weak in dramatic values, making his direction strictly conventional and without imagination: 'the commonplace lines on which the story developed gives the entire picture an atmosphere of artificiality'.[22] Perhaps part of the reason may have been that many of the characters of the smart set at Longchamp were thought to be 'unsavoury types' and the dubious moral tone made 'the spectator view their proceedings with an unsympathetic eye'.[23]

The appearance of the duo Harry Terry and Scotch Kelly was somewhat incongruous and only provided some cheap humour, which was not admired, suggesting 'Shepherd's Bush rather than Longchamp'.[24] Although there were some luxurious apartment interiors, the settings were regarded as ordinary and the masked ball looked as if it was staged on a somewhat meagre scale. Equally, although Conway's outfits for Isabel Jeans reflected her earlier glamour in previous Rat films, the costumes for what were intended to be other well-dressed attendees at Longchamp and the cabaret troupe were not exactly eye-catching or effective.

Undoubtedly the star of the show was the attractive Ivor Novello but his performance was criticised by some as being indifferent as he tended to play himself rather than demonstrate any empathy with the character of the Rat. But others felt he was a commanding figure animated by the spirit of revenge and his reckless ferocity kept interest alive throughout.

However, he did appear more content playing the suave society figure at the beginning of the film rather than the Rat of old. Mabel Poulton's role was a simple one and she worked hard to make the underworld sweetheart vivacious and true to type and at the end had an opportunity for a display of emotional intensity. In marked contrast was the glamorous and dangerous Isabel Jeans in the unpleasant role of the wife. For some she was inanimate and ordinary, while for others she was excellent. Marie Ault as Mère Colline was as usual, the colourful and amusing bartender.

Shortly after the trade show, Gainsborough decided to revise the film and add sound effects and dialogue sequences using the British Acoustic system. This was accomplished at the Wembley studio of British Talking Pictures in June 1929, complete with a special musical score by Billy Trytel and his band, who had recently returned from America where he had done something similar for Victor Saville's *Kitty*. However, the process was not an easy one for Mabel Poulton and she was extremely nervous. She was in the projection room at the Wembley studio with Bill O'Bryen when she heard herself on the screen for the first time: 'Oh surely that's not how I really sound!' she wailed and burst into tears.[25] In contrast, Isabel Jeans refused to do her talking parts until she was absolutely satisfied that her voice was suited to the medium. She underwent various tests but she shone, no doubt due to her stage training.

When the sound version of *The Return of the Rat* was screened in late July it was viewed as having no ascertainable advantage over the original other than Ivor Novello's voice, which of course many would want to hear. For some critics this was not enough and generally the sound dialogue, although clear, was too deliberate and each artist 'was determined that people in the next street should hear every word'.[26] The silent version was thought better and described as a 'highly coloured drama of the cheapest order' but it has entertainment value whereas the talkie version was 'merely annoying'.[27] For others the Longchamp races, the duel and the cabaret gained immensely from the inclusion of sound effects. The introduction of dialogue, particularly with the quarrel between The Rat and his faithless wife (Isabel Jeans), his welcome by the café owner (Marie Ault) and the love passages with the Rat's new sweetheart (Mabel Poulton), were also thought to be noteworthy and advantageously devised. As a silent film, it was a loosely strung series of exciting situations but now with dialogue it had become a grimly realistic drama 'transmuted from lead to silver and occasionally gold'.[28]

After completing work on the silent version of *The Return of the Rat*, Cutts was contemplating directing a new and more intensive version of *The Wonderful*

Story, which had been his first film in 1922. The intention was to make a talkie with dialogue written by A. Neil Lyons as a Graham Cutts' Picture produced by British Talking Pictures in association with Gainsborough. It was to be filmed at the Wembley studio of British Talking Pictures in the summer of 1929 but if the film was ever made, it was not released. That was the end of Cutts' association with Gainsborough and it would be a while before he made another picture.

Taxi For Two

Following the departure of Adrian Brunel, Michael Balcon appointed a new director in the form of the Hungarian Alexander Esway in late 1928. His real name was Sandor Ezry Esway and he was educated for the Diplomatic Service in Hungary and served in the Hungarian military. This background was later admired, tongue-in-cheek, since there was definite 'room for "diplomatic" film directors' in London.[29] During the post-war turmoil he was arrested by revolutionaries and was sentenced to fifteen years but got out of prison in fifteen days, an accomplishment thought to be equally invaluable for completing films on time. For some reason Esway's thoughts turned to the movies and he went to Hollywood, where he became technical adviser to Erich von Stroheim but then went back to Europe and moved to Berlin in 1922. There he joined UFA, directing and writing scenarios before visiting London in late 1923, where he married Hedwig Heyer, a German national. Shortly after the marriage the couple visited New York and presumably returned to Germany before moving to London in late 1928.

Alexander Esway

Described as 'a pleasant young man with enthusiasm and some charmingly quaint English expressions'[30] he was signed to make *Taxi For Two*, based on his own story and scenario about a shop girl and her two admirers. Starring Mabel Poulton, Gordon Harker and John Stuart (who had made an earlier appearance in Alfred Hitchcock's *The Pleasure Garden* and had now become one of the most sought after male leads), filming took place at the Islington studio from mid-January into February 1929.

It was a simple story about little Molly (Mabel Poulton), a sales girl who finds a valuable necklace, which she returns to Lady Devenish and gains a reward. She also meets her son Jack (John Stuart), who poses as a chauffeur in order to cultivate her friendship. His good looks and refined manners win her heart. Molly buys a taxi with the reward and persuades Jack to drive it. Albert (Gordon Harker), an elderly shop assistant, is also in love with Molly and not happy when he learns of her affair. She treats her devoted admirer with scant courtesy and in a moment of jealousy, Albert reveals the truth about Jack to Molly. At first she is annoyed but it is not long before the young lovers are happily reconciled.

One of the first big scenes was filmed in Harrods by cameraman James Wilson, with Molly the shop girl and a convincing but spurious floorwalker played by Claude Maxted helping a querulous customer look through an enormous pile of silk stockings. As things get out of hand Jack rescues Molly from a scolding. Mabel Poulton's dressing room was a trying-on cabinet in the men's underwear department. Esway's fractured English put everyone in a good humour, especially a number of real Harrods' girls who had been pressed into service. Bill O'Bryen, Gainsborough's publicity manager, was in attendance to watch proceedings with a cluster of journalists.

Esway completed *Taxi For Two* by mid-February and in March it was announced that he would begin work on his second film, *Soho*, and that, perhaps not surprisingly, filming would take place in the streets between Shaftesbury Avenue and Oxford Street. *Soho* was designed to be a talkie with sound effects and special music written by the famous musical comedy composer Vivian Ellis, whose numbers had scored such a success in the stage shows *By the Way* (1925) and *Mr Cinders* (1929). Although the project was kept going throughout 1929, it never materialised.

The trade show for *Taxi For Two* was delayed and it was decided instead to add dialogue sequences. This was begun at the end of August 1929 but the American director Denison Clift was brought in to work on the speech sequences. Finally, the trade show of *Taxi For Two* was given in November 1929 and it was described as being a 'bright innocuous trifle with a simple, yet appealing Cinderella-like theme and amusing cockney humour'.[31]

The picture was partly constructed to display the talent of Mabel Poulton 'in the particular line of comedy in which she always shines and her impersonation of the self-reliant slangy little cockney employed as a salesgirl is quite up to the level of her previous performances'.[32] Vivacious and in turn peppery and affectionate, her cockney lisp made the dialogue more amusing.

Further good characterisation was provided by the two male leads: John Stuart as Jack was an excellent lover and effectively conducted himself in a gentlemanly manner, while Gordon Harker gave a clever characterisation as Albert, winning sympathy as the sorely tried but faithful admirer.

The story was seen as feeble in quality and much padding had been applied, some of which was superfluous. There were too many unconvincing incidents, starting with Molly's neglect to hand over the necklace to the office for lost properties and then the subsequent ploy of her slipping on a banana skin, picking up a *Daily Telegraph* and seeing an advertisement offering a £250 reward for the necklace. Credulity was further stretched when Molly went to retrieve the reward by pushing aside the butler, walking straight into Lady Devenish's boudoir and being immediately handed a cheque while the susceptible son falls in love at first sight. Despite these flaws, Esway made the most of the possibilities presented by the novelettish story and gave the simple love theme full play. The cockney humour and the good cast 'succeeded in unfolding the picture in a manner that should prove diverting to the masses'.[33]

The City of Play

In addition to signing Alexander Esway, Michael Balcon also engaged the celebrated American director Denison Clift, who was a great friend of Graham Cutts and had 'a strong sense of story values, being an author and dramatist of proved success'.[34]

Denison Clift

His appointment was of major significance since he had a tried-and-tested legacy of directing many successful British films and his stature in the British film industry was considerable. Born in San Francisco and educated at Stanford University, Clift entered Hollywood in 1917 on the literary side of the business and was initially attached to Cecil B. DeMille and Thomas Ince before joining Fox in 1919 as production editor. In this capacity he also wrote scenarios and produced several films. In the summer of 1920 he made a trip to Europe and liked it so much that he returned in late 1921, signing a contract with Ideal to direct a series of pictures in London. He was determined to make these films the premier pictures of Great Britain and was 'to be given all the resources and money to produce the highest standard of workmanship'.[35]

Clift became an early advocate of progressing the British film industry forward and was convinced that Britain had 'every resource and every opportunity to place her in the forefront of world picture production'. He also believed that stories with a British temperament, atmosphere and viewpoint should be made in Britain to preserve their original strength and flavour, adding: 'British technique must advance so that the standard of production here will make the English versions of such subjects unsurpassed in the international market.'[36]

Over the next three years he made eleven pictures, his last being *The Loves of Mary Queen of Scots* (1923), starring Fay Compton, before returning to Hollywood and another contract with Fox.

After a three-year stay, he returned to the UK in late 1927 and initially worked for BIP and made *Paradise* (1928) with Betty Balfour, before joining Gainsborough. Clift's first Gainsborough production, *The City of Play*, was based on an original story he had written about a villainous hypnotist who makes a girl under his influence give a nightly parachute dive until his death releases her from his spell. It was originally set in the Coney Island pleasure ground but transferred to a Viennese setting, evincing a pseudo-continental atmosphere.

At the end of January 1929, Clift and art director Alan MacNab travelled to the Continent to seek out locations and ideas for atmosphere in Berlin's Luna Park and the famous Prater amusement park in Vienna, stopping at Prague and Dresden. At the latter, there was a disagreement with the authorities; police and customs officers confiscated their cameras and the contents, saying that the negatives must be developed and viewed before they could release them.

Back in London casting was complete by the end of February. Initially, the female lead was to be played by Mabel Poulton but instead the part was allocated to Chili Bouchier, an 'interesting little exotic British girl'[37], giving her the biggest opportunity she had received to date. Filming began at the Islington studio in early February and continued through May, with a scenario completed by Denison Clift. Ariel (Chili Bouchier) is a timid little trapeze artiste and dancing girl in a continental circus.

One of the sensations of the show is when someone leaps by parachute from a lofty ladder. In performing this, a man is killed and the proprietor has difficulty in finding someone new to do it. Tambarini (Lawson Butt), an Italian member of the troupe, offers to find someone. He exercises his hypnotic powers over Ariel and under his influence he gets her to jump from the tower. Richard Von Rolf (Patrick Aherne), a young Austrian officer, falls in love with her but realises something is wrong and tries to induce her to leave the show with him. Tambarini surprises them and puts Ariel in a trance, during which she assures Von Rolf that she is not in love with him and he sends her off to do a sensational parachute jump. He fights Von Rolf, leaving him wounded on the floor. Emerging from the dressing room he is confronted by a tame boa, let loose by jealous snake charmer called Zelah, a former lover of Tambarini. He is frightened to death and so releases Ariel and the wounded hero Von Rolf saves her.

PAT AHERNE

LAWSON BUTT

OLAF HYTTEN

CHILI BOUCHIER

JAMES CAREW

ANDREWS ENGELMAN

LEILA DRESNER

The City of Play

WRITTEN & DIRECTED BY DENISON CLIFT
A Gainsborough Picture distributed by W.& F.

Two scenes from *The City of Play* (1929)
Above: Chili Bouchier
Below: the Viennese fairground scene

A huge set was constructed to feature a big Viennese fairground with freaks and sideshows; a vast cavernous mouth of a giant was the entrance hall. The script called for Leila Dresner (who played Zelah, the snake charmer) to lure Lawson Butt up to her room, let loose the snake and leave it to strangle him. Denison Clift wanted the largest snake in the country and so via British Instructional Films, who have the sole rights to film animals from the zoo, he loaned a nineteen-foot boa and its keepers for the part. Lawson Butt hated snakes and this particular boa was fierce and hissed so loud, it could be heard all over the studio. The sequence had to be filmed six or seven times but once complete, everyone let out a large cheer!

In another scene there was mild panic when an accident occurred. The floor of the studio collapsed under the weight of Mary, a twenty-ton elephant, who fell ten feet into the cellar dock, together with a dozen people. Luckily no one was injured and Mary was unruffled and winking with docile enjoyment. A gangplank was quickly put into position and the calm and collected elephant strolled back up to the floor level. Denison Clift announced a break for lunch so the floor could be mended before the retake could be made. In early April Clift took his unit to Paris to film some special thrilling scenes of a parachute descent from the Eiffel Tower that formed the latter part of the picture.

With the silent film completed, it was decided to add some dialogue written by Angus MacPhail towards the end of the film in August 1929, making *The City of Play* part-talkie, and a trade show was given in November 1929. Although it was thought to have a popular touch and the circus scenes added interest, it was perceived as being an unsophisticated melodrama that was neither convincing nor interesting, with a thin story that represented an 'average proposition for the undiscriminating'.[38] Despite the deficiencies of the plot, Clift did not make the most of the opportunities presented and his characterisation was often thought to be ineffectual. The intrusion of sound towards the end was also viewed as bewildering and it was thought that the picture would have been better as just a silent, which was originally intended. Most of the cast failed to distinguish themselves. Chili Bouchier was not given much opportunity and although she was attractive and clearly showed ability, she lacked the charm and experience to lend much interest. Pat Aherne was a weak and uninspired hero and the only good performance came from Lawson Butt as Tambarini.

Although Clift's debut for Gainsborough was given only a lukewarm reception he was to direct a second picture and in the summer of 1929 he went on a trip to Nice and Venice to study suitable locations for a new talkie, which he was preparing in script form. However, by the autumn he was in New York for the opening of his new play called *Scotland Yard* and then moved to Hollywood, where it was revealed he was to direct talkies. Later, in the spring of 1930, he was signed to Paramount to write and direct. His contract with Gainsborough was clearly abandoned.

19 JOURNEY'S END AND GRAPPLING WITH THE PROBLEM OF SOUND

The period 1927–30 has been described as the most momentous in British films, with the 'Quota Act', the foundations of big-scale film combines, including Gaumont-British, and then the advent of the talkies. Like all major film companies Gainsborough went through enormous transition. Despite the flotation of 1928, things were not exactly easy for a number of reasons. One issue was that Michael Balcon did not enjoy the continuity of repeatedly working with specific directors. With the departure of Graham Cutts and Alfred Hitchcock in 1927, he used a variety of directors such as Géza von Bolváry, Miles Mander, T. Hayes Hunter, James A. Fitzpatrick, Maurice Elvey, Alexander Esway and Denison Clift but none of them stayed long, with the exception of Hayes Hunter, who made two features and Adrian Brunel, who made five features before leaving in late 1928. Perhaps, with the return of Graham Cutts in the summer of 1928, Balcon hoped he would go back to the stability of earlier days, but this proved elusive.

When Victor Saville rejoined Balcon at Gainsborough in late 1929 it must have been a blessing.

The Landscape of the Talkies

By far the biggest challenge for Gainsborough Pictures was the advent of the talkies. Michael Balcon later admitted, 'Frankly, we were all caught on the hop – and I am afraid, slow on the uptake as well. It is hard to believe now that there were people who thought this novelty of talking films would never oust the silent film.'[1] From the outset, anything to do with sound film changed rapidly and unexpectedly from week to week. Opinions and comments went out of date as soon as they had been aired and confusion about everything endured for a while, but one thing was clear: Europe and Britain proceeded more slowly and conservatively in adjusting to the new conditions than America and the British trade were largely sceptical of the permanency of the talking innovation. For example, in May 1929, *Picturegoer* wrote of 'The Peril of the Talkies' and said, 'It is of course inconceivable for several reasons that the silent film will die – at any rate for many years,'[2] while *The Stage*, referring to the talkies, observed, 'The spreading of the craze has not altered our opinion that talking pictures are more or less a passing novelty.'[3]

But not everyone agreed with these sentiments. When J.C. Williams of World Wide Pictures visited London in May 1929, he announced that the silent film was dead. He derided the idea that synchronisation of musical accompaniment with the film would make silent pictures any more acceptable, and made it clear that what was needed was full dialogue pictures. He also asserted that the confusion over the different sound systems would be resolved in favour of the sound on film system.

Herbert Wilcox was also more enthusiastic. In late 1928 he went to Hollywood to investigate the possibilities of sound and made the talkie *Black Waters* (1929), directed by Marshall Neilan. On his return to London he declared: 'It will be five years before the talking picture nears perfection and ten before it is anywhere near life-like.'[4] But despite the flaws he firmly believed that talkies would sweep the field.[5]

Throughout 1928, and particularly 1929, the talkies caused much unsettlement, especially for shareholders of the various film companies, and even Gaumont-British witnessed the temporary decline of their shares. The cost of installing new equipment for film studios and cinemas was considerable. Sir Oswald Stoll observed, 'The sound picture innovation and the incursion of high finance materially disturbed the entertainment situation.'[6]

It was no surprise that the change to sound was difficult because everything was in a state of flux and complicated by a variety of different systems of recording and reproducing equipment that made choice difficult. In terms of recording, the distinction between the rival systems of sound on film and disc was the main cause of confusion and experimentation. The sound on film systems gave weak or poor sound and although discs gave better definition, they were more difficult to synchronise.

The major American systems that rose to prominence were the sound on film system used by RCA's Photophone, Western Electric, which ran both the Warner's Vitaphone separate disc system and the Fox-Movietone sound on film system. In the UK Phonofilm, also a sound-on-film system, was acquired by British Talking Pictures in late 1928 and the British Acoustic system, of Gaumont-British, ultilised a soundtrack on a separate strip of film which had to be synchronised with the actual film strip, which proved cumbersome.

RCA and Western Electric registered companies in Britain to market their equipment and in June 1929, Western Electric sent a first group of fifty engineers to the UK to begin a whirlwind installation campaign to put their system into 130 British cinemas. The British Phonofilm system was fitted in forty cinemas by late 1928, and by the middle of 1930 British Acoustic had installed their equipment in over 250 theatres, but eventually the majority of cinemas were wired by Western Electric. At the same time the choice of recording system stabilised in 1930 in favour of sound on film. As a result, Western Electric abandoned separate discs in December 1931 and British Acoustic abandoned using a separate sound film strip in December 1929.

Balcon noted that in 1928 he, like many others, was deceived into believing that sound was a passing phase: 'We hastened our financial doom by making *A South Sea Bubble, The Firstborn, The Wrecker, The Crooked Billet* and *Balaclava*, which even as silent films were not particularly distinguished.'[7] In fact, this is not entirely accurate because being part of the Gaumont-British combine, he was aware of British Acoustic, a Gaumont subsidiary, and their efforts to develop synchronised sound. And, as we have seen, Gainsborough were the first to attempt to use the system to add sound to some of their pictures in 1928, starting with *The Wrecker* (1929) and then *The Lady of the Lake* (1931), *Balaclava* (1930) and *The Crooked Billet* (1930). This process was a difficult one and clearly the system faltered since all of these pictures were delayed.[8]

The flaws in the British Acoustic system were amply described by Adrian Brunel, who made two sound shorts for Gainsborough called *In a Monastery Garden* and *Life on H.M.S. Rodney* using the British Acoustic system, which did not turn out well. At the premiere of *In a Monastery Garden* in late 1928, Brunel said: 'The sound blared out – and it was out of synchronisation, being about five seconds behind the picture. The effect was excruciating.'[9] Interestingly, by mid-1929 British Acoustic must have solved some of its earlier problems because it was used to synchronise the sound effects and dialogue in Cutts' *The Return of the Rat* and for Maurice Elvey's full talkie *High Treason* (a Gaumont production). But most of the films in transition from silent to sound were synchronised using the RCA system, which Gainsborough adopted following British International Pictures and many others, although Herbert Wilcox at B&D equipped his studio with Western Electric.

Output in 1930 showed some interesting statistics, proving the fact that talkies were overtaking silents. Of the 717 films given a trade show, 524 were talkies and only 193 were silent. Of these only eighty-two were British talkies (mostly sound on film), comprising fifty-six made with RCA, ten with Western Electric and ten with British Acoustic.

The first two British talkies shown in the UK were actually made in America by Herbert Wilcox with *Black Waters* (trade show May 1929) and Victor Saville with *Kitty* (trade show June 1929). The first true British talkie was Alfred Hitchcock's *Blackmail* (trade show June 1929), followed by Maurice Elvey's *High Treason* (trade show August 1929).

One major benefit of the rush to make talkies was that the British had the unique asset of many actors and actresses who spoke well, often due to their stage training. Soon it would not be enough just to have intelligent 'good lookers' but they would also have to demonstrate good recording voices. When J.C. Williams of World Wide Pictures visited London in May 1929 he said that there was a definite vogue in America for the English voice. The American director Denison Clift also thought that London was in an enviable position regarding actors and actresses who had presence and the command of pure speech: 'England boasts many of the finest artists of the speaking stage and has unlimited talent to draw upon for the talkies...'[10]

There were of course other concerns. The Quota Act was meant to revitalise the industry but now, because of the transition to sound, there had been a substantial drop in the number of pictures in production as producers struggled to make structural adjustments in order to create talkies. Studio plans and personnel were severely dislocated due to the shortage of recording equipment, delays in transit, installation and experimentation and consequently all production activity was stalled. The commercial politics of production had become distinct against the creative artistry of making entertainment – 'the imposition of talkies is diverting the studio brains into the complex questions of effective apparatus and the clash of the enormous financial interests which aim at control of the means of presenting films. Picture making, it seems, has become a secondary consideration'.[11]

Another important factor of the introduction of dialogue into film was the need for scripts to be far more detailed, creative and carefully prepared. For some this was already part of their skill set – for example, Victor Saville had 'always been an intelligent minority of directors who have always taken great pains to have a carefully written script before starting to shoot'.[12] Gainsborough, well aware of the importance of this new skill, engaged the services of novelist A. Neil Lyons to provide the conversational footage for *The Return of the Rat* (1929) and other talkies.

Despite the unsettling nature of the introduction of sound, by mid-1929 it was acknowledged that there was 'a great deal of work being done in getting talkie studios into being, grafting talking sequences into silent pictures and preparing for a steady stream of talking films this autumn in England'.[13]

Gainsborough's Global Footing and The Installation of Sound

Even though the diversion of what to do with the new sound technology took up considerable time and effort, Michael Balcon was energetically involved in some interesting new distribution deals that firmly put Gainsborough on a global footing. In early 1929 contracts representing £30,000 worth of foreign business were signed, including an agreement with Franco Films to distribute in France and Belgium, the International Pictures Company of Shanghai for China, Hong Kong and Macau, Kinema Limited for South Africa, Peter Fraser of Koba for Japan, the Anglo-American film Corporation for most of South America and British and Dominion Film Proprietary Limited for Australasia. Other agreements were placed for Germany, Austria, Hungary, Czechoslovakia, Yugoslavia, Balkan states, Norway, Sweden, Denmark, Finland and other important distribution deals were being negotiated for the US, Canada, India, Burma and Ceylon.

Next, Gainsborough entered an arrangement with World Wide Pictures, the new American distribution company under the aegis of directors J.D. Williams and John Maxwell. World Wide were to distribute all present Gainsborough product through the US and Canada (including *Downhill*, *Easy Virtue* and *A South Sea Bubble*). *The Constant Nymph* had been purchased by United Motion Picture Producers Limited, the forerunner to World Wide, but since the Hays Office failed to remove a ban, the contract was terminated.

Further, on a trip to Berlin in March 1929 with other executives of Gaumont-British, Balcon signed a deal with his German partners Fellner & Somlo to make two Anglo-German subjects. The first, *Bride 68* (original title *Das Land ohne Frauen*), was directed by Carmine Gallone with Conrad Veidt, Elga Brink and Clifford McLaglen and the second, *The Hound of the Baskervilles* was directed by Richard Oswald and starred Carlyle Blackwell as Sherlock Holmes.

When Bill O'Bryen, head of publicity and casting, decided to leave Gainsborough to become publicity chief for Fox Films in early March 1929, Balcon must have been devastated since he had been a huge asset. The first studio representative to place studio visits from the press on a sensible and established basis, he worked effectively 'with great intelligence and tact'.[14] Hugely popular, his personal network and skill was not to be found in any other studio. Shortly afterwards George Hopton, the general manager at Gainsborough, died suddenly and O'Bryen was persuaded not to leave Gainsborough after all. A month later Harold Boxall, formerly studio manager, who had a wide general knowledge of production and had worked at Islington since the inception of the studio under FPLBPL, was appointed to replace Hopton.

One significant film that Gainsborough secured in early 1929 was a special screen feature about Major Henry Segrave and his world land speed record. With Harry Ham in charge of production and Walter Blakley on camera they filmed Segrave getting ready to depart London with scenes in West End streets, at the Islington studio, the Golden Arrow showroom, the Southampton docks and then on board the liner *Majestic*, which departed 31st January 1929. On arrival in New York on 6th February, they filmed Segrave's reception by Mayor Walker and finally, the thrill of the race itself on Daytona Beach, Florida, on 11th March 1929, where he made the world's land speed record of 231 miles an hour. On his return to London Segrave was knighted by King George V.

By the late spring of 1929, Balcon was moving towards adopting the RCA system, with plans to convert the Islington studio into sound floors. He also announced that they would no longer make silent films and the recently made pictures would be given dialogue effects and synchronised music. His plan was to ensure that the next Gainsborough production would be an all-talkie starring Ivor Novello and was being prepared by Denison Clift. One idea was to make a screen version of Gerald du Maurier's play *Fame*, playing at St James's Theatre. There were also negotiations taking place to send a unit to the US to make an all-talkie picture.

According to Balcon it was 'now life or death to equip ourselves for sound'[15] but whatever system was finally chosen would require a long wait for the equipment to arrive and be installed. After spending over a year of valuable time and money trying to utilise the British Acoustic system, which had finally been abandoned, Gainsborough decided that the European systems were insufficiently developed and decided to go with RCA. This was partly because they thought that films made on an American sound process would have easier access to the American markets, which in the end proved to be a fallacy, and perhaps because they felt that after their frustration with British Acoustic, a sound-on-film system would be more practical.

Most people at Gainsborough were pretty ignorant when it came to the technical side of the sound innovation but luckily a young man named Percy Baynham Honri (real name Thompson) wrote a letter in which he claimed some knowledge. Balcon snapped him up and made him the company's recording man. Honri came from a showbiz family and had served an apprenticeship with Stoll before joining the British Broadcasting Corporation, where he ended up in research and development. Although his experience of sound films was not profound, it was greater than anyone else and he clearly understood the new technology. Balcon took him and George Gunn (chief electrician) to New York (from mid-May to mid-June 1929) with the aim of learning about the RCA system at their studio and getting RCA to give them some priority in delivery. He must also have taken all the necessary material and film for *The Wrecker* and *Balaclava* since both films were synchronised by RCA in their studio at this time. Balcon was also negotiating a deal to make talkies in America.

While the group were away in New York work began with characteristic energy and initiative to convert Islington 'from a noisy studio for silent film to a silent studio for noisy films'.[16] Since the building was immediately adjacent to a marble works, where noisy machinery was in operation the interior had to be completely soundproofed. After careful planning, new floating walls and floors were decided upon. First of all a shell was created inside the existing studio with the old walls and floors being covered with two thick layers of insulating quilting made of double layers of fibrous Colatex material. Battons were then introduced, on which new floors and walls were constructed. These were then covered in another layer of insulating material, with the result that the new floors and walls were at no point in direct contact with the original structure. The ceiling was ingeniously cut off from sound with drapes that also lined the interior. The ventilation system was carefully isolated from the structure itself by canvas channels so that no transmitted noise would be detectable and a monitor room was placed at one end of the floor. Work began on converting studio No. 2 first before studio No. 1 but when finished, the old studio was almost unrecognisable and there was 'a cathedral calm on entering the double entrance'.[17]

Balcon arrived back from America in the middle of June and at a meeting of the Gainsborough board discussed his activities at the RCA studio, the synchronisation of the silent pictures, the progress on converting the studio to sound and the agreement to install the RCA sound recording apparatus. Further big news was that he had made a major deal with Tiffany-Stahl Productions and Sono-Art Productions in America. However, it was not until the end of July 1929 that the RCA apparatus arrived and was installed, tested and ready to use. Shortly afterwards (and to perhaps test the water) Victor Saville directed a musical short called *Armistice* (trade show November 1929), featuring the band of the Coldstream Guards and the Welsh Male Voice Choir. Based on a poem by John McCrae it was a rather uninspiring vision of some of the songs made famous during the First World War.

The first major projects were the sound conversion of *The Crooked Billet*, *The City of Play* and *Taxi for Two*. Gainsborough were congratulated on their achievement: 'The period the company has just passed has been one of an exceptionally trying character. Talking pictures have involved all sorts of new trading difficulties and the provision of new studio plant and the acquisition of a new technique. It is very gratifying that Gainsborough have tackled these problems in so practical and so bold a manner'.[18]

At the first meeting of Gainsborough Pictures (1928) Limited in August 1929 with C.M. Woolf, chairman, presiding, the accounts covering the period up to 30th April 1929 showed a net profit of £12,125. Balcon said the meeting was a far from happy one.[19] Woolf described the past year as a crucial one – 'particularly in this country'[20] – and explained that when the company realised the definite mood of development in regard to sound films, the production of silent pictures was halted and a nucleus of technical staff were sent to America for training in sound technology. He added that the new conditions with talking pictures must eventually benefit the British producer. Every effort had been made to equip the Islington studio with the result that one complete RCA recording unit had already been installed and would shortly be functioning. And finally, Balcon's deal with Tiffany-Stahl was regarded as a positive move, enabling them to break 'into the American market in no uncertain fashion'.[21]

The Second Kiss

During his visit to Berlin, it is likely that Michael Balcon met representatives from another Berlin-based film production company because in early April 1929 Herman Millakowsky, in charge of Greenbaum GMBH, paid a visit to London for discussions. A few weeks later Gainsborough entered into a new continental contract with Greenbaum to produce six joint pictures. Some would be made in England, others in Germany, all would have an international director and cast and they would be talkies with dialogue in two languages. The production chief of Greenbaum was George Watt, who had gained experience in the US and the Continent, and had been chief assistant to Erich Pommer of UFA. According to reports once existing contracts in Germany were terminated, presumably with Fellner & Somlo, the arrangement with Greenbaum would be an exclusive one.

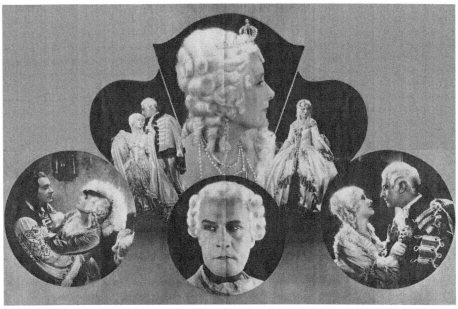

Some scenes from *The Second Kiss* (1930)

The first picture, directed by Erich Waschneck, was called *The Second Kiss* (*The Ring of the Empress* or *Der Gunstling von Schonbrunn*) and began filming at the beginning of May 1929 with Iván Petrovich and Lil Dagover. A delightful romantic comedy, it followed the story of how a gallant adventurer and Austrian nobleman Baron Von Trenck (Iván Petrovich) rescues Maria (Lil Dagover) and her maid Franzi from robbers and entertains them at his castle. She rewards him with a kiss and an amethyst ring but Maria guards her identity and claims to be the wife of the court jeweller in Vienna when in fact she is Theresa, Empress of Austria Empress. He follows them back to Vienna and discovers that she is indeed the Empress. Von Trenck's followers are arrested for disturbing the peace and duly imprisoned; he appeals to the Empress. After being granted an interview, he recognises the lady of the ring. She insists that he forms his followers into a regiment and he is promoted to colonel. The Royal Consort discovers Trenck wearing the ring of the Empress and both the Empress and Franzi make efforts to recover it. Trenck is sentenced to imprisonment for duelling but the Empress contrives his escape, retrieves her ring and sees that he finds happiness with Franzi.

On completion in September, the film was given a trade show in April 1930 and was described as 'a delicately handled and well characterised costume romance'[22] that could not 'fail to please a cultivated audience'[23] and was praised for its picturesque staging, faithful period detail, romantic theme, intelligent direction and aesthetic appeal. It was thought that Erik Waschneck 'handled the delicate theme with restraint' with a 'wonderful sense of pictorial values'.[24] Although slight and slow in development, the story was played in the spirit of light-hearted gaiety that almost made it light opera, with song numbers and musical accompaniment. Indeed, the Tobis sound recording was thought to be highly efficient, with natural and clear tones but sometimes the players' elocution was hampered by the use of English, which appeared to be an unfamiliar language.

The characterisation was vital and succeeded in maintaining interest with the handsome Iván Petrovich giving a dashing and attractive performance, while Lil Dagover looked extremely beautiful and behaved in a manner befitting an empress, though edged with an interesting sense of aristocratic humour.

Some scenes from *The Second Kiss* (1930)

Woman to Woman

Following Michael Balcon's visit to America in mid-1929, Gainsborough's New American arrangement with Tiffany-Stahl Productions was announced in late June 1929 with a deal to produce two pictures: a talkie remake of *Woman to Woman* and a picturisation of the successful play, *Journey's End*. The Tiffany-Stahl contract was perhaps the largest ever written for a British company in giving a minimum guarantee of $135,000 for *Woman to Woman* and $230,000 for *Journey's End* with an equal split of costs and profit.

Tiffany Productions had been founded in 1921 by Mae Murray, her husband, director Robert Z. Leonard and Maurice H. Hoffman. After Murray and Leonard divorced in 1925, John M. Stahl became the director of Tiffany and renamed the company Tiffany-Stahl Productions. Bank-rolled by Mr Young of Detroit, a wealthy manufacturer of automobile parts, Stahl acquired the former Reliance-Majestic Studio at 4516 Sunset Boulevard, Los Angeles, in 1927. The contract did not endure after the departure of Stahl in late 1929.

Woman to Woman, directed by Victor Saville in association with Burlington Films, marked the renewed working relationship with Saville and Balcon, indicating that Balcon was hoping to secure Saville as a fully-fledged Gainsborough director. The script dialogue was ably handled from the modern point of view by Michael Morton, the original author, and the music, sound script and continuity was by Nicholas Fodor. Saville's chief concern was to find an actress to play Deloryse who could sing, dance, was capable of deeply emotional acting and combined unusual good looks and a slight foreign accent. Luckily, Betty Compson, who played the original role, was available and more than willing to participate. When Saville arrived in Hollywood at the beginning of July 1929, he was given a warm welcome and completed filming in twenty-four days at the Tiffany-Stahl studio during July and August, and was back home in late September with two prints of the completed film.

The film was turned around quickly and given a trade show in November 1929, where it was described as 'the best British talkie made in America'[25] with exceedingly good sets but lacking the same captivation as the silent version.[26] Saville did not appear to get the most out of his players nor did he bring out the full appeal of the story. Betty Compson dominated the film, securing all the sympathy, and she sang and danced with beauty and grace. Although her acting was admired, making *Woman to Woman* a real woman's picture, somehow she did not rise to the same emotional heights achieved in the silent version and her voice, though pleasant, illustrated her lack of experience. George Barraud was weak as the husband, and although he had a pleasant voice he was somewhat wooden. Equally, Juliette Compton was thought to be too unsympathetic and equally wooden as the wife.

Feeling rather pleased that the entire production took only twenty-five days to complete, on his return to London Saville was full of ideas gleaned in America and described American studio organisation as efficient and nearly perfect: 'The activities of each department dovetail so wonderfully that everything works smoothly and is therefore much more economical,' he said. [27] He really thought that what was done in Hollywood could be done in London but much change was needed to achieve such a result. It was believed that he would work on another joint Gainsborough-Burlington production.

A scene from *Woman to Woman* (1929)
with Juliette Compton and Betty Compson

In addition to Balcon's deal with Tiffany-Stahl, he had also agreed to jointly produce other pictures with Sono-Art productions. Sono-Art was headed by Otto. E. Goebel and George W. Weeks, the producers of *The Rainbow Man* (1929), and Weeks was well known in the industry and had been general manager of FPL (Paramount) before forming Sono-Art in early 1929, utilising the Metropolitan studio in Hollywood.

The situation became more interesting when in September 1929 there was a merger between Gainsborough's American distributor, World Wide Pictures (run by J.D. Williams and John Maxwell), and Sono-Art. George W. Weeks was made acting vice-president and general manager and the new company, known as Sono-Art-World Wide Pictures Inc., was intended as an international producing-distribution combine. The company would continue to distribute British International Pictures and Gainsborough and at the same time agreed to produce six pictures for Gainsborough, three to be made in America and three in London.

At the end of 1929 it was announced that there would be two joint productions: *Swannee River* and *Sawdust and Satin*. The latter was to be directed by T. Hayes Hunter and would star Jacqueline Logan and Frankie Darro. Neither film appeared to go into production.

Journey's End

The second Tiffany-Stahl joint production was *Journey's End*, based on Robert Sherriff's wartime play set in the trenches. The script for the play had been championed by a young stage director called James Whale, who persuaded the London Stage Society to produce it for two nights at the end of 1928 (the central character was played by the young and little-known Laurence Olivier). Whale then persuaded actor and producer Maurice Browne to raise funds to stage the play at the Savoy Theatre on 21 January 1929, with the new lead of Colin Clive. It became a huge hit, transferred to the Prince of Wales and within a year had been staged in many of the capital cities of the world. In New York, the play enjoyed an even greater success and was a constant source of discussion, indicating a good American market for a film version.

From the outset Michael Balcon knew that it would make a good subject as a talkie and he was determined to acquire the rights in the face of stiff competition from several other British and American producers. Luckily, Sherriff and Brown, who controlled the rights, wanted to preserve the spirit of the play by having the film made by a British company, who they believed would understand the hearts and minds of the characters. Welsh-Pearson Elder and Gainsborough became the frontrunners and in the end they decided to combine forces and acquired the rights for £15,000, an unprecedented sum in 1929.

At the time it was thought that Gainsborough would be able to film *Journey's End* at the Islington studio, but the delay in installing the RCA sound equipment precipitated a change of plan. With Balcon retaining complete artistic control, it was decided to make the film with Tiffany-Stahl in their Hollywood studio, with James Whale as director. V. Gareth Gundrey, who had written the script for *Balaclava*, was secured, severing his brief connection with BIP. It was almost certainly thought that his wartime experiences would provide an invaluable perspective. Gundrey had reached the rank of captain in the Third Welch Regiment and had been awarded the Military Cross, having fought in and survived the Battle of Passchendaele in 1917. He was wounded in November 1918, just before the Armistice, and had his leg amputated as a result. But when James Whale read Gundrey's script he rejected it and then Maurice Brown supported Whale and there was a deadlock. A script was needed that would prove acceptable to the guardians of the play or the deal was off. At first, Gundrey was asked to leave for New York to confer with Brown and Whale, but then Balcon changed his mind and decided it would be better to send George Pearson from Welsh-Pearson Elder. Pearson related that the meeting before his departure to discuss the issues with Balcon and Gundrey was 'sad and embarrassing'.[28]

Pearson was given instructions to arrange the re-writing of the script that would be agreeable to all, to supervise the filming by James Whale (who had little experience of actual directing) and to see that there was no distortion of Sherriff's work during production. He arrived in New York on 12th July, made his way to Hollywood and returned a month later.

A scene from *Journey's End* (1930)

A scene from *Journey's End* (1930)

On the trip across the Atlantic, Pearson made his own comments about Gundrey's script. Although he thought it was technically good, it 'over-elaborated much that only needed the utter simplicity of the play'.[29] Once in Hollywood, Whale and Pearson secured Moncure March, who had served in the Great War and whose experiences paralleled the characters of the play, to revise the script, which was finally accepted by all concerned. One of the key points of both the play and the film was the marvellous characterisation and so the next hurdle was the casting of six men, each symbolising a type and class (there were no woman or love interest in the film). Luckily, although he was still appearing in the play in London, Colin Clive was allowed to leave for eight weeks to recreate onscreen his role as Captain Denis Stanhope, the chief character in what was seen as a powerful anti-war story.

With many significant scenes taking place in one set (a dug-out), the staging was simpler than many movies and filming took place from mid-November through to December 1929. Even though Pearson had to endure considerable Hollywood studio politics he resisted many superfluous demands and the result was a huge global success.

At the trade show in April 1930 the picture was hailed a triumph, the finest film ever shown and 'a great picture, one of the most moving and sincere the screen has given us'.[30] Like the play, it was a drama of stark realism played out between Stanhope (Colin Clive), a shell-shocked company commander, and Raleigh (David Manners), a young lieutenant who used to worship him at school and whose sister is in love with him. After three years in the fighting line and proving himself a leader,

Stanhope's nerves have frayed under the constant pressure but he keeps going by drinking whisky. He fears that Raleigh will report unfavourably to his sister, and so resents him and friction between them evolves, which only ends when Raleigh is killed in an attack. Various other characters peppered proceedings, including second in command Lieutenant Osborne (Ian MacLaren), who was in contrast to the nervy activity and devotion to duty expressed by Stanhope, a coward called Hibbert (Anthony Bushell) and the humour of Captain Trotter (Billy Bevan).

Thankfully, in directing the film it was thought that Pearson and Whale resisted every temptation to depart from the dignified spirit permeating the play but added new touches of atmosphere. Colin Clive's character dominated and he was so vibrant that he carried 'the spectator into his very mentality',[31] giving a performance that was an even greater achievement than the one onstage. The recording was exceptionally good – the voices audible to the slightest inflection – and the sound effects produced a realistic atmosphere, particularly for the fatal trench raid.

The association with Welsh-Pearson proved a good one and in early 1930 more joint ventures were announced, including a talkie version of *Squibs* with Betty Balfour (in the end realised by Julius Hagen and Henry Edwards in 1935) and another to feature Sir Harry Lauder.

The Fox Pictures debacle with Gaumont-British

In mid-April 1929 Isadore and Maurice Ostrer, joint managing directors of Gaumont-British, made a six-week trip to America, overlapping somewhat with Michael Balcon's visit to New York. Ostensibly their trip was to accompany booking agent William Morris in making a survey of the American talkie industry, to negotiate film rights to some Broadway plays and to engage American players for British talkies but they also had a secret mission.

William Fox of Fox Pictures had made an offer to the Ostrer brothers to buy the Gaumont-British empire and although his offer had been refused they were interested in selling part of the company. In early 1929, the Ostrer brothers had formed a controlling company called Metropolis and Bradford Trust that owned 65% of the ordinary share capital of Gaumont-British. William Fox was seemingly more interested in the theatre stock of the company since Gaumont-British controlled over 300 out of 4,000 cinemas producing gross receipts equal to a quarter of the entire gross receipts of all theatres in the UK. Fox wanted a share of this part of the business. During personal negotiations in Hollywood the Ostrer brothers sold 49% of shares to William Fox, retained 49% and appointed Lord Lee of Fareham as chairman, with 2% of shares to safeguard the interests of both parties. Thus, William Fox bought a substantial, but not controlling interest in the company although for some reason he believed he had bought a 65% controlling share. As a condition of the sale it was agreed that Fox would install sound equipment in all of Gaumont-British cinemas from Electrical Research Products.

For months afterwards there were denials that Fox had acquired any interest in Gaumont-British and a boardroom battle ensued. The Bromhead brothers, original owners of Gaumont and on the board of Gaumont-British, were not pleased and asserted their knowledge about the deal that was still being kept secret. This acrimonious, behind-the-scenes struggle was fought with denials and accusations and compounded by public and government anxiety at the idea of an American firm taking over a big British company. The Bromheads called a general meeting of the board and, with backing from the British Board of Trade, made sure that while foreign nationals could own shares they could not hold a controlling interest. In early August 1929 they resigned and the news was no less than a bombshell. Gaumont-British was quickly reorganised, with Isadore Ostrer becoming chairman, Mark Ostrer vice chairman and with the addition of C.M. Woolf and Will Evans as joint managing directors.

Confusion then reigned over the nature of Fox's shareholding in Gaumont-British, which carried on for years. Matters were compounded by huge changes in the Fox Picture Corporation. William Fox had made extensive new investments in his chain of film theatres but with the Wall Street Crash of late 1929, his incapacitation through a car accident and the threat of anti-trust action, his movie empire was on the verge of collapse. There was a long drawn-out legal battle, during which Paramount attempted to acquire the Fox holdings in Gaumont-British in early 1930 but failed.

Finally, in April 1930 William Fox was forced to sell his interests in the company and was ousted out. Harley Clarke and his syndicate bought the company and he became president. However the controversy over the Gaumont-British shares continued unabated and the relationship between the two companies was fraught. In the 1930s discord and litigation ensued.

Gainsborough's New Lease of Life

At the beginning of January 1930, Michael Balcon reflected on the problems and prospects for 1930. [32] Finally, the turmoil of 1929 as Gainsborough struggled to adapt to the problem of sound had been overcome. The output of silent pictures that had almost become worthless had been tinkered into marketability by adding some dialogue and sound effects, the Islington studio had been successful converted to sound and now they were trying to make British talking pictures a commercial proposition throughout the world. They were even thinking constructively about how to manufacture multi-lingual talking pictures in order to cater for all markets and the problem of colour.

Gainsborough's upcoming programme for 1930 was considered the most ambitious to date. Although only eight new dialogue and synchronised films were specified, they had in fact sixteen pictures in production or scheduled for production. *The City of Play, Taxi for Two, The Second Kiss, Balaclava* and *The Crooked Billet* were all part-talkie pictures and nearing completion. They were also due to go into production with *Woman to Woman, Journey's End, Symphony in Two Flats, Gipsy*

Melody (based on an original story by Nicholas Fodor and a joint venture with Burlington Films), *The Bill of Divorcement*, *A Night in Montmartre* (based on an original play by Miles Malleson and Walter Peacock), *Soho* (with a musical score written by Vivian Ellis), *Just For a Song (Jack and Jill/ Variety)*, *Sugar and Spice (The Gainsborough Picture Show)* and *The Gainsborough Gems.*

Sugar and Spice

In the autumn of 1929, Michael Balcon engaged Alexander Oumansky as director for a projected musical project. Oumansky had been part of Diaghileff's Russian ballet before becoming ballet master for the stage shows put on as a precursor to a movie presentation at The Capitol Theatre in New York. In mid-1925 he took up the post of general production manager for the Samuel Rachmann Film Company to introduce American-style stage shows into movie-theatres of seven Germany cities, including the flagship UFA Palast Am Zoo in Berlin. Sometime in 1929 he had been lured to London and in late 1929 was working on the stage and dance numbers for BIP's *Harmony Heaven* (1930).

The project was announced in September 1929 as *The Gainsborough Picture Show* and was planned to be a musical, all-singing, all-dancing, intimate revue. With J.W. Dodd as assistant director, casting took place to secure an array of 'variety' turns and attached to the project were some of the finest songwriters in the country who were preparing special numbers, including Vivian Ellis, Jay Whidden, H. Gordon and Billy Trytel, with numbers such as 'Parisian Doll', 'Sunshine of My Heart', 'To You' and 'I am so in Love with You'.

At first Ivor Novello was cast in the lead role alongside other well-known stage personalities such as Rebla, Gordon Harker, Roy Royston, Elsie Carlisle, Iris Rowe, the Barrie Sisters, Ross and Sargent and Johnny Nitt. Eventually the scale of the project was abandoned, perhaps because Ivor Novello was not available, and six revuettes were filmed between October and December 1929 by Claude L. McDonnell. They were ready for screening at the beginning of 1930 under the collective banner of *Sugar and Spice* but were, in fact, six shorts. These were titled *Toyland, Classic Versus Jazz, Black and White Revue, Gypsy Land, Plantation* and *On the Lido* and featured a chorus of twelve Gainsborough girls, Hal Swain's Kit Kat Band, Lewis Hardcastle's Troupe, Ross and Sargent, Johnny Nite, Elsie Carlisle, Peggy White, the Prince Sisters, the Barrie Twins, The Plaza Boys, Colombo Brothers, Iris Rowe and many more.

Just for a Song

Just for A Song started out as *Jack and Jill*, an original story of backstage life treated from a music-hall angle. Written by Angus McPhail in late 1929, it was re-titled *Variety* for a short while. It was conceived as an all-talkie with sound effects and special music written by Jay Whidden and was to be one of Gainsborough's first musical productions. Casting began in early October by Victor Saville, who engaged as leads Roy Royston and Constance Carpenter, both musical comedy stars at Daly's Theatre, along with Cyril Richard (who had made a big success in BIP's *Blackmail*) and the well-known light opera star Lilian Davies in her film debut.

Filming took place from the end of October through December 1929 at the Islington studio, with V. Gareth Gundrey as director. Gundrey, one of the original Gaumont production trio with Victor Saville and Maurice Elvey, had worked on the script for *Balaclava* with Elvey in 1928 and had worked extensively with Saville. He had signed a contract with Gainsborough to produce a series of pictures, of which this was the first. The dialogue was being supervised by Milton Rosmer who it was thought might become a Gainsborough director.

A British drama of vaudeville life, developed on familiar American lines, *Just For a Song* was the story of two young variety artistes from the country named Jack (Roy Royston) and Jill (Constance Carpenter), who secure an engagement with a circuit of theatres through their agent, Moss (Nick Adams). The booking manager Craddock (Cyril Richard) falls in love with Jill and schemes to separate her from Jack by inducing another artist, Norma (Lilian Davies), to persuade Jack to write a song for her. Jack compromises himself with her and Jill breaks off their partnership. Craddock thinks that he has scored a victory but Moss intervenes and succeeds in reuniting the couple.

Gundrey started shooting all the variety acts and stage scenes first and then by mid-November he began work on the actual story. One of the big scenes was a charity music hall performance by numerous artists with a set of proscenium of a typical music hall and Louis Levy and orchestra on one side of a band pit. The acts included The Mangan Tillerettes in a speciality number called 'The Orchid', the comedy juggler Rebla, Sid Seymour and his Mad Hatters Orchestra and Roy Royston doing eccentric dances and then dances with Constance Carpenter.

Just for a Song was given a trade show in March 1930 and was thought to be unpretentious, providing exceptional individual characterisation, good realistic atmosphere, a pleasing love story, plenty of humour, a number of tuneful melodies, varied music hall acts and 'sufficient intrigue of a very sensational kind to keep up the interest'.[33] Gundrey unfolded the story clearly and effectively, and although on a familiar theme that lacked originality, the inclusion of proper music hall stars lent variety without interfering in the development of the main theme. However, the colour sequences were crude and lacked brilliance but the RCA sound recording was good and did justice to the quality of the speaking voices.

Gainsborough Gems for JMG

Another series of shorts, collectively titled *Gainsborough Gems*, was made in late 1929 and quickly released in January 1930. Referred to as the first 'sound revuettes' to be made by a British company for quota purposes, the fifteen short subjects were made for Jury-Metro-Goldwyn and were similar to MGM's successful movietone acts. Each film featured well-known artists from the British stage and concert halls, with a variety of singing, dancing and musical items. The acts comprised Mattini and his band, the singing of Ena Reiss, the dancing of Daphne de Win, Billies Barnes, star of Charlot's Revue, George Mozart the celebrated vaudeville artiste in a sketch called 'Married Life', the Hardcastle Negro Troupe, Hal Swain the celebrated dance band leader presenting his saxophone sextette, Al Starita, another dance band celebrity, Paul Mandell and his band, Elsie Percival and partner, the Walsh Brothers, Madame Phillipova and the Balalaika Orchestra and finally, Dick Henderson, fresh from his American tour.

The Fire and the End of an Era

Ivor Novello's first talkie was to be based on his play, *A Symphony in Two Flats*, but the ongoing saga of when shooting would commence continued through the latter part of 1929, with starting dates shifting constantly. Perhaps part of the delay was that they were waiting for the stage show to end but it was so successful that it ran for months at the New Theatre. Originally titled *Encore*, it was confirmed that filming would begin at the Islington studio in November 1929, but it was further delayed until 24th January 1930 as the stage production drew to a close. The production was to be directed by V. Gareth Gundrey and was to have a novel casting structure. Since the film was a joint production with Sono-Art-World-Wide, they had sent over the American star Jacqueline Logan, whom they had under contract, to be the female lead in an American version, but Benita Hume was assigned her original stage part in the film for the British version.

Scenes were being filmed for *Balaclava* in the Islington studio during Saturday, 18th January 1930 when fire broke out at about 1.40pm. Most of the staff and players were at lunch in the studio restaurant. Raynham Henri noticed smoke and flames coming from the upper No. 2 studio and rang the studio fire alarm. The fire was in the sound recording rooms at the far end of studio No. 2 and had started because William Shand had been given the job of impregnating some wire coils for the recording apparatus with paraffin wax. This was done in an electric double saucepan with water in one compartment, wax in the other. He forgot to switch off the heater when he went to lunch so the water boiled away and the wax burst into flames.

On hearing the alarm, the studio fire brigade comprising George Gunn and William Shand got to work to tackle the fire and ran out the reels of hose from a hydrant. The actor Cyril McLaglen tried to help but the place was dark and full of smoke so Gunn sent him off to turn the hydrant on. Then the windows shattered and flames ignited the drapes around the floor used to deaden the sound. It soon got out of control and within a few minutes the whole upper part of the studio buildings was burning. As Gunn and Shand were running the hose down a narrow passage the accumulated gases in the recording room exploded, blew the doors open and shot flames straight at them. The goods lift was immobilised as the fire had cut off the electric power and was on the floor below but its upper gates were just accessible. They managed to open it and jumped in but Gunn climbed down the trellis gates, got his finger jammed in the trellis and couldn't move. He passed out and then fell, minus part of his finger. When he awoke, he groped his way out. Gunn, Shand and Thomas Gobbett, another member of the technical staff, received first-degree burns but Shand was so badly burnt and in shock that he did not survive.

The blaze presented scenes similar to those witnessed during a wartime air raid. Actors and actresses dressed as Highland soldiers and Russian peasants fled down the emergency stairs and ground-floor workers lent a hand until it became too much. They fled into the smoke-filled streets and joined hundreds of nearby tenants who feared to retire lest the ninety-floor high wall of the studio should collapse on the roofs of their dwellings. It proved to be one of the most spectacular fires in London for many years. Michael Balcon was in the West End having lunch with Bill O'Bryen prior to taking in the international rugby match at Twickenham when he was called to the telephone and raced to the scene, joining C.M. Woolf.

Despite the arrival of many fire engines the destruction was speedy and at great risk studio staff and fireman salvaged cameras, other apparatus and a great deal of valuable property, although much was destroyed. The entire upper floor, including the dressing rooms and the recently completed upper ground No. 2 sound-proofed studio was completely destroyed, along with all the newly installed sound recording apparatus. But the old ground floor No. 1 studio remained relatively unscathed and no film was lost, except the film that was actually on the sound recording camera at the time of the fire. The storage vaults and cutting rooms were left untouched.

The blaze was devastating to both Gainsborough and Michael Balcon and in a few hours they 'were robbed of the fruits of many months careful thought and labour'.[34] They not only lost a member of staff but also their first fully-equipped soundproof studio, along with all the brand new sound apparatus.

The company had spent much time in deciding how to move forward and which sound system to use. Everything had been bought and installed, many alternations and improvements had been made and everyone was in a confident mood to move forward with the new programme of talkies but now all production plans were in jeopardy and work on *Balaclava* was temporarily interrupted. Three imminent productions were immediately postponed. These were *Revue August 1914* to star the comedian Ernie Lotinga, Basil Dean's Associated Talking Pictures version of *Escape* (1930) and an unspecified picture by Adrian Brunel with Betty Balfour.

The indomitable spirit of Michael Balcon inspired all his staff and associates and thankfully, everyone rallied round so that within ten days of the fire Gainsborough were back in business and the filming of *Balaclava* resumed at Estree Many productions were transferred to the Elstree studio, where Gainsborough had already hired space to film Victor Saville's *A Warm Corner* (1930) and *The Sport of Kings* (1931), both featuring the well-known comedian Leslie Henson.

Finally, Bill O'Bryan, who was in charge of casting and publicity, resigned in February 1930 and went into partnership with the Albermarle New Service, where his unique experience of casting and close personal contact with all the leading stage and film artists and journalists in London and the provinces would be highly invaluable. 'Shan' Balcon combined his existing duties as production manager with that of casting, while Hugh Percival, O'Bryen's capable assistant, was promoted to run the publicity department. However, O'Bryen's departure and that of J.W. Dodds, assistant director, along with other impending changes in studio personnel, was unfortunate as it gave rise to much speculation concerning the future of Gainsborough. Balcon stressed that the company would continue its activities, some disturbance in studio personnel was inevitable and plans for rebuilding the studio were under serious consideration.

At a board meeting of Gainsborough Pictures held on 7th February 1930, chairman C.M. Woolf announced that Simon Rowson of Ideal and W.J. Gell, managing director of Gaumont, would join the board. Although Michael Balcon made assurances that Gainsborough would continue as a separate unit under the Gaumont-British banner, this move fuelled further rumours that had started in late 1929, that a major consolidation programme was being considered. One train of thought was that there would be a fusion of identity and picture making activity at Gaumont's Shepherd's Bush studio and Gainsborough's Islington studio.

C.M. Woolf, as chairman of Gainsborough and the W&F film service, joint managing director of Gaumont-British and with many other business interests, was now in a position of considerable power and influence. It would appear that he had plans to consolidate the film production units under the banners of Gainsborough, Gaumont and British and Dominion, which would result in the largest film production combine in the country. Meanwhile, backroom drama and intrigue continued, with denials by various other directors. As all these issues surfaced Michael Balcon was ordered to take time away from the business. He needed a period of rest from the damaging effects of a series of domestic and business worries in which family illness and personal nervous strain were followed by the heavy shock of the Islington studio fire. He and his wife went to Madeira for a few weeks, leaving his brother, 'Shan' Balcon, in charge.

With many of its part-silent, part-talkie films being released in 1930, including *Balaclava* (1930), along with its first steps in full talkie production such as *Woman to Woman* (1929), *The Gainsborough Gems* (1930), *Just for a Song* (1930), *Sugar & Spice* (1930) and *Journey's End* (1930), Gainsborough had finally bridged the gap between silent and sound films. The stage was set for another phase in the life of the Islington studio, Michael Balcon and Gainsborough Pictures as they entered the 1930s and the realm of the talkies

The Gainsborough or Islington Studio

ACKNOWLEDGEMENTS

I would like to thank the following people:
Sarah Currant and all the staff at the British Film Institute Library
Janice Healey for all her advice and helpful information
Jane Donovan for her remarkable editing and patience
My 'marketing' and 'ideas' team of Colin, Jane, Phil, Tim, Shaun, Mimi, Clive and Cindy
My London hosts – Cindy & Andy, Robert, Bill and Denise and Denise
The Ronald Grand Archive for the cover image of the Islington studio and other images
Brian Twist for his images from the J.W. Mitchell Collection
Townly Cooke for his images
Nick Baker Findlay (son of Patricia Cutts) for a photo of Graham Cutts
All other photographs and images are from the author's extensive private collection

BIBLIOGRAPHY

Affron, Charles. *Lillian Gish: Her Legend, Her Life* (2001)

Allen, Virginia. *Gordon Conway: Fashioning a New Woman* (1997)

Allvine, Glendon. *The Greatest Fox of Them All* (1969)

Balcon, Michael. *Michael Balcon Presents: A Lifetime in Films* (1969)

Bergfelder, Tim and Christian Cargnelli. *Destination London: German-Speaking Emigrés and British Cinema 1925–1950* (2008)

Bouchier, Chili. *Shooting Star: The Last of the Silent Film Stars* (1996)

Brinson, Charmian and Richard Dove and Jennifer Taylor. *Immortal Austria: Austrians in Exile in Britain* (2007)

Brunel, Adrian. *Nice Work: Thirty Years in British Films* (1949)

Chapman, Gary. *Stars of the British Silent Screen* (forthcoming, 2014)

Cook, Pam (ed.). *Gainsborough Pictures: Rethinking British Cinema* (1997)

Curthoys, Ann and Marliyn Lake (eds.). *Connected Worlds: History in Transnational Perspective.*

Draper, Chris. Islington's Cinemas and Film Studios (c.1989)

Ede, Laurie N. *British Film Design: A History* (2010)

Foster, Jonathan. *The Death Ray: The Secret Life of Harry Grindell Matthews* (2009)

Golden, Eve. *Golden Images: 41 Essays on Silent Film Stars (2001)*

Haver, Ronald. *David O. Selznick's Hollywood* (1980)

Hicks, Seymour. *Hail Fellow Well Met* (1949)

Hitchcock O'Connell, Pat and Laurent Bouzereau. *Alma Hitchcock: The Woman Behind the Man* (2003)

June. *The Glass Ladder* (1960)

Kear, Lynn and James King. *Evelyn Brent: The Life and Films of Hollywood's Lady Crook* (2009)

Kohn, Mark. *Dope Girls* (1992)

Kreimeier, Klaus. *The Ufa Story: A History of Germany's Greatest Film Company 1918–1945* (1996)

Low, Rachael. *Film Making in 1930s Britain* (1985)

—. *The History of the British Film, 1914–1918* (1950)

—. *The History of the British Film, 1906–1914* (1948)

—. *The History of the British Film, 1918–1929* (1971)

McGillan, Patrick. *Alfred Hitchcock: A Life in Darkness and Light* (2003)

Moseley, Roy. *Evergreen: Victor Saville in His Own Words* (2000)

Munday, John. *The British Musical Film* (2007)

Musser, Charles. *Before the Nickelodeon: Edwin S. Porter and the Edison Manufacturing Company (1991)*

Noble, Peter. *Ivor Novello: Man of the Theatre* (1952)

Pearson, George. *Flashback: The Autobiography of a Film Maker* (1957)

Powell, Michael. *A Life in Movies* (2000)

Rotha, Paul. *Film Till Now: A Survey of the Cinema* (1951)

Slattery-Christy, David. *In Search of Ruritania* (2006)

Spoto, Donald. *The Life of Alfred Hitchcock: The Dark Side of Genius* (1999)

Steer ,Valentina. *The Secrets of the Cinema* (1920)

Taylor, John Russell. *Hitch: The Life and Times of Alfred Hitchcock* (1978)

Thomson, David. *Showman: The Life of David O. Selznick* (1994)

Travis, Doris Eaton. *The Days We Danced: The Story of My Theatrical Family from Florenz Ziegfeld to Arthur Murray and Beyond* (2003)

Vogel, Michelle. *Olive Thomas: The Life and Death of a Silent Film Beauty* (2007)

Warren, Patricia. *British Studios: An Illustrated History* (1995)

Webb, Paul. *Ivor Novello: A Portrait of a Star* (2005)

Wilcox, Herbert. *Twenty Thousand Sunsets: The Autobiography of Herbert Wilcox* (1967)

Wilson, Sandy. *Ivor* (1978)

SOURCES

In order to create this history I have conducted extensive research at the British Film Institute Library using a variety of sources but focused mainly on the trade press. In addition, a variety of relevant books covering the period and many valuable online resources have been consulted.

I have given a list of all these sources below but have only specified the specific source of quotes.

I have not included a filmography. All of this information can be obtained online. For all specific details of each film mentioned in this book, please visit the Internet Movie Database or the BFI's Screenonline.

Websites

Ancestry (http://home.ancestry.com)
British Film Institute Screenonline (http://www.screenonline.org.uk)
Cinetecadelfriuli (http://www.cinetecadelfriuli.org)
Internet Movie Database (http://www.imdb.com)
Jazz Age Club (http://www.jazzageclub.com)
Lantern (http://lantern.mediahist.org)
Lili Damita (http://filmstarpostcards.blogspot.co.uk/2013/08/lily-damita.html)
Madonna of the Screen by Greta Groat (http://www.stanford.edu/~gdegroat/AJ/essay.htm)
Nick Redfern's Research into Film/Claude Hamilton Verity (http://nickredfern.wordpress.com/category/claude-hamilton-verity-2)
Nita Naldi (http://nitanaldi.com)
San Francisco Silent Film Festival (http://www.silentfilm.org)
Screensnapshots (http:/screensnapshots.blogspot.co.uk)
The Death Ray: the Secret Life of Harry Grindell Matthews (http://www.harrygrindellmatthews.com)
The Stage Archive (https://archive.thestage.co.uk)
Will of Memory (http://www.willofmemory.com)

Journals/Magazines/Newspapers

Cinema
Eve
Evening Standard
Exhibitors Daily Review
Film Weekly
Hollywood Filmograph
Kinematograph Weekly
Motion Picture News
Motion Picture Studio
Movie-Land
New York Dramatic Mirror
New York Times
Photoplay
Picture Show
Picture World
Projection Engineering
Singapore Free Press
Stoll's Editorial News
The Bioscope
The Educational Screen
The Film Daily
The Gramophone
The Guardian
Pictures and Picturegoer / The Picturegoer
The Referee
The Stage
The Stage Yearbook
The Times
Theatre World
Variety

Sources for All Quotes

1 Famous Players-Lasky's London Experiment

1 *The Picturegoer*, 10th to 17th May 1919 and *New York Times*, 16th May 1919.
2 *Kinematograph Weekly*, 30th October 1919.
3 *New York Times*, 16th May 1919.
4 *The Film Daily*, 1st July 1919.
5 *Kinematograph Weekly*, 9th September 1920.
6 *The Picturegoer*, 25th October 1920.
7 *The Picturegoer*, 18th October 1919.
8 *New York Times*, 30th November 1919.
9 *Film Daily*, 27th August 1919.
10 *Kinematograph Weekly*, 20th November 1919.

2 The Islington Studio

1 *Motion Picture Studio*, 9th July 1921.
2 Ibid.
3 Ibid.
4 Ibid.
5 *Kinematograph Weekly*,19th August 1920.
6 Ibid.
7 Ibid.
8 *The Picturegoer*, August 1921.
9 Ibid.
10 Ibid.

3 Famous Players-Lasky: The British Films

1 *The Bioscope*, 2nd December 1920.
2 *Kinematograph Weekly*, 6th May 1920.
3 *The Picturegoer*, 15th May 1920.
4 *Kinematograph Weekly*, 17th June 1920.
5 *The Picturegoer*, 2nd July 1920.
6 *The Picturegoer*, 10th July 1920.
7 *Alfred Hitchcock: A Life in Darkness and Light* by Patrick McGillan.
8 *The Picturegoer*, March 1926.
9 *Kinematograph Weekly*, 2nd December 1920.
10 *The Pictures and Picturegoer*, 25th September 1920.
11 *Kinematograph Weekly*, 23rd September 1920.
12 *Pictures and Picturegoer*, 23rd October 1920.
13 *Kinematograph Weekly*, 23rd September 1920.
14 *The Bioscope*, 30th June 1921.
15 *Kinematograph Weekly*, 2nd December 1920.

16 *Kinematograph Weekly*, 14th October 1920.
17 *Motion Picture Studio*, 18th June 1921.
18 *Motion Picture Studio*, 5th November 1921.
19 *The Bioscope*, 3rd November 1921.
20 *Motion Picture Studio*, 23rd July 1921.
21 *The Life of Alfred Hitchcock: The Dark Side of Genius* by Donald Spoto
22 *Kinematograph Weekly*, 29th September 1921.
23 *The Bioscope*, 6th October 1921.
24 Ibid.
25 *Kinematograph Weekly*, 29th September 1921.
26 *Motion Picture Studio*, 26th November 1921.
27 *The Picturegoer*, February 1924.
28 *Wellington Evening Post* from *The Daily Mail*, 3rd June 1921.
29 *The Stage*, 25th August 1921.
30 *Alfred Hitchcock: A Life in Darkness and Light* by Patrick McGillan.
31 *The Life of Alfred Hitchcock: The Dark Side of Genius* by Donald Spoto.
32 *Kinematograph Weekly*, 20th October 1921.
33 *Motion Picture Studio*, 8th October 1921.
34 *The Bioscope*, 25th May 1922.
35 *Kinematograph Weekly*, 25th May 1922.
36 Ibid.
37 *Kinematograph Weekly*, 5th January 1922.

4 Change is in the Air

1 *Motion Picture Studio*, 7th January 1922.
2 *The Stage*, 23rd June 1921.
3 *Movie-Land*, 3rd January 1921.
4 *Motion Picture Studio*, 18th June 1921.
5 *The Stage*, 6th October 1921.
6 *The Stage*, 9th September 1926.
7 *Alfred Hitchcock: A Life in Darkness and Light* by Patrick McGillan.
8 *The Bioscope*, 25th May 1922.
9 *Kinematograph Weekly* 24th August 1922
10 *The Bioscope*, 21st September 1922.
11 Ibid.
12 *The Days We Danced: The Story of My Theatrical Family from Florenz Ziegfeld to Arthur Murray and Beyond* by Doris Eaton Travis.

5 Graham Wilcox's Wonderful Story

1 *Twenty-Five Thousand Sunsets* by Herbert Wilcox.

2 Ibid.
3 *The Bioscope*, 1st June 1922.
4 *Kinematograph Weekly*, 1st June 1922.
5 *The Picturegoer*, March 1923.
6 *Kinematograph Weekly*, 1st June 1922.
7 *The Picturegoer*, January 1923.
8 *The Bioscope*, 1st June 1922.
9 *The Picturegoer*, January 1923.
10 *Kinematograph Weekly*, 30th March 1922.
11 *Kinematograph Weekly*, 18th May 1922.
12 *The Picturegoer*, January 1923.
13 *Motion Picture Studio*, 1st July 1922.
14 *Picture Show*, 9th September 1922.
15 *Picture Show*, 2nd September 1922.
16 *The Picturegoer*, October 1926.
17 *The Picturegoer*, September 1922.
18 *Variety*, 15th December 1922.
19 *Kinematograph Weekly*, 16th November 1922.
20 *The Picturegoer*, January 1923.
21 *The Picturegoer*, January 1923.
22 Ibid.
23 *Motion Picture Studio*, 26th August 1922.
24 *Kinematograph Weekly*, 5th October 1922.
25 *The Picturegoer*, January 1923.
26 *Variety*, 22nd February 1923.
27 *The Bioscope*, 1st February 1923.
28 *Kinematograph Weekly*, 1st February 1923.
29 *The Bioscope*, 1st February 1923.
30 *Kinematograph Weekly*, 1st February 1923.
31 *Variety*, 22nd February 1923.
32 *The Bioscope*, 1st February 1923.
33 *Hitch: The Life and Times of Alfred Hitchcock* by John Russell Taylor.

6 Welsh-Pearson Tip-Toe in with Betty Balfour

1 *The History of British Film 1918–1930* by Rachel Low.
2 *The Picturegoer*, 25th September 1926.
3 *The Picturegoer*, 16th October 1920.
4 *Motion Picture Studio*, 26th May 1923.
5 Ibid.
6 *Motion Picture Studio*, 7th July 1923.
7 *Flashback: The Autobiography of a Film Maker* by George Pearson.
8 *Kinematograph Weekly*, 4th October 1923.
9 *Kinematograph Weekly*, 20th December 1923.
10 *Motion Picture Studio*, 15th December 1923.
11 *The Bioscope*, 20th December 1923.
12 *Flashback: The Autobiography of a Film Maker* by George Pearson.
13 *Kinematograph Weekly*, 27th March 1924.

14 *Kinematograph Weekly*, 3rd July 1924.
15 *The Bioscope*, 3rd July 1924.
16 Ibid.

7 Balcon-Saville-Freedman

1 *Michael Balcon Presents: A Lifetime in Films* by Michael Balcon.
2 *Nice Work: Thirty Years in British Films* by Adrian Brunel.
3 *Motion Picture Studio*, 14th April 1923.
4 *The Bioscope*, 10th May 1923.
5 *Motion Picture Studio*, 14th April 1923.
6 *Michael Balcon: A Lifetime in Films* by Michael Balcon.
7 *Hitch: The Life and Times of Alfred Hitchcock* by John Russell Taylor.
8 *Motion Picture Studio*, 2nd June 1923.
9 Ibid.
10 *Alfred Hitchcock: A Life in Darkness and Light* by Patrick McGillan.
11 *Picture World*, 26th April 1924.
12 *Motion Picture Studio*, 2th April 1923.
13 *Cinema*, 7th June 1923.
14 *The Bioscope*, 14th June 1923.
15 *The Bioscope*, 6th September 1923.
16 *Evergreen: Victor Saville in His Own Words* by Roy Moseley.
17 *Kinematograph Weekly*, 15th November 1923.
18 *Variety*, 2nd April 1922.
19 *Motion Picture Studio*, 17th November 1923.
20 *Kinematograph Weekly*, 15th November 1923.
21 *Motion Picture Studio*, 17th November 1923.
22 *The Bioscope*, 15th November 1923.
23 *Kinematograph Weekly*, 8th November 1923.
24 *Variety*, 2nd April 1924.
25 *The Bioscope*, 1st November 1923.
26 *The Bioscope*, 15th November 1923.
27 *Showman: The Life of David O. Selznick* by David Thomson.
28 *Motion Picture Studio*, 29th December 1923.
29 *Motion Picture Studio*, 17th August 1923.
30 *Motion Picture Studio*, 23rd February 1924.
31 *Kinematograph Weekly*, 21st February 1924.
32 *The Bioscope*, 21st February 1924.
33 *Kinematograph Weekly*, 21st February 1924.
34 *Alfred Hitchcock: A Life in Darkness and Light* by Patrick McGillan.
35 *Hitch: The Life and Times of Alfred Hitchcock* by John Russell Taylor.
36 *The History of British Film, 1918–1929* by Rachel Low.
37 *The Stage*, 31st March 1927.

38 *Hitch: The Life and Times of Alfred Hitchcock* by John Russell Taylor.
39 *The Life of Alfred Hitchcock: The Dark Side of Genius* by Donald Spoto.
40 *Hitch: The Life and Times of Alfred Hitchcock* by John Russell Taylor.
41 *The Bioscope*, 10th January 1924.
42 *Kinematograph Weekly*, 10th January 1924.

8 A Passionate Adventure and the Formation of Gainsborough Pictures

1 *The Bioscope*, 7 February 1924.
2 *Alfred Hitchcock: A Life in Darkness and Light* by Patrick McGillan.
3 *Showman: The Life of David O. Selznick* by David Thomson.
4 Madonna of the Screen by Greta Groat http://www.stanford.edu/~gdegroat/AJ/essay.htm
5 *The Picturegoer*, August 1924.
6 *The Bioscope*, 10th April 1924.
7 *The Bioscope*, 20th March 1924.
8 *The Bioscope*, 10th April 1924.
9 *Kinematograph Weekly*, 26th April 1924.
10 *The Bioscope*, 21st August 1924.
11 *Kinematograph Weekly*, 21st August 1924.
12 *The Picturegoer*, October 1924.
13 *The Bioscope*, 21st August 1924.
14 *Kinematograph Weekly*, 19th June 1924.
15 *The Film Renter and Moving Picture News* January 1925 in *Gainsborough Pictures: Rethinking British Cinema*, edited by Pam Cook.
16 *Kinematograph Weekly*, 2nd October 1924.
17 *Kinematograph Weekly*, 29th January 1925.
18 *Kinematograph Weekly*, 22nd January 1925.
19 *The Bioscope*, 22nd January 1925.
20 The Ufa Story: A History of Germany's Greatest Film Company 1918–1945 by Klaus Kreimeier.
21 *Alfred Hitchcock: A Life in Darkness and Light* by Patrick McGillan and *Hitch: The Life and Times of Alfred Hitchcock* by John Russell Taylor.
22 *The Life of Alfred Hitchcock: The Dark Side of Genius* by Donald Spoto.
23 *Hitch: The Life and Times of Alfred Hitchcock* by John Russell Taylor.
24 *Gainsborough Pictures: Rethinking British Cinema*, edited by Pam Cook.
25 *Hitch: The Life and Times of Alfred Hitchcock* by John Russell Taylor.
26 Ibid.

27 *The Picturegoer*, June 1925.
28 *The Picturegoer* June 1925, *Kinematograph Weekly*, 23rd April 1925 and *The Bioscope*, 23rd April 1925.
29 *The Bioscope*, 23rd April 1925.
30 *Kinematograph Weekly*, 23rd April 1925.

9 The Hitch-Cutts' Divide

1 *Kinematograph Weekly*, 26th February 1925.
2 *Hitch: The Life and Times of Alfred Hitchcock* by John Russell Taylor.
3 *Kinematograph Weekly*, 29th January 1925.
4 *Hitch: The Life and Times of Alfred Hitchcock* by John Russell Taylor.
5 Ibid.
6 *Kinematograph Weekly*, 26th February 1925.
7 *Alfred Hitchcock: A Life in Darkness and Light* by Patrick McGillan.
8 *Kinematograph Weekly*, 19th March 1925.
9 *The Bioscope*, 12th November 1925.
10 *Variety*, 3rd November 1926.
11 *Hitch: The Life and Times of Alfred Hitchcock* by John Russell Taylor.
12 *The Ufa Story: A History of Germany's Greatest Film Company 1918–1945* by Klaus Kreimeier.
13 *The Life of Alfred Hitchcock: The Dark Side of Genius* by Donald Spoto.
14 *Michael Balcon Presents: A Lifetime in Films* by Michael Balcon.
15 *The Picturegoer*, August 1925.
16 Ibid.
17 *The Picturegoer*, October 1926.
18 *Theatre World*, October 1925.
19 *Ivor* by Sandy Wilson.
20 *Theatre World*, October 1925.
21 *The Bioscope*, 10th September 1925.
22 *Kinematograph Weekly*, 10th September 1925.
23 Ibid.
24 *The Picturegoer*, February 1926.
25 The Picturegoer, October 1927.
26 The Bioscope, 3rd December 1925.
27 *The Life of Alfred Hitchcock: The Dark Side of Genius* by Donald Spoto.
28 Ibid.
29 Ibid.
30 *The Bioscope*, 26th March 1926.
31 *Kinematograph Weekly*, 18th March 1926.
32 *The Bioscope*, 26th March 1926.
33 *Kinematograph Weekly*, 25th March 1926.
34 *The Bioscope*, 27th August 1925.

35 *Hollywood and the Culture Elite: How the Movies Became American* by Peter Decherney.
36 *Kinematograph Weekly*, 22nd October 1925.
37 Ibid.
38 *The Bioscope*, 18th February 1926.
39 *Kinematograph Weekly*, 18th February 1926.
40 *The Bioscope*, 18th February 1926.
41 *Lilian Gish: Her Legend, Her Life* by Charles Affron.
42 *Twenty Thousand Sunsets: The Autobiography of Herbert Wilcox* by Herbert Wilcox.
43 *Variety*, 27th January 1926.
44 *Film Daily*, 14th January 1926.
45 *Twenty Thousand Sunsets: The Autobiography of Herbert Wilcox* by Herbert Wilcox.
46 *The Bioscope*, 4th March 1926.
47 *The Bioscope*, 22nd October 1925.
48 *Kinematograph Weekly*, 8th October 1925.
49 *The Picturegoer*, December 1925.
50 http://nitanaldi.com
51 *The Bioscope*, 7th October 1926.
52 *Kinematograph Weekly*, 7th October 1926.

10 Gainsborough's Progress

1 *The Bioscope*, 5th November 1925.
2 Ibid.
3 Ibid.
4 *The Bioscope*, 7th January 1926.
5 Ibid.
6 *Michael Balcon Presents: A Lifetime in Films* by Michael Balcon.
7 Overview of Crossing the Great Saraganda on the BFI – http://www.screenonline.org.uk/film/id/440503/index.html
8 *Kinematograph Weekly*, 7th January 1926.
9 *The Bioscope*, 7th January 1926.
10 *Kinematograph Weekly*, 11th March 1926.
11 Ibid.
12 *The Bioscope*, 1st April 1926, p.18/ *Washington Sunday Star*, 14th March 1926.
13 *The Film Daily*, 19th July 1926.
14 *The Picturegoer*, May 1926.
15 *The Glass Ladder* by June.
16 Ibid.
17 Ibid.
18 *The Picturegoer*, October 1926.
19 *The Picturegoer*, March 1926.
20 Ibid.
21 *Nice Work: Thirty Years in British Films* by Adrian Brunel.
22 *The Picturegoer*, May 1926.

23 *The Life of Alfred Hitchcock: The Dark Side of Genius* by Donald Spoto.
24 Ibid.
25 *Hitch: The Life and Times of Alfred Hitchcock* by John Russell Taylor.
26 *Michael Balcon Presents: A Lifetime in Films* by Michael Balcon.
27 *The Life of Alfred Hitchcock: The Dark Side of Genius* by Donald Spoto.
28 Ibid.
29 *Kinematograph Weekly*, 16th September 1926.
30 *The Bioscope*, 16th September 1926.
31 *Eve*, 2nd February 1927.
32 *The Bioscope*, 10th June 1926.
33 *The Bioscope*, 15th July 1926.
34 *The Picturegoer*, October 1926.
35 Ibid.
36 Ibid.

11 The Restructuring of Gainsborough

1 *The Bioscope*, 1st July 1926.
2 See Chapter 10.
3 *Alfred Hitchcock: A Life in Darkness and Light* by Patrick McGillan.
4 *Kinematograph Weekly*, 23rd September 1926.
5 *Kinematograph Weekly*, 22nd July 1926.
6 Ibid.
7 *The Stage*, 9th September 1926.
8 *The Bioscope*, 15th July 1926.
9 Sale of contract between Ivor Novello and Gainsborough on ebay.co.uk.
10 *The Bioscope*, 30th September 1926.
11 *The Stage*, 9th June 1927.
12 *Nice Work: Thirty Years in British Films* by Adrian Brunel.
13 *The Bioscope*, 10th April 1927.
14 *The Bioscope*, 9th December 1926.
15 *The Bioscope*, 16th December 1926.
16 *The Bioscope*, 20th January 1927.
17 *The Picturegoer*, April 1927.
18 Ibid.
19 *The Stage*, 26th May 1927.
20 *The Picturegoer*, April 1927.

12 Coward's Wit

1 *The Bioscope*, 15th July 1926.
2 *Kinematograph Weekly*, 26th August 1926.
3 *Kinematograph Weekly*, 16th December 1926.
4 *Michael Balcon Presents: A Lifetime in Films* by Michael Balcon.
5 *Kinematograph Weekly*, 5th May 1927.

6 *The Bioscope*, 5th May 1927.

7 *The Film Daily*, 20th January 1929.

8 *The Stage*, 12th May 1927.

9 *The Stage*, 31st March 1927.

10 *Kinematograph Weekly*, 24th March 1927.

11 Ibid.

12 *The Bioscope*, 28th April 1927.

13 *Kinematograph Weekly*, 1st September 1927.

14 *Nice Work: Thirty Years in British Films* by Adrian Brunel.

15 *Kinematograph Weekly*, 29th March 1928.

16 *The Bioscope*, 29th March 1928

17 *Theatre World*, May 1928.

18 *The Picturegoer*, August 1927.

13 The Gaumont-British Combine

1 *Kinematograph Weekly*, 17th March 1927.

2 Ibid.

3 Ibid.

4 *The Stage*, 31st March 1927.

5 Sale of contract between Ivor Novello and Gainsborough on ebay.co.uk.

6 *The Stage*, 23rd June 1927.

7 *The Bioscope*, 18th June 1927.

8 Ibid.

9 *Kinematograph Weekly*, 15th September 1927.

10 Ibid.

11 *Kinematograph Weekly*, 30th May 1929.

12 *The Picturegoer*, October 1927.

13 Ibid.

14 Ibid.

15 *Kinematograph Weekly*, 10th November 1927.

16 *Kinematograph Weekly*, 11th August 1927.

17 *The Picturegoer*, September 1928.

18 *Kinematograph* Weekly, 4th August 1927.

19 *The Picturegoer*, September 1928.

20 *Nice Work: Thirty Years in British Films* by Adrian Brunel.

21 *Kinematograph Weekly*, 5th January 1928.

22 *The Bioscope*, 5th January 1928.

23 *The Bioscope*, 2nd February 1928.

24 *Kinematograph Weekly*, 23rd February 1928.

25 *The Bioscope*, 23rd February 1928.

26 *Theatre World*, April 1928.

27 *The Bioscope*, 23rd February 1928.

28 *Theatre World*, April 1928.

29 *Michael Balcon Presents: A Lifetime in Films* by Michael Balcon.

30 *The Picturegoer*, May 1928.

14 An Interlude with Cutts

1 See Chapter 12.

2 *Kinematograph Weekly*, 15th September 1927.

3 See *Gordon Conway: Fashioning a New Woman* by Raye Virginia Allen.

4 *Film Weekly*, 2nd September 1929.

5 *Theatre World*, February 1928

6 *Kinematograph Weekly*, 22nd December 1927.

7 *Kinematograph Weekly*, 26th August 1928.

8 *The Picturegoer*, May 1928.

15 Walter West's Flutters

1 *The Stage*, 15th March 1928.

2 *The Bioscope*, 15th March 1928.

3 *Kinematograph Weekly*, 4th October 1928.

4 Ibid.

5 *Kinematograph Weekly*, 26th September 1929.

16 The Bubble Breaks with the 'Quota Act' and British Lion Growls

1 See Chapter 3.

2 *The Picturegoer*, August 1928.

3 *Michael Balcon Presents: A Lifetime in Films* by Michael Balcon.

4 *The Bioscope*, 1st September 1927.

5 *The Bioscope*, 15th March 1928.

6 *The Stage*, 28th December 1928.

7 *Kinematograph Weekly*, 15th March 1928.

8 *The Bioscope*, 8th January 1929.

9 *Variety*, 12th June 1929

10 *The Bioscope*, 26th January 1928.

11 *The Bioscope*, 5th April 1928.

12 *The Stage*, 26th July 1928.

13 Ibid.

14 *Ivor* by Sandy Wilson.

15 *Shooting Star: The Last of the Silent Film Stars* by Chili Bouchier.

16 *Kinematograph Weekly*, 6th September 1928.

17 The Reorganisation of Gainsborough and a Last Gasp of Silents

1 *Hitch: The Life and Times of Alfred Hitchcock* by John Russell Taylor.

2 The Bioscope British film number December 1928.

3 *Nice Work: Thirty Years in British Films* by Adrian Brunel.

4 *The Bioscope*, 11th July 1928.

5 *Nice Work: Thirty Years in British Films* by

Adrian Brunel.
6 *Kinematograph Weekly*, 6th December 1928.
7 *Kinematograph Weekly*, 20th September 1928.
8 *In Search of Ruritania* by David Slattery-Christy.
9 *The Bioscope*, 19th September 1928.
10 *A Life in Movies* by Michael Powell.
11 Ibid.
12 *Kinematograph Weekly*, 13th December 1928.
13 Ibid.
14 *The Bioscope*, 12th December 1928.
15 *New York Times*, 13th January 1929.
16 *Film Till Now: A Survey of the Cinema* by
  Paul Rotha.
17 http://www.cinetecadelfriuli.org
18 http://screensnapshots.blogspot.co.uk

**18 Gainsborough's Hybrid Silent –
Talkies**

1 *The Bioscope British Film Number*, December 1928
2 See Chapter 19.
3 *Kinematograph Weekly*, 23rd August 1928.
4 *The Stage*, 25th July 1929.
5 *Kinematograph Weekly*, 26th July 1928.
6 *Motion Picture News*, 25th August 1928.
7 *The Educational Screen*, February 1931.
8 *Motion Picture News*, 25th October 1930.
9 Ibid.
10 *The Bioscope*, 20th May 1931.
11 *Kinematograph Weekly*, 21st May 1931.
12 *The History of British Film 1918–1930* by
Rachael Low.
13 *Kinematograph Weekly*, 17th April 1930.
14 *The Bioscope*, 16th April 1930.
15 *Kinematograph Weekly*, 17th April 1930.
16 *Nice Work: Thirty Years in British Films* by
  Adrian Brunel.
17 *The Bioscope*, 26th March 1930.
18 *Kinematograph Weekly*, 27th March 1930.
19 *The Bioscope British Film Number*, December 1929.
20 *Kinematograph Weekly*, 10th January 1929.
21 *The Stage*, 9th May 1929.
22 *The Bioscope*, 1st May 1929.
23 Ibid.
24 *Kinematograph Weekly*, 2nd May 1929.
25 *Michael Balcon Presents: A Lifetime in Films* by
Michael Balcon.
26 *The Stage*, 1st August 1929.
27 *The Stage*, 1st August 1929
28 *The Bioscope*, 24th July 1929.
29 *The Bioscope*, 22nd January 1929.
30 *Kinematograph Weekly*, 17th January 1929.

31 *Kinematograph Weekly*, 21st November 1929.
32 *The Bioscope*, 20th November 1929.
33 *Kinematograph Weekly*, 21st November 1929.
34 *Kinematograph Weekly*, 3rd January 1929.
35 *The Bioscope*, 24th November 1921.
36 *Motion Picture Studio*, 11th February 1922.
37 *Kinematograph Weekly*, 28th February 1929.
38 *Kinematograph Weekly*, 14th November
1929.

**19 Journey's End and Grappling with the
Problem of Sound**

1 *Michael Balcon Presents: A Lifetime in Films* by
  Michael Balcon.
2 *The Picturegoer*, May 1929.
3 *The Stage*, 18th April 1929.
4 *The Bioscope*, 20th February 1929.
5 *Film Weekly*, 11th March 1929.
6 *The Stage*, 7th November 1929.
7 *Michael Balcon Presents: A Lifetime in Films* by
  Michael Balcon.
8 See Chapter 18.
9 *Nice Work* by Adrian Brunel.
10 *The Film Daily*, 16th October 1929.
11 *Kinematograph Weekly*, 2nd May 1929.
12 *Kinematograph Weekly*, 9th May 1929.
13 *The Picturegoer*, July 1929.
14 *Kinematograph Weekly*, 7th March 1929.
15 *Michael Balcon Presents; A Lifetime in Films* by
  Michael Balcon.
16 *The Bioscope*, 15th May 1929.
17 *Kinematograph Weekly*, 27th June 1929.
18 *The Bioscope*, 26th June 1929.
19 *Michael Balcon Presents: A Lifetime in Films* by
  Michael Balcon.
20 *The Bioscope*, 14th August 1929.
21 Ibid.
22 *Kinematograph Weekly*, 17th April 1930.
23 *The Bioscope*, 16th April 1930.
24 Ibid.
25 *The Bioscope*, 20th November 1929.
26 For a full description of the silent version
  including the plot, see Chapter 7.
27 *The Bioscope*, 2nd October 1929.
28 *Flashback* by George Pearson.
29 Ibid.
30 *Kinematograph Weekly*, 17th April 1930.
31 Ibid.
32 *The Bioscope*, 1st January 1930
33 *The Bioscope*, 12th March 1930.
34 *The Bioscope*, 29th January 1930.

INDEX

Forthcoming titles from Edditt Publishing

www.eddittpublishing.com

Visit the website for information about other Jazz Age titles.
Check out www.jazzageclub.com
(Jazz Age Club on Facebook)

**Stars of the British Silent Screen
by Gary Chapman**

Forthcoming
Hardback £25 ISBN 9781909230064
Paperback £12.99 ISBN 9781909230071
Apple e-book (Epub) £8.99 ISBN 9781909230088
Amazon Kindle e-book (Mobi) £8.99 9781909230095

**The first ever study of British silent film as seen
through the lives and achievements of its glittering
array of stars.**

A general introductory chapter examines the trends and themes leading up to the
introduction of sound, but the bulk of the book will be personality led. Each biographical
sketch will include, where possible, life histories, comments from interviews, a career
discussion and descriptions of their roles in key films, plus photographs.

Some of the stars featured include: Gerald Ames, Marie Ault, Betty Balfour, Clive Brook,
Hilda Bayley, Estelle Brody, Fay Compton, Gladys Cooper, Ivy Close, Ivy Duke, Josephine
Earle, Isobel Elsom, Henry Edwards, Lilian Hall Davis, Violet Hopson, Isabel Jeans,
Matheson Lang, Flora Le Breton, Malvina Longfellow, Victor McLaglen, Joan Morgan,
Owen Nares, Guy Newall, Ivor Novello, Mary Odette, Mabel Poulton, Stuart Rome, John
Stuart, Alma Taylor, Malcolm Tod, Queenie Thomas and Chrissie White.

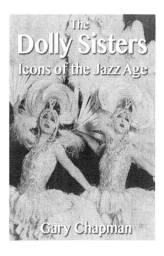

The Dolly Sisters: Icons of the Jazz Age
by Gary Chapman

Already published
£12.99 paperback, ISBN 978-1-909230-03-3
£7.99 Apple e-book ISBN 978-1-909230-04-0
£7.99 Amazon Kindle e-book ISBN 978-1-909230-05-7

A dizzying cocktail of delight, extravagance and pathos. Teeming with fantastic and fascinating stories from the Jazz Age of the twenties and thirties, it tells a true story every bit as dramatic and engrossing as the best fiction.

The rags to riches story of identical twins Jenny and Rosie is set against the glittering backdrop of high society in America and Europe before the onset of the Second World War. They had a colourful life where nature's duplicity enabled a highly successful career as dancers which made them 'stars'. And yet, lurking behind their glamorous story of fame, fortune, mistaken identity, millionaires, love and sisterly devotion - that made them legends - is another of rivalry, duplicity and tragedy.

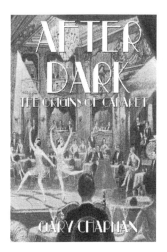

After Dark: The Origins of Cabaret
by Gary Chapman

Forthcoming
Hardback £25 ISBN 9781909230170
Paperback £12.99 ISBN 9781909230187
Apple e-book (Epub) £8.99 ISBN 9781909230194
Amazon Kindle e-book (Mobi) £8.99 9781909230200

A peek behind the completely hidden world of late night supper entertainment explaining its origins and development focused on the period 1910-1930 when cabaret and the dancing craze attained its fullest expression on both sides of the Atlantic.

This history of a unique form of entertainment, explores its ebbs and flows as it develops into a thriving art form in the 20s and explores the transatlantic network of nightlife in major European and American cities. It contains descriptions of all the main cabaret venues in London, Paris, New York and elsewhere and detail about the cabaret entertainers who became huge stars. There are numerous photographs of the cabaret venues, programmes, adverts and performers.

Dolly Tree : A Dream of Beauty
by Gary Chapman

Forthcoming
Hardback £25 ISBN 9781909230132
Paperback £12.99 ISBN 9781909230149
Apple e-book (Epub) £8.99 ISBN 9781909230156
Amazon Kindle e-book (Mobi) £8.99 9781909230163

The first biography of a costume designer, famous on both sides of the Atlantic, for her extravagant creations that appeared in stage shows, cabaret, couture and film in the glamorous 20s and 30s.

Famous on both sides of the Atlantic, for her extravagant creations that appeared in stage shows, cabaret, couture and film in the glamorous 20s and 30s, Dolly Tree (1899-1962) forged a successful career during the 1920s and 1930s and was a prime example of the New Woman. Her artistic flair touched so many stage and screen personalities that even if you have never heard of her before you will be familiar with her elegant creations for such movie stars as Myrna Loy, Jean Harlow, Judy Garland, Maureen O'Sullivan and other MGM starlets. She was also responsible for creating the quintessential 1890s look for Mae West that made her famous.

Part One covers her early life, her appearances as an actress during World War 1, her early illustration work, her emergence as a dress designer in London, Paris and New York and as house designer for Peron Couture. Part Two follows her departure from New York to Los Angeles and her work at Fox Film Corporation and then MGM during the 1930s.

Dolly Tree's creative genius had a profound impact on fashion and her modern approach to dress designing with its chic air of simplicity has given her creations a timeless quality that can still be glimpsed at in modern couture.